PLYMOUTH
BRONZE AGE TO TODAY
How Dartmoor Tin put Britain's Ocean City on the Map

CHRIS ROBINSON

with

KEITH LOZE

JAMES McFARLANE

British Library Cataloguing in Publication Data

Chris Robinson
Mining Local History
Plymouth Bronze Age to Today
How Dartmoor Tin put Britain's Ocean City on the Map

A catalogue record for this book is available from the British Library
ISBN 978-1-9160190-2-7

Written and illustrated by Chris Robinson
Layout Chris Robinson
Cover design: Ben Robinson Cover photo: Roy Perring
© Chris Robinson 2019

First published 2019

Also available:
Victorian Plymouth
Plymouth's Great War
Plymouth in the Twenties & Thirties
Plymouth in the Forties & Fifties
Plymouth in the Fifties & Sixties
Plymouth in the Seventies
The Story of Plymouth Hoe, Barbican and City Centre - Then & Now

Published by
Pen & Ink Publishing
34 New Street, Plymouth PL1 2NA
Tel: 01752 228120 /705337
www.chrisrobinson.co.uk

Printed and bound in Great Britain by
Deltor Communications Ltd
Long Acre, Saltash, Cornwall
PL12 6LZ

CONTENTS

Foreword 4

Acknowledgements 5

Introduction 7

PART ONE: SCRATCHING THE SURFACE

ONCE UPON A TIME IN THE WEST 11

WHAT DID THE ROMANS EVER DO FOR US 31

1066 AND ALL THAT 43

PLYMPTON BECOMES A STANNARY TOWN 57

COMPETITION TIME 69

PART TWO: GOING UNDERGROUND

THE AGE OF THE GENTLEMAN TINNER 79

NINETEENTH CENTURY A DRAINING EXPERIENCE 89

PART THREE: TWENTIETH CENTURY – FOXED?

HARD TIMES: INTRODUCING TUNGSTEN 152

HEMERDON – SHAFTED AGAIN 166

TO BE OR NOT TO BE? 187

MAKING INROADS 193

CAN YOU DIG IT? 207

CRYING WOLF? 223

ON THE BALL – AND UNDER THE BALL? 248

Mining Glossary 252

Bibliography 254

Foreword

David Buckingham, at Hooten Wheals on the O Brook near Hexworthy. November 2019

Having a lifelong interest in Dartmoor, its antiquities and mining remains, I was naturally very interested when Chris Robinson first started talking about writing this book. Like many others I was saddened to learn that Wolf Minerals, the company that was developing the first mine in England for over 45 years and the sponsors of the book project, had gone into administration. Sad too for all those others whose livelihood at that stage depended on the continuation of exploiting the tungsten deposit at Hemerdon.

Chris had, by that stage, already outlined to us the narrative thread behind the book – of how tin streaming on Dartmoor had created an early economy and comparatively vibrant community around the sources of the tin-bearing rivers of that granite range, giving the area a history stretching back some 4000 years.

All of the standard Plymouth history books produced in the twentieth century suggest a formal commencement of mining activities in this area in the twelfth century, so here was an opportunity to reappraise our early history with two of my great passions at the forefront.

It was therefore not a difficult decision for me and ultimately the rest of our board of directors of the Plymouth Barbican Trust to agree to support the completion of this book. Not only is the Trust deeply committed to preserving the threatened historic fabric of this city – we have owned and maintained over 20 key, listed buildings in and around the Barbican for over 60 years and were instrumental in saving the area from the post-war bulldozers – but we also consider promoting projects that enhance or advance our understanding of city's heritage.

The well-known historian Crispin Gill was a founder member of the Plymouth Barbican Association (as it was originally known) and Crispin's New History of Plymouth, published in 1993, was the last full scale attempt to provide a comprehensive story of the city, however he too suggested a date of 1156 for the recognised commencement of mining activities in this area.

And so I am sure that he would have welcomed this addition to the local book shelves. Doubtless there are those that will question Chris's assertion that the Cassiterides – the Tin Islands talked about by ancient historians – referred to Plymouth Sound, at the mouths of the Tamar and the Plym. However the theory is well argued, particularly in the light of recent findings off the coast of Egypt and Syria where large numbers of tin ingots have been examined using the latest technology and been shown to hail from Dartmoor and/or Cornwall.

One wonders how much more technological advancement will enable one to open up the secrets of the past, but until such time Chris's review of what we do know will give everyone a clearer insight to what has gone before than we have ever had, and I, and the Barbican Trust, are very pleased to have been able to help by ensuring that the book could be completed and end up in your hands today.

David Buckingham

David Buckingham
Chairman of the Plymouth Barbican Trust
November 2019

Acknowledgements

James McFarlane and Chris Robinson with early on-site finds, posing for a publicity shot.

David Cobbold, holding a large piece of ore containing tungsten, at Drakelands

Back in September 2017 I had an email from Elaine Budd of Wolf Minerals at Drakelands, she wrote: *'As part of my role, I am keen to explore the Mining Heritage in Plymouth and for that to be available to the wider community alongside the archaeological findings on site here at Drakelands.*

'Would you be interested in discussing the possibility of undertaking some research and subsequently producing a short publication on this subject?'

Always interested in having an opportunity to explore a part of the city's heritage that I'm not too familiar with, I readily agreed and in October a meeting was set up at Hemerdon with James McFarlane, who had joined the Drakelands operation as their Geology Superintendent two years earlier. James had already compiled extensive historial research on the backstory of the mine and we had an animated discussion about how we might contrive to produce an illustrated book on the subject.

Little did either of us think that a year later Wolf would be having to call in the administrators and the 250-strong workforce would be stood down and the mine closed. By that stage the book, which had, by mutual agreement, already become a much bigger project than at first envisaged, was roughly at the half way stage. Already I had learned more about the

early history of this part of the world than ever known before, and gained a better understanding of mining in the area than I had ever imagined I would. For much of this I am greatly indebted to someone who has been an acquaintance for many years, a drinking buddy, a family friend and a real mining enthusiast, Keith Loze.

Keith has been with me throughout this journey, and has provided numerous books, articles and contacts, along with a mass of manuscripts notes and feedback for this book.

Another life-long mineral and mining enthusiast and historian is Owen Baker, who incidentally produced Plymouth's first Then & Now style book back in 1976. Owen has a wonderful collection of documents, manuscript notes and mineral samples from just about every mine in the immediate Plymouth area, espeically Dartmoor tin. He very kindly gave us full access to all of it. Likewise, David Cobbold, the current incumbent of the Newnham estate and owner of part of the land that Drakelands sits on, allowed us to borrow a suitcase full of documents relating to mining activities on the estate over the last two hundred years or so. Similarly Sukey and Kate at Hemerdon House were extremely generous with their time, allowing me to spend a full day in the wonderful library there.

Clockwise from the top left: A favourite at the Miners' Arms, Tungsten Tipple, Elaine Budd, Keith Loze and a team from Wolf Minerals outside the Miners' Arms, enjoying a sundowner, including Jeff Harrison and James McFarlane.

Elizabeth Parsons, the daughter of the Second World War Mill Superintendent at Hemerdon, Jack Partington, similarly freely availed us of her father's diaries and papers, which remarkably she had kept and which have proved invaluable. Elizabeth was one of many charming people with links to the mine that we met at the Miners' Arms at the beginning of this project.

Sue Burkhill, one of the parish councillors at Shaugh, introduced me to a number of interesting residents who had stories and photographs. Violet Pummell at Galva House, who had written pieces on Hemerdon for the *South Devon Times*, was equally helpful as was John McIver who has a great knowledge of the area and its residents.

We have also had full access to the archives of the *Western Morning News* and *Plymouth Herald*, a lot of which are currently in the custody of the Plymouth Barbican Trust, who have very generously sponsored the writing of the second half of this book, following the unfortunate exit of Wolf Minerals. To them I owe a huge 'thank you'.

I would also like to thank Ernie Hoblyn, Tom Greeves, Sandy Gerard, Phil Newman, Eileen Fox and all those others who have written extensively on the ancient history of Dartmoor and its mining heritage.

With regard to the more recent story Keith and I would like to thank John Abraham, Paul Lister, Jane Charley, and Andy Sarosi for sharing memories, photographs and documents from the AMAX period and John Briggs and especially Jeff Harrison for steering us through the Wolf years. Another former Wolf man, and still involved today, James McFarlane collected together some remarkable documentation and if and when the mine is eventually successful his role will have been a key part of it, as he has been in producing this book. Others we'd like to thank include, in no particular order: Brian Brett and, Doug Westaway of Kelly Mine, Len Jones, Tony Brooks, Keith Haines, Chris Bailey, Norman Gay, Steve Roberts, Margaret Grimbly, Mike Grigg, Bob Le Marchant, Wesley Ashton, John Boulden, Stephen Holley, Clive Charlton, Tommy Hatwell, artifact photographs, and Roy Perring for the splendid cover shot which comes as close to summing up what the book is all about in one image as we can think of.

Thanks too to, Calstock Archive, AC Archaeology, Threlkeld Quarry and Mining Museum, British Geological Survey, Devon County Planning Department (especially Sue Penaluna), Wolf Minerals, the South West Image Bank, the National Trust, Plymouth Motor Club, the British Newspaper Archive, Wikipedia, Ancestry.com and Sir Tim Berners-Lee.

And then there are those who have already read this before you – the proof reading team that is Bill Bugler, Rob Warren, Gloria Dixon, Owen Baker, Keith Loze, Trish Greathead and last but not least, my long suffering wife and publisher, Clare Robinson, who has not only read the whole thing and put up with an at times irritable and irritating author, but has also hand-coloured a number of the illustrations.

CJR & KRL *November 2019*

Introduction

As I write these notes, Plymouth is gearing up to celebrate 400 years since the sailing of the Mayflower 1620-2020, a story that has a strong resonance with the people of that great nation on the other side of the Atlantic, but which is essentially a tale of happenstance for Plymouth, as the Separatists on board the Mayflower – and the Speedwell – never intended to set foot in Plymouth, and were probably somewhat anxious on account of it. Their journey was already running late and winter was closing in fast, making their crossing all the more dangerous. While here, however, they would have encountered many men who were experienced in terms of Atlantic crossings, be they fishermen operating in and out of Newfoundland, or traders and would-be colonists who had been looking for commercial opportunities several thousand miles away. Few other ports in Britain would have boasted such a collection of hardy sailors, but then Plymouth had been either trading or welcoming seaborne traders for hundreds, even thousands of years before that.

Written evidence of mining in Devon and Cornwall takes us back to 1156, but physical evidence of tin mining and tin trading takes us back to at least the second millennium BC. We have long suspected that there was a healthy trade being carried out with civilisations from the eastern shores of the Mediterranean thousands of years ago and exciting recent discoveries are starting to provide hard evidence that there would have been no Bronze Age without tin from Cornwall and Dartmoor. The vast granite intrusions of this part of the Westcountry have long been responsible for rich mineral deposits and the unique geology of Drakelands, Hemerdon, is because the rocks there are even older than the Dartmoor rocks that it sits alongside.

Remarkably, it wasn't until the beginning of the nineteenth century that scholars in this country really started to examine what we now call Dartmoor National Park and wonder at the hundreds of hut circles that sit on the fringes of the rivers that run south off the moor towards the English Channel. Why there? What attracted people to this barren part of the world?

Well back then it wasn't barren, it was forested, and back then there was a huge amount of alluvial tin just sitting in the beds of those rivers. Extraction was comparatively easy: the ore being more dense than ordinary rocks meant that it didn't move easily, but when eroded from the host granite, that waste material now made its merry way downstream, towards the sea, leaving the tin behind.

2013: Recording archaeological data on Crownhill Down, possibly a cairn, now buried beneath the Mine Waste Facility.

For hundreds, nay thousands, of years this process brought economic prosperity and consequently communities to the area and it is only recently through Bronze Age finds like those at Whitehorse Hill on Dartmoor, like those unearthed by various archaeological surveys of Hemerdon and Crownhill Down, and more recently still at Sherford, that we are able to build up a really good picture of just how prosperous and how well populated this area was. Mount Batten has long been renowned for the Bronze Age material found there, and it has long been claimed by academics that this is where our early ancestors would have lived. It is after all an obvious point at which to trade goods produced in Devon and Cornwall, as it is within easy reach of the Tamar and the Plym which, long before the age of modern roads, were the principal motorways of their day.

Ships coming from thousands of miles away, from the Middle East needed our tin, because it is the vital second element that gives us bronze – copper being the other – and several thousand years ago, there were few known sources of tin, apart from Asia and Cornwall and Dartmoor.

Curiously enough among the many consequences claimed as result of this trading relationship with those early civilisations in the Middle East is the suggestion that those people living around here became more civilised too, wearing clothes and jewellery unknown to other parts of the UK and that we started building not only stone hut circles but houses with cob walls, a phenomenon common to the Middle East and the South West but relatively rare anywhere else in England.

There is even speculation that our celebrated clotted cream may have been a process picked up from our Mediterranean visitors, there is a product from Tyre that bears a greater similarity to clotted cream than anything else in Britain or Western Europe.

Such was the extent of this trade that when, in the twelfth century, the cleric Geoffrey of Monmouth, was looking to create a backstory for Britain, he came up with a narrative that saw Brutus land on the banks of the Dart, at Totnes, with an army of Trojans, whom he marched down to Plymouth, to do battle with the Wessex giants on Plymouth Hoe.

During the course of that gripping encounter, Corineus, leading warrior of the Trojan army, threw Gogmagog, the Wessex giant, off the cliff at Lambhay (the name apparently means 'giant's leap') giving victory to Brutus, who then rewarded Cornieus with the tip of Wessex, which he renamed Cornwall in Corineus' honour, while Brutus went on to take Albion, which he renamed Britain in his own honour.

All entirely untrue … fake news from the Middle Ages. And yet why do you suppose he sited that story here, if it wasn't for the true story of tin that underpinned the early history of this part of the world.

Certainly it was a story that our ancestors liked to celebrate, because

a couple of hundred years later, when Plympton, which had become an important stannary town on the back of all this mining and trading eventually became so silted up from the fall out of this activity that the once busy trading port and the river that it served was no longer navigable. Before long traders became fed up of waiting for high tides in order to trade out of Plympton and opted to do their commerce around Sutton Harbour instead. At that time Sutton was made up of three separate areas, Sutton Raf, Sutton Valletort and Sutton Prior. The first two were owned by reasonably wealthy landowners, but the most valuable part was held by the Priors of Plympton – hence Sutton Prior. In 1439 the Act of Incorporation, only the second ever granted in the country, saw the three Suttons become one, and it was around this time that the name Plymouth was formally adopted.

And to celebrate their new found independence, what do you suppose the people of Plymouth did? Buying into Geoffrey of Monmouth's fake news, they created two giant figures, one bigger than the other, on Plymouth Hoe – and there they remained for some 200 years, until after the fallout of the Civil War and the Restoration of the Monarchy in 1660, the Citadel was built on the Hoe and all trace of the giants disappeared. We do know that from time to time, men had been employed to tidy the figures up, but no known image of the figures exists, which is a pity because even if that story isn't true it seems as though its rooted in something very real indeed. Tin streaming continued to take place on the Moors until relatively recent times, but, by the nineteenth century more and more mining was being done underground, and given the known geology of the area, local landowners, or at least the major local landowners, began to turn their thoughts to what lay beneath the grassy slopes. Few of our landed gentry were not sucked into the notion that there might be vast riches buried beneath and mines were opened by Lord Morley at Mount Batten, Lord Lopes at Maristow, the Strodes at Newnham, the Woollcombes at Hemerdon, the Gennys family at Whitleigh …

None of their mines were successful, unlike those around Tavistock where the Bedford family made a vast fortune and the ancient Stannary Town of Tavistock enjoyed something of a renaissance. Such is not to say that the landowners lost money, generally it was the shareholders that lost out, while the labourers, lawyers and landowners all profited from the experience, some to a much greater extent than the others.

The story of the nineteenth-century gentleman tinner occupies the middle section of this book and is full of false hopes, false promises and failed projects. By the end of the Victorian age and the first flush of the Industrial Revolution, metal mining had become a largely forgotten industry on the fringes of Plymouth, but then came something of a revival with the discovery worldwide of the value of a hitherto little know mineral called tungsten. First mentioned in the 1780s and first discovered locally in the 1860s it wasn't really until the beginning of the twentieth century that anyone really started to appreciate its potential. Quick off the starting blocks were the Germans who, realising that they could make tools with a harder cutting edge, missiles with greater penetration potential and armaments with more effective protection, started buying up all the tungsten they could find in Cornwall. They also bought and operated their own mine in Cumbria. It took the British Government some time to cotton on to this and it wasn't until just before the start of what would become the Great War that they put a stop to this particular export trade and started to think in terms of using the stuff themselves.

Before the end of what we now call the First World War, they had overseen the opening of a tungsten mine at Hemerdon, but for a wide variety of reasons, reneged on their pledge to keep it going after the war had ended. Despite a little bit of interest, nothing that significant happened at Hemerdon again until we were on the verge of war again at the end of the 1930s. Again the Government got involved, and again, even before the end of the war, they abandoned the project.

In the Korean War it was considered again, but without much enthusiasm. The same could not be said of Canadian Bill Richardson who got very excited about the potential of the Hemerdon tungsten deposit. He wrote to the Prime Minister, he wrote to the Queen, he wrote to Prince Philip, he wrote to all the major mining companies he could think of, and although he attracted a degree of interest, he failed to find the financial backing he needed.

A few years later, though, AMAX, one of the companies who had come over, from Canada, to see what all the fuss was about, took on the leases for the mine and threw some major resources at examining the potential of Hemerdon.

They spent millions of pounds, drilling, testing and complying with all the restrictions that Devon County Council, Plymouth City Council and the South Hams Council put in their way.

Eventually they secured the much needed permissions, but by then the price of tungsten had fallen to such a level that it was not viable to actually contemplate constructing a mine and working the deposit.

Enter Humphrey Hale, a Brit, with Devon ancestry, who went out to Australia in the early 1990s hoping to make a fortune as a gold miner. In 2007 he was asked to become the managing director for the then newly formed Wolf Minerals. The fledgling company had a handful of mining interests in New South Wales, but were looking for something bigger and better.

Through an old university friend Humphrey, who was actually sent to look

2013: The archaeological excavation team reveal what may have been a tinner's hut at Hemerdon.

for uranium, he came to learn about the tungsten deposits at Hemerdon. Within a few years and with tens of millions of Australian dollars pledged by Australian banks and investment companies, Wolf came here and built the biggest mine that Hemerdon had ever seen. It was the first metal mine to be built in England for almost 50 years and now at last with all that money behind them and after spending £160 million, surely it would work this time?

Chris Robinson
Plymouth
November 2019

9

Grimspound round house, with sheltered doorway and surrounding pound wall.

PART ONE: SCRATCHING THE SURFACE
ONCE UPON A TIME IN THE WEST

Tin, it is claimed, once held a value and strategic importance similar to that of oil. In his paper *Tin Deposits and the Early History of Bronze* the eminent Canadian geologist Bob Cathro wrote: *'Judging by how much effort went into finding it, the price of tin must have been extremely high.*
'It became an indispensable commodity, worth scouring the world for and going to war over, and it occupies a special place in the history of mining, economic geology, agriculture, warfare, art, and human development. Gold and silver could finance a war, but bronze could win it.'

'The early occupation of Dartmoor by man was prompted by the presence of tin,' stated 43-year-old Robert Burnard in his Presidential Address to the Plymouth Institution in 1891.
'We find on Dartmoor pre-historic antiquities which undoubtedly belong to the Bronze Age, and where most abundant stores of tin appear to have lain there, are to be found the remains of the thickest population.
'He streamed the valleys for the precious metal, hunted the red deer, and nightly kept his cattle and sheep in stone enclosures capped with peat hedges, so as to secure them from the predatory animals which must at that time have infested some of the tree-clad clitters and wild vastnesses of the Moor.'
Significantly, of over 1,000 hut circles referenced by Burnard (in 2017 the figure is more like 5,000), the vast majority, almost 800 of them, occur in the southern part of the Moor – that is south of a straight line from two miles west of Cox Tor to Ilsington on the east. In those distant days of pre-history, well over 2,000 years ago, the tin on the Moor was remarkably easy to locate and extract, as

it sat in the shallow beds of rivers and streams. It was found in the form of tinstone or cassiterite (oxide of tin) and appeared as heavy black sand and gravel, the result of millions of years of erosion as the dense material was separated out of parent lodes by wind, rain and river flow.
Almost all our ancestors had to do was shovel it, sieve it and swap it: swap it for something that was of more immediate practical use to them.
As tin was an essential element of bronze and as that alloy was central to the latest phase of human development, later to be dubbed the Bronze Age, there was a ready market for their product, particularly as, apart from certain areas of Cornwall, there was no ready supply of tin known at that time anywhere else in Western Europe.
And so, it was, according to some of our earliest historians, that traders came from as far afield as Phoenicia – that purple patch (the word comes from the Greek Phoinike – literally 'purple land'), the fertile crescent of the Eastern Mediterranean, marked-out by what is now Syria, Lebannon and northern Israel to seek out the Cassiterides – the Tin Islands.
Of course back then there were no roads along which our Dartmoor residents would carry their booty, but that mattered not as all of the rivers ultimately led to the sea.
Rivers were the routeways of the day: if you walked along the riverbank you were unlikely to get lost and anyway you could doubtless float and steer your cargo to the coast. Thus it was comparatively easy for our Dartmoor residents to make their way to the sea and service their customers.

Robert Burnard was born on 12 July 1848. His father Charles, had founded the Plymouth-based chemical company Burnard, Lack & Algar and was Mayor of Plymouth in 1881-82.
Robert was destined to became a partner of the firm when it was removed from Sutton Harbour to the Cattewater. It was the dredging of the adjacent waterfront that led to his interest in archaeology and the impact that tin-streaming had had on the area.

Furnace chimney Har Tor Blowing House N

Charles Burnard (top left) clearly infused his son (top right) with an interest in Dartmoor at an early age and in 1883 they were founder members of the Dartmoor Preservation Society.

Dartmoor wasn't really thought to be worthy of serious consideration prior to the end of the eighteenth century. The notable early antiquaries – Leland, Camden and Stukely – who wrote of prehistoric remains around the country, didn't mention any of the ancient monuments on Dartmoor. The first generation of historian geographers of Devon – Hooker, Risdon, Westcote and Pole – writing in the early seventeenth century, didn't date Dartmoor any further back than the Middle Ages. Map makers were similarly oblivious to Dartmoor's distant past and Benjamin Donn's comparatively detailed Map of the County of Devon published in 1789 conspicuously lacks any archaeological features. Cornish clergyman Richard Polwhele provided the proper first local reference to an ancient Dartmoor location when he wrote a description of Grimspound in 1797 – and 'speculated wildly about the purpose for which it had been built'. (Barber)

A major landmark in the development of Dartmoor studies, however, came in 1830 with the publication of the first volume of the Transactions of the Plymouth Institution, which included Samuel Rowe's 'Antiquarian Investigations in the Forest of Dartmoor, Devon.'

The Plymouth Institution itself was a relatively new body (1812) and the work was a combined effort on the part of Samuel Rowe, John Prideaux, Major Hamilton Smith and Hemerdon resident Henry Woollcombe.

Their fieldwork represented an attempt to list and locate all types of ancient monument on Dartmoor. It was revised by Rowe who, like Polwhele was a vicar as well as an antiquarian, in 1846, as A Perambulation of Dartmoor and reprinted ten years later, three years after his death. In 1895 the work was thoroughly revisited and expanded by Samuel's nephew, J Brooking Rowe.

Har Tor Blowing House S. another view of access

Bellaford Cyclopean Bridge by F. Reynolds J. Shattock & R.B. on the pier July 1888.

A painting from a series of images of Samuel Rowe's fieldwork team in the 1820s.

At Merrivale there is evidence of widespread streaming for tin which in later years 'probably contributed its quota of ore to the two blowing-houses in the valley of the Walkham' attests Burnard.

He adds: 'The remains in the Har Tor valley are not so perfect nor so extensive as those at Merrivale, and consist of a single stone avenue, in fair preservation, leading from two small circles down to the River Meavy.

'Fifty yards south of the western termination is a cairn, and across the Har Tor brook, on the commencement of the slope leading to Cramber Tor, is an imperfect enclosure, still containing about a dozen hut circles.

'Within a radius of a mile from this avenue there are nearly a hundred hut circles, some in ruined enclosures, and others detached.

'The whole district has been streamed for tin from end to end. A comparatively modern [remember his findings were published in 1891] blowing house is situated close to the junction of the Meavy and Har Tor brooks, and some of the shallow workings cross the stone avenue and are palpably of later date.'

By way of clarifying the situation he continued, 'It is not for a moment intended to imply that the existing mining remains are coeval with the avenues, for each succeeding race of tinners have obliterated the "spoils" of the former; but where tin has evidently been most abundant there are the most prolific signs of human occupation.

'This is illustrated most forcibly by the valley of the Plym above Cadaford (Cadover) Bridge where streaming remains are very abundant; for including Trowlesworthy and Ditsworthy Warrens, there are no less than five groups of hut circles containing over one hundred examples, besides ruins of enclosures, cairns, kistvaens, &c.'

Burnard then went on to discuss the likely dates ascribed to the Bronze Age and quoted Dr John Evans who, in 1881, suggested that the era most likely began around 1200 or 1400 BC in this country: 'It is a question,' moved Evans, 'whether this antiquity will meet all the necessities of the case; for we can hardly imagine the Phoenicians, or those who traded with them, landing in Britain and spontaneously discovering tin. On the contrary, it must have been from a knowledge that the inhabitants of Britain were already producers of this valuable metal that the commerce with them originated ... If, therefore, the Phoenician intercourse direct or indirect, commenced about 1500 BC, the knowledge of the use of tin, and probably also of copper, dates back in Britain to a still earlier epoch.'

Taking his cue from Evans, who was a major figure in postulating dates for the Stone, Iron and Bronze ages, Burnard reasoned that given the probable antiquity of the Bronze Age was from 3,000 to 4,000 years ago, 'the production of tin in Devon and Cornwall must be as old.

'Given we find on Dartmoor pre-historic antiquities which undoubtedly belong to the Bronze Age, and where most abundant stores of tin appear to have lain there are to be found the remains of the thickest population.'

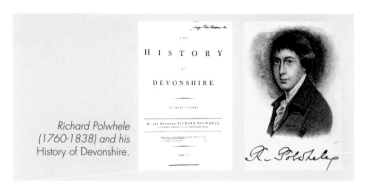

Richard Polwhele (1760-1838) and his History of Devonshire.

All of which led Burnard to his conclusion that the early occupation of Dartmoor was due to the presence of tin.

For Burnard the lack of clear evidence was not an issue: 'The disintegrating character of the Dartmoor climate, the destruction of ancient monuments and buildings, and appropriation of the stone for walls, gate posts, &c., by succeeding relays of natives, have wrought havoc with antiquarian evidence, and prevented the realization of chronological sequence.'

Clearly the logical place to site any 'modern mine' would be where tin had previously easily been found: 'In this district several modern mines have been sunk on the sites of ancient workings – they are known as Vitifer, Birch Tor, Bushdown, Watern Hill and Golden Dagger. With the exception of Golden Dagger, they are all "knacked".'

Around Grimspound, however, are to be found plenty of traces of 'busy mining operations,' and Burnard singled the area out as 'a fine example of an ancient fortified shelter. It is in the thick of stream works and deep open cuttings.' With some 24 hut circles within the site as a whole it is easy to imagine a community of around 100 people – given 'the moderate allowance of four persons per hut.'

As Hill & McAlister stated in 1906, 'most of the tin bearing placers occcur in rivers which drain to the south [of Dartmoor] this is due to tilting of the region towards the south during the Tertiary Period.'

The mouths of the main rivers that rose on the moor, Dartmouth, Teignmouth, Salcombe and Plymouth fed into accessible harbours, only then there was no settlement of consequence nestled around what would become Sutton (the sud-ton or south town of the Walkhampton Hundred) and which would only, post-Middle Ages evolve into Plymouth.

Rather the earliest settlers at the mouth of the river we now call the Plym (originally perhaps the Mew or the Cad) were living in the caves high above the northern bank of the river at Cattedown or at the end of the high ridge that ran along the southern bank – Hawe Stert (Hawe being the high ridge and stert marking the end of it). We now know it as Mount Batten and it would appear that our Phoenician friends may well have known it as Iktin (Diodorus) or Ictis, the main trading-post of the Tin Islands, or the Cassiterides.

'If Ictis is an actual place, then Mount Batten has a claim to the name both on archaeological and topographical grounds,' wrote Professor Barry Cunliffe after a major archaeological investigation of the site in 1988. However, he added somewhat enigmatically, *'the matter is beyond proof.'* Indeed it is a debate that has raged for hundreds of years. St Michael's Mount has also been suggested as a possible location for Ictis, but although there was plenty of tin in that area at that time, there were no adjacent islands that could be interpreted as the Tin Islands.

Pliny and Ptolemy referred to the Cassiterides but didn't say where they were, avers Malcolm Todd in *The South West to 1000AD*. *'The islands were mythical, though the commodity that gave them a name was real enough. There is nothing to support the romantic notion that Phoenicians or Carthaginian entrepreneurs concerned themselves with any form of commerce in British waters.'*

Once again this is something that is probably impossible to prove ... either way.

Anyone sailing into Mount Batten 500 years ago, let alone 2,500 years ago would be hard pressed to say for sure that they weren't sailing into a veritable archipelago. They would have already passed the island we call the Mewstone (which appears to enjoy the same name derivation as Meavy, which feeds into the Plym, coming from the Old English *maew*

which refers to the sound of a gull, historically the 'sea mew') and the island that now sports the name of local seafaring hero Sir Francis Drake (the first Englishman to circumnavigate the globe).

To the west they would see the Rame Peninsula, island-like in appearance from the sea and the Sound, that is without further investigation, as the mouth of the Tamar snakes around behind Mount Edgcumbe to Millbrook. Above that sits the modern community of Torpoint itself, a virtual island being bounded by the River Lynher to the north.

The Stonehouse peninsula too, prior to the infilling of Stonehouse Creek along with large tracts of Millbay, would have looked to the casual waterborne observer like an island, and with Millbay spilling over into the great Sourpool behind, the Hoe (the high ridge on the north-western banks of the Plym) would have looked like a rapidly rising land mass surrounded by water – after all Sutton Harbour extended further westwards than it does today.

In those dim distant pre-historic times the lower reaches of the Plym had streams feeding into it all the way up to Plympton and beyond. The creeks at Tothill, Laira and Marsh Mills on the western banks have only been infilled in the last 200 years or so, as have, to a greater or lesser extent, the inlets on the eastern side, at Hooe, Pomphlett and Chelson Meadow. And all of this before the tailings from the tin industry from the earliest times

onward have been gradually silting up the Plym and the Tory Brook.

Time was when ships could sail within a stone's throw of Plympton Castle – doubtless part of the reason for the Normans choosing the location in the first place, and the Tory was navigable to a point just below the Iron Age encampment of Boringdon.

In the absence of Google Earth, the work of the Ordnance Survey cartographers, and any other accurate means of mapping the world, who would have known that Plymouth Sound wasn't surrounded by islands? Just like the Golfe du Morbihan and countless other Mediterranean locations. Let us not forget that our earliest maps were unbelievably crude by almost any standards.

Maybe the reason that mention of the Cassiterides faded into oblivion is that after the phrase had been coined it wasn't long before it was realised that these weren't really islands after all. However, Ictis, as a trading-point for tin, remained at the heart that self-same area and trade continued.

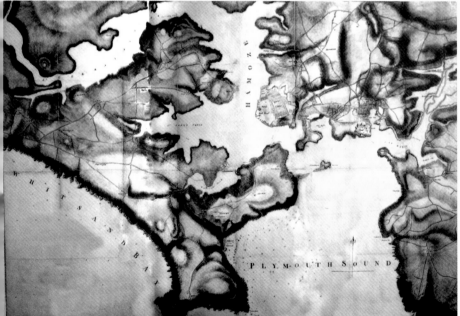

So keen were the Phoenicians to conceal from the Greeks and Romans their navigation of British waters that Strabo (c.64 BC to c.24 AD) records a story about a Phoenician mariner who on finding that a Roman vessel was on his track in pursuit, rather than let his pursuer discover the secret passage ran his ship aground and destroyed it. On returning home the mariner's patriotism was rewarded. He was hailed as a hero and the cost of the loss of his ship was met by the public treasury.

However, as Geoffrey Chowen noted in his 1863 Account of the rise and progress of mining in the counties of Devonshire from the time of the Phoenicians to the present, 'eventually other maritime powers shared with the Phoenicians the trade of these regions.'

He later adds: 'we learn from Pliny, that 330 years before Christ, a Greek colonist of Marseilles, Pytheas, who was their most celebrated navigator, had the good fortune to discover the Cassiterides, at that time ten in number, abounding in lead and tin.' Certainly it's easy to see how the land masses bordering Plymouth Sound could have looked like ten islands, and more readily so than the Isles of Scilly where there are more like 100 separate land masses of varying sizes.

Furthermore, Chowen adds: 'lead was well known to the western Britons, and there is every reason to believe that the ore was obtained in large quantities from the banks of the Tamar, now the site of the Tamar mines.'

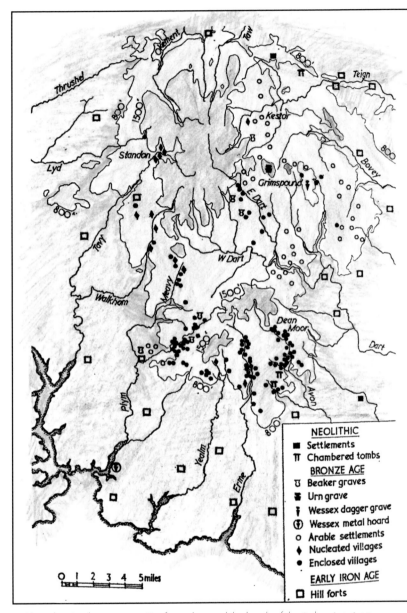

Map showing how communities formed around the heads of the tin bearing rivers of Dartmoor. The map is based on figures 20, 22 and 23 in Exeter and its Region published by the University of Exeter for the British Association in 1969, from the chapter 'Prehistoric and Roman Settlement' by Lady Fox © Exeter University.

Cunliffe's work in the 1980s revealed a number of Bronze Age finds, despite the fact that the early inhabited part of the Mount Batten peninsula, on the northern side, sheltered from the south-westerly winds and hidden from the view of potential aggressors, was devastated by the wholesale quarrying of that part of the headland during the first half of the nineteenth century.

Just a little further up the river at the more sheltered haven of Oreston there was found, in 1868 a substantial hoard of bronze weapons and instruments *'each representing the stock in trade of the itinerant bronzesmith active late in the Wessex Culture period, probably in the fourteenth century BC,'* wrote the soft-spoken Scotsman, and then curator of the Plymouth City Museum, James Barber in 1970.

He continued: *'The siting of this hoard on the estuary of the Plym, a natural highway from the sea to the Moor at a time when transport by water was the general rule, since thick forest occupied most low-lying ground and all river valleys, must surely be significant.*

'The hoard comprised 16 flanged axe heads with typical crescent-shaped cutting edges, three dagger blades, a tanged spearhead and a chisel.'

So was Mount Batten once Ictis? Todd does concede that Ictis, which was later described in some detail by Diodorus, did exist.

Diodorus of Sicily, the Greek historian was writing sometime between 60 and 30BC when he said:

'The inhabitants of Britain who dwell about the promontory known as Belerium (more or less defined by the west Cornwall of today) are especially hospitable to strangers and have adopted a civilized manner of life because of their intercourse with merchants of other peoples. They it is who work the tin, treating the bed which bears it in an ingenious manner.

'This bed, being like rock, contains earthy seams and in them the workers quarry the ore, which they then melt down and cleanse of its impurities. Then they work the tin into pieces the size of knuckle-bones and convey it to an island which lies off Britain and is called Ictis; for at the time of ebb-tide the space between this island and the mainland becomes dry and they can take the tin in large quantities over to the island on their wagons.

'(And a peculiar thing happens in the case of the neighbouring islands which lie between Europe and Britain, for at flood-tide the passages between them and the mainland run full and they have the appearance of islands, but at ebb-tide the sea recedes and leaves dry a large space, and at that time they look like peninsulas.)

'On the island of Ictis the merchants purchase the tin of the natives and carry it from there across the Strait to Galatia or Gaul; and finally, making their way on foot through Gaul for some thirty days, they bring their wares on horseback to the mouth of the river Rhone.'

Very much reduced in size and scale over the last few hundred years or so, there is good evidence to suggest that Mount Batten – Howe Stert – was once a tidal island, however, its slowly emerging narrow isthmus has been significantly widened by the gradual silting up of the Plym.

Browsing through the 1,300-page, lavishly illustrated *Chronicle of Britain and Ireland* published in 1992, it's interesting to read that under the dateline 700 BC: *'With trading ships plying from Spain and France, the western settlement of Mount Batten [Plymouth] has become Britain's largest port. It is a thriving harbour which exports precious metals brought from the moors rich in ore a few miles to the north and west.*

'These exports include tin, silver, copper and gold, all of which are traded for bronze tools and other finished metal products from the other side of the channel and Spain.'

Intriguingly the account goes on to say that the *'port is helped by a strange but well-known local phenomenon: at high tide certain areas of the coastline become islands, and Mount Batten, one of these areas, is then easily accessible by ship.*

'Greek travellers and traders who have come this way speak enthusiastically of a port called Ictis, which may well be Mount Batten. It is certainly a vibrant trading post, which locals say has been active for 200 years.'

It is hard to imagine that many other 'islands' off the coast of Cornwall, Devon or anywhere else for that matter, could have been accessed by a cartload of heavy ore, via a sandy or muddy crossing, no matter how it was pushed or pulled!

In this context it's also worth quoting another find referenced by James Barber, in 1970: that of *'bronze implements, scrap metal, and founder's ingots of the eighth and seventh century BC ... discovered at Mount Batten at the mouth of the Plym, close to where the Wessex Culture Oreston hoard was found.'*

Notwithstanding all these significant finds, the naysayers will tell us there is no evidence for the early tin-streaming of the moorland rivers that feed into the Plym, but the answer here would appear obvious enough: early tin streaming was relatively easy and left little in the way of scarring or adjacent workings and if, and where, such workings did exist all traces would almost certainly have been obliterated by the later reworking of those very same sites.

Nor does it help that the acid soil conditions of the Moor are harmful to any metal objects that may have been buried or discarded there.

The one seemingly incontrovertible fact is that, as James Barber put it, *'the monumental record of Dartmoor begins with the Bronze Age, from shortly before 2,000 to around 500 BC.'*

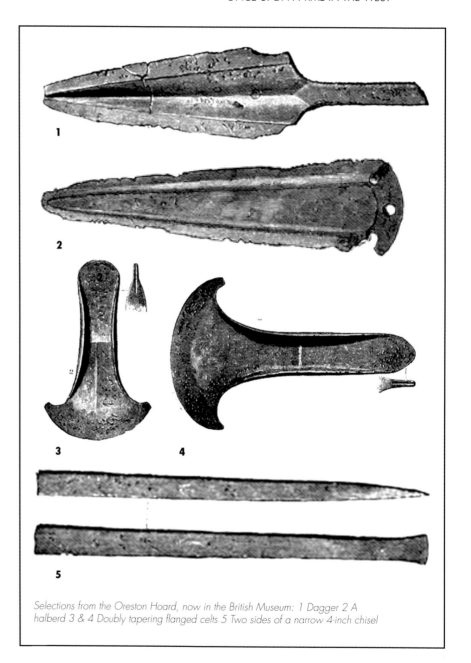

Selections from the Oreston Hoard, now in the British Museum: 1 Dagger 2 A halberd 3 & 4 Doubly tapering flanged celts 5 Two sides of a narrow 4-inch chisel

Even today, with centuries of land reclamation and building the area looks like an archipelago.

And so the question that inevitably arises from that, is, if it wasn't for the tin, why else would people have settled here, and, in particular, why would they have chosen to set up home on the banks of rivers that for thousands of years were associated with the mineral cassiterite from which we obtain tin?

Sir Stafford Northcote
1818-87
Antiquarian and politician.
Served as Chancellor of the
Exchequer 1874-80 and Foreign
Secretary 1885-86. One of only
two people to hold the office of
First Lord of the Treasury without
becoming Prime Minister.

There is no obvious alternative answer to the question, other than that the people who came here, came here for the tin. Who were they and where did they come from? The suggestion is that they were the Beaker Folk, and surface finds have yielded a good many arrow heads typical of those introduced by the itinerant Beaker people.

The Beakers are so named on account of the pottery vessels – beakers – that have typically been found in their burial chambers or kistvaens.

A particularly good example was found at Watern Down. The skeleton of the deceased had long since decayed – the acid soil attacking the collagen and calcium in much the same way as it does metal. A similar discovery at Fernworthy yielded a flint knife, lignite cloak button and a seriously decomposed remnant of a copper – not bronze – knife, with a wooden hilt.

These are by no means isolated discoveries and their proximity to watercourses that would have been rich in alluvial tin are too marked to have been coincidental.

Tin undoubtedly came from this region, there were little or no alternative sources at the time and there is another nice piece of local legend that has long since been cited to add weight to the argument.

To return to the age of the Victorian gentleman antiquarian we find Sir Stafford Henry Northcote, President of the British Archaeological Association, addressing the body's 18th Annual Congress in Exeter Guildhall in August 1861.

After some general opening remarks about the Association and the Advantages of Archaeology, Sir Stafford, who came from an ancient local family that could trace their ancestry back to Galfridas de Northcote who settled in the county in 1103, set about enlightening his audience with insights about Devon: *'It is here, if anywhere, we are to look for the earliest traces of the original inhabitants of this land of Britain.'*

Referencing Orpheus and Herodotus, the accounts of the Cassiterides – the tin islands – and the trade in that metal between Cornwall and Devonshire and the ancient world he suggests that he should not lay *'too much stress upon all the legends and traditions connected by this intercourse. But undoubtedly there are a great many circumstances, small in themselves, yet all bearing the same direction, which seem to point to a connection between this south-west of England and an eastern origin.*

'I dare say,' opined the 42-year-old Member of Parliament, *'that I should provoke a smile at my credulity, though I do not desire to be thought so very low in the depths of ignorance as that, (a comment that was greeted with laughter) if I referred to old legends about the colonisation of this country by Brutus and the Trojans who came with him, but the legend is worth some consideration.'*

Writing towards the end of the first millennium AD our ancient scribes created a back story to explain the evolution of British history and the monarchy.

That story was concocted around a mythical figure Brutus, the Trojan great-great grandson of the goddess of love, Aphrodite who, having accidentally murdered his father, was exiled to Greece from where he liberated the descendents of the once-captive Trojans and led them to this country sometime around 1103 BC.

Totnes, 23 miles to the east of Plymouth, has been cited as his entry point to these islands, but so too has Plymouth. Plymouth is also said to have been the location for the great battle that Brutus' leading warrior, Corineas, fought with Gogmagog. The latter was a fearsome giant, whom, it was claimed, could wield an uprooted oak as a weapon. However in the struggle between them, after Gogmagog had broken three of Corineas's ribs, the enraged Trojan lifted Gogmagog aloft and threw him off the nearest cliff on to the rocks below – a feat commemorated in the name Lam-Goemagot, Goemagot's Leap, today known as Lambhay Hill on the edge of Sutton Pool where Plymouth's medieval castle was later built.

Following on from this glorious victory the story goes that Brutus went on to take Albion, which was renamed Britain in his honour. Meanwhile, Corineas was rewarded with the western peninsula of Albion, which became Cornwall – in his honour.

In later years, apparently to commemorate the Incorporation of the Borough of Plymouth in 1439, massive representations of the giants were hewn into the grassy seaward slope of the Hoe where they remained and were maintained for the next 200 years.

Charles Newington's impression of what the Plymouth Giants may have looked like.

Geoffrey of Monmouth, produced his History of the Kings of Britain sometime around 1135.

*George Rawlinson, 1812-1902
M.A., F.R.G.S. (Canon of Canterbury
and Camden Professor of Ancient
History at the University of Oxford)
Photographed c.1899. His
elder brother, Sir Henry Creswick
Rawlinson was a leading Orientalist
and has been described as the Father
of Assyriology.*

Now while this is undoubtedly the stuff of myth and legend, the question that presents itself is: did the fact that Plymouth Hoe overlooks Mount Batten, Hawe Stert, or Ictis, as it may once have been known, have any bearing on the ancients choosing to land Brutus here in their made-up story that was set firmly towards the end of the actual Bronze Age? A time when tin from this very area was such a crucial element of that age and in the economic success of the great powers of the Mediterranean, of which Troy had been one.

We will probably never know for sure. What we do know, thanks to the detailed research commissioned by Wolf Minerals published in January 2016 by AC Archaeology, is that the Hemerdon site – specifically the eleven cairns investigated on Crownhill Down – have established that the area was utilised for the siting of '*ritual monuments from the Beaker period and early Bronze Age, potentially continuing as late as the late Bronze Age.*

'*Together they have provided an extensive and broad range of examples that provide a rare and recently unparalleled scale of results covering prehistoric ritual practice.*'

Although there was not a great number of actual artefacts discovered, such finds as there were, were significant: dating from the Early to Middle Bronze Age the hoard is made up of a variety of material types that include bronze, pottery, worked stone, worked flint and faience.

'*The Beaker pottery along with the associated flint and worked stone finds are a rare and important group. Indeed, the beakers themselves are rare examples to be recovered from Devon, with only around ten examples known at present.*'

Certainly the number of cairns (piles of stones serving as burial markers and monuments) and tumuli (a mound of earth created over the top of a grave or set of graves) is significant and as Simon Hughes noted in his paper on the Hemerdon Project, '*they appear to surround the tinwork, running east-west across the Down and into the Tory Brook Valley.*

'*This may indicate the importance of the tin resource during the Bronze Age and presents the possibility of comparable relationships across the tin-rich uplands.*'

Writing in 1890 Professor George Rawlinson, in his book *Phoenicia*, talks of large profits arising from the copious supplies of tin and lead being imported into Greece and Asia from the Cassiterides and speaks of the local inhabitants here being '*clad in black cloaks, and in tunics reaching to the feet, with girdles round their waists, and that they walked with staves, and were bearded like goats,*' and further that they '*subsisted by means of their cattle, and for the most part led a wandering life.*'

An interesting observation, particularly in the light of the fact that Julius Caesar and other Roman historians, several centuries later were describing the peoples of Britain as being '*in a wretched state of barbarism … the use of clothes being scarcely known. Only those peoples living on the south coast appear to have covered their nakedness with the skins of beasts, and then only, it seems, in order not to offend the strangers they were trading with, rather than any idea of decency.*'

In more recent years, the availability of geochemical procedures, x-rays, fluorescence analysis and radiocarbon dating have enabled researchers to make more accurate assessments of what can be found on Dartmoor – and off the coast of Devon – and in almost every instance they give credence to the views of our Victorian forebears.

The most recent discoveries revealed by the detailed inspection of an ancient cist on Dartmoor have proved to be of international significance. Dubbed the Whitehorse Hill cist, the artefacts retrieved from this exceptionally well-preserved stone burial chamber included the partially cremated remains of a young person, most likely female, aged between 15 and 25, placed in a basket of woven lime bast and wrapped in an animal pelt, thought to be from a species of bear once native to this country but extinct for over 1,000 years.

The radiocarbon dating of the find suggests a date of more like 4,000 years ago, that is from around 1800 to 1600 BC.

It was the kind of find that Jane Marchand, the chief archaeologist of Dartmoor National Park Authority, never expected to see in her lifetime: '*The last Dartmoor burial with grave goods was back in the days of the Victorian gentlemen antiquarians. This is the first scientifically excavated burial on the moor, and the most significant ever.*'

As well as yielding evidence of relatively sophisticated clothing the finds revealed the earliest known examples of turned wood to be found in Britain, as well as the greatest hoard of beads ever found on the Moor. '*Previously we had eight beads from Dartmoor, now we have 200,*' enthused Marchand.

A necklace, belt and bracelet between them produced the most exciting finds, primarily because one of the beads was of amber from the Baltic and another was made of tin, as were 34 studs on the leather-fringed, nettle fibre belt. Although, in the words of Dr Alison Sheridan (a specialist in Neolithic and Bronze Age Britain) '*it is uncertain how far the burial of*

Located in what is now a very isolated spot, on one of the highest and most remote parts of Dartmoor, the Whitehorse Hill cist wasn't really expected to yield anything of great interest, and when first identified such material as was contained within did not look overly promising. The stone box was buried beneath a mound of peat and the fur and the blanket inside it were covered in a wet black sludgy mess. However as it was lifted out of position a bead fell out and the archaeological team realised that they were on to something rather special. Just how special couldn't be fully appreciated for quite some time. It took a year just to clean and freeze dry the basket before its treasures could be removed and treated in their own right. But as the fabrics, the beads and the jewellery came to be identified so the discoveries took on major significance, containing not only the earliest examples of wood-turning ever found in Britain, but also containing the earliest evidence of tin-working in the southwest.

21

artefacts in a Dartmoor cist indicates local tinworking,' the archaeologists are convinced that the tin bead at least, made part from a rolled and flattened ingot, was made locally. As such it constitutes the earliest evidence to date of tin smelting in Britain.

There have been other pre-Roman finds in the area that add to the local tin story, notably the finds in Moor Sand Bay just east of Salcombe. While initial discoveries in the late 1970s produced a number of copper alloy and gold artefacts, subsequent investigation a little further out to sea, uncovered some 42 ingots of pure tin (and 282 copper ingots) with speculative dates of 1000 to 800 BC.

Then, in 1991, at what is assumed to be another shipwreck site in Bigbury Bay, just off Mothecombe, near the mouth of the Erme, another 40 tin ingots were found. Most of these weighed in at a little less than 3lb (1.5kg) although eight of them clocked in at somewhere between 9-15lb (4-7kg).

The dating of these items has proved a little more difficult and Henrietta Quinnell, (an Honorary University Fellow at Exeter writing in a paper Dartmoor and Prehistoric to Early Medieval Tinworking) suggests that it could be *'anywhere within the prehistoric to the Early Medieval periods.'* Interestingly enough it also would appear that the two ingot finds have rather different smelting and refining traditions.

Another, early positive identification was found near the source of the Avon from the enclosed settlement of Dean Moor. Here, back in the mid-1950s, a small but significant globule of smelted tin was found *'within a burnt spread around a hearth'* in one hut, and in another a cassiterite pebble was discovered having been trodden into the floor. Given that the ceramic

finds from the same site have now been dated rather confidently to the period 1300 to 1100 BC, then here again we have reason to suppose that tin was being worked on the moor over 3,000 years ago.

Given the importance and value attached to the metal, logic suggests that this industry would have continued unabated through the centuries and certainly through the period of Roman occupation, however Quinnell concludes that there is currently *'very little evidence for the working of Dartmoor tin before the full Medieval period.*

'But,' she adds a little more optimistically, *'it is highly likely that data for this will be forthcoming in the future.'*

Quinnell's comment leads us nicely into another section of Sir Stafford Northcote's presidential address of 1861. Having dealt with tales of Phoenicia and Troy and Rome (he suggested that the Romans didn't have too much to do in the far west of England as the area was already relatively civilised compared to the rest of the country), he contended that *'there are many other small evidences of the same connection.*

'Some of them,' he averred, *'may perhaps be fanciful; others have something in them'* and, anticipating Quinnell by more than 150 years expressed the hope that *'those who come here with the power and the habit of testing and sifting evidence, will enable us to judge for ourselves how far these matters have any real worth.'*

Sir Stafford then went on to speak of the evidence of place-names. *'Polwhele, who is perhaps our best local historian traces Phoenician origin in everything – in names, in places, in everything to be found in the West of England … Because we do know that the science of etymology, the comparison of one language with another, often affords the means of ascertaining the connection between one people and another. [this comment eliciting a hearty 'hear hear' from his audience]*

'I should be glad to know if there is any truth in the origin which he ascribes to the names Hartland Point, Start Point, Belston and others, he supposes to contain traces of Phoenician worship – Start Point referring to Astarte, Hartland Point to Hercules, and Belston to Belus.

'He speaks of double pillars at Hartland and Start Point, and connects them with the Phoenician worship of the sun and moon; and with the celebrated Phoenician pillars of Hercules. We know that at Cadiz, a point to which they attained in Spain, there were two pillars – the two pillars of Hercules, one of the great landmarks of the ancient world. These were pillars connected no doubt with Phoenician worship. Polwhele supposes there were two pillars at Hartland Point; and speaks of there being the remains of such pillars at Start Point even now.

'I do not know whether such is the case; but it is matter for the curious to enquire into. Polwhele sees in these double pillars traces of the Phoenician worship being introduced into this country.'

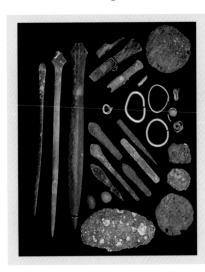

Part of the fabulous Salcombe hoard that contained some 320 gold, copper alloy and tin ornaments, weapons and ingots from the Bronze Age which were recovered from the seabed off the South Devon Coast by the South-West Maritime Archaeology Group and sold to the British Museum for £29,000.

Northcote then went on to talk about the early remains on Dartmoor, an area that was then starting to attract major interest among the archaeological community and, picking up on Polwhele's point 30 years later, John Lloyd Warden Page in his book *An Exploration of Dartmoor and Its Antiquities* (Seeley & Co., London 1892) notes that: *'Several tors having the prefix Bel have had their etymology traced to Belus or Baal, whom the Phoenicians worshipped as the Sun-god, while Ham Tor has been assigned to their deity Ammon.'*

In this context Page later adds a footnote quoting Crossing (*Amid Devonia's Alps* p.193) where he observes that Bel Tor, Belstone, Bellaford and Bala Brook, etc., are in close proximity to ancient mine workings – or bals.

'Is this not better than Druids?' Page asks. Given that the first use of the term bal – used to describe a mine, first occurs around 1600 AD the answer must surely be no, indeed is it not more likely that the term bal or ball derives from those bel locations?

Meanwhile to go back to that meeting in Exeter in 1861 we find Stafford Northcote still in full flow, now invoking Shakespeare in his attempt to demonstrate that by adducing trifles that may appear *'light as air'* in themselves, are when taken together can appear as *'confirmations strong as proofs of holy writ: Othello Act III, Scene III.'*

Northcote's latest witness in his attempt to affirm a Phoenician connection with Devon was *'another departed friend, Mr Richard Ford.'*

As it happens, Ford's daughter, Georgina, had married Sir Stafford's brother, Henry. More importantly, however, shortly after his own wedding Mr Richard Ford had decamped to Spain for four years and it was there that he formulated his essay on Cob Walls which would later appear in the *Quarterly Review* in 1837.

'This learned article,' opined Sir Stafford, *'may have faded from the memory of some of you, but it is quite worth refreshing your recollection of it.*

'He traces the origin of cob to the very earliest times; and he traces it curiously enough from the Phoenicians along both sides of the Mediterranean sea, at Carthage and in Spain, and then he brings it over, leaps over, from the Pillars of Hercules to the South West of England.

'Here there certainly does seem some reason to suppose that this institution (for it really is a county institution) of cob walls (laughter) – may have come to us from these same people – the Phoenicians ("hear, hear").'

Again this may not seem like a significant piece of archaeological evidence, but it remains true that Devon has, historically, always had the greatest number of cob-walled buildings in Britain, with Cornwall and Dorset not far behind, and some are very ancient indeed. As for the rest of the country, such structures are something of a rarity.

Sir Stafford was still not done, however, he had yet another crowd-pleasing trifle with which to entertain his audience and to act as a tourist pitch to those listening who had perhaps not been to the county before.

'There is one matter which, under any circumstances, I recommend our visitors to make themselves acquainted with, whether it is of Phoenician antiquity or not ... I mean our clouted (sic) cream.'

Another ripple of laughter rang out around the room.

'It is,' enthused the speaker, *'a very good thing in itself ("hear, hear" and more laughter). Therefore they will not be doing any harm in investigating it rather carefully.*

'But,' he went on forcibly, *'it is said that clouted cream is to be found nowhere except in the West of England, and in the neighbourhood of Tyre.*

Typical Devon cob house, Sheepwash, from Baring-Goulds Book of Devon 5th Edition 1935

Left: Rodda's Clotted Cream, in production since 1890.

'There are some curious little circumstances connected with it. We know the old name of cheese, which appears to been something like compressed milk, or Tyre, and butter. Then in the composition of the stuff which they make in India – ghee – they put in sour milk called "tyre".' Northcote continued: 'A description is given in one of the ancient writers, Pliny I think, of the way of making butter, and of substance which he calls oxygala, a very close relative of clouted cream. He mentions that butter was not originally known to the Greeks or Romans, who acquired it from the barbarous nations. According to his description, the ancients made oxygala exactly in the way that we make clouted cream, by warming the milk over the fire.'

Some 150 years later the *Oxford Companion to Food* concurs. Following the folklore tradition they too suggest that clotted cream *'may have been introduced to Cornwall (and Devon of course!) by Phoenician traders in search of tin.*

'It is similar to kaymak, a Near Eastern delicacy that is made throughout the Middle East, southeast Europe, Iran, Afghanistan, India and Turkey.'

Before Sir Stafford wrapped up this section of his presidential address he referred to a then recent discovery of glass and glass beads on Haldon Hill some of the earliest examples of which were made in Tyre and the likes of which were found in the much more recent Whitehorse Hill find referred to above. These finds led modern archaeologists to speculate in a similar way.

As Sir Stafford himself put it: *'I dare say half these things are worth nothing; but they still seem to tend one way ...'*

Indeed they do, and today as we look back from the twenty-first century there seems even more reason to support the views of our ancient scribes, notably one Aylett Sammes.

Sammes was a seventeenth-century English antiquary, whose seminal work *Britannia Antiqua* (published in 1676) was one of a number of early historical works in the library of our Hemerdon resident and Dartmoor pioneer, Henry Woollcombe.

Borrowing here and there from the slightly earlier endeavours of Samuel Bochart, who died a decade before Sammes went to press, and whose texts were only ever published in Latin, Sammes put forward what was, on the surface at least, a fairly convincing and comprehensive account of the impact of the Phoenicians on the place-names of our Welsh and Western shores.

And, underpinning all of that was the Phoencians' prime motive for visiting these shores in the first place – tin.

Sammes argues that the Cassiterides ultimately became a generic term for the British Isles, but not under that incarnation of the name, rather in the original Phoenician – Bratanac. Bratanac he suggests means, in Phoenician, the Country of Tin (or as it appears throughout his text – tynn): the Brit element coming from Bretta, the Spanish word for earth which in turn had been conferred upon the indigenous Iberi (as the Phoenicians had dubbed the Spanish thereby giving us Iberia with Iberi here meaning 'Diggers in Mines'). The relevance here being that, according to Sammes, the Phoenician route to Westcountry tin was through Spain.

The 'anac' element argued Sammes *'Anciently signifying Tynn among the Phoenicians.'* Evidencing an easy transition from Bratanac to Britannia, Sammes claims that the Greeks later translated the Phoenician 'Country of Tynn' into their own language as Cassiterides, literally 'the Tin Islands'.

Sammes, however, fell foul of the notion then prevalent among the ancient academics that the Tin Islands were the Isles of Scilly and their main trading point, Ictis was St Michael's Mount. However the Isles are not tin-rich and as Paul Ashbee puts it forcibly in his *Ancient Scilly* (1974): *'It is impossible that Scillonian tin could have been of any consequence in the ancient world.'*

Polwhele concurred and was among the first to point the finger closer to home. Reasoning that the Isles of Scilly were too far west, too remote and lacking the substantial tin resources to be found either side of the Tamar and the Plym, he proposed that an island in Plymouth Sound would be a more logical location for Ictis.

'That our idea of the convenience of such a central spot to the tin traders of Devon and Cornwall, is perfectly just, seems evinced in the strongest manner, by the actual meetings of the Devonshire and Cornish miners on Hengstone-down, at no great distance from our island, for the purpose of renewing the remembrance of their unwritten laws (their traditional observances of high antiquity) and of settling various points, in which both parties were interested, either as tin-manufacturers or merchants. Periodical associations of this kind were natural.'

Writing in 1797, Polwhele quoted Richard Carew's 1602 Survey where the latter noted that there was a saying among country folk that:
Hengston-downe well ywrought, Is worth London towne, deare bought.
This he averred *'grewe from the store of tynne, in former times, there digged up: But this gainfull plentie is now fallen to a scant saving scarcitie.'*

Left: Title page from Sammes' Britannia Anitqua.
Above: Early depictions of Phoencian ships.

Recent revelations certainly provide the most compelling argument to date that we are on the verge of establishing beyond reasonable doubt that the tin trade, whether it was from Cornwall or south-west Dartmoor, was being conducted with the Middle East all those years ago. Essentially the latest examination of tin ingots found off Kfar Samir, Israel, suggests that the material dates from 1300-1200 BC and originated in ore formed around 291 million years ago – which according to one of the leaders of the research team, Dr Daniel Berger, rules out sources in Anatolia, central Asia and Egypt, which formed much earlier or later. Furthermore the elemental composition, according to Berger's paper published in the peer-reviewed, open-access scientific journal produced by the Public Library of Science, PLOS ONE, 'is quite similar to those of the Salcombe ingots.'

A few of the ingots investigated were found by a fisherman, Adib Shehade, off the shore of Kfar Samir (north), in the 1970s. Remarkably he retrieved 30 rectangular ingots, which he subsequently sold to a local tinsmith who used some of the tin to repair car radiators. Fortunately, however, four of them were bought by the University of Haifa.

In the 1980s there was another spectacular find, off the coast of Turkey. This was said to be an Uluburun ship, which sank shortly before 1318 BC and amongst the items in its cargo were glass ingots, faience, resin, items fashioned out of gold, silver, ivory and amber, 10 tons of copper ingots and a ton of tin. There have been other less striking finds in recent years, but then, quite remarkably, in 2014 a further ten tin ingots were found by a team of archaeologists, including Ehud Galili of Haifa University, off the coast of Haifa in Kfar Samir (south).

The find was part of a wider discovery dubbed a 'Neolithic Atlantis' by the media as it came from the remains of a 7,700-year-old village that sat underwater some 220 yards offshore beneath 16 ft of seawater. Among the items retrieved from the site were some of the oldest wooden artefacts in the world, evidence of olive oil production ... and ancient tin.

Drawing together samples from these and other finds, Berger and the team at the Curt Engelhorn Centre for Archaeometry in Germany, looked at some 215 tin ingots weighing almost one and a half tons and concluded that the tin was likely to have originated in Cornwall and Devon.

Picking up on the story *The Times* of Israel noted how 'archaeologists have found evidence of tin mining in Cornwall and Devon as early as 2000 BC' and affirmed that 'ancient methods of mining the metal, such as sifting river water, leave few or no artefacts, meaning the metal may have been harvested from these areas or even earlier.'

Meanwhile, Berger and his team felt that it was 'no accident that that the shift in the tin trade from the Near East to Europe and Cornwall in particular, documented by the isotopic and chemical evidence, corresponds to the demise of the Minoans and the rise of the Mycenaeans c.1430 BCE.

'Unlike the Minoans, the Mycenaeans sailed west and established several trading ports in southern Italy, Sicily, Sardinia and south Iberia, which served as gateways to new trading routes to Britain and the European interior.'

Top: Dr Daniel Berger. Middle: Ehud Galili of Haifa University working on the submerged village off the coast of Israel. Photo: Dr Jonathan Benjamin courtesy of Dr Ehud Galili, University of Haifa and Israel Antiquities Authority. Bottom: Three of the ingots of tin from Cornwall or Devon. Photo Ehud Galili

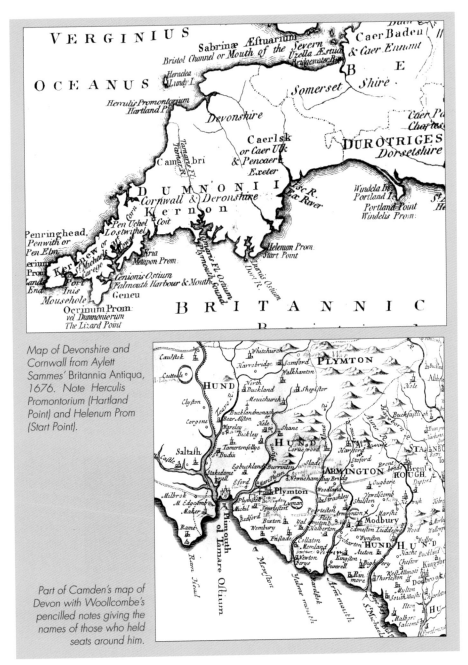

Map of Devonshire and Cornwall from Aylett Sammes' Britannia Antiqua, 1676. Note Herculis Promontorium (Hartland Point) and Helenum Prom (Start Point).

Part of Camden's map of Devon with Woollcombe's pencilled notes giving the names of those who held seats around him.

In another footnote Powhele references the figure now regarded as the father of British local history, John Leland, who, in 1542, and then in his late-thirties, visited the West Country and made the following observation locally: 'By the river of Tamar from the hedde north north est issuying owt towarde the sowthe, the contrey being hilly, is fertile of corne & gresse with sum tynne workes wrougt by violens of water. Hengiston beyng a hy hylle, and nere Tamar, in the east part, baryn of his self, yet is fertile by yelding of tynne both bi water & dry workes.'

Polwhele picks up the story again: 'If then, the Devonshire and Cornish miners were in the habit of consulting their mutual convenience, by such meetings at a central spot, is it not fair to conclude, that they had a regard also to the common advantage, in the actual exportation of their tin, and that they conveyed this metal to some port of traffick, equally commodious to both parties? This port was some island on their coasts: and where can an island be found more accessible to both parties?'

For further evidence Polwhele wrote: 'Let us add to this, the vestiges of ancient tin-works in its vicinity.

'We are informed, from records, that "all the old mines on Dartmoor, are on its western side towards the Tamar." This is a curious circumstance. And there is no doubt but the traces of old tin-works are chiefly on the west side of the forest. Here are strong marks of both shode and stream-works. The boldest vestiges also, of our ancient Cornish mines, are very near the Tamar. It is natural, therefore, to conjecture, that the greater abundance of tin on the banks of the Tamar, would give a proportionate consequence to the adventurers of the neighbourhood; and the weight of interest thus irresistibly acquired, would render their own district the principal seat of commerce.'

In order to identify the island at the heart of this commercial activity, as we have mentioned already, Polwhele quotes Diadorus as saying 'The space between Ictis and the main land becomes an isthmus at the reflux of the tide.'

'Such, even now,' wrote Polwhele, 'may almost be said of St Nicholas (Drake's Island); since "from this island a range of rocks reacheth over to the south west shore, discovered at the low water of spring tides.

'It is remarkable that this range of rocks is called the Bridge. Nor have I a doubt that in the time of our historian this bridge was passable: and great quantities of tin from the west, were probably carried over it in Cornish waggons.'

'… it seems reasonable to suppose that these ledges of rock towards the sea, were once covered with strata of gravel and sand and earth, forming a part of the isle of St Nicholas; but that these different layers were removed in a course of time from their foundation of rock, fretted away by the gradual fluctuation of the sea , disturbed and tumbled into the deep from the mining of subterraneous waters, divulsed and dashed to atoms amidst earthquakes and the violence of the tempest.'

Whilst it is difficult to state with any degree of certainty that such a passable bridge ever existed between Mount Edgcumbe and St Nicholas Island, their appears to be no archaeological evidence for any Bronze Age occupation of the isle, whereas there is, as we have already seen, clear testimony for the suggestion that Mount Batten, just a few hundred yards to the east of Drake's Island, was Ictis of the Ancients – the Bronze Age trading-post between the sailors from the Mediterranean and the native population – the Dunmonii.

Interestingly enough, here is another name that Aylett Sammes suggests came from our overseas visitors: *'the Inhabitants of Cornwal (sic) and Devonshire, in which two Counties the Phoenicians were very conversant, by reason of their abounding Tynn, derived their name from the Phoenicians.*

'Upon this account some have derived them from Moina, in the British Tongue signifying Mines, but the Question is, whence the Dan or Dun proceeds? For Solinus calls them Dunmonii; Ptolomy, Damnonii, and in other Copies (Cambden saith) trulier Daumonii, although I think the transposition is very easie and usual and hides not at all the Original Dan or Dun.'

He continued, *'In the Ancient British Language, as also in the Phoenician, Dun or Tun (for in composition we find both waies) signifies a Hill ... from Dun or Tun, or Monia, signifying Hills of Tynn; I find that both waies that they are of a Phoenician Derivation.'*

Sammes then turns his attention on the *'first Country of the Dunmonii Westward – Cornwal – shooting into the Sea ... the Name of which Country, if we examine the Original of it, and what at this day it is called by the Inhabitants ... we shall find it could be called so by none but the Phoenicians. To prove this, let us consider it is agreed unto by all hands, that it received its Name from being like a Horn, running smaller and smaller, with little Promontories as if they were horned on either side: And this is brought from Korn, Plural, Kern, signifying Horns in the British Language.*

'Now as this Kern or Korn is derived from the Phoenician Cheren, signifying the same, so the manner of calling Places after sort came from them also, a thing so frequent in Eastern Countries to call any Corner or Angle made, by the name of Horn; As for Example, Cyprus called Cerastis ... that we are not to doubt but Cornwal, called Kernaw by the Inhabitants, proceeds from the Phoenician here.'

Mentioning in passing that Corsica was, *'from its having so many Promontories, called Carnatha, by the Phoenicians,'* Sammes took his Cornwall/Kernow line further by adding: *'That Cornwal was called Kernaw by them rather than the Inhabitants, will appear, Firstly, Because there is no other Promontory in this Island so called, notwithstanding the*

Grignion's engraving of John Leland, reputedly taken from a bust of the sixteenth-century antiquary at All Souls College, Oxford.

British Language was in use through the whole ... There are other Places that run into the Sea as much like a Horn as this, which, in my judgement, is an evident sign of the Phoenicians in this part of England above others.

'Secondly, Because it is more natural to imagine, that Sailers (to whom the shapes of Countries appear at a distance, more than to the Inhabitants), should give the Name, than those that only ply'd upon the Shoars in small Carows, or Leather and Wicker Boats, as the Britains did.'

Having dealt with the main name elements Sammes went on to suggest, somewhat questionably, countless other Cornish connections with the language of the Phoenician folk, foremost among them one of the most common place name elements in that county – Pen.

'We find many places begin with Pen, namely, such as are of a High scituation (sic), which, without dispute, is an Argument, that Pen, a Hill in the British Language, came from the Phoenician Pinnah, signifying the same thing, because we find it most used in those parts of England the Phoenicians frequented most; nay through all this Island we shall scarce meet with any Northward, when on the West and South Coasts, we cannot go six or eight miles but we find them.

'To instance the south-side of Cornwal only: Penrose, Pensansm Pengersick, Penrose again, Penwarren, Pendennis, Penkeivel, Penwyn, Pentuan, Penrock, to which may be added that infinite number of Towns, beginning with Tre, as Treewose, Trenowth, Tregenno, Trewarveneth, Trevascus, Trenona, Trewaridreth, Trewargan, Tergermin, Treliscick, Trefuses, Tregamian, Tremadart, Tregonoc, which those verysame Parts can have no other account given of them if they proceed not from the Phoenician Tira, and by contraction, Tra, signifying a Castle, so that they were Forts built by them to secure their Trade.'

Interesting observations indeed, particularly when considering the two, admittedly much later, forts located near the mouths of the Tamar and the

The term Bronze Age doesn't appear to have been coined until after the exploration of Dartmoor began in earnest.

The man credited with the phrase is the English banker, politician, philanthropist and polymath, Sir John Lubbock, who in his seminal work of 1865, Pre-Historic Times, came up with the terms Palaeolithic and Neolithic to describe the Old and New Stone Ages. A near neighbour of Charles Darwin, with whom he had extensive correspondence, Lubbock also spoke of the Bronze Age and the Iron Age.

In 1871 Lubbock purchased land at Avebury to prevent part of its ancient stone circle being built on and some years later when elevated to the peerage he took the title of Baron Avebury in the County of Wiltshire.

In 1874 he introduced a bill into Parliament that would later become the Ancient Monuments Act of 1884.

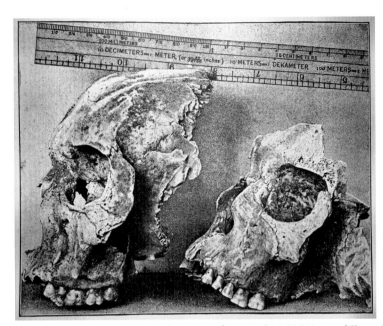

Paleolithic Plymouthians (sic) – Cattedown Cave (from Worth's 1890 History of Plymouth)

Plym, are at Trematon and Plympton (which Gilbert Dyer of Exeter in his book *A Restoration of the Ancient Modes of bestowing Names on the Rivers, Hills, &c. of Britain* (1805) suggested was a compound one of three syllables: pen, leim or lim and ton meaning the enclosed space at the port head).

The view was endorsed by Baring-Gould almost a century later when he wrote in his *Book of Devon* (1899) that *'Plym is not the name of the river which has its mouth where the town squats. Plym is the contraction for Pen-lynn, the head of the lake, and was given originally to Plympton, where are the remains of a castle and where are still to be seen the iron rings to which vessels were moored.'*

Indeed in March 2010 an archaeological work by J Austin of Exeter Archaeology *'clearly demonstrated that the former quay wall lies preserved beneath Market Road, on a broadly similar alignment to it.'*

No dating evidence was recovered so it was not possible to say whether this was the earliest quay wall or a later one, however its proximity to the Priory site suggests that it probably dates from at least the first millennium. Sammes enlisted a number of other Phoenician terms in support of his thesis and while in recent years there has been much debate about whether there was ever a definable state known as Phoenicia, the question is largely irrelevant. As long as the area encompassed by the generic term Phoenicia and the Levatine mariners who sailed from those parts had a common language, the issue is principally an academic one.

As indeed is the issue of what constitutes the Bronze Age itself.

The term 'bronze' to describe that alloy that generally runs to eight parts copper one part tin, doesn't appear at all in Western Literature until the sixteenth century while, as we have seen, the expression 'Bronze Age' is much later still, being first deployed by John Lubbock in 1865.

Based on a series of lectures he delivered to the Royal Institution in the summer of 1864 Lubbock published his *Pre-Historic Times, as Illustrated by Ancient Remains, and the Manners and Customs of Modern Savages* the following year and in it he also coined the terms Paleolithic and Neolithic. The former relates to that time *'when many shared the possession of Europe with the Mammoth, the Cave bear, the Wooly-haired rhinoceros and other extinct animals'*, while the latter describes *'the later or polished Stone age; a period characterized by beautiful weapons and instruments made of flint and other kinds of stone, in which, however we find no trace of the knowledge of any metal, excepting gold, which seems to have been sometimes used for ornaments.'*

Certainly the finds from the caves at Cattedown give us plenty of evidence of the mouth of the Plym being inhabited in the Palaeolithic era, with human remains being found alongside traces of lion, hyena, rhinoceros and woolly mammoth.

There is no reason to suppose that such human occupation of the area has not been consistent from that day to this.

Furthermore, additional evidence of the ancients' existence around the mouth of the Plym is to be found on the opposite bank of the river, above Oreston on the landward route connecting Mount Batten to Dartmoor. For it is there we find the only known man-made structure surviving today within the modern Plymouth boundary in the shape of the tumulus – the Bronze Age barrow – that gives its name to Burrow Hill.

It would appear that until relatively recently there were two other earthen burial mounds in the same vicinity but these were bulldozed in the levelling out of the field.

Such mounds were introduced into this country by the Beaker people around 1800 BC, at the very dawn of the Bronze Age.

Bronze coinage, after generations of copper coinage Britain went bronze in 1860.

Among the many finds from the archaeological digs at Crownhill Down have been these three gems. Top left: One of three bronze axes of the Middle Bronze Age. Bottom left: Faience bead. Right: A viirtually whole, but fragmented Bearker pot of the early Bronze Age.
There were several bags of pottery sherds, most from the Middle Bronze Age along with a number of flint tools from a Beaker grave assemblage, as well as other flint flakes, most probably dating from the Bronze Age..

Meanwhile, it's interesting to note that around the very time that the notion of a Bronze Age (or Bronze Period as Daniel Wilson had described it a little earlier, in 1851, in his *Prehistoric Annals of Scotland*) was gaining currency in Britain, the Government was preparing to refashion the old copper penny with a lighter, bronze version.

First issued in 1860, the new bronze penny, and indeed bronze halfpenny, sported, like its earlier incarnation, the monarch's head on the obverse and a depiction of Britannia on the reverse but now there was a new element added to the mix – a small but recognisable image of the Eddystone lighthouse behind Britannia. Was this a pure coincidence or was it a deliberate nod in the direction of the Cassiterides, the Tin Islands, just south of which the Eddystone sits, below Plymouth Sound, the veritable hub of the commercial exportation of tin, without which there would have been no Bronze Age?

Although, of course, in its unmarked state, who knows how many trading vessels were lost on those treacherous red rocks of the Eddystone Reef.

The first light was not erected there until the late-eighteenth century and Smeaton's tower itself – the one depicted on the new coinage – had just celebrated its centenary (1759-1859).

Today an iconic feature on Plymouth Hoe, where it was re-erected after the construction of the present Douglass Lighthouse on the reef, and although it disappeared from the bronze penny in 1895, it returned in 1937 and stayed there until decimalization.

Of course, as well as the introduction of small value bronze coins (nevertheless destined to be forever referred to as coppers), the nineteenth century also witnessed something of a revival of tin mining in the area. However, before we can look at that we must assess the scant material that we have on mining activities in the area between the Bronze Age and the Victorian era.

29

A reconstructed prehistoric settlement c.3000 BC © Dartmoor National Park

WHAT DID THE ROMANS EVER DO FOR US?

If an accurate picture of Bronze Age activity in the South West is difficult to paint with any real degree of certainty from a twenty-first-century perspective, the situation barely improves as we move forward in time. However, it is by now seemingly incontrovertible to suggest that something was happening around the upper reaches of the Plym by the time that the Iron Age arrived and that that activity was almost certainly centred around alluvial tin streaming.

We have already mentioned Boringdon Camp, let us now consider it in more detail. Described by Slater and Pearson in their 1985 *Survey of Boringdon Camp* (in the proceedings of the Devon Archaeological Society) *'as a large circular enclosure with a single entrance in the eastern part of its main circuit'* this is one of a number of Iron Age or Romano-British (c.600 BC to 400 AD) structures in the area.

With a 'rectilinear annexe to the southeast' apparently acting as an outwork, it is a curious and impressive structure. Roland Smith, writing a decade after Slater and Pearson, was uncertain of its origins. *'Whether the enclosure represents a permanent occupation site, a fortified place of refuge, or an elaborate defensible stock enclosure is as yet undetermined.'* Brooking Rowe, on the other hand, writing at the dawn of the twentieth century was a little less circumspect: *'There can be but little question that the place known as the Castle Ring, or Boringdon Camp, is Celtic, and of much earlier date than anything now remaining at Plympton. The name Boringdon, Burrington, Burraton,'* he continued, *'and its variations, Bury Down – mean the earthwork fortress on the hill.*

'This fortress stands high – five hundred feet above sea level – and it commands the valleys below, those of the Plym and the Torry Brook.' Back then it was clearly a vantage point of some significance as these two rivers were much more navigable and important than they are today, or even in Brooking Rowe's day. As he noted: *'An old woman of Plympton, who died about the year 1834 at the age of 94, used to say that her mother had told her that she recollected vessels coming to the quay opposite the Church of St Mary where there was a boathouse. Other old persons still alive remember boats coming very far up what are now the marshes, west of the road leading from Plympton St Mary bridge to Underwood ... even now, sometimes with very heavy rain, or a rapid thaw after snow, and a flowing tide, the lower parts of Plympton are inundated by the overflow of the stream. That there is very much less land in these valleys covered with water than in former days is certain.'*

Indeed: although no doubt Brooking Rowe would be amazed to see the amount of development that has now taken place over those spaces prone to inundation.

But if the area has changed so much in the last 300 years, what would it have looked like 1,000 years ago?

'While now the estuary is two miles from Plympton, in early times the tidal waters flowed nearly up to it, and at high tide, even in medieval times, it would seem that they washed the walls of the castle.'

The very mound of which Brooking Rowe observed, *'as pointed out to us by a distinguished engineer officer'* ... *'is in a direct line with Boringdon Camp.'*

Clearly the detritus generated by the extensive tin mining of the upper reaches of the Plym contributed massively to the silting up of the lower reaches of the river and the Plym Estuary itself, making it difficult to imagine just how navigable the waterways were two or even three thousand years ago.

In this context it's interesting to note that former Plymouth City Council Archaeological Officer, Keith Ray, in the mid-1990s wrote of a *'very much smaller, and as yet unproven contemporary (with Boringdon Camp) enclosure may have stood at the western end of a high hill spur very much closer to the centre of Plympton.*

'This site is attested only historically, through a local name that appears in the nineteenth century and whose derivation is unknown. It has been identified as 'Crana Castle' (Plympton Documents Part 1: Stevens) a place known as 'Crownhill' in the nineteenth century, as revealed by field names in the 1842 Tithe Award.'

'Crana Castle is likely to be the site of a kind of Iron Age enclosure known as a 'promontory fort'. The most dramatic of such sites are in the coastal locations and within southwestern Britain they are most common in Cornwall.'

The idea behind them was to protect what became an enclosed space from easy attack and as Ray was keen to point out: *'The topography certainly favours such an interpretation. Although the very end of the spur has been lost to quarrying, the hill clearly dropped away sharply to the west and north.'*

Typically hill forts were thrown up to protect communities and to allow them to protect the source of whatever it was that drove their local economy, and, not surprisingly perhaps, tin-rich Devon and Cornwall each have more than any other English County with Devon being the slightly more heavily populated. Somerset, Wiltshire and Dorset are the next in line indicating that the Westcountry was at that time the most developed part of England, although it's worth noting that there are a lot in Wales too, and along the Scottish borderline. For this area, however, the inference that presents itself is that the South-west was more advanced than the rest of the country, and that foremost among the theories for this was the trading with, and the influence of, the merchants from the Mediterranean and mainland Europe.

The natives of the eastern parts of what we now call England were less sophisticated.

Calling themselves, as Mr Camden had it, the Cumero, they were known to those on the other side of the Channel as painted people, the Bryths or Brits, hence Britains as Aylett Sammes argued again in his *Antiqua Britannia.*

The men of the western regions *'Cornwal and Devonshire'* where *'Mettal most abounded. The description of which is given by Strabo. They are Inhabited (saies he) by Men wearing black Garments, clad in side Coats descending to their Ankles, going with Staves like the Furies in Tragedies; Mines they have of Tynn and Lead, which they exchange for Earthen-Pots, Salt, and Brazen ware.'*

Top left: Artist's impression of a civilised Ancient Britain from Aylett Sammes's Britannia Antiqua Illustrata. *Right: Artist's impression of Bronze Age man based on recent finds at Sherford. Above: Still from 'The Life of Marghwen' with clothing and accessories based on the findings in the Whitehorse Hill kist © Dartmoor National Park.*

That the trading and general interaction with foreigners encouraged a more 'civilised' society is further evidenced in that the natives living away from the sea coasts went about naked.

Pomponius Mela, regarded as the first Roman geographer, wrote around 43AD of them that their *'bodies are dyed with Woad; whether it be to make a gallant shew, or for what else, is uncertain.'*

'Dio Nicæus, out of Xiphilin's Epitome, concerning the Britains in the North part of the Island,' we read in Sammes, noted that *'They till no ground, but live upon prey and hunting, and the fruit of trees: Fish (though they have it in very great plenty) they will not taste. They dwell in tents, naked, and unshod. They use their wives in common, and bring up all the children among them.'*

Pliny, also writing in the first century AD in his *Naturalis Historia*, a work that very much became a template for subsequent encylopedias wrote that the Britains *'There groweth an Herb in Gaul like unto Plantain, named Glastum, that is, Woad, with the juyce of which the Women of Britain, as well married Wives, as their young Daughters, anoint and dye their Bodies all over.'*

Gaius Julius Solinus writing around 250 AD in *De mirabilibus mundi* (*The Wonder of the World*), attested *'That the Country is partly Peopled with Barbarians, who, by the means of Artificial Incisions of divers forms, have, from their Childhood, sundry figures of Beasts printed upon them, and having these Characters deeply engraven on their Bodies, as the Man grows in stature, so do these painted Characters also. Neither do these Savage Nations think any thing shews their Courage more, than undergoing these lasting Stars, by which their Limbs drink in much Paint or Colour.'*

There has been some debate about the accuracy of some of these accounts, but Julius Caesar himself, the first Roman to give an account of the British, noted that those he initially encountered *'did stain themselves with Woad, which createth a blew colour, to make themselves more terrible to their enemies in fight.'*

The notion that our Westcountry ancestors were not only wearing clothes, as the Whitehorse finds testify (the finds have been radiocarbon dated between 1800-1600 BC) but that they also appear to have tilled the ground and had sophisticated settlements suggesting a degree of civilisation that eluded much of the rest of the country.

Strabo, incidentally, also notes that *'Some of them for want of skill, can make no Cheese, although they have plenty of Milk.'* An observation that resonates with the earlier contention that Devon and Cornwall's clotted cream production was an art learned from our early trading visitors.

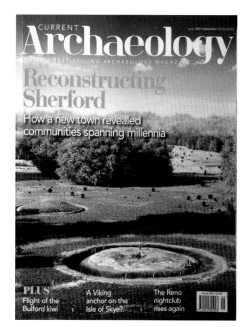

Recent finds at the vast development site for Sherford village, just below the A38 route that separates Plympton from Plymstock, suggest a vast Bronze Age settlement that went on to host a substantial Romano-British community well into the first millennium. Top right: Limestone structure thought maybe to have been a Romano-British corn-dryer. Above: Artist's reconstruction of Bronze Age barrows unearthed at Sherford.

Meanwhile, later finds support the notion that *'activity in the Plymouth area during the centuries of Roman administration of Britain was very probably much more considerable than has been appreciated hitherto'* (Ray 1995). *'In general, the number and density of well-attested coin finds of the period is greater in the Plymouth area than anywhere else in Devon apart from Exeter and the east of the county bordering Somerset and Dorset.'*

As far as Plympton itself is concerned the finds have been *'primarily from areas bordering the former tidal inlet that stretched from the Plym at Saltram right up to Market Road, at least into the eighteenth century'. (ibid)*

Among the Roman coins found in the late nineteenth century, *'mainly adjacent to the ancient shore line'* RH Worth included examples found of Alexander Severus, Antoninus Pius, Constans, Domitan, Nero, Trajan Decius, Vespasian all at Mount Batten; Hadrian, Alexander Severus and Antonius Pius at Cattedown, Victorinus at Staddon; Carus and Magnetius at Millbay, as well as various others dotted around the area, among them a couple of unidentified pieces from Plympton.

Alexander Severus 222-235AD

Antonius Pius 138-161 AD

Nero 54-68AD

Hadrian 117-138AD

Worth's sketch of the Roman Bronze figure of Mercury found at Hooe in April 1888.

Worth also mentioned a discovery made at Hooe, in April 1888, around the time he was working on his second edition of the *History of Plymouth*. Unearthed in a garden in Hooe, at Plymstock, it was a figure of Mercury – god of merchandise and patron of merchants.

'It is two and one-eighth inches in height ...'

'There is full reason to believe that this figure was one of the gods of a Roman merchant; and the little landlocked harbour of Hooe at once suggests itself as an admirably adapted for a trading post.'

Somewhat intriguingly, it is possible that we know the name of at least one of our Roman traders, Lucius Mancus, for that is the name scratched on one of the sherds found at Mount Batten

This certainly would appear to be in line with Brooking Rowe's contention that *'it is not altogether improbable that we have at Plympton the outlines of a Roman camp, and that a Roman fortification of some kind was in existence there. It is not likely that the Norman would have raised such a mound as now exists; and in such a position as this, if he had not found an earthwork ready to his hand, instead of the round shell keep, the remains of which we have, he would have erected a rectangular one, as he generally did, unless he was able to erect his new building on an existing superstructure, to the outlines of which it was made to conform.*

'The rectangular form of the enclosure is some evidence in support of such a theory. A Roman road ran near it.'

Adducing further potential evidence he added: *'It is said that the remains of a galley, presumably Roman, but as to which we have no particulars, were found in the Torry Brook valley, and the names of places nearby – the Ridge Lane, Ridgeway, Voss and Dark Street Lane – tell we think, a story of a Roman settlement here.'*

On the subject of the galley, however, Worth was a little more specific and a little more sceptical: *'Mr JC Bellamy recorded that the remains of a Roman galley had been found in excavating Newnham Park but with no proof of identification (another account – more reasonably – calls the vessel a canoe).'*

Referring again to St Maurice Castle, Brooking Rowe wrote: *'The mound is certainly not Roman, but the regular form of the enclosure, the shape of the base court, the proximity of the great road, the importance of the position and the fact of there being a Romano-British population in the immediate neighbourhood, seem to afford some evidence in support of the idea that there was a Roman work of some kind here, perhaps placed by the Roman soldier upon the defensive fort of the Damnonii (sic).'*

Whatever form the settlement around Plympton took during the Roman occupation there can be little doubt that extensive trade was being conducted with our Latin overlords, particularly as they had long since been seeking the source of the Phoenician tin.

'The mystery was so well preserved that Julius Caesar when he landed in Britain was not aware that he had come to the land "whence tin came", although the helmets, shields, and breastplates of his centurions were composed of some ten per cent of the metal from Cornwall' averred EL Bowley in *The Fortunate Islands* in 1945.

Bowley was principally concerned with Cornwall and Isles of Scilly, yet, as George Lewis noted in 1907: while one *'would naturally be led to believe that the Romans would not have failed to seize properties of such value, yet scarcely a trace of their presence has been found in the older mines, or even in Cornwall itself ...'*

Indeed, that was the perceived wisdom throughout much of the twentieth century.

In the 1972 edition of WG Hoskin's *Devon*, first published in 1954, we find the celebrated local historian stating that the *'Romans made little impact anywhere in Devon, except at Exeter which they founded in the reign of Nero (54-68 AD) and which became the south-western terminus of their great frontier road, the Fosse Way ...'*

He continued, *'Despite many attempts to prove the existence of Roman roads west of Exeter (and attempts inter alia to establish Totnes as a Roman town) there is, as yet, no evidence for Roman occupation beyond the Exe. The sum total of Roman or Romano-British occupation is meagre.'*

Meanwhile, writing in 1970's *Dartmoor A New Study*, James Barber somewhat guardedly wrote: *'There is ... no evidence at present for settled habitation on Dartmoor between about 400 BC and the period of the first Anglo-Saxon settlements about AD 700.'*

Later still, Helen Harris in the *Industrial Archaeology of Dartmoor* published in 1992, in a stance adopted by many others, ventured to suggest that *'It is in the south-west of Dartmoor that tin first appears in known records ... in the middle of the twelfth century.*

'In 1168,' she writes, *'it was worked at Sheepstor near the Plym at Brisworthy, but it is not known under what circumstances or by whom it was first found,'* However, as there could have been no Bronze Age without the tin from Dartmoor and Cornwall, the need for written records to be brought to the table to convince the sceptics when we are essentially dealing with a pre-literate society is never going to be easy.

Shifting the focus a little nearer the present mining activity, the 1979 *Archaeological Survey of An Area Surrounding Hemerdon Ball* overseen by Chris Edwards suggested that there was no shortage of proof of early activity in the area: *'the most important evidence of prehistoric settlement on Crownhill Down is to be found on its crest where a well-defined system of rectilinear enclosures run from south to north ... and east to west from the present western field wall of Crownhill Down and Heathfowl Cottages (both now ruins) to "Old Bottle Hill Leat".'*

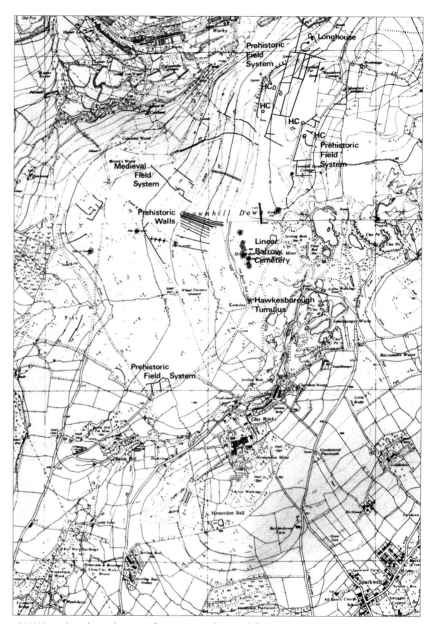

AMAX's archaeological survey of mine site and Crownhill Down.

RADIO CARBON TESTING
Willard Libby 1908-80. The American chemist who won the Nobel Prize for Chemistry in 1960 for his contributions to the team that had been developing the process since the 1940s. The process has revolutionised archaeology and palaeontology. Libby also discovered that just as organic compounds could be dated using carbon-14, so tritium could be used for dating water ... and hence wine.
During the war he worked on a gaseous diffusion process for uranium enrichment and later worked with Edward Teller developing the Hydrogen bomb. A participant in the Atoms for Peace programme, Libby, in his later years, at the University of California, worked towards improving the state's air pollution.

'It contains,' he continued, 'four hut circles, a hut platform and a cairn as well as evidence of subsequent medieval settlement in the form of remodelled prehistoric banks, two longhouses and four associated outbuildings.' Clearly it is difficult to precisely date these finds but there is no reason not to suppose continuous occupation, neither is their any reason to assume that their presence here was due to anything other than tin. But again, like the Phoenician issue itself, the evidence is circumstantial and hypothetical rather than written or empirical.

Thus we follow Lewis and many others who have come after him by 'passing from the Roman period to that of the Saxon regime in England,' where 'we find distinct evidence in the discovery of Anglo-Saxon bracelets and ornaments in old workings, that tin mining was not suffered to lapse, either before or after Athelstan's conquest of Cornwall in 937.'

Support for this contention came early in the twenty-first century when Thorndycraft, Pirrie and Brown published their paper on the *Alluvial Records of Medieval and Prehistoric Tin Mining on Dartmoor* in *Geoarchaeology* in 2004.

There they revealed evidence for post-Roman activity gleaned from a core of material 'taken from a palaeochannel far down the Erme Valley a little distance up from the normal tidal limit.'

Henrietta Quinnell assessing the findings puts it thus: 'The sequence in the core was analysed for its chemistry and a layer of sandy silt, interspersed between two peat deposits, showed heightened tin concentrations ... The beginning and end of this silt deposition was radiocarbon dated between AD 245-366.

'Both the increase in sandy silt and its heightened tin concentrations were considered consistent with, and therefore potentially dating, tin streaming further up the Erme Valley. This therefore suggests an episode of tinworking at some date in the late-Roman to early post-Roman periods.'

Clearly with the advantage of radiocarbon dating, modern archaeologists have been better able to assess their findings and 'prove' the antiquity of objects and materials with a reasonable degree of accuracy.

Interestingly enough the Erme would appear to have been one of the 15 place-names west of Exeter or Isca Dumnoniorum, to have been mentioned in the seventh-century Ravenna Cosmography – a massive 'road map' of the known world from India to Ireland, that was compiled by a priest at Ravenna in Northern Italy. Based on a collection of old sources, we find Duriarna – literally the 'fort on the River Arnos.' (In Gover, Mawer and Stenton's *Place-Names of Devon*, we read that Professor Max Förster compares the German river name Erms, earlier Armisa, suggesting that there may have been a British Arma. It appears as Irym and Hyrm in twelfth century documents and as Arme Haven according to Leland 1550).

'Each of the rivers of southern Dartmoor (Tavy/Tamar, Plym, Erme, Avon, Dart and Teign) were likely to have been used as communication routes to the moor, from coastal markets,' says leading Dartmoor authority, Tom Greeves, in his online resource *The Romans on Dartmoor*.

Greeves lists a remarkable number of Roman finds from all over the National Park, the sheer weight of which he postulates, points to tinworking remaining 'the most likely focus of Roman interest in Dartmoor.'

The Plym we have already dealt with, but if we widen our scope, to the other rivers, among the great many pieces of evidence Greeves introduces to the debate is the discovery in 1991-92 of 40 tin ingots from a wreck site off the mouth of the River Erme.

'These are most likely to be of Roman date, and one possibility is that the boat had just set off with a cargo of Dartmoor tin. The variety of shapes suggest independent tin smelters.'

Greeves also states that 'importation of amphorae from the Mediterranean, presumably containing oil and wine, in the immediate post-Roman period (5th and 6th centuries AD) is now known from two locations which seem to have been the sites of beach markets at the mouths of the Erme (Mothecombe) and Avon (Bantham) two Dartmoor rivers rich in tin, which is likely to have been traded in exchange.'

Amphorae, the classic two-handled traditionally Greek and Roman narrow-necked jars or jugs, were used in the transportation of all manner of goods and their presence, along with coins, distinctive pottery and exotic goods, 'filtering out even on to the higher moor' are all now pointing to one inevitable conclusion regarding activity across almost all of Dartmoor.

Okehampton and the area around it, it would appear, was a particularly busy spot:

'On the site of Okehampton Castle, a Roman sherd plus 16 pieces of tile, including one from a bath hypocaust, and building mortar, "strongly suggest the presence of a Romanised building in the immediate vicinity".'

Then there are the 200 or so coins dated around AD 320-330 that were found back in 1897 under a rock in Okehampton Park. Remember there were no cheque books, bank cards or banks in those days and large quantities of coins were 'hidden' for safety – which was fine as long as nothing happened to the person who had hidden them or their ability to remember where they had hidden them.

Meanwhile, 'at Chichacott, just north-east of Okehampton, a 1st -2nd-century Roman fort has been confirmed,' adds Greeves.

Moving south again, to what was destined to become, like Plympton, one of four Devon stannary towns – Chagford – we learn, from Greeves again, that 'in 2002-3 several sherds of Roman pottery dating to about AD 100 were found in the excavation of a roundhouse (hut circle) on the edge of the moor at Teigncombe, just above Chagford.'

Later he mentions 'a superbly crafted porphyritic stone bowl dating from 5th-7th century AD' that 'was found at Holy Street near Chagford in 1987, buried in a field which shows traces of possible house platforms. 'This high status object,' he adds, 'must reflect a relatively wealthy settlement.'

'Dartmoor,' Greeves concludes, 'can now be seen as an integral part of the Roman province of Dumnonia, and new discoveries are bound to reinforce this picture in the next few decades.'

So we no longer have to cling on to such slender threads as the oft-quoted seventh-century life of St John, patriarch of Alexandria, which mentions tin as a commodity obtained by a voyage to Britain.

Moreover, as John, the Almoner, died in 616 AD, and it appears that this account of his life was not put together for another 300 years, it's hardly a first-hand account – but it does make more sense in the light of recent discoveries than it perhaps did in the past.

The problem is that we have very little in the way of first-hand accounts for anything that took place in or before the first millennium and so it is an area heavily reliant on archaeological finds that indicate activity and contact. Among those post-Roman nuggets that are documented though are many that have a degree of resonance if not direct relevance.

It is recorded that in 838 a great battle took place at Hingston Down. The people of Cornwall fought alongside 'a great ship army' of Vikings and against the West Saxons led by Egbert, King of Wessex. Egbert had, over the previous two decades or so, raided Cornwall from east to west and his victory at Hingston Down would appear to have consolidated his conquest of the last bit of West Devon.

It is interesting that the battle should have been at Hingston Down,

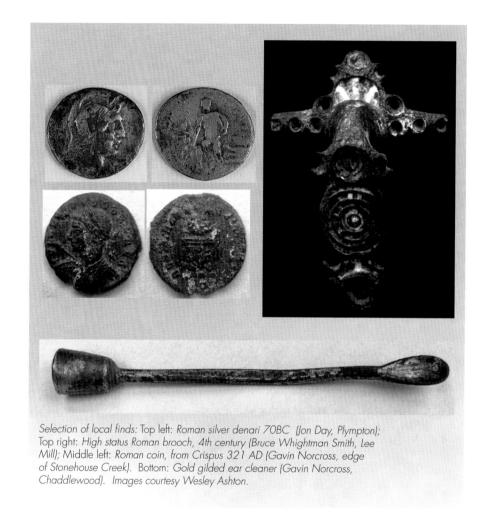

Selection of local finds: Top left: Roman silver denari 70BC (Jon Day, Plympton); Top right: High status Roman brooch, 4th century (Bruce Whightman Smith, Lee Mill); Middle left: Roman coin, from Crispus 321 AD (Gavin Norcross, edge of Stonehouse Creek). Bottom: Gold gilded ear cleaner (Gavin Norcross, Chaddlewood). Images courtesy Wesley Ashton.

traditionally the meeting-place between the tinners of Cornwall and Devon. Could it have been that that valuable metal had been in part the reason for the conflict being staged at that location, or was it pure coincidence? Geraint, the last effective King of the Dumnonii (the people of Devon and Cornwall), had, incidentally, perished back in 710 following defeat at the Battle of Llongborth (Langport?) against the West Saxons, while the last King of Cornwall (which had become the one remaining bastion of the Dumnonii), was Dugarth, who died in 875.

Not long after that Athelstan succeeded his father Edward as King of the Anglo Saxons. He expelled the Cornish from Exeter and established a new boundary at the River Tamar – previously it had been the Exe.

The impact of Athelstan's success was to be an enduring one, and while we don't know the exact context of the image here, of Athelstan presenting a book to St Cuthbert, it is interesting to reflect for a moment on the influence of religious houses up and down the country.

Given that books and documents then were the source of all knowledge and accepting Sir Francis Bacon's sixteenth-century contention that *'knowledge itself is power'* then for the most part such tomes as there were, were to be found in those religious houses, generally chained to the shelves of the library. And of course, at this point in time, all books, documents, maps, plans and other manuscript material was precisely that – handwritten. Any copies would have been copied by hand, and the number of people who were capable of performing such a task was a very small one indeed and they were generally men of the cloth, religious figures. Indeed it was a prerequisite of taking holy orders that candidates could read and write.

Furthermore most texts were written in Latin, a legacy of the Roman occupation, and although more people could speak – and read – that tongue, it was, nevertheless, a fraction of what was already a very small fraction of the population.

King Alfred (871-899), who didn't learn to read until he was 40, became a keen advocate of literacy and wanted to establish a school where sons of noblemen and even ordinary boys could learn such a skill. Essentially he believed the reading was the road to a better understanding of the Bible and thus wisdom. He promoted the development of the Anglo-Saxon Chronicle in 891 and through it we know more about him than any other Anglo-Saxon king. English as a written language was very much in its infancy still and most laws and regal pronouncements were handed down by word of mouth, as 'the King's word.' But another of Alfred's motives was that lay officials, like judges, should be able to read.

But in reality few outside the Church, or its satellite bodies, were literate and even fewer had books and such books as there were tended to be religious in nature. Furthermore, such was their value that they tended to be mentioned individually in wills.

Athelstan was evidently one of the first kings to be literate and was something of a book collector, but he appears not to have held on to all of the books that he acquired and there was no royal library.

Athelstan presenting a book to St Cuthbert – the illustration, which comes from Bede's Life of St Cuthbert *is the earliest surviving portrait of an English king, although he is widely regarded as the first English king.* Opposite page: *Ethelred the Unready*

Curiously enough it was one area where women were often better read than men, although again, only among the great and the good.

Levels of literacy throughout the Anglo-Saxon period were low; however, if a community was to be regulated it needed rules and as society became more complex so it became more essential that statutes and other legal matters should be formally recorded, if not by laymen then by churchmen. Wulfstan, who was appointed Bishop of London in 996, understood this and was personally instrumental in starting to codify the law formally:

'At our synodical council ... these legal statutes were urgently issued by King Aethelred, and all the magnates ... swore that they would observe them faithfully; and therefore ... I have committed them to writing for the memory of posterity, and the benefit of men now and in the future.'

As the inhabitants of random collections of hut circles formed themselves into towns and villages, so someone had to take the lead in civic matters and, based on the Christian model, that was the friar, the prior, the man of the cloth, the cleric ... the clerk.

'Clerk' in the original sense was *'man in a religious order, cleric, clergyman'.* As the scholarship of the Middle Ages was practically limited to the clergy, and these performed all the writing, notarial, and secretarial work of the time, the name *'clerk'* came to be the equivalent to *'scholar'*, and specially applicable to a notary, secretary, recorder, accountant, or penman.' (*A New English Dictionary on Historical Principles*; Founded mainly on the material collected by The Philological Society. Oxford 1893) Remember everything, even the Bible, then had to be copied by hand, and when St Augustine decided to make his mission the re-establishment of Christianity in England in 597, monasticism became an important part of life on these islands. Furthermore, as the scripture of Christianity spread and everyone bought into it, the church became fantastically rich.

'In Medieval England, the belief in Heaven and Hell was total. Medieval Peasants were taught that the only way to Heaven and salvation was via the Church. Therefore people worked on Church land for free. Money dues were paid to the church for baptism, marriage and death. Also every year, each family paid a tenth of its yearly worth to the Church – known as tithes. Such an income made the Church fabulously wealthy and powerful. It gained vast areas of land and it was on this land that monasteries were built.' (CN Trueman, *Medieval Monasteries* 2015)

Cornwall led the way and a number of the county's monasteries claim roots dating back to the sixth century.

In Plympton we find the first local indication of such an establishment with the founding of a late-Saxon monastery.

'Plympton Priory was one of the most ancient and notable religious houses in Devon,' wrote Worth in his 1895 *History of Devonshire.*

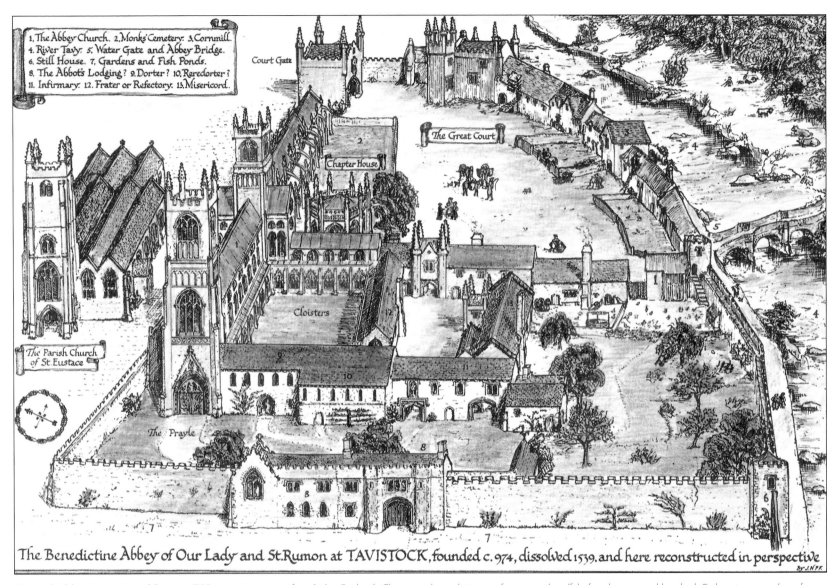

1. The Abbey Church. 2. Monks' Cemetery. 3. Cornmill.
4. River Tavy. 5. Water Gate and Abbey Bridge.
6. Still House. 7. Gardens and Fish Ponds.
8. The Abbot's Lodging? 9. Dorter? 10. Reredorter?
11. Infirmary. 12. Frater or Refectory. 13. Misericord.

Court Gate

The Great Court

Chapter House

The Parish Church of St. Eustace

Cloisters

The Prayle

The Benedictine Abbey of Our Lady and St. Rumon at TAVISTOCK, founded c.974, dissolved 1539, and here reconstructed in perspective

By J.N.P.K.

Tavistock Abbey. It is estimated that over 700 monasteries were founded in England. They varied greatly in size, from just a handful of souls to several hundred. Embracing a number of different religious orders, each had its own philosophy, identity, layout and design. Almost a third of these institutions belonged to the order of St Augustine, including Plympton Priory.

The canons who held two hides of the Plintona manor under William, were the successors of men who had been seated there in all probability for a longer period than any other religious (house) in Devon outside Exeter.
'There is yet extant a copy of a Saxon document of reasonable authenticity, dated 904, which records a grant by Eadweard the Elder to Asser, Bishop of Sherborne, and the convent there, of twelve manors, by way of exchange for the monastery which in the Saxon tongue is called "Plymentun".'
Such a date places the foundation some 70 years earlier than the Benedictine Abbey at Tavistock (974) on the banks of the Tavy, and over a century before the other Benedictine establishment overlooking the Dart at Buckfast. Each was perhaps a reflection on the importance of the tin rivers to the local economies, with Plympton at the top of the pecking order. It was destined to become the wealthiest monastic house in Devon and the fourth wealthiest establishment of the Augustinian Order in England and Wales. And what, if not tin and the trade surrounding it, would have underpinned that wealth?
It is perhaps no coincidence that, during the reign of Athelstan *'a stannary court was in existence … when all dues had to be paid to the sovereign on all tin mined.'* (Frank Booker – *Dartmoor A New History*)
Athelstan reigned as King of the Saxons 924-927, but more significantly as the first King of the English from 927 until 939. Was it the unification that occasioned the King to make such a demand or were such dues already being claimed?
Booker suggests that *'some form of Stannary organisation was in existence before this date'* however, the date he gives is 950, a decade or so after Athelston's death, but he doesn't give his source so it could be from around the time that the Plympton monastery was founded.
It is perhaps also not without significance that, later that same century, in 997, when the Vikings made, what would be the last of their *'periodic seaborne invasions of Devon'* (Gill) they attacked and burned Tavistock Abbey on their way up to Lydford.
Brooking Rowe, incidentally, references one of the earlier Viking raids: *'we may be sure the Lord of Plympton sailed forth with his men in 851, when the tidings that the Danes had landed, not far off, at Wembury, and joined the men of Devonshire, fought against the heathen men, and, as the Saxon chronicle says, at Wic gean beorge (Wembury) made great slaughter and gained the victory.'*

The home sides weren't always successful, however, as we learn that the Benedictine monks at Exeter Monastery (founded by Athelstan in 932) were repeatedly forced to flee on account of Danish raids. They were apparently recalled by King Canute in 1019.
The Danish/Viking raids had been troublesome over a long period of time but had become particularly problematic from the 980s and following the Battle of Maldon in 991 Aethelred was compelled to pay tribute, or Danegeld – protection money in effect – to the Danish king. Not that that stopped the raids and, in 1002, Aethelred apparently ordered a cull of Danish settlers in an action that became know as the St Brice's Day massacre.
That certainly didn't put an end to hostilities however as it seems as though one of the victims was Gunhilde, said to be the sister of King Sweyn of Denmark and wife of Pallig Tokesen, the Danish Ealdorman (Sheriff) of Devon. Tokesen also appears to have been a victim of the massacre. Small wonder then that King Sweyn invaded the country in 1013 and replaced Aethelred (who fled to Normandy) until a year or two after Sweyn's death in 1014.
However, to return to the assault on Lydford. This was *'a famous town'* during Aethelred's time, and had its own mint – coins were inscribed with LVD, LVDA and LVDAN. Prior to the Conquest and during the reign of Edward the Confessor – Aethelred's son – this was, after Exeter, the most populous place in the County, and taxed on a par with London … and the reason for that was undoubtedly because the parish included pretty much the whole of the tin-rich area of Dartmoor.

The seal of Plympton Priory.

Section of the Bayeaux Tapestry depicting the English King being struck in the eye with an arrow.

1066 AND ALL THAT

Edward the Confessor died on 5 January 1066. Edward had no heir, prompting his brother-in-law, Harold Godwinson, Earl of Essex, to stage a coup and the following day he had himself crowned King of England. Later that same month Harold married Edith, the widow of King Gruffudd ap Llywelyn of Wales and sister of the Earls Edwin and Morcar.

Later in the year Harold's disgruntled brother, Tostig, upset at the lack of support he had received in the face of the Northern Rebellion which had forced him into exile on the continent the previous year, joined forces with the King of Norway and invaded the north-east of England.

After initial successes along the coast of Cleveland, and at York, Tostig and the Norwegian King, Harold Hadrada, were met at Stamford Bridge where both men were killed in battle along with Tostig's brother-in-law.

For King Harold it meant an end to northern challenge to his power, but it didn't mean an end to his immediate problems and the following month he had to face a more difficult challenge posed by Edward the Confessor's distant cousin, William of Normandy.

Asserting that he had already been promised the English crown by Edward and claiming that Tostig had accepted the arrangement two years earlier on a visit to Normandy, William mounted a massive assault on the south coast.

Advance units arrived in Hastings in October, little more than a couple of weeks after Harold had done battle in the north. Many of the English forces were exhausted from their long march south, and, overall, armed with a motley collection of arms, the tired foot-soldiers were always going to struggle against the fresh force of well-organised archers and mounted cavalry that confronted them. Failing to capitalise on an early advantage the home side was slaughtered and the English king was killed.

Thereafter the Normans swiftly made their presence felt across the south of England and on 25 December 1066, William of Normandy was crowned King of England.

The following year, according to a later addition to the Anglo-Saxon chronicle, William *'imposed a heavy tax on the unfortunate people; but, notwithstanding, he let his men plunder all the country which they passed through.'*

The first major insurrection against the new king came from one of the most significant cities in the country – Exeter. King Harold's mother, the former Queen, Gytha, who had held a lot of land in the county, was foremost among the rebels. William personally led the attack against the city and many Englishmen joined his army. After an 18-day siege, in which the losses on both sides were heavy, the city requested a negotiated peace and William, aware of the strength of the city walls agreed terms: he then built a small castle within the walls and left.

This was by no means an isolated incident, and William moved around the country imposing his will in no uncertain terms. However his most significant display of authority came at the midwinter of 1085, when again, according to the celebrated chronicle, William was in Gloucester: *'... the king convened a large meeting, and very deep consultation with his council, about this land; how it was occupied, and by what sort of people. Then sent he his men over all England into each shire; commissioning them to find out "how many hundreds of hides were in the shire, what land the king himself had, and what stock upon the land; or, what dues he ought to have by the year from the shire".'*

The manorial system is said to date from the late Roman occupation and it covered much of Europe. Essentially a manor was a self-supporting area of land held by a Lord who, in most cases, lived in a manor house, with his servants. The other inhabitants on the manor were serfs or villeins, people who worked the land and were largely under control of the Lord of the Manor. Each manor had three main constituent parts: the demesne, controlled by the Lord for benefit of his immediate household and his dependents; serf or villein holdings - occupied by peasants who were obliged to provide the Lord with either services (labour), produce or cash or a combination of the same; and free peasant land, which was not exactly free, as there was a rent to pay, but there was no obligation beyond that, other than they were expected to behave within certain parameters and were subject to manorial courts.
Of course, even the Lords were holding land at the providence of the King and in many cases the Lords themselves would place someone – a baron or one of his tenants – to oversee the manor.
In some instances the King would hold some of his manors directly, while it has been estimated that perhaps as much as 25% of the land was held by the Church.
The Lord of the Manor had other sources of income in addition to those described above – notably charges for using the mill, the bakery, the wine press etc. the right to hunt or let animals, especially pigs, feed in his woodland. There was also the income from the manorial courts – villeins and serfs had recourse to the courts but had to pay for the privilege – and the one off payment (like the modern key money) that might be charged when, for example, one villein died and a new tenant took over. The majority of this income supported the Lord of the Manor, but some of it would always end up in the King's coffers.

From Winchester, which had been an administrative centre and seat of power from the Iron Age onwards, the King's men were sent out across the country to collate answers to the following list of questions:

What is each manor called?
Who held it in the time of King Edward (in 1066)?
Who holds it now (in 1086)?
How many hides are there (what is its tax assessment)?
How many plough(team)s* on the demesne (local lord's own land) and among the men (rest of the village)?
How many free men, sokemen, villeins, cotta[ge]rs, slaves?
How much woodland, meadow, pasture, mills, fisheries?
How much has been added to or taken away from the manor?
How much was the whole worth (1066) and how much now (1086)?
How much had or has each freeman and each sokeman?
And whether more can be had than is had (in other words, can the manor raise more tax revenue)?

Remarkably the King's men acquitted their task extremely efficiently and by the end of 1086 their work was done – although one or two areas in the north of England, that had proved troublesome to his predecessor, were surveyed in a little less detail.
Written principally in Latin (as opposed to the Old English of the Anglo-Saxon Chronicle) the results were written up in a tome that was initially known as the *Liber de Wintonia – the Book of Winchester –* it was also referred to as the *Winchester Roll* or the *King's Roll* but was restyled as *Domesday Book* (or *Doomsday Book*) towards the end of the twelfth century. This was on account of it being the final word in terms of land ownership: *"for as the sentence of that strict and terrible last account cannot be evaded by any skilful subterfuge, so when this book is appealed to … its sentence cannot be put quashed or set aside with impunity. That is why we have called the book* The Book of Judgement *… because its decisions, like those of the Last Judgement, are unalterable. (Richard FitzNigel, 1179)*

A truly remarkable document, the like of which was not attempted again in this country for almost 800 years, the survey informs us that the population of England at that time was in the region of one to one and a half million and for Devon on its own, around 70,000.

For the Plympton and Plymouth area the survey paints an interesting picture of life in the area 1,000 years ago. Plymouth, or at least the area embraced by the immediate post-war boundary of the City, was a collection of some 18 or so scattered manors a number of which were already part of the rapidly growing parish system which had been steadily evolving over the previous two or three hundred years.

The county of Devon had been created sometime before 800 AD and, reflecting the increasing need for some sort of local government, the counties were divided into hundreds. The heart of the area we now know as Plymouth was then the Manor of Sutton – the 'sud' 'ton' or south town of the Walkhampton Hundred and Sutton, along with Maker originally, and King's Tamerton were at that time, treated as a unit and were, prior to 1066, 'in the Lordship of King Edward and belong to the King.'

Strategically placed at the mouths of the Tamar and the Plym it is easy to see why the King would be particularly interested in these manors for not only were they key elements in protecting everything up river of the Sound but also they would have been comparatively wealthy on account of their maritime trading.

Whatever the reasoning it is interesting to read that unlike the rest of the county where revenue collecting was relatively standard 'these three manors paid one night's revenue' – in other words, this was a fixed rent, fixed on the amount of food needed to support the King and his household for one night. From similar examples this figure would appear to have been in the region of £100, which may seem rather modest, but when you allow for inflation it's more like £200,000!

Among the other manors within the Walkhampton – later the Roborough – Hundred were Burrington, Compton, Efford, Eggbuckland, Honicknowle, Lipson, Manadon, Mutley, Stoke, Stonehouse, Whitleigh, Widey, and Weston Peverell, as well as a number of more disparate settlements like Buckland Monachorum, Bere Ferrers, Tamerton Foliot and Bickleigh. Crispin Gill in his *Plymouth A New History*, suggests that *'there were something like two hundred families living on the*

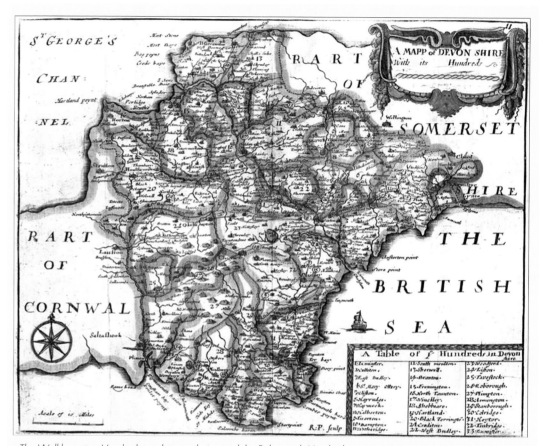

The Walkhampton Hundred was later re-designated the Roborough Hundred.
A Hundred was a subdivision of county which in turn was thought once to have referred to a 100 (or maybe 120 hides): a hide being an area of land of no specific dimension but one which it was deemed could support a family.

For almost 1000 years, up until 1844, with but a brief break, Maker was officially part of Devon. It is thought that it might have been part of the exchange effected by Edward the Elder with the Bishop of Sherborne in the first decade of the tenth century when Plympton also changed hands.

Odo, shown with club in hand, rallies Duke William's troops during the Battle of Hastings
The Latin text reads: HIC ODO EP[ISCOPU]S BACULU[M] TENENS CONFORTAT PUEROS
("Here Bishop Odo, holding a club, gives support to the boys").

William of Normandy:
Surnames are a relatively modern
phenomenon. The Romans were quite
keen on them but during the middle ages
they fell out of favour and faded out. In the
later middle ages they came back. Initially
in the form of bynames – in other words
a description of someone's occupation or
place of residence.

Geoffrey of Mobray (Montbray) was appointed to the newly created see of Coutances in 1049 and was one of William's right hand men, both in religious and political terms. A warrior-prelate, he was at the Battle of Hastings, and was present at William's Coronation. Geoffrey's reward was a sizeable fief spread over 12 counties. Geoffrey also took a leading role in the suppression of English rebellions in 1069.

Along with Bishop Odo of Bayeux, the Duke of Kent and William's half-brother, Geoffrey was part of the inner circle through which he hoped to maintain stability in the Church and the wider political arena, not to mention the physical suppression of insurgency generally.

15,000 odd acres of farmland scattered through the 31 manors, 150 farms, and 72 smallholdings.'

He further noted that spread through the manors were around 450 acres of small woodlands, plus four very large woods, each over a mile long.

Oddly enough the Devon Hundreds immediately to the east of Sutton, were similarly structured: elongated areas stretching north from around the mouth of one of south west Dartmoor's tin-yielding rivers: the Plym, Yealm, Erme, Avon and Dart – surely not a coincidence.

The Plympton Hundred itself was full of manors that doubtless in part owed their existence to tin and its related trading activities, including around Hemerdon: Elfordleigh, Shaugh Prior, Coldstone and Woodford. Then around the lower reaches of the Plym: Plymstock, Sherford, Hooe, Goosewell and Staddiscombe.

Hemerdon was in the hands of Roald Dubbed, one of 50 or so major landowners who between them owned the whole of Devon. Some of them, like the King himself, who had the lion's share – owned land all over the country not just county.

Roald leased Hemerdon to Walter (surnames were not common at that time), and prior to 1066 it had been in the hands of Goda. Roald held 30 different Devon manors and Hemerdon was one of the more modest of them, although, with just two villagers and a couple of smallholders, it did have a comparatively large expanse of pasture – some 60 acres.

Roald also had Whitchurch and Train within the Roborough Hundred, and like most of the major Devon landowners, he had a house in Exeter.

Exeter at that time was one of the largest centres of population in the country and was mentioned in the same context as York, Winchester and London. The King himself owned 300 houses in Exeter, the Bishop of Exeter had almost 50. Baldwin, the Sheriff of Devon, had a number of properties in the city, as did the Walter of Douain, Ralph of Pomeroy, William Cheever, the Church of Battle Holds and the Bishop of Countances.

Overall the Church as a whole held around 25% of the county and the country and among the other principal local landowners to have a house in Exeter was the Abbot of Tavistock. Tavistock was deemed to be a relatively poor religious house, nationally at that time, but was, nevertheless, a comparatively affluent one in local terms. However second only to Exeter in the county in 1066 was Crediton, where there was a population of some 246 villagers, 73 smallholders and 40 slaves (Devon incidentally had one of the highest ratios of slaves in the country – one-in-five of the population).

Oddly enough, the seat of power in the county had moved from Crediton to Exeter just 16 years before the Conquest.

Barnstaple, Totnes and Lydford were next in line of significance – note again the tin connection with the latter two – and the King held all three, although Judhael held Totnes from him.

Essentially the King held most of the wealthy manors including, from among the next group of highest tax yielding manors (all of them between £20 and £50 a year) Silverton, North Molton, South Tawton, Hartland and Chillington. Before 1066 the last three were in the hands of Gytha, King Edward's mother, and North Molton was part of Edward's wife's – Queen Edith's – property portfolio.

By comparison, all of these manors, along with a great many others, were much bigger than Sutton or King's Tamerton, each of which paid 20 shillings by weight.

Interestingly enough Plympton, the then eminently navigable port further up the Plym from Sutton, paid a great deal more – £13.10s. As did the manor of Ermington sitting on the Erme and Yealmpton on the Yealm only a pound less at £12.10s. Even Diptford on the Avon was more valuable in mere monetary terms, paying £7.5s to the King.

In almost every instance the wording of the *Domesday* text in this context read *'by weight and assayed'* … and it's tempting to want to read this as a reference to tin, but rather it appears that *'payment by weight was obviously designed to compensate for light or worn coins'*, there was also the issue with poor quality coinage. Norman silver coinage in the early eleventh century was typically only around 55-65% fine, while previously it had not only been a little heavier but more like 75% fine.

Curiously there was another qualitative measure that was mentioned here and there that also has a resonance with the tin industry, as we find reference to payments being *'weighed and assayed'* and *'smelted and weighed'* and *'blanched'* – an obvious parallel notion to that of tin being smelted, and the later *'white rent'* that was introduced after a second smelting yielding white tin.

List of those holding land in Devonshire 1087

I King William	XXVII Richard son of Count Gilbert
II Bishop of Exeter	XXVIII Rober of Bully
III Bishop of Countances	XXIX Robert of Albermarle
IIII Glastonbury Church	XXX Robert Bastard
V Tavistock Church	XXXI Richard son of Thorolf
VI Buckfast Church	XXXII Ralph of Limesy
VII Horton Church	XXXIII Ralph Pagnell
VIII Cranborne Church	XXXIIII Ralph of Feugeres
IX Battle Church	XXXV Ralph of Pomeroy
X St Mary's Church, Rouen	XXXVI Roald Dubbed
XI Mont St Michel Church	XXXVII Theobald son of Berner
XII St Stephen's Church, Caen	XXXVIII Thurstan son of Rolf
XIII Holy Trinity Church, Caen	XXXIX Alfred of Spain
XIIII Earl Hugh	XL Alfred the Breton
XV The Count of Mortain	XLI Ansger
XVI Baldwin the Sheriff	XLII Aiulf
XVII Iudhael of Totnes	XLIII Odo son of Gamelin
XVIII William of Mohun	XLIIII Osbern of Sacey
XIX William Cheever	XLV The wife of Hervey of Hellean
XX William of Falaise	XLVI Gerald the Chaplain
XXI William of Poilley	XLVII Gerard
XXII William of Eu	XVIII Godbold
XXIII Walter of Douai	XLIX Nicholas
XXIIII Walter of Claville	L Fulchere
XV Walter	LI Haimeric
XXVI Gotshelm	LII William & others of the King's servants
	LIII Colwin & others of the King's thanes

With over 50 mints operating around the country the quality of coinage was frequently an issue and it was not unknown for severe punishments to have been executed. In 1124 Bishop Roger of Salisbury rounded up 94 minters who had been adjudged guilty of debasing the royal currency and shortly after Christmas the men were blinded and castrated on the orders of King Henry I. Henry later found himself embarrassed when a number of his knights were paid in coins made almost entirely of tin and not silver. More than 240 coiners were identified and many were similarly punished.

Perquisite: Legally the casual profits that come to the lord of the manor over and above his regular income source, but more generally the profit attached to a particular office or position in addition to salary or wages. Historically it would appear that 1,000 years ago this included a revenue stream from gold and silver mines and perhaps other mining operations too – iron, tin and salt.

Archbishop Lanfranc's third ecclesiastical council at Winchester in 1076 had decreed that henceforth all members of the priesthood be celibate, although conceding that priests who already had wives could keep them. The move was by no means universally popular.
But then, in 1102, Anselm, the Bishop of Canterbury, managed to pass a ruling that all priests should be celibate, even those who already had wives – or mistresses. Furthermore, priests were banned from attending drinking-parties, growing their hair long and indulging in homosexual practices.

But as with most knowledge of this period, although the production of the *Domesday Book* did much to enhance our understanding of life in the eleventh century there are still plenty of questions unanswered – one of the biggest of which, in the context of this book is 'why is there no mention of Devon tin mines or tin miners in *Domesday*?'

JM Kemble, in his two volumes on the Saxons in England, suggested that mines were a regalian right of the Anglo-Saxon Kings and therefore the idea has been mooted that there was no need to record ownership details or revenues due because these belonged to the King anyway. Certainly mines of gold and silver have long since consistently been regarded as Crown perquisites.

Another observation has been that the survey generally did not record activity that was not directly related to the land and farming, hence it was not just mining that was not recorded, but also fishing – apart from those land-based fisheries.

Whatever the situation was in 1087, we struggle to find authentic documentary evidence for the arrangement until another 70 years had passed and the relatively newly crowned Henry II innovated a claim to the stannaries – the tin-producing areas of Devon and Cornwall.

At that time most of the tin came from Dartmoor:

'*In the twelfth century the rich alluvial deposits of southwest Devon had produced nearly all the tin of Europe and whatever there was of Cornish mining lay near the Devon boundary.*' (George Randall Lewis – *The Stannaries* 1907)

Through it all the importance of Plympton had grown and it was the centre of two major incidents in the early part of that century.

In 1121 the Saxon monastery was suppressed by Bishop Warelwast, a nephew of William the Conqueror. According to Leland this was because members of the religious community there, essentially a dean and four canons, when asked, '*wold not leve their concubines.*'

Consequently they were unceremoniously kicked out, with their wives.

In its place Warelwast founded what would become known as the Augustinian Priory of St Peter and St Paul, with an impressive, but sadly long since gone, Priory Church in which Warelwast himself was eventually buried.

The Priory Church took the best part of 50 years to complete and in that time it is thought that Plympton's Norman castle had largely been built … and destroyed.

Another indicator of the increasing wealth of the area, the castle is said to have been completed during the lordship of Richard de Redvers, a descendant of Baldwin of Moeles, who was, in turn, a companion of the Conqueror. However following the death of William's son, Henry I, in 1135, Richard de Redver's son, another Baldwin, opted to support Henry's daughter, Matilda, in an attempt to overthrow her cousin Stephen, who had already highjacked the throne.

The consequence of this was a protracted civil war over the next decade or so, one of the first encounters of which was at Plympton when the newly crowned King Stephen sent down some 200 men and a large body of archers to lay waste to Baldwin's castle.

Baldwin's life was spared, but he was banished from the Kingdom. It wasn't until 1148 that Matilda finally abandoned her attempt to take the throne.

Meanwhile, our attention now turns to Brisworthy in the Upper Plym Valley. Mentioned in *Domesday* as Brittenesworth(y) this was part of Richard de Mewy's (Meavy) holdings and sits just three miles northeast of Shaugh Prior and 300 metres from Ringmore stone row and cairn circle:

'There are records of the extraction of tin here in the Pipe Roll of 1156,' write the not always reliable Mary and Jessica Walmesley in *The Old Men of The Moor.*

'By Norman times it must have been a busy little settlement for there was a rabbit warren at Truslesworthy, scattered among the ruins of Coomzeage enclosures, and hut circles on either side of the infant Plym.'

The reference to rabbits here is almost as interesting to the reference to tin, as, while we may surmise that tin mining had been going on in this area for hundreds, perhaps thousands of years, the rabbit was a relatively recent introduction to the area.

It was the Romans who first introduced domesticated versions of the 'small digging hares' to these shores and it was in 1135 that we find that St Michael's Island (as Drake's Island in Plymouth Sound was then known) was granted, along with all its rabbits, by Walter de Valletorta to the Priors of Plympton.

Quite why the rabbits warranted a special mention we do not know, but there can be little doubt that in remote locations, away from everyday animal husbandry, the rabbit was an important source of food … and warm clothing. However, the only creatures enumerated in *Domesday* are those of value and consequently relatively large: cattle, sheep, pigs, goats and oxen. Fish appear only under the generic term of fisheries and it would seem that the Normans were the first to farm rabbits on English soil.

But the farming of tin, or rather collecting the taxes on the same, was altogether more profitable and, from the middle of the twelfth century, the revenues achievable showed a remarkable increase, as did the indigenous population (the number of people living in England more than doubled in the twelfth and thirteenth century).

Samson de Tracey was granted land at Truslesworthy (Trowlesworthy?) for a rabbit warren in the thirteenth century and in time the humble coney came to be the main motif of the tinner's craft.

Rabbits ran around 'the bosses at Widecombe and Chagford, and many another parish church in Devon, but as far as this writer has been able to discover, 'Tinner's Rabbits' are not to be found anywhere else in England,' (Walmesley).

The Walmesleys were writing in the pre-internet days of the 1980s and while their contention may have been acceptable at that time, the information readily available today is a little more illuminating. The South West undoubtedly hosts an unusual abundance of churches sporting the motif (over 30) including, significantly another of the Devon stannary towns – Tavistock – but there are isolated examples elsewhere – Chester, Suffolk and Scarborough. They also appear in churches in Northern Germany.

However, the earliest examples are to be found in Chinese cave temples, dating from the sixth and seventh centuries, and the symbol is said to have Buddhist connotations. The suggestion is that the design 'representing peace and tranquility' was spread by ancient traders transporting silks and ceramics bearing the motif along the Silk Road. This raises many possibilities foremost among which are either that it was then introduced by traders arriving from the Middle East, exchanging their goods for our tin, or that it somehow was arrived at independently and spontaneously by Devon tinners.

While rabbits may have provided a staple foodstuff for the miners, and churches may have benefitted handsomely from the tin trade the synergy is simple, as it was no great leap of faith to see the three rabbits as a symbol of the Holy Trinity – 'One in Three and Three in One.'

There are many other fascinating theories put forward for the design, in many other cultural contexts, and doubtless part of it's enduring popularity would appear to be the circular form which, as an ancient German riddle describes it, shows: 'Three hares sharing three ears, Yet every one of them has two.'

Clockwise from the top: South Tawton Church roof boss; Paderborn Cathedral window, Germany; Castle Inn window, Lydford; Pewter plate.
Right: The Three Hares: Greeves, Andrew, Chapman.

William de Wrotham was almost certainly a member of the Royal Household. He held a number of significant posts within the Church and outside of it. Named as the first Lord Warden of the Stannaries he also was effectively in charge of the King's navy for many years and held the office of Archdeacon of Taunton, among many other roles. Described as 'one of the greatest of the King's clerks' William appears to have died sometime around 1217.

'From 1156 to 1160 the tax on output, 30d. per thousand-weight in Devon and 5s. in Cornwall, was farmed by the Sheriff of Devon for the annual sum of £16.13s.4d showing a production of about 133 thousand weight of tin.'

These records appear to suggest that tin production at that particular time was relatively modest: *'It would seem,'* wrote George Randall Lewis, in 1907, *'that in 1156 the production of tin was small and for the most part confined to western Devon.'*

Lewis then added, *'During succeeding decades the farm was raised from time to time to keep pace with the increasing yield of the mines. Using the same basis of estimate, the yield rose to 183 thousand weight in 1163, 533 in 1169, and 640 in 1171.*

'During the later years of Henry II's reign, the mines were farmed by the sheriffs in conjunction with several associates, as in the years 1174-76, when William Bulzun, Alan Furnell, and Juel de Espreton shared the farm between them.'

There were steadily growing revenues to be made farming tin and although not all of it went directly to the King, as from time to time he would sell his rights or give them away in lieu of debts or some favour or other, there can be no doubt that it was in the King's interests to encourage mining activities.

At that time regulation was relatively straightforward, miners were still, in socio-economic terms, relatively close to the villein class.

'They were subject to the same customary payments and services, owed suit to the manor and hundred courts. Around the industry, however, had already grown a certain customary law, not only for miners, but for smelters and dealers, and of this the provision, which perhaps more than any other tended to raise the tinner above the ordinary agricultural labourer, was the so-called right of bounding.' (Lewis)

This provision meant that the poorest villein could potentially become his own master, simply by laying claim to a piece of land, registering its boundaries in a court and then setting to work. The potential for mayhem was obvious and the situation frequently caused conflict. But the Royal purse was hungry for the rewards as were those around all this mining activity who benefitted from the commerce that followed in its wake. Indicative of the new-found prosperity of the immediate area we find Tavistock being created a borough at the beginning of the twelfth century, in 1116, and Plympton at the end of it, in 1194.

The following year, 1195, the new King, Richard the Lionheart, in addition to the tax collected on his behalf, decided to do a bit of tin trading and traded some £90 worth of tin purchased on his behalf by his collectors. It would appear that the venture was a success and in 1197 he repeated the exercise, only this time on a bigger scale: he cleared £352.6s.10d (around £700,000 in today's terms) on the transaction.

All of this in addition to the sums he was raising from the mines on the Royal Manors, the sale of export licences and the customs' duties on said exports.

It was a situation that increasingly called for better monitoring processes, hence no doubt the decision taken that same year to appoint William de Wrotham to administer the Royal Stannaries, or tin mines.

The appointment was made by the then Archbishop of Canterbury, Hubert Walter, who also served as Justiciar – the King's chief minister and roughly equivalent to today's Prime Minister although there was as yet no parliament – and the following year William was placed in charge of tin production with an office that was later styled as Lord Warden of the Stannaries.

Other offices were added to De Wrotham's post almost immediately: Sheriff of Devon, 1198; and Sheriff of Cornwall, 1199; and then Warden of the newly rebuilt Lydford Castle. William's impact was significant and sudden and in his first year he brought £1,100 into the Royal coffers.

One of his first tasks had been to regulate the weights used to weigh tin at the first smelting. To that end he accepted the findings of a court in Devon and another in Cornwall and then appointed two men to take charge of the correct weights – and then another man, a clerk, to keep the paperwork, and his superiors, in check.

William also issued an ordinance forbidding the purchase, sale, or removal of tin of the first smelting from the stannaries or from the location appointed for its weighing and stamping, until it had passed through the hands of the keepers and clerks *'of the weigh and stamp of the farm.'*

A second directive prohibited the holding back of any tin of the first smelting for more than two weeks unless it had been properly weighed and stamped.

Once again this procedure was to be carried out by the aforementioned officials, who not only weighed the tin but also stamped each block with the Royal arms. They also kept a record – in triplicate – of each block:

how much it weighed; who owned it and how much tax had been paid. De Wrotham also imposed a new duty of one mark in each county on each thousand-weight of tin, as it emerged from the second, more refined smelting and for ease of administration it was decreed that no one was to hold back tin from the first smelting for longer than 13 weeks.

The two county seats, Exeter and Bodmin were designated permanent weighing and stamping centres, while other places were named from year to year by the Warden and necessary venues chosen and hired at the King's expense.

For the tinners themselves, of course, this must have involved no inconsiderable expense, just in moving the metal from mine to weighing station. Nor was life especially easy for the keepers of the weights and the clerk, as large sums of money were at stake and the stamping hammer had to be securely kept when not in use.

Precisely because of the nature of the business in hand the two keepers were inevitably men of substantial property in their own right, while the clerk, with his triplicate parchment rolls, wore the King's livery and was paid out of the Royal coffers.

So that everything was crossed checked, the keepers made out tallies and chirographs too and these were then handed over to the Warden who accounted for everything to the Exchequer.

Clearly for many minor miners this was a cumbersome process – and a difficult and expensive one, especially as the taxes had to be paid before they could take their tin away. Although, of course, it wasn't always the miner who presented the tin. In an early letter from De Wrotham we find him dividing stannary people into distinct categories: diggers, smelters, ore buyers and tin dealers.

Often we find that the men that actually sourced the material were unable to properly capitalise on their findings and as they could often go through lean periods, particularly as legitimate opportunities for selling their products were few and far between, they could often go hungry and were therefore easy prey for those looking for tin at rock bottom prices. Small wonder that 'from early times' there had been *systematic shipping of tin from smelting-house direct to purchasers.'* (Lewis)

Hence another of De Wrotham's early measures, compelling ship's masters not to receive tin on board without the Warden's licence.

'Smuggling, nevertheless, seems to have proceeded with unabated activity for centuries,' asserts Lewis, who cites numerous examples. He adds: *'It was not confined to one class of the community, but was indulged in by merchants, sailors, blowers and miners, without distinction. Many methods were taken to avoid payment. Occasionally the stamp was counterfeited, but more often the tin was run into small bars and sold either to wandering chapmen (itinerant vendors or pedlars) or to sailors from the coast.'*

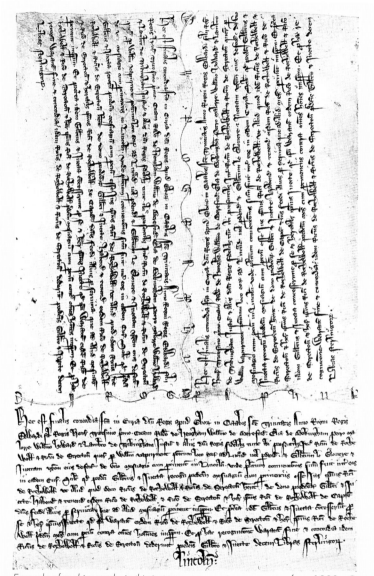

Example of a chirograph, in this instance a property conveyance from 1303. One piece of parchment contains triplicate versions of the text. The two at the top were intended for the two parties to the transaction while the third was to be held by the court that had overseen the transaction. They would be cut along the wavy lines in order to establish authenticity.

Charles Allston Collins (1828–73) Berengaria's alarm for the safety of her husband, Richard the Lionheart. Berengaria became famous as the only English queen never to have visited England when she was queen. She lived mostly in France in lands owned by Richard. Basque-born, she was the daughter of Sancho VI of Navarre and Sancha of Castile.

Nevertheless, there was a substantial, legitimate export trade and in 1198 the Chamberlain of London was charged with £379.18s., received in fines from merchants of London, for leave to export tin (Lewis).

It is not altogether clear just how much the increases in the amount of tin going through the King's books reflected an increase in vigilance or an increase in production but most likely it was a combination of the two. Certainly the figure for 1199 at over 900 thousand-weight was heading towards double what it was in 1195 when the figure for Cornwall was just 256 thousand weight and no figure for Devon appeared – although Walmesley, citing a Pipe Roll Survey, notes that *'more than 254 thousand weight of Dartmoor tin was despatched to La Rochelle to adulterate the coinage in which Richard Coeur de Lion paid his troops.'*

One thing we do know about King Richard is that with all his overseas crusading and warring he twice drained the country's resources – the second time just to raise his own ransom. We also know that in his ten years as English King he spent but six months in England and that his last breath was taken in central France, on soil then held in his and his successor's name.

Tragically, it was while attacking the castle of a rebellious French count that 41-year-old Richard was shot in the shoulder with an arrow from a crossbow: the wound festered and less than two weeks later he died. John, his younger brother, who was also then on the other side of the Channel, made the journey across to London where he was crowned at Westminster. The following year King John entered a politically motivated marriage with 12-year-old Isabella, daughter and heiress of Audemar Taillefer, Count of Angouleme. And then, in 1201, in an attempt to protect another important aspect of his sovereignty, he issued the first charter of the stannaries.

A landmark document, the fact that it was the first of its kind should not detract from the fact that in essence it served to confirm a number of ancient privileges; notably of *'digging tin and turfs for smelting it at all times, freely and peaceably and without hindrance from any man, everywhere in the moors and in the fees of bishops, abbots, and counts ... and of buying faggots to smelt the tin without waste of forest, and of diverting streams for their works, and in the stannaries, just as by ancient usage they have been wont to do.'*

The new legislation went much further though and went on to describe how, in true continental style, miners were not to be subjected to the jurisdiction of magistrates or coroners, but only their warden:

'We have granted that the chief warden of the stannaries and his bailiffs through him have, over the aforesaid tinners, plenary power to do them justice, and to hold them to the law, and that they be received by them in our prisons, if it shall happen that any of the aforesaid tinners ought to be seized or imprisoned for the law; and if it shall happen that one of them be a fugitive or an outlaw, then let his chattels be delivered to us through the hand of the warden of our stannaries, for the tinners are of our farm and always in our demesne.'

In other words the King had a vested interest in miners being free to find tin and no men but the King's men were to stand in their way, as long as the tinners paid their taxes. The charter states clearly *'that they were not to be called from their work save by the warden, and this fact seems to preclude any possibility of their being drawn upon by the lords of the manors (ibid).'*

Local manorial lords, not surprisingly, were less than happy with a situation whereby any villein could leave his service by claiming to be a miner, particularly after Devon and Cornwall were deforested in 1204.

Interestingly enough this is another area that De Wrotham was granted rights to – overseeing the royal forests in Devon and Cornwall.
Up until that point the whole of Devon had been regarded as a royal forest – that is an area reserved by the King for hunting. However, permission to deforest the county did not extend to the whole of Devon, rather just the area *'up to the metes of the ancient regardes of Dertemore and Exmoor'* (that is everything except Dartmoor and Exmoor was freed from forest law). Of course the deforestation would have had an enormous impact on this area. Already the fall-out from the tin industry had had a massive impact on the Tamar and the Plym.

Not only had thousands of years of tin mining occasioned massive silting up of the lower reaches of these and other tin-yielding rivers rising on Dartmoor, but sea level had been gradually falling as well.
It has been estimated (Fitzpatrick 1991) that in the Bronze Age sea levels were some three metres (10ft) lower than they are today and that even in Roman times they were around two metres (6.5ft) lower. Factor these statistics into the upper reaches of the Plym Estuary today and you get some idea of how much deeper the waterways must have been in order for boats to be able to sail up to Plympton Prior or Colebrook.

Crownhill Down looking West, note the scarring casued by centuries of tin streaming.

The deforestation of Dartmoor was prompted by King John's loss of Normandy and desire to raise funds quickly. Devon 'up to the metes of the ancient regardes of Dertemore and Exmore, as these regardes were in the time of King Henry the First' was sold for 5,000 marks, Cornwall for 2,200. The idea, from an investment perspective, was to enable land to be brought into cultivation, however it also made the prospect of mining the land much easier.

It also helps explain why, by this time, Plympton was starting to struggle as a port: *'Though Devon slates were still shipped to Southampton from Plympton late in the twelfth century, it soon ceased to be a port, and shipping began to move to the Canon's quay at Sutton. In 1211 a cargo of bacon was carried from Portsmouth to Plymouth. The great port had been born.'* (Walmesley)

It's interesting in this context to note one of the other roles held by our friend William De Wrotham, as from 1206 to 1215 he was, to all intents and purposes, also in charge of King John's navy – effectively the First Lord of the Admiralty, long before such a role existed.

De Wrotham helped develop Portsmouth as a royal dockyard and in late 1213 he was overseeing the activities of the seaports along the south-west coast and the Cinque Ports.

Clearly he sat very close to the English power base and was heavily involved with a wide variety of matters that touched this region.

By this time Devon and Cornwall had for many years been treated as two distinct entities and here Lewis has an interesting theory: *'It is possible that the motives for the separation of the Cornish tinners from those of Devon in matters of administration were based on racial difference. While the Devon tinners apparently sprang from Anglo-Saxon stock, the miners of Cornwall formed a remnant of the Celtic race.'*

Whatever the rationale, it would appear that it was the 1201 charter that led to the *'division of the mining districts into several provinces or "stannaries".'* (Lewis) Although quite when they came into play is less clear. Furthermore, the position of Warden of the Stannaries appears to have been a little less than consistent for some years after the death of De Wrotham.

Isabella, the Queen-Dowager, received the Devon stannaries in 1217 and seven years later Berengaria, Richard the Lionheart's widow, briefly held the stannaries … apparently in part payment for a debt.

In between times, in 1220, it would appear that the Devon stannaries were granted to Waleran the Teuton, who, for a rent of 200 marks (£123), became the new warden. Fifteen years later, we find Richard de Tragford is only paying 90 marks (£60) for the same privilege (plus a £10 tithe to the Bishop of Exeter).

The situation with the Cornish stannaries appears equally inconsistent throughout the thirteenth century, however, in Devon, from 1243 onwards, it seems that the stannaries were accounted for to the King and around the same time the old notion of 'farming' tin was replaced by a new tax known as 'profits of the small stamp.'

The stannary revenues from the county were accounted for by a 'clerk warden' who either received a salary from the King, or from the warden to whom the King had leased the mines.

Samuel Prout (1783-1852): Plymbridge.

The revenues and trading activities appear to be relatively healthy throughout this period and the general prosperity was reflected in a number of different developments.

In 1238 we first find mention of Morwellham, although it had doubtless been in existence long before that. A little further to the east, that same year, appears the first documentary evidence of Plym Bridge and it was presumably no small coincidence that in March 1241 Baldwin de Redvers made Plympton Erle (now St Maurice) a borough and granted the burgesses a market and fairs (although it has already enjoyed a market since 1194). Not long after that Sutton itself was granted a market, a gesture that effectively made Sutton a town. The official document was signed by King Henry III on 27 January 1254. At that time the King was wintering in the French fortress town of Bazas with his council, then made up of the Bishops of Bath and Hereford, the Earl of Hereford and Essex, the Earl of Warwick and others, including John Maunsel, provost of Beverley, John de Burgo, John son of Alan, Roberto de Sancto Johanne, Roger de Sumery, William de Grey, William Gernun, Imbert Pugeys and Ralph de Bakepuz.

The identity of the individual who actually presented the petition to the royal party on that occasion is not recorded but the suspicion is that it was the Prior Baldwin from Plympton because it was the Prior and Convent of Plympton who by that charter were henceforth permitted to hold a weekly market at Sutton on Thursdays, plus a yearly fair on the eve, the day, and the day after of the Feast of St John the Baptist.

English Patent Roll (27 January 1254) Market Charter of Sutton Prior (PRO)

It is perhaps not surprising therefore that within a generation (that is by 1288) Plympton Priory had become the second wealthiest religious house in Devon. However, there had already been mutterings from malcontents. The people at Plympton felt that the new market at Sutton had taken trade away from them, meanwhile, John Valletort claimed that he was the actual Lord of the Manor for Sutton. The situation came to a head at a couple of inquiries held in Exeter the upshot of which was the passing of a number of binding observations/decisions, namely that:

Sutton was on the coast of the port of Plymouth, but not part of the King's soil; part of Sutton belonged to the Priors of Plympton where they had assize of bread and ale and some rents; part of Sutton south of the coast (essentially south of what is now known as the Parade) belonged to John Valletort, where he was entitled to certain rents, although the Abbot of Buckland had assize of bread and ale; while the port of Plymouth was the King's land and it paid £4 per annum to the Exchequer.

Most importantly as far as Sutton was concerned, it was the judge's verdict that *'it would prejudice neither the King nor anyone else if Sutton were made a free borough and its inhabitants free burgesses.'* (Gill)

One can imagine that the King's interest in the area was moving up the Tamar and Tavy a little at that time, following the discovery of silver at Bere Alston in 1290. Henry III had already issued a writ to the sheriff of Devon making it quite clear that the rights to any mines found on the King's land yielding gold, silver and copper in the county were vested in the King and no one else and in 1289 Edward I's men were directed to work his mines of silver, copper, lead and iron, that had just been found in Ireland.

Five years later, however, following the attempt by the French King, Philip IV, to seize Edward's possessions in Western France, the English King's attention was re-focussed once again.

An fleet was assembled in Portsmouth to take an army over to Gascony. Scattered off the coast of Cornwall, the fleet reassembled in Plymouth and

The deforestation of Devon was confirmed in 1217 by Henry III, who 22 years later conferred the Forest of Dartmoor, along with the Manor of Lydford, on his brother, Richard, Earl of Cornwall. From that point onwards the area technically became a 'chase' although nominally nothing changed.

The following year, 1240, anxious to settle a dispute with a few knights who owned land adjoining the Forest of Dartmoor, he issued a writ directing the Sheriff and a dozen Devon knights to perambulate the said forest to determine its exact bounds.

Thus it was that on 24 July 1240 what has since become known as 'The 1240 Perambulation' took place. Collated into one grand plan, the original has long since been lost but a number of near-contemporary copies are still around. Edmund, Richard's son, inherited the forest, but when he died Dartmoor reverted to the Crown.

the Earl of Lancaster, the King's brother, sailed with it. There were further expeditions in 1296 and 1297, also from Plymouth, which effectively marked the start of the port's long association with the Crown and the Navy. Indeed Plymouth was rapidly becoming the major port on the south-west coast.

Plympton, however, was, as yet, wealthier still and when the King himself arrived in the county, in April 1297, it was at Plympton Priory that he set up court, notwithstanding the royal right of being accommodated at the expense of Sutton, King's Tamerton and Maker mentioned 200 years earlier in *Domesday*.

Not without his problems in Wales (under Madog ap Llywelyn) and Scotland (William Wallace and Robert Bruce), the 55-year-old Warrior King spent two months at the Priory, *'almost ruining them in the process'* (Walmesley), but then Edward almost ruined the country, spending a hefty £750,000 over a four-year period, defending his kingdom … not always successfully.

Plympton St Maurice with it's medieval church and Norman castle, believed to have been constructed on the site of an earlier fortification.

PLYMPTON BECOMES A STANNARY TOWN

Regrator: Someone who buys commodities in advance in order to sell them for a greater price later.

Meanwhile, back in Devon, we are left to piece together the ongoing progress of the Dartmoor tin industry through what scant documentation exists. It would seem that a 1240 reference to 'la Dryeworke' (Dry Lake – a tinner's gully) is only the second specific reference to a tin-mining location on Dartmoor, but then the document that the reference appears in is the first reference we have to a number of places on the moor.

Even this nugget of information reveals very little of the scale of the operations on Dartmoor and around its perimeters, although an interesting entry in the Exchequer accounts of 1302 shows that there were some 134 Devon tinners presenting their yields to the officials, of which the vast majority, 109 (over 80%) produced less than a thousand weight each (half a ton); while 16 produced between half a ton and a ton; seven produced over a ton; one more than two tons and just one who managed just a little short of five tons.

Whether the larger amounts were from workings involving more than one tinner is unclear, but it certainly appears to suggest that the general pattern was for men to be working in relatively small units, if not alone. The situation was very similar in Cornwall and remained much the same throughout the fourteenth century, although famously there was the example of Abraham the Tinner, who, in 1357, was imprisoned for clogging up the Fowey at Lostwithiel.

From the paperwork generated by the case it appears that Abraham's tin-mining enterprise included some seven named workings, including four streamworks, which together involved over 300 persons – men, women and children.

'He was not a small-scale, semi-subsistence miner, but a proto-capitalist whose principal resource would have been the skill and the muscle-power of those 300 people.' (Herring)

The fact that Abraham was imprisoned illustrates the extent to which the industry was already impacting on the tin-yielding rivers. *'Much of the material removed from ... streamworks was taken in suspension down river to be dropped where the waters slowed in the middle and tidal reaches of the Fowey, Lynher, Tamar and Camel, silting up formerly navigable channels at great cost to trading towns.'* (Herring)

The towns at the mouths of the Dartmoor rivers, where arguably mining had, to that point, a longer and more active history, suffered, as we have already seen in the case of Plympton, the same fate. However, judging by the records of the fourteenth, fifteenth and sixteenth century, it was seldom that anything other than legal lip service was paid to address the problem. Devon does, however, appear to have been better regulated at times and the instance of Abraham the capitalist tinner is by no means unique on

Jewish heretics being burned at the stake.

William the Conqueror had originally brought in a community of Jewish financiers from Rouen in 1070. His rationale being that as Christians were banned from lending money, the Jews, with their expertise and ability to finance major projects would play a vital role in the King's economic strategies for expanding trade, and building castles and monasteries.

The move worked for the King, and the community expanded rapidly setting up bases in most major towns and cities around the country. Towards the end of the twelfth century, however, the relationship was soured by brutal anti-Jewish protests, culminating in a massive massacre of over 150 Jews in York, in 1190.

The situation simmered down somewhat in the years that followed but in 1255 all Jews were expelled from Leicester and 20 years later the community was required by statute to give up their traditional role as money lenders.

Whether it was their failure to comply, or that enforced loans, high taxes and property confiscations had left the Jews with nothing more to give, or simple anti-Semitic prejudice is unclear, but the bottom line was that the 3,000 strong community was forced to leave England and all of their property was forfeit.

Curiously enough Harold Bayley in his book Archaic England (1919) picking up on the notion that 'entire sentences of archaic Hebraisms are to be found in the now obsolete Cornish language' and that 'certain of the western tin mines were farmed by Jews' says 'yet there is a tradition among Cornish tinners that the '"Saracens", a term still broadly applied to any foreigner, were not allowed to advance further than the coast lest they should discover the districts whence tin was brought.' He added, 'the entire absence of any finds of Phoenician coins is an inference that this tradition is well founded, for it is hardly credible that had the "Finicians" penetrated far inland or settled to any extent in the country some of their familiar coins would not have come to light.'

the other side of the Tamar. As Lewis notes 'there was the case in 1342 of "certain of the wealthier tinners of Cornwall," Michael de Trenewyth, Michael his son, John Billyon, Hervey his son, Ralf Reslack, Walter le Beare, John Carnignon, and William Scarlet, who are said to have "usurped divers stannaries by force and duress, and to have compelled stannary men to work in these contrary to their will, for a penny for every other day, or a bit more, whereas before they worked 20d or more worth of tin per day, and for a long time have prevented tinners from whitening and selling their tin worked by them; wherefore the stannary men have ceased working and some of them are impoverished".'

In a later chapter Lewis adds: 'In Cornwall with true laissez-faire spirit the English mineral law left the unorganised tinners to a much greater extent unprotected, and handed them over to the tender mercies of the middlemen and regrator.'

In the 1340s they also, along with the rest of the South West, experienced the dire consequences of the plague that spread from Central Asia and killed 30-60% of Europe's population in a four-year period. Overall the death toll in England was at the lower end of the scale but nevertheless would have been most devastating around our ports and trading routes.

Tin mining had recently been given a massive boost with the issue of Edward I's Charters of 1305. Measures which gave tinners a licence to dig … wherever they thought they might find tin: 'They may dig tyn & turves for melting of tyn everywhere in our lands moors and wastes & of all other persons whatsoever … and the waters & water courses for the works of the Stannaryes to turn where & as often as need shall be & buys bushment for the melting of tyn as of old tyme hath bin accustomed to be done …' (A true Copie of the Charter or grants made by King Edward the first, in 1305 – quoted in Hambling)

Prompted no doubt by a royal desire to increase the Crown's revenues the charters had the effect of extending the stannaries and reversing the minor blip in fortunes that appears to have taken place in the 1290s, either a consequence of Richard of Cornwall taxing the miners too hard or perhaps as a consequence of the banishment of Jews from England in 1290, by Edward I. Lewis suggests that, as the Jewish community financed a lot of English commerce, this move 'may have seriously upset the machinery by which the mines were promoted.'

Hambling writing in 1995 picks up this theme: 'Records of the twelfth and thirteenth century show that Jews were closely concerned with early mining in Devon, though whether as traders in tin, financiers of mining ventures, or as miners themselves is not clear.' He adds: 'As late as the nineteenth century, remains of medieval tinners' buildings on Dartmoor were commonly called Jews' Houses.'

Alternatively, Jim Bolton (*The Medieval English Economy*) suggests that a *'crisis of overproduction in Europe'* was responsible for the reduction in the output of tin locally.

Whatever, the new measures confirmed the Devon/Cornwall split, and the freedom from ordinary taxes enjoyed by the tinners on the King's ancient demesnes – although it appears that all tinners were, in practice, exempt. Under the terms of the charter tinners did not have to pay tolls and market dues at fairs and ports on their own goods or the general levy or the tenth and fifteenth levy. Having said that they were liable to *'taxation of a special nature at the will of the Crown and without the mediation of Parliament* (Lewis).'

The King also affirmed in the 1305 charter the Royal right of the pre-emption of all the tin mined in Devon and Cornwall. These rights were regularly used as a financial tool and just a few years later, in 1312, his son, Edward II passed on those rights to the Florentine Bardi, Italians to whom he owed money. Then, in 1314, Edward made over his rights of preemption (the right to buy all the tin) to the Genoese businessman Antonio Pessaigne, who subsequently incurred the wrath of the tinners by requiring them to take all their tin to Lostwithiel at their own expense.

Consider if you will the plight of the miner having to transport half a ton of tin or more by packhorse across unmade roads to what was then the chief stannary town in Cornwall.

To compound matters Pessaigne then weighed the tin with his own weights and paid them around half the market rate.

Naturally, unhappy with these arrangements, the tinners, notwithstanding the Royal commissions, sold their tin to whoever they wanted to *and 'maltreated the patentees factors'* … in other words they were somewhat less than courteous towards the Italian's men!

Eventually the King was persuaded to revoke the patent. However, that did not stop further abuses of the pre-emption over the next two decades, including that by Edward, the Black Prince in 1347. Newly appointed the first ever Duke of Cornwall, the teenage Prince promptly sold his rights to a German merchant, Tideman of Limberg, in return for a rent of 3,500 marks (£2,340). Not surprisingly the tinners and merchants were, once again, less than happy.

The following year local tinners had the perfect opportunity to express their feelings as the Prince, returning from Gascony, where there was a brief period of peace, dined at Plympton with the Prior before moving on. The Prince didn't stay long but he was to return to the area on a number of occasions. Over the rest of the century Plymouth was to experience suffering at the hands of the French as a series of Breton raids gradually increased in their severity.

"Edward The Black Prince receives the grant of Aquitaine from his father King Edward III" Initial letter "E" on a page of illuminated manuscript, date: 1390; British Library, shelfmark: Cotton MS Nero D VI, f.31r. British Library On-line gallery

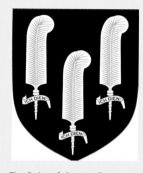

The Duke of Cornwall exercised jurisdiction over all of the Cornwall and Devon stannaries, although in reality the Devon element was little more than Dartmoor.
In practice the whole system rested on the shoulders of the Warden, or Lord Warden of the Stannaries, who, in turn, invariably tended to delegate his judicial powers to his vice-warden and the stewards. Beneath them sat the lower stannary courts, with their stewards and juries of miners.

Edward of Woodstock, the Black Prince, was born in June 1330, the eldest son of Edward III and Phillipa of Hainault. He was created Prince of Wales before reaching his teens in 1343 and became the first English Duke with his subsequent appointment as the Duke of Cornwall. Celebrated as a great military leader, he never held the throne, as he predeceased his father. Achieving great victories against the French in the Hundred Years War, his Black Prince nickname was conferred posthumously and is thought possibly to derive from his black shield and black armour – although there is also a suggestion that it was on account of his brutality towards the French.
As Duke of Cornwall the young prince also enjoyed the honour of Trematon and any royal claims to the rapidly expanding town of Plymouth were also his along with the newly styled Duchy of Cornwall – indeed the Duchy has remained the property of the Sovereign's eldest son ever since.
The now familiar badge depicts three ostrich feathers said to have been a tribute to King John of Bohemia who died alongside the Prince and his father at the Battle of Crecy in 1346. The motto 'Ich Dien' – I serve' also dates from this time and formed the motif for the Prince's 'shield for peace' that he is thought to have used when jousting.

The first of these occurred two years after the Prince's visit and the last, and most devastating, took place in 1403 when it was estimated that some 600 houses were destroyed.

Plymouth, by the middle of the fourteenth century, had become one of the 25 largest towns in England, a remarkable feat considering that at the time of Domesday, Sutton, around which it grew, wasn't even one of the 25 largest manors in Devon. The growth, in part, reflected the burgeoning of the port as a naval base and gradual transcendence of the town over Plympton as the latter became increasingly less viable as a port, principally on account of the accrual of silt from the very mining that had brought its prosperity.

As yet its glory days were not entirely over. In 1355 having been appointed Lieutenant of Gascony, Prince Edward was again in the area. Orders to convene fleets at Plymouth and Southampton were issued in April and ships began to arrive in port in May. Vessels wanting to leave Plymouth had to be well-defended, and local men were required to be armed in case of attack. Archers marched hundreds of miles to muster in the port as did other fighting men from all parts of the country.

Locally the population more than doubled as the Prince, residing from the end of July to the beginning of September at the Priory at Plympton, watched over the preparations. With him a retinue of Knights (Audley, Stafford, Chandos and Loring) and Earls (Suffolk, Oxford, Warwick and Salisbury) all making their demands on the limited resources of the area. In all it said that a force of around 3,000 was assembled: 1,000 men-at-arms, 1,000 horse archers, 300-400 foot archers and 170 Welshmen. Many of the men were convicts, being held for rape, theft, abduction and – in over 100 cases – murder, all of them hoping to win a pardon.

It must have been an interesting summer and a prosperous one for some, although many of those local merchants who sold their goods to the army had to wait a long time before they were paid.

Nevertheless, the activity provided a massive boon to the local money-go-round that summer and on through the winter, as the Prince rested in Bordeaux and ordered supplies from Plymouth.

In March 1357 after a successful campaign in France and victory at Poitiers, the Prince returned to the port and brought with him a prize captive – the King of France, who was subsequently ransomed for three million gold crowns.

The following year, en route for Bordeaux and also attending to the affairs of his duchy, the Prince ordered a warship to be built in Plymouth. There were further royal visits to the area in 1362 and 1364, and, by 1377, it is estimated that Plymouth had eclipsed Exeter in size and boasted a population of around 1,700.

Plympton, meanwhile, had become a fully fledged Stannary town, along with Tavistock, Chagford and Ashburton. Plympton was not originally selected with the others in 1305. However, after the appointment of the reigning Abbot of Tavistock as Warden of the Devon Stannaries … and Keeper of the Port of Dartmouth, it was not all was plain sailing for Tavistock. The appointment, which appears to have been for ten years, was beset with *'a series contradictory grants made to people, other than the abbot'* (Walmesley) and this coupled with *'a disastrous vacancy prolonged over three years (1324-27) … wrecked the prosperity enjoyed by the Abbey under Robert Champeon (ibid).'*

Tavistock had indeed witnessed a sustained period of growth. A new parish church dedicated to St Eustace had been erected in the thirteenth century and in 1318, shortly after Tavistock had become a Stannary town, the church was enlarged. A few years earlier, on 29 October 1311 the parish church in Plympton, just east of the castle, was dedicated and the cemetery there reconciled. It's interesting in this context that Paul Hambling (*The Dartmoor Stannaries*) suggests there were *'prominent religious guilds attached to many Devon parish churches. 'The accounts of the Chagford churchwardens show that the Guilds of St Michael, St Katherine, St Mary and several others were all deeply involved in mining ventures. That may explain,'* he adds, *'the tradition that many Devon churches were rebuilt in the fifteenth century with wealth derived from tin.'*

With Tavistock experiencing difficulties, the burgesses of Plympton, jealous of the former's status, looked to usurp its position and *'tried by devious measures to have the coinage removed from Tavistock, so that their own town could take its place (Walmesley).'*

In their petition the burgesses argued that Plympton was better suited as a stannary town because it was a maritime town, with direct access to trading routes, whereas Tavistock was a long way inland thus transport costs were high. *'Their petition was successful (after all, the jury who made the decision was largely drawn from men living near Plympton) (Gill).'*

It also doubtless helped that the man who held the Honour of Plympton, Hugh de Courtenay, was able to bring his personal influence to bear on the King. Tavistock protested and in the end both were retained. Plympton was formally accepted as Devon's fourth Stannary albeit the smallest in terms of its bounds. Cornwall at that time had five stannary towns – Bodmin, Liskeard, Lostwithiel, Helston and Truro.

Curiously enough, one of the early acts under Edward III, who succeeded his father in 1327, was to designate Ashburton as the staple town for tin in Devon, while Lostwithiel was re-designated the staple town in Cornwall, following a number of years when it had lost out to Bodmin. In 1328 however, the year Plympton became a Stannary town, all staples were abolished and for the best part of 40 years *'the export of tin was entirely unregulated.'* (Lewis)

Certainly in the 1340s there is record of considerable shipments of tin by Florentine merchants via London and indeed London was rapidly becoming a significant market for tin generally, thanks in large measure to the capital becoming, almost overnight, the centre of the English pewter industry. Pewter had been around since the Bronze Age. Although used widely for decorative items and tableware by the Egyptians and, later, by the Romans, it didn't really come into its own in Europe until the Middle Ages: *'An English pewter industry developed rapidly to supply ecclesiastical, noble and middle-class households with pewter vessels which were fast replacing the copper and clay utensils previously used,'* writes Bolton, who cites examples of a pewterer at work in Norfolk by 1340, York in 1348, and a *'considerable if illegal industry in Cornwall itself, using uncoined tin.'* However, it was London that the trade mainly gravitated towards and pretty soon it seems the pewterers there had the industry more or less sewn up. As the self-styled 'Craft of Pewterers' a group issued an *'elaborate code of ordinances, designed in true medieval spirit for the enforcement of a high standard of purity of material and skill in workmanship.'* (Lewis)

By the end of the century the London company had a practical monopoly of pewter exports and the trade, which seems to have been made up of

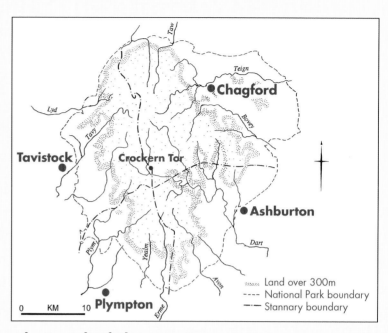

The Bounds of Plympton Stannary

From full sea mark at Plymouth to the Old Quay and so up the street called St Andrews St and so up to the Old Town, all the dwellings on the west side being in Tavystock Court, and so the highway to Uddletor Rock (Yelverton Rock) from thence to Horrabridge and so the highway to Yennadon Cross and so by the long hedge to woodland which divideth the parish of Meavy and Walkhampton to Creeby foot and thence ascending the river of Meavy to Reedapit lake from thence to Blewstone from thence to Horradill head from thence to Broken Burrow from thence to plain lodge from thence to Crane Tor from thence to Turragott Stone nr Woollake Haw from thence to St Peter's Cross and so watershut the top of the hill towards Pyles' Beacon from thence to Modbury Steeple and from thence to St Michaelborrow. (From a seventeenth-century Strode document)

Pewter

An alloy of tin, there have, historically, been three main variants of pewter: 'fine', which was about 99% tin with around 1% of copper and was mainly used for tableware; 'trifle' used for holloware and made up of fine metal with around 4% lead; and 'lay' or 'ley' metal, which was used to make items that were not in normal contact with food or drink and which contained around 15% lead.

'tin in vessel, small bars, and an assortment of pewter mugs plates, and candelabra, had reached considerable height in 1402 (ibid).'
The London guild soon proved itself not only to be the largest but it controlled the supervision of the entire manufacture elsewhere in England. Given then that more than 90% of the content of pewter was from tin, this was to have interesting ramifications for the Stannaries.
'By the early 1370s one in 20 of the male population of Devon was involved directly in tinworking, with many ancillary activities involved as well – such as charcoal making from peat or wood.' (Greeves/Fox)
The question, however, was, were all those who claimed to be tinners actually tinners? This issue, along with one or two others, came to a head in 1376 when two petitions were presented to Parliament.
It was claimed that even those tinners not working on royal demesnes were claiming stannary privileges and that furthermore it wasn't just the labouring tinners but their employers too, who were pleading freedom of the mines. It was also said that certain tinners were having cases heard at stannary courts about disputes that didn't even relate to the tinner's workplace, Royal or not. And that furthermore the Warden was allowing tinners, imprisoned for felony at both Lostwithiel and Lydford, to run free and that the stannary jails were receiving villeins who their masters were about to imprison for arrears, and was treating them so well that they were refusing to return to their lords and masters.
For its part Parliament was somewhat vague and evasive in its response. Under the terms of the 1305 charter, tinners, they said, were free to work in the lands of all parties; although they conceded that disputes arising outside of areas where mining was taking place should not be heard in stannary courts and that the term 'tinner' should only be applied to manual workers in the tin works themselves and only for as long as they worked there.
At the end of the fourteenth century the statistics for Devon were much as they had been at the beginning: in 1394, in Devon, out of 109 tinners presenting material at the coinages, only six produced more than half a ton of tin, and four years later out of 123 tinners, 17 produced between half a ton and a ton and only five brought in more than a ton. As Lewis notes when commenting on these figures: *'the significant feature is the great number of men whose income from tin must have been exceedingly small.'* Assuming of course, that all the tin produced, was dealt with via the proper channels.
The outlook could not have been all that gloomy though.
Bolton, observing that England's principal exports at this time were cloth and wool, notes that the *'only other product of note was tin, sold either as rods or blocks of pure ore, or made up into pewter vessels.'*
He then adds: *'The opening up of new mines in central Europe reduced*

Map showing distribution of tinners in Devon in 1373 (from Eileen Fox, 1999).

demand for English tin in Germany, but the Italians more than made up for any loss in that sector. From Southampton and later London, the Genoese and Venetians shipped large quantities of tin to the Mediterranean and beyond to Asia Minor.'
In one year, towards the end of the fourteenth century, he showed that the Genoese and Catalans shipped more than a third of the tin presented for coinage in Cornwall and Devon. It would appear that the principal route was for the tin to reach Southampton via coasting traffic from the southwest and then to be taken by road to London.

Plymouth's new Corporation Seal

With Plympton increasingly difficult to access by water, this worked wonders for Plymouth and it was perhaps no great surprise to find that in 1439 the town's petition for borough status was successful and at last it achieved total independence from the Priors of Plympton. A new corporation seal proclaimed it now to be the King's burgess town, and the combination of being a strategic part of the country's ability to launch attacks and the necessity of being able to defend itself, had been recognised.

Significantly Plymouth was the first town in Devon to be incorporated (Totnes followed in 1505 and Exeter in 1537), and it was also the first town in England to be incorporated by an Act of Parliament.

The tin trade at this stage was still relatively buoyant. Newman, in his 1994-study demonstrated that from the middle of the fifteenth century through to the dawn of the eighteenth century of 14 farms investigated in an area of south-west Dartmoor all had evidenced that at least one tinner had lived there at some point.

It was also around the middle of the fifteenth century that Walmesley suggests that the 'Gentlemen Tinners' started to take a serious interest in the profits of the industry: *'they began to strike up partnerships with "Labouring Tinners" … and this probably suited the latter.'*

'Previously they had entered when and where they pleased, dug tin, and handed back a share of it. Now the days of feudalism were drawing to a close and it was better all round, to make peaceful arrangements.

'The tinners' families were often ordinary tenants of the manor, and if things got out of hand it could be awkward for them. Besides the tinners themselves were often short of money, for they could only sell four times a year at the coinages, and they were glad of the opportunity to sell at other times to the local tin dealers, who were ready to make advances, though probably at lower than coinage prices. It suited them well to go to the local gentry, work out and register pitches at the tin court, and share their profits with the landowners.'

It was in this context that Walmesley introduced the *'solid reliable Devon family'* the Strodes, who inherited the ancient manor of Newnham, through marriage, in the early fifteenth century, into the local tin narrative.

Certainly it is true that mining and the selling of tin had become increasingly regulated and the centuries-old stannary court arrangements were in need of overhaul.

Given that tin had long been regarded as a Royal metal and that the crown was therefore keen to protect its production – and tax it – it is clear that there had been some form of safeguarding of tinners' rights before the Charter of 1305 and indeed those of 1198. The former, however, forged a split between Cornwall and Devon and so the traditional tinners' meeting place on Hingston Down was abandoned in favour of Crockern Tor, east of the Tamar.

Over and above the more regular Stannary Courts, where individual cases were heard, these were Stannary Parliament meets, where tinners convened, amid much ceremony, to draw up a code of conduct for the industry that might later evolve into law.

The date for the first recorded Parliament was 11 September 1494, although there were almost certainly earlier assemblies, indeed there was a 'Great Court' held in 1474.

Located quite centrally for the four Devon stannary towns and very central in terms of Dartmoor itself, Crockern Tor could be an inhospitable host if the weather was not favourable. It was an open-air affair. There was a very large, thin, granite slab that served as a table on the top of the tor and it was surrounded by stone seats with one, the Lord Warden's seat, being at the head of the table and surmounted by a stone canopy.

An elevated, isolated spot, the tor would attract a large crowd for these assemblies, each of the four Stannaries sending 24 jurats, who together with the Lord Warden (or as in 1494, the vice-warden, Sir John Stepcote) and his men would constitute a gathering of over 100, without the attendant servants, observers, relations and refreshment providers, all of whom would have arrived on foot or on horseback.

Walmesley paints a fanciful picture: *'At the groups of farms and tenements of Prince Hall, Bellever, Dunnabridge, Broom Park, Brownberry, Huccaby, Hexworthy and Sherberton, there must have been a great brewing and baking, and airing of linen come Parliament time. For several days, perhaps the best part of a week, judging by the length of the agenda, these usually quiet places would be crowded with men and horses. So they must have looked to the Parliament as a time of excitement, a break in the day-to-day round, and a welcome addition to their income.'*

Perhaps so, but as we only have record of ten assemblies in over 210 years – all but three of them were spread across the sixteenth century – it would be hard to allocate too much excitement to these proceedings.

List of Plympton jurats at the 1510 Crockern Tor Parliament

William at Hele
William Rede
William Odymer
William Tyllon
William Forde
William Brusey
William Chidston
William Wyet
John Beare
John Mede
John Peke at Hele
John Scobell
Robert Batin
Robert Hamme
Richard Rose
Richard Pommerie
Nickolas Bragge
Nickolas Combe
Jurdeay Bragg
Walter Adam
Elias Efford
Andrew
Roger Eggecombe

Interestingly enough nearly one in four of the men present were named William, one in three were named John with more than a quarter of the other names being shared by Robert, Richard and Thomas. The use of surnames appears almost universal and 400 years on from Domesday there appears to be no hint of Anglo-Saxon names.

However, those that we do know of are relatively well documented and happily from the 1510 assembly we have the names of all the stannators, including, obviously enough, those from Plympton *(see left)*.

As it transpires only Ashburton and Tavistock supplied the full complement, with Chagford and Plympton each sending only 23 men to the table. Among the Plympton deputation was Roger Eggecombe - a relative perhaps of Richard Edgecumbe (the spellings of that surname are still variable today) who was appointed Sheriff of Devon in 1494, and is therefore a plausible candidate to have been Lord Warden at that time.

No agenda survives from the 1494 congregation, however, we have a record of the 1510 assembly. At that Assembly they began by stating that all previous statutes be declared null and void, and that the court should affirm the laws they were about to pass – all of them, incidentally, in plain English, so that everyone understood what was being said. The use of Latin was vetoed. Some of the measures were clearly formal ratifications of what had been agreed in the past but others would have broken new ground.

Anxious to assert their independence, the stannators further insisted that only those cases concerning life, land and limb should not be referred to the Lord Warden or his court. Tinners rights, inter alia, the rights and titles to workings, the position on partnerships, and the rights of children and widows to inherit, were all discussed, as were the marking of ingots and the penalties liable for those who refused to pay fines.

Another of the 37 enactments affirmed by the 1510 Parliament was the "tinners' ancient right" to dig tin in any place in Devon where found, and also *to carry water to the works'* with a fine of £40 to be imposed upon anyone who obstructed the tinners in the exercise of this right, including it seems the Sheriff or the Baliff.

Before starting to dig, however, the tinner had to first set his bounds – not a problem on the Duchy land, but requiring permission of the owner on 'foreign' land, this is an area outside the Royal demesne. Furthermore, tinners were not permitted to subvert trees or woods in any private grounds. Tinners were also not allowed to bound any stream works, nor were they permitted to mine works within the bounds of stream works.

'The actual (bounding) process consisted in marking the angles of the area desired to be enclosed by small holes and heaps of turf, or else by poles erected at each corner, with a furze bush at the top.' (Lewis)

When the tinner had settled upon his holding and had pitched his bounds, he then had to have them registered in the steward's book at the nearest stannary court and then have them announced at three successive sessions.

Assuming the tinner's claims were not contested, he became entitled to his 'writ of possession' and his right became absolute, and, in Devon at least, this became real property which he could pass on to his heir.

As might be expected it was incumbent on the tinner to keep his bounds in good order and quite a bit of legislation was generated by attempts to determine when a bounded area could be deemed vacant or void.

Bounding was the most fundamental of the tinner's privileges, underpinning the whole notion of free mining. In the earliest of the charters it was referred to as an 'ancient custom' and it is impossible to say when and where it originated.

By the very nature of the measures being deployed we get a fairly clear picture of the state of tin mining at the dawn of the sixteenth century.

Certainly evidence for the Duchy suggests that up to this point, most of the tin from Cornwall was still being shovelled from alluvial deposits – from shallow pits drained by trenches or by the simplest of water wheels.

'Often,' wrote Lewis, in 1907, *'a single Cornishman, aided possibly by his son, could manage a stream work, and there may still be seen in Cornwall small affairs of this sort which yield a fair profit.'*

And don't assume that a fair profit was predicated on a detailed examination of the end of year balance sheets. As Lewis later suggests, *'it is doubtful if the free miners in any part of England ever kept written accounts of any sort, as the total lack of any mine document of this nature makes it seem probable that with the characteristic happy-go-lucky methods prevalent even in modern Cornish mines (remember he was writing over 100 years ago) the medieval free miners squared their accounts by the use of pebbles,'* a practice it seems they were still using in the late-1700s.

For the first two or three thousand years the extraction of tin from Dartmoor and Cornwall was a relatively simple and straightforward process. Rich deposits of cassiterite (oxide of tin) or tinstone, as it was also known, had been eroded out of granite tin lodes by rain and spring water over millions of years. Thus the heavy black material came to be found in the river beds and valley beds buried, at no great depth, beneath lighter material and all the early tinners had to do was shovel it.

The process was called streaming – alluvial mining – and over time almost every stream on Dartmoor was worked on, the tinners creating mounds of debris along the banks of these rivers and streams. Customarily the tinstone that had been thus unearthed would be washed – that is crushed and rinsed to remove as much waste as possible – in two 'wash' sessions each year, one in May, the other in September.

Traditionally it seems that the amount of tin yielded in May was higher, presumably on account of there being more rinsing rainwater available over the winter. It will be apparent from this that it was the waste material from the streaming process that, over thousands of years of alluvial mining, tended to get lodged where the upper tidal reaches of the sea met the downstream waters of the river.

Inevitably this tended to be at the very point around which a community had grown up over time, initially because rivers were the principal highways for getting around before roads were good enough to support wheeled transport and locations situated at the mouths of large rivers became important trading ports. However, for rivers where there was a great deal of 'streaming' taking place upstream of such estuaries, the ports, in time, became severely compromised by this activity. Plympton itself being a prime example of how a once thriving port could be reduced to a community living on the edge of extensive mud flats or marshlands.

Nor was the situation eased when such simple alluvial mining gave way, firstly to eluvial mining, where the weathered tinstone although not actually in the stream bed had, nevertheless, been weathered away from the parent lode and then secondly, on to the digging of open pits and shafts before the new technology spawned by the Industrial Revolution allowed for the deep underground mining of Dartmoor in the eighteenth and nineteenth centuries.

In the very early days the ore could easily have been ground down with a pestle and mortar, however once the easily available material had been exhausted so the eluvial and less eroded metal-bearing rocks were turned to and heavier handed treatment was required. Crazing mills, deploying heavy circular millstones were introduced. Initially man-powered, then later horse, then water-powered, these mills in time gave way to knacking, or knocking, mills. Essentially these worked on the same pestle and mortar principal but these were mechanised affairs generally comprising 'two or three heavy, iron-shod posts called stamps, working up and down in a frame and pounding the ore beneath them. Powered by a small waterwheel, the stamps could hammer the largest chunks of ore to a fine gravel ready for the crazing mill.' (Hambling) The practice was further refined towards the end of the sixteenth century when it was realised that the ore could be crushed to powder if water was introduced into the stamping process.

The tinner was then left with what was known as black tin which could be sold at that point, particularly if the tinner was desperate for money. However such sales had to be made at the 'wash' or before witnesses. Black tin could not be taken out of the country and only recognised tinners were allowed to hold stocks of such unsmelted material. The smelting too had to be done at a designated time and place, in the presence of one of the King's designated officers, who would weigh, stamp and tax what was now white tin. Prior to the Charters of 1305 and the creation of the Stannary towns this would have happened on appointed days in local market towns. Edward I's legislation, however, meant that henceforth those Stannary towns would be fixed as Tavistock, Chagford and Ashburton, and as we have seen from 1328 onwards, Plympton as well. By that time the tinners' ability to smelt his own tin had improved substantially and a new structure started appearing on the Dartmoor landscape – the blowing house 'a small stone building containing

Washing for tin, 1556.

a granite furnace with bellows powered by a waterwheel. Layers of crushed ore and charcoal in the furnace were brought to a high temperature by the steady blast of air, liquid tin drained into a stone trough or 'float' below, and from there was ladled into stone moulds.' (Hambling) The resulting tin ingot typically weighed in the region of 100-200 lbs and most tinners, it appears, produced a little less than 5-8 ingots a year.

The Strode coat of arms on the wall at Newnham today. A family tree suggests they originated with Reginald Strode – of Ermington – great great grandfather of Richard Strode.
It is curious to see the prominence of three conies –three rabbits – on the badge. This would appear to be extremely rare in English heraldry, maybe even unique and suggests a possible link with the three tinners' rabbits and thus perhaps a suggestion that the Strode wealth was at least partly based, at that point in time, on mining. Certainly the Strodes had a share in almost all the tinworks in the Plympton district.

Clearly this was hardly an exact, or even an exacting process. Tin-mining was still largely a simple process even when scaled up to a larger operation. However, as we have already seen with the case of Abraham the proto-capitalist tinner, the fallout from the activity was of great concern to those living downstream of mining operations, hence the measures passed in later sixteenth-century gatherings at Crockern Tor forbidding the sinking of shafts within 24-feet of the highway, or *'so situated as to choke the rivers and havens with their refuse.'*

Legislation which, for one particular Plympton resident affected by the issue, came a little too late. The resident in question was Richard Strode of Newnham.

Described as a tinner himself, although one struggles with the notion he actually got his hands dirty, Strode was, like a growing number of his peers, a man who had clear interests in the mining industry and almost certainly employed a number of manual labourers – in other words, the archetypal gentleman tinner. He was, however, unhappy that the

The remains of Plympton Priory

streaming works of the Dartmoor tinners generally was affecting the viability of ports like Plympton and, as MP for the town, with the help of some fellow members, he put forward a bill to the national Parliament dealing with *'the perishing, hurting, and destroying of rivers, portes, havens and crekes in the county of Devon,'* occasioned by tinners' silt.

The Act represented, inevitably, a restriction on the standard practices of the Dartmoor tinners and not surprisingly they took exception to it. In the Stannary Court Strode was taken to task by *'an influential competitor'* and fined £40 by each of the Devon stannary courts.

The Plympton man refused to pay and was consequently arrested and imprisoned in the stannary gaol *'in a dungeon and deep pitte under the grounde in the Castell of Lidforde'* where he languished for *'thre wekes and more.'* (quoted in Brooking Rowe 1906)

However, as an MP, collector of fifteenths and therefore an officer of the King, he was able to sue for a writ of privilege in the Court of Exchequer, and obtain his liberty. Whereupon he headed back up to Westminster and induced Parliament to pass an Act freeing him from the consequences of the judgement of the Stannary Court.

'Strode's Case', as it has since become known, also granted him and, historically ever after his fellow MPs, immunity from prosecution related to his Parliamentary activities.

As such it is one of the earliest, oft-quoted and most important legal cases regarding Parliamentary privilege.

In his defence Strode's original protests were clearly well-founded. Official statistics show that Devon's tin production reached a peak in 1524 of over 470 thousand weight of tin, yielding over £368 of coinage duty, and although there was a slow decline thereafter, production throughout the sixteenth century was consistently well in excess of previously measured amounts. Great news for some but not those living downstream and at the next meeting of the Stannary Parliament at Crockern Tor, in 1532, Strode, who bought a substantial piece of waterfront at Lambhay, on the fringe of Sutton Pool, was vindicated as it was ordained that:

'... every Person or Persons that hereafter shall Work in any Stream Works, or cause any Stream Work to be Wrought, that they and everyone of them Convey and Carry, or cause to be conveyed and carried, the Gravel, Ruble, and Sands, into old Hatches, Tipittes, miry places, or other convenient place, from the said great Rivers, so that the said Gravel, Ruble or Sands be not conveyed to the said Havens of Dartmouth and Plimouth ...' (Newman quoting Radford 1930)

Certainly Strode had plenty of reason to be concerned. Former Plymouth Local Studies Librarian, and mining historian, Owen Baker, examined the Strode Collection in the City Archives (now part of The Box) and identified more than 100 share certificates, mostly sixteenth century, which show that the Strodes held a share in almost all the tinworks in the Plympton district. *'Each of these tinworks or bounds had their own name registered in the Stannary Court at Plympton. It is impossible to accurately locate some of them,'* wrote Baker in an unpublished manuscript, *'but they tend to fall into general groupings as follows:*

Newnham Park, the Strode family home, late eighteenth century, by the Rev John Swete. The Strode family had long been seated at Newnham which stood about a mile to the south-east of Loughtor. After William Strode (1512-79) married Elizabeth Courtenay, the heiress of Loughtor, the decision was taken to move the principal residence to Loughtor. A new mansion house was built and given the name Newnham Park.

Hemerdon Area
Great Hemerdon Bale
West Hemerdon Bale
Drakeland Beame
Little Bottle Hill
Great Bottle Hill
Lobb Beame

Crownhill Down
Many pits divided into two groups: North Crownhill and South Crownhill At South Crownhill there were early workings called Hawkesborough (modern Hookspray) and Bonewood Combe (Bude farm) and these extended west into Fernehyll Wode or Vernhill Beame. In the deerpark to the south lay The Parke Worke and to the north and west of Fernhill lay:

> Furzeparke Tinwork
> Somerley
> Heath Beme
> Heath Beme Coombe
> Elverley (Elfordleigh)

Sparkwell Area
Goodamore Beame
Lower Goodamore
Sparkwell
Burchland Beame
Backmore Pits
Bickford Beame

All of these Hawkesborough related sites were in time to evolve into Wheal Sidney, while Lobb Beame was a forerunner of Wheal Mary Hutchings and Drakeland Beam, Little Bottle Hill and Great Bottle Hill would become Bottle Hill Mine.

The 1532 order was apparently repeated at the 1536 convocation, but it would appear that the call, even if it was heeded, came too late for some. Observing the state of Plympton Priory a few years later, John Leland, one of Henry VIII's chaplains wrote: *'The lower and first buildinges of the court of the Priorie be almost clean choked with the sands that Torey Brooke bringeth from the tynne workes.'*

'Plymtoun Mary,' noted Leland, *'stondeth not apon Plym River ... but it stondeth on Torey Brooke, by the Est Ripe of it,'* and, having ridden about half a mile along the course of the Torry Brook, he commented that its *'color is always redde by the Sand that it rennith on and caryeth from the Tynne Workes with it.'*

Of course at that precise time the Priory had recently been dissolved by Henry VIII, along with countless others the length and breadth of the country.

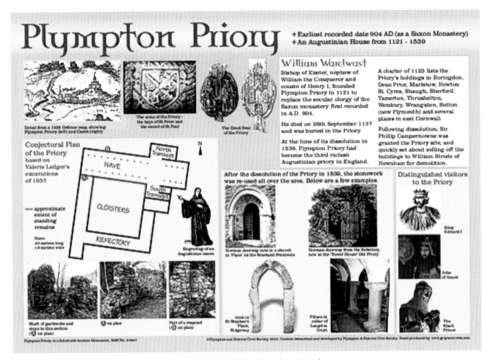

The Plympton Priory information panel by Graphic Words

More significantly, at the time of the Dissolution this great Augustinian foundation had been *'so enriched with liberal gifts by the Redverses and Valletorts and other benefactors, that it was the wealthiest house in the West, with revenues valued at £912.12s.8d (Worth).'*

Rich indeed, as that figure then was comfortably more than three times the annual coinage dues for Devon. Sadly, however, there is very little trace of the magnificent Priory church, or its ancillary domestic buildings, to be seen today – although the site is evident and there are indications of some of the structures. Shortly after Richard Strode's encounter with the Stannary Court we find William Strode of Lughtorr – Loughtor being the original name of Newnham Park – cited in a deposition made in April 1539, by John Edward.

Edward, stating himself to be a business partner of Strode, claimed to have pitched a tinwork called Hethbeme (Heath Beme) back in 1527, having 'given warning' to one John More of Plympton and certainly there is among the Strode papers a letter of attorney of Richard (not William) for possession of a tinworks in Plympton – although it may not have been the same one. 'Botelhylle tinworks' is also referred to in a document from that year.

But to return to Edward's testimony, he states that *'nine or ten years later two others named Wat Rowe and John Brusey gave notice that they too had made a pitch at Hethbeme. And so it was that Edward and Strode went up to the disputed site to meet the new claimants ... who were conspicuous by their absence.'*

Master Strode then called upon the bystanders – they had evidently taken witnesses with them – to confirm that no one had appeared to contest the claim. But then they noticed a *'multitude of person'* had assembled at Somerley Cross nearby. Whereupon Strode proposed *'Goe we al neer unto them to knowe what they meane and the cause of there assembly.'*

As the Strode party advanced towards Somerley Cross so Brusy, Rowe and company came to meet them.

In the discussion that followed it was agreed that the newcomers, Rowe and Brusy, should have a one-eighth share of the site. New boundaries were set in turf and it was agreed that the larger part henceforth be known as Great Hethbeme and the smaller, Litel Hethbeme.

Interestingly enough, another document from the collection, this one from 1595, relates another encounter, this one at a Tincourt, when a tinner wanted to lodge a claim for a piece of ground to work on. Here we read that William Am *'tooke one Phillipp Strode, gentleman, by the arme and gave him warnings of the Pitch of a certain tinworke called Littell Holt,'* evidently because the previous owner had stopped working this particular Plympton St Maurice facility.

The sixteenth century witnessed a significant change in such documentation. In the early Tudor period records were produced in Latin, during the reign of Queen Elizabeth, some were in Latin and some were in English, by the beginning of the seventeenth century the use of English had become standard.

COMPETITION TIME

This was, of course, a time of major social upheaval and change, and one of the benefactors was the Warden of the Stannaries, Henry Courtenay, whom Henry VIII had created feudal baron of Okehampton, feudal baron of Plympton and Marquess of Exeter, in 1525.

Henry's father and grandfather had already held the hereditary post of Earl of Devon, as well as Warden of the Stannaries. Admittedly his grandfather had incurred the displeasure of Henry VII and had been incarcerated in the Tower of London, but Henry, who was also a grandson of King Edward IV, had won the support of Henry VIII, who was also his first cousin, and the title had been reinstated.

Thus it was that by the late 1530s Henry Courtenay was administering most of the West of England, but somehow, partly through his antipathy to Thomas Cromwell, and despite the fact that his second wife, Gertrude Blount, was an unrepentant Roman Catholic, he became implicated in what was known as the Exeter Conspiracy and he was beheaded with a sword on Tower Hill on 9 December 1538. The Earldom of Devon was forfeited and his lands in Cornwall annexed by the Duchy of Cornwall. There were other difficulties for the area too.

Throughout the Roman Empire period, and indeed a little before it, other sources of tin had been found on the Iberian Peninsula and along the Germany/Czech border – the Erzgebirge. Tuscany and the Balkans also became somewhat more minor sources, but happily the ever growing demand for pewter kept everyone busy. As long as the London pewterers could get their tin cheaper than their European counterparts, on the grounds of it being more readily available, and as long as demand for London pewter remained high, on the grounds that it was superior to that made by their mainland competitors, all was well.

'Early in the sixteenth century, however, the art was improved in France and Flanders by runaway English apprentices; the German stannaries attained a considerable output; the monopoly of Cornwall was broken; and the growing competition from continental pewterers was so keenly felt in England, that the statute passed in 1534 not only prohibited the purchase of foreign pewter and authorised its seizure wherever found, but forbade the taking of alien apprentices, forbade any alien to become a pewterer in England, and considered as aliens all English pewterers who travelled or remained abroad.' (Lewis)

Saxon and Bohemian tin mines achieved their greatest output in the sixteenth century, but the Thirty Years' War (1618-48) largely put paid to their success. Initially the war was fought between Catholics and Protestants in Bohemia, but later drew in Denmark, Sweden and France.

Henry Courtenay, KG, shown 2nd from left wearing a mantle displaying his arms, detail from procession of Garter Knights in the Black Book of the Garter, c.1535, Royal Collection, Windsor.

The London pewterers had had it their way for some considerable time, but as it was primarily a soft metal, pewter utensils had a tendency to have a shorter lifespan than caterers, ale house and inn keepers, would have liked and consequently those in such trades were always on the lookout for cheaper pewter, even if it wasn't all that pure.

'In the long run the body of consumers is the best judge of what is good for it, and the London pewterers, by refusing to meet the demand, doomed their trade to eventual decay.' (Lewis)

And the demand was certainly there. One estimate (from Homer: *'Exeter Pewterers from the Fourteenth Century to about 1750'* in the *Transactions of the Devonshire Association*), suggests that around this time there was around 12lbs of pewter in circulation for every man woman and child in England, what is more in the late sixteenth century there appears to have been a *'flourishing business in France in the manufacture of knick-knacks from an alloy of tin and lead.'* (Lewis)

Tom Greeves, in 2016, quoted Blake, writing 100 years earlier in the *Transactions of the Devonshire Association*, as asserting that, around 1600, tinworking in Devon was still considered to be more important than maritime activity.

Nevertheless, it seems many miners in Devon and Cornwall struggled to make ends meet. Nor were they helped by the moneylenders, the merchant buyers or the mine owners.

Sir Walter Raleigh

Interest rates fluctuated wildly, at one point they were as high as 40%. In an attempt to improve the situation Queen Elizabeth, during her period of preemption, loaned out £8,000 a year without interest.

Wages were relatively low, labourers working for as little as £3 per annum, undoubtedly stressful when compared to the daily subsistence cost for a man and his family of around tuppence ... before any allowance was made for clothing and rent.

In 1601, Sir Walter Raleigh, who had been appointed Lord Warden of the Stannaries some 16 years earlier, claimed that through the judicious exercise of preemption he effectively managed to double the weekly wage of the average tinner from two shillings to four shillings. A notion corroborated by the Cornish antiquary Richard Carew who asserted that at that time the daily rate for a labourer – or hireling – was 8d per day. Based on a six-day week that would equate to 48 old pence, or four shillings, a week, which, assuming that there was work available all year round, would yield an annual income of nearer £10 per annum.

An improvement it might have been, but, according to one report, which found echoes in the account of Thomas Beare, a veteran tinner of the time and a stannary official, these were still starvation wages for the 10-12,000 tinners of the lowest class. Small wonder that Carew later came to call them *'the roughest and most mutinous men in England.'*

'The wretchedness of their existence became proverbial. They lived in hovels and bred like rabbits. Working as they did in four-hour shifts, that being as much as a miner could endure in the ill-ventilated shafts and levels, their life was irregular and broken. Tippling and ale-houses abounded most in the parishes richest in tin.' (Lewis)

Under such circumstances it's perhaps no surprise that miners looked to sell on the black market or to degrade their product. According to Stannary Law, all tin sold was required to be marked and although the fines for selling corrupt, lower quality tin, were severe – the blower could be pilloried or fined, the owner of the block would forfeit the block and pay a fine to the Duke – the practice went on.

Nor did it help that a lot of the tin mining was now being done underground.

Whereas 300 years earlier almost all of the West Devon and Cornwall output was obtained from stream works, the situation had changed. Miners were now being forced underground to obtain tin which, according to Beare, was inferior to stream tin. The miners had been better off financially back then and their working conditions had been better too.

By the end of the sixteenth century the mines were starting to get so deep that the drainage engines of the day couldn't cope with the amount of water seeping in.

Tinners were coming back up to the surface to find work, but not to find

Either the mine owners would find themselves needing to borrow funds at a punishing rate of interest or, through the process of preemption, needing to sell their tin in advance of production ... whatever the eventual price. This bond inevitably favoured the lenders and the merchant buyers, and put the mine owner in a position where he would then contract the miner to produce a fixed quantity of tin, more often than not an unrealistic amount, forcing the miner ultimately to accept payment in tin which, inevitably, he would end up having to sell at a lower price and would therefore need to borrow money at an uncomfortable rate of interest to survive.

tin: instead of digging in the dark they were turning back to husbandry. Not surprisingly the amount of tin produced went into decline. From 1605 the Dutch started exporting tin from Malacca in the East Indies (it had long been mined there but it had been pretty much off the radar as far as Europe was concerned).

Most of this Malaccan tin found a ready market in China but it was said that around 100 tons of it came into Europe each year and was partially responsible for the breaking of the British monopoly, although following the formation of the Levant and East India Company in the last years of Elizabeth's reign there was still a lot English tin going out to the East.

Nevertheless, the pressures on the West Country tinners were increasing and then the screw was turned even further when the London pewterers demanded, as manufacturers, that they should be able to buy tin for less than it was on sale to the general public.

Needless to say the London pewterers were not desperately well liked in the South West and their popularity ratings weren't exactly helped by their engaging the services of an assayer in London and their attempts to try each block of tin before it was made into pewter. Faulty pieces were sent back and wrong-doers were prosecuted in the stannary courts at the company's expense.

At one point Henry Cowes, a London pewterer, appointed Deputy Assay-master by Charles I was dispatched to Cornwall 'to reform sundry abuses in that office' and to look for bad tin.

'In view of the fact that the tinners, entrenched behind their own judiciary, were as completely a unit in opposing the enforcement of the inspection laws as the pewterers were in demanding it, one can hardly be surprised at the bad blood there was between the two.' (Lewis)

There were bad feelings too in Plymouth which found itself in something of a dilemma, having taken over from Plympton as the point at which local tin was dispatched, with Tin Street (now part of Vauxhall Street) and Tin Lane giving us a major clue to where that activity may have taken place, the town was now starting to suffer significantly from the issues that caused the latter's demise.

In 1638 we read that the 'harbor is of late years much decayed and quared up with gravell, sand and stones and ballast which appeared playnly to be occasioned by the great quantity of sand and earth which dyvers tynners working in a Tynneworkes called Clasiewell and other works and Tynne Milles neare the rivers of Plym and Mewe, which fall into the said harbour convey out of their said works and Mylles into the said rivers.' Better known today as Crazy Well Pool, Clasiwell was, in its day, a substantial openwork on the moor and one can but wonder just how much material had come down stream from it. But this was a process that had been going on for thousands, not just hundreds, of years on the banks of the moorland rivers feeding into the Plym so it is hard to implicate any one of the many operations in isolation.

Irritating as it doubtless was to the merchants of the time, Plymouth was about to face a much bigger problem, with the outbreak of the Civil War, at the beginning of 1642.

The decade had begun well as far as the local tin mining industry was concerned as the previous year Parliament did away with the tin monopoly with the passing of the Stannary Act of 1641.

Over the next few years Plymouth found itself besieged continuously by Royalist forces. Notably it became one of the few, if not the only, major town to successfully hold out against the King. Most of the wealth in the town was 'new money', accumulated by Elizabethan merchants and privateers, like Drake, Hawkins and Raleigh. There was no indigenous landed gentry in the town, but there were many surrounding the town, and men like William Woollcombe 'of the parish of Plympton St Mary,' were self-professed Royalists.

According to a letter dated 26 September 1643, from John Digby, Earl of Bristol, and advisor to the King, Woollcombe had 'paid £30 towards

Humphrey Woollcombe (left), in the first History of Plymouth, written but not formally published at the beginning of the nineteenth century wrote:
"What the Merchandize was at this early period in which they bartered it is difficult now to ascertain. The subject on which this Council was summoned probably formed a principal article, wool and woolfels; to this may be added most probably tin, and one circumstance that corroborates this supposition as the name of one of our streets being Tin Street which is an Ancient name.
"It may probably occur to everyone that Tin Quay is another proof but this Quay is a very modern one and gained its name from its proximity to Tin Street. Prior to its enlargement it was called Half Moon Quay."

John Webster (1610–82), also known as Johannes Hyphastes, was an English cleric, physician and chemist with occult interests, a proponent of astrology and a sceptic about witchcraft. He is known for controversial works.

It is interesting to speculate about the incidental activities in the area around the time of the Civil War, and it is possible, but by no means probable, that one of the members of the Parliamentary contingent based here was one of Cromwell's surgeons cum army chaplains – John Webster.

Yorkshire born Webster was 33 in 1643 and before the Civil War he worked as a teacher in Lancashire. Claiming to have studied under Johannes Huniades, the Hungarian alchemist who lectured at Cambridge University, Webster also styled himself Johannes - Johannes Hyphastes.

Over the course of his lifetime he wrote a number of interesting and challenging works on a variety of subjects, not least of which was Mettallographias – An History of Metals – which was published in 1671.

Within the book, which runs to several hundred pages, there is a substantial section on Tin. The source for the information that Webster gives on the subject is credited to 'one Thomas Creber of Plimpton St Mary, in Devonshire'.

Did Webster meet him here or elsewhere? And when? Clearly it was most likely to have been sometime between 1640 and 1670 and whatever the circumstances of their encounter, the substance of what was imparted during their exchange – it may of course have been in letter form – gives us a fascinating insight into the industry at that time. After all, Creber appears to have had tin running through his veins as he was described as 'one (and all his ancestors before him) that had wrought in the Tin-mines and these

particulars,' writes Webster, 'I had from him.

1. The Hills where they get tin Ore, near that place where he lived, are called Yelsborrow and Woollack.

2. Black stones that hold Tin, they call Tin-stones, and lie either in a load, or in a string.

3. There is other Tin Ore that is softer, and lies in a dun stones, and is of a yellowish colour, but will melt neer both alike.

4. Pure Ore, which they call Corn Tin, being found in grains, and is the hardest to melt.

5. Another place they call Armed Pit, which hold Ore they call Zill Tin, which is as small as Grit or Sand, and needeth nothing but washing, and is most easily melted of all other sorts of Tin Ore, and lieth in Chalk and Clay; and this small Ore, because it is rich, they call it fatty Ore.

6. The black stones, if they find them at the top, do continue in the whole Mine or Work. Sometimes it is in that they call strings, running through the earth, or stones, like small twigs or strings: and sometimes it is all in one, like a great branch or trunk, which they call a Lode. Sometimes it runneth in Spar, sometimes in a black stone that will strike fire, sometimes in white stones that are soft.

7. Their smelting houses roofs, after certain years they pull down, and find store of Ore in that stuff, that in their former meltings was forced from the fire.

8. The Corn Ore is found at the bottom of the Hills, being there digged into, and lieth sometimes in one sort of earth, and sometimes in another. And the Zill Ore is found in the same order.

9. The uppermost part of their Work they call Cooping; and if it be good or rich, the Lode or Strings underneath are good: If bad or indifferent, those underneath, are sometime good, and sometime bad.

10. They call that part of the mineral, that is found washed down, or otherwise brought down into the Valleys, Shoad.

11. They have a thing they call Mundick, sometimes found in the Ore, which they separate lest it should spoil the Ore; some of it is yellow, which is the worst, and sometimes of other colours; and the Mundick after smelting the Ore, is blackish and hard. Of it Mr Boyl saith thus, Mundick I have had of a fine golden colour; but though it be affirmed to hold no Metal; yet I found it in weight, and otherwise, to differ from Marchasites, and the Mine men think of a poysonous nature.

12. They have a thing they call Maxy, mixt with the Ore, which cannot be separated by the water, but by the fire, and then smells very ill, and is a blewish colour.

13. Lastly, They also find something like bright Ore, which they call Shim.

And thus much of this Metal, seeing there is no need to speak of any Medicaments prepared forth of it, because I have not had experience of any such.'

In his pre-amble to his discourse on Thomas Creber's account of tin mining in the Plympton area he states: 'That the ancient Britons practised these Tin-works' and then referenced the Historian Pliny, who reporteth, that the Britans fetched Tin out of the Isle Icta in Wicker Boats, covered and stitched about with Leather.' And further that: 'the Britains who inhabited this part, digged Tin out of stony ground and at a low Water carried the same in Carts to certain islands adjoining.' Did Webster then deliberately look for someone in the Plympton area because he believed that the Cassiterides were at the mouths of the Plym and Tamar?

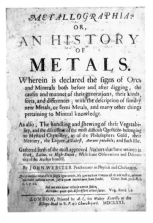

the maintenance of the Royal army on the understanding that none of 'his Majesty's loving subjects and soldiers of what degree or quality soever they be, not to plunder or pillage him, the said W Wolcombe, either in his goods or estate or molest or trouble his person or family for any pretence whatsoever.'

Woollcombe was right to be concerned, for after the Royalists were successfully repelled from their boldest of attacks on Plymouth in early December 1643, Sir Richard Grenville took over the King's forces locally. Prince Maurice, who had led that Sabbath Day assault, moved to attack Lyme Regis, while Grenville set about plundering the houses of the local Parliamentary gentry.

Grenville, who had been engaged in the Siege of Plymouth earlier in the war, had withdrawn to Cornwall where he helped to frustrate the advancing Parliamentarians.

A fiery character of noble birth, Grenville's marriage had ended acrimoniously and he had ended up in prison on account of a couple of lawsuits, one brought by his wife. Elected MP for Fowey in 1628, early in the Civil War, Grenville had garnered men and money to support the Parliamentary cause but had then marched for the King instead, earning himself the nickname 'Skellum' – scoundrel.

Tasked with leading the offensive against Plymouth, having despoiled large properties from Lanhydrock to Buckland Abbey (formerly the home of his grandfather), stealing revenues and hanging villagers in the process, Grenville made his way to Marsh Mills, to make camp in the meadows there on the Plympton side. It was to be his base for the next year or so, even though through the ravages of plague and cold he kept losing men to the burial yard of Plympton St Mary.

In the event Grenville's last major offensive was launched in January 1645, when he set an army of 6000 men against the whole line of Plymouth's defences. Hundreds of men were lost as the attempt failed once again. The cost in manpower and money was becoming a major problem for the Royal cause. Later that year the King preempted large consignments of tin, which were shipped to Ostend that they might be sold for the benefit of the Royal party.

In the meantime, further supplies of Cornish tin were deployed to help fund the Royalist cause at home. The Cornish were anxious to protect their Royalist privileges, particularly with regard to the Stannaries and the Duchy, and it appears that Grenville, at one stage, was recommending a plan to the Prince that would have created an almost independent Cornwall. As it transpired the Stannaries were almost ruined by the war bleeding into Cornwall, but Parliament managed to hold the western counties and they farmed out what little revenue there was from tin to members of their own party.

A grandson of the Sir Richard Grenville who had sailed with the Revenge, this Richard was by all account a man with a violent temper who often found himself in troubled waters, mainly of his own creation.

His story was the basis, 300 years later, for Daphne Du Maurier's 1948 novel, The King's General.

Sir John Granville was a kinsman of Sir Richard Grenville – he allegedly changed the spelling of this name to emphasise his Norman roots although he was perhaps keen to distance himself from Skellum Grenville. Knighted in 1643 by Charles II when he was but 15 – the King was just a year or two older – Sir John, a loyal servant of the King, was a key figure in rallying support at home for the Restoration.

The amount of revenue generated by Dartmoor mining operations dwindled significantly during the early years of the war and no Devon tin at all was registered as being coined in the last few years of the conflict.

It would also appear that while this was happening one particular Parliamentarian, John Webster was, seemingly in his spare time, conducting a review of the history of metals, including, obviously enough tin, and that much of the information gleaned for that specific section came from a Plympton man – Thomas Creber *(see opposite page)*.

Meanwhile, it's of no small consequence that for the whole of the interregnum (1650-60), more or less from the first period of the Commonwealth to the Restoration, the practice of preemption was allowed to lapse. This laissez-faire approach on the part of Cromwell and company saw the abolition of coinage duty alongside the scrapping of preemption and led almost immediately to the dawn of a new era: *'The preemption being resigned by the farmers, the price of tin rose. Multitudes of tradesmen left their callings for that of mining. Still the prices rose. Old, abandoned works were filled again and new ones taken.'* (Tinners Grievance 1697)

Locally we find reference to Agnes and John Jutsham of Shaw (Shaugh?) leasing Cuccold Tin Works from William Strode in August 1647, Sir Richard Strode of Newingham (Newnham), conveying a sett of tin works at Blacktor to Matthew Yandall in 1654, and another sett, at Vinlake, to Cornish tinners, William Coryn and Renald Loggett, in 1670. In the meantime, in 1661, John Elford of Longstone, Nicholas Hele of Shaugh and others conveyed a sett to Henry Creber, while other Strode lessees included Benjamin and Margaret Surfe at Bottle Hill and another apparent husband and wife team, Agnes and John Jutsham of Shaugh, who, earlier, in August 1647, had leased the curiously named Cuccold Tin Works at Plympton St Mary. The situation was simple: as tinners could now sell whenever they wanted and at the best price, there was renewed interest in the industry.

The price doubled in no time, rising rapidly from £3 to £6 per hundred-weight. Sadly these glory days were to be short-lived as the Restoration of the Monarchy was accompanied by the reintroduction of coinage duties and preemption ... although the man granted the lease of both appears not to have exercised his privilege. That man was Sir John Granville, one of the King's most trusted supporters. Granville had worked stealthily in England throughout the Protectorate as Prince Charles' foremost representative as the young royal languished in exile. Upon the Restoration, Charles lost little time in rewarding those who had been of great service to him and for Sir John that meant that he effectively became the most powerful man in Devon and Cornwall.

The 32-year-old was made Earl of Bath, Lord Lieutenant of Cornwall, Governor of Plymouth and Lord Warden of the Stannaries.

Whether or not Granville chose to exercise his rights with regard to coinage and preemption, it didn't stop the price of tin falling in the aftermath of the Restoration: from a peak of around £6.5s to a price of nearer £4.2s in 1666, which was roughly where it had been 50 years earlier.

Curiously enough 1666 was also the year that an unnamed stonemason carved the legend 'John Earl of Bath' into the foundation stone of the massive new fortification that Charles II had commissioned for Plymouth – the Royal Citadel upon the Hoe. Never again would the town defy the Royalist cause, indeed it's position with regard to the Royalist cause was soon to be tested.

Little could the Earl of Bath have imagined in 1666 that he would have a major part to play in the next significant development for the English monarchy. But this is how events unfolded as, given the absence of a legitimate son or daughter of Charles, and the flight of his Catholic brother, King James, Parliament offered the Protestant William (Sovereign Prince of Orange) and his wife Mary (granddaughter of Charles I) the throne.

The offer, it should be noted, was conditional on the couple signing a 'Declaration of Rights' a document that affirmed certain rights of relating to the power of Parliament while at the same time imposing restrictions on the power of the Monarchy.

Notably it was Sir John Granville who arrested the Commander of the Garrison in Plymouth and surrendered the Citadel to the Royal Couple, thereby ensuring Plymouth's place in history as the first town to proclaim for the new King and Queen.

Parliament might have been gradually becoming more powerful, but it hadn't been getting its own way on everything, neither was the Crown. In 1679 a bill had been introduced into Parliament to remodel the Stannary Parliament. It appears to have come in the wake of the Cornish convocation's refusal to agree with the King over the matter of preemption. Among the proposals contained within the bill was that no-one should be elected to the Stannary Parliament unless they enjoyed a freehold worth £400 a year – or in the case of a tinner, of £2,000.

This was a massive amount when considering the average annual income of a common tinner had fallen to around £12 per annum.

The bill failed but its intent was clear and doubtless was in the minds of the Cornish Convocation of 1687 when they said *'that able fit men if they be not miners, if they have parts and be maintainers of mines, and known by the barmaster or his deputy to understand well the custom of the mines, ought to serve for jurors, especially in the difficult and weighty matters and cases.'*

It was about electing people that understood the industry, not just the wealthy or those that had made a lot of money from mining. Clearly the revenues being generated from the mining activities on Dartmoor and around Plympton were falling way behind those accruing west of the Tamar.

Back in the early sixteenth century Devon's production rate was running at around 25-35% of Cornwall's figures, in the second half of the century it had dropped to 12-24% without the Cornish figures, then averaging around 1,000 thousand weight (1,200 lbs), changing all that much.

During the seventeenth century the Devon figures fell away further and seldom went beyond 10% of the output in Cornwall, while by the latter stages of that period something less than 1% was more the norm.

Around the turn of the seventeenth/eighteenth centuries there was a slight resurgence with a peak yield recorded in 1706 when the Devon output was recorded as being 123,636 lbs of tin, but even then that was barely 4% of the 3,200,000 lbs of Cornish tin being registered. In terms of coinage duties raised that yielded a sum of £96.11.9d across the Devon stannaries, compared to sum of £6,400 across Cornwall.

It is likely that part of that boom in 1706 was driven by the activities at Drakeland. The mine was worked by Richard Osbourne seemingly in partnership with John Elford esquire. As part of the Newnham estate it will come as no surprise to learn that Sidney Strode had a share in the enterprise.

Clearly Strode appears to have invested quite heavily and on the collapse of the venture, he presented Osbourne, in December 1713, with a claim of £10.15s, as a *'distraint for his share'*. Strode also wanted a return of the following tools, a list which makes for interesting reading in its own right:

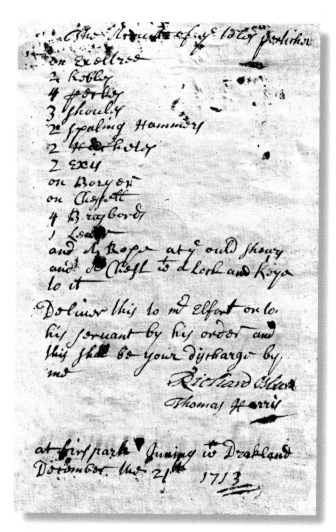

2 Kibbles
3 Shovels
2 Spalling hammers
1 Boryer
1 Chisel
4 Brayboards
1 Rope … and a chest with a lock and key to it.

Two years later the Strode family leased a sett *'within the tinwork or mine called Bottle Hill situate in the Bowling Green there'* to John Lang of Tavistock and James Mager of Plympton (Shorten 1985).

Mager was by all accounts a working tinner and had discovered a copper lode adjoining the tin there – our first reference to Botelhyll tinworke dates back to 1527 and it was doubtless active long before that.

Permission was granted to work a sett that was *'5 fathoms in breadth by 40 fathoms in length, that is to say, 15 fathoms to the west, and 25 fathoms to the east of the shaft that is now on the said work.'*

It appears that the royalty rate due to be paid to the mineral owner had been fixed at one-ninth … to be settled monthly or as soon as 20 tons or ore were ready for sale.

'This,' writes Shorten in Plympton's Metal Mines, *'is the first mention of copper at Bottle Hill, but it is evident that shaft mining had been carried out on the lodes for some time.'* This was also the last documented reference to Bottle Hill for some time, so we can only presume that the venture was not a great success.

For all of the doom and gloom in Devon, life on the other side of the county divide was looking up.

In 1710 the Cornish recorded a peak-to-date total of £9,600, compared with the Devon peak of £368.9.1d way back in 1524.

The problem was a local one, clearly the Dartmoor rivers had long since been stripped bare and, east of the Tamar, the prospect of underground activity was not looking like being particularly popular or productive in the eighteenth century.

The major obstacle was water. Water was everywhere as the shafts were sunk deeper. Various attempts had been made to address the issue. John Coster, a Bristol man, promoted a waterwheel that was 40ft in diameter and could take the place of half a dozen smaller ones used on a single mine, but this was still old technology and not desperately effective. The situation required a more radical solution.

Back in 1675 Sir Samuel Morland had patented an early kind of water-pump though it would appear to have been 100 years or more before it was used in any mine, but there was an even greater engine of salvation on the scene and about to make its presence felt – the steam engine.

Morland had examined the potential of steam power himself, but the origins of this hugely significant contribution to mining and to the wider world came from the brain

Samuel Morland (1625-95) was secretary to John Thurloe, the espionage chief in Cromwell's Commonwealth, but apparently became a double agent after learning of Thurloe's plot with Richard Cromwell to assassinate Prince Charles. He became embroiled in espionage and cryptography himself.
Following the Restoration in 1660 Morland was made a baronet and given a minor role at court.
A life-long friend of Samuel Pepys, Morland was something of a polymath and as well as his water-pump, initially produced to improve the water supply to Windsor Castle, he also experimented with using gunpower to create a vacuum that would suck in water (a crude early internal combustion engine), an adding machine, a mathematical multiplying machine and an early form of the megaphone – the Harrington Vamping Horn.

CAPTAIN THOMAS SAVERY.

THE INVENTOR OF THE

STEAM ENGINE.

Thomas Savery's (c1650-1715) steam pump or steam engine, was the first such device to be commercially available and contributed greatly to solving the problems of mine drainage on the one hand and improved public water supplies on the other. A military engineer – he was a captain when his book was published – Savery took out other patents including one for polishing glass or marble, and another for the 'rowing of ships with greater ease and expedition than hitherto.' Requiring the use of capstan driven paddle-wheels the idea was rejected by the Admiralty following an unfavourable report from Edmund Dummer, the man who was responsible for the King's new Dockyard on the banks of the Tamar – at what was to become Devonport.

THE

MINER'S FRIEND;

OR,

An Engine

TO

RAISE WATER BY FIRE,

DESCRIBED.

AND OF THE MANNER OF FIXING IT IN MINES;

WITH AN ACCOUNT OF THE SEVERAL OTHER USES IT
IS APPLICABLE UNTO; AND AN

ANSWER TO THE OBJECTIONS MADE AGAINST IT.

BY

THOMAS SAVERY, GENT.

Pigri est ingenii contentum esse his, quæ ab aliis inventa sunt.
SENECA.

LONDON: PRINTED FOR S. CROUCH, AT THE CORNER
OF POPE'S HEAD-ALLEY IN CORNHILL. 1702.

REPRINTED, 1827.

of a 48-year-old man, born within walking distance of Hemerdon – Thomas Savery from Shilstone, Modbury.

On 2 July 1698 Savery patented a steam pump: *'A new invention for raising of water and occasioning motion to all sorts of mill work by the impellent force of fire, which will be of great use and advantage for draining mines, serving towns with water, and for the working of all sorts of mills where they have not the benefit of water nor constant winds.'*

The following summer, on 14 June 1699, at Gresham College, he demonstrated his machine to the Royal Society and a spectacle which, by all accounts, met with their approval. Indeed they published an account of the engine in Volume 21 of their *Philosophical Transactions* later that year, a gesture for which Savery gave his *'most humble and hearty thanks'* three years later when he published his own account in: *The Miner's Friend; or, An Engine to Raise Water By Fire, Described, And Of The Manner Of Fixing It In Mines; with an account of the several other uses it is applicable unto; and an answer to the objections made against it.*

Before thanking the Society, however, Savery was at pains to thank the King, George III, to whom the inventor had given a personal

demonstration at Hampton Court and as a consequence received via Royal Assent a patent and Act of Parliament, *'to pursue and perfect the same.'*

Three years down the line Savery informed the King that his invention was now *'fully completed and put in practice in your dominions, with that repeated success and applause, that it not to be doubted but it will be of universal benefit and use to all your Majesty's subjects.'*

The task had not been an easy one to complete, as Savery explained in his section dedicated to the Royal Society: *'I have met with great difficulties, and expense, to instruct handicraft artificers to form my engine according to my design; but my workmen, after so much experience are become masters of the thing, that they oblige themselves to deliver what engines they make me exactly tight and fit for service, and as such I dare warrant them to any body that has occasion for them.'*

Nevertheless, he was very aware of the scepticism that his invention was bound to excite. Addressing his next remarks to The Gentlemen Adventurers in the Mines of England he wrote:

'I am very sensible a great many among you do as yet look on my invention of raising water by the impellent force of fire, a useless sort of project, that never can answer my designs or pretentions; and that it is altogether impossible that such an engine as this can be wrought under ground, and succeed in the raising of water, and draining your mines, so as to deserve any encouragement from you.'

However, Savery was clearly very confident of his machine and after 40 pages or so of explanation and illustration of his machine he provided a very prescient vision of what was then at least half-a-century away – the Industrial Revolution.

'I hope, when it is considered how far this engine of mine differs from the bare pretensions of ignorant or designing men, and that any persons may see what my engine will perform by they contract for it, there will be found no ground for the least suspicion in any person concerned to employ them in mines; but, to the contrary, afford us a generous encouragement in business so conducive to the increasing the mining trade, and thereby enrich themselves and the nation, and increase the king's revenue.

'I could heartily wish all miners, for their own as well as their country's interest, were good mechanics, and truly understood the nature, use, and application of all kinds of engines; for I am sure those that do will be my best friends, without expecting that horse, or men, or any other strength, can or will do more than what nature and the laws of motion has allowed them.'

Unfortunately for Savery his machine was not without its problems and the Gentlemen Miners of the Southwest were to prove slow on the uptake and it would be sometime before this new technology was fully embraced in Devon or Cornwall. Partly it was because of the long term reliability, partly it was the lack of availability of any substantial supply of coal locally, partly because its capabilities were limited and partly, doubtless, the cost.

Mining was becoming beyond the means of most ordinary miners.

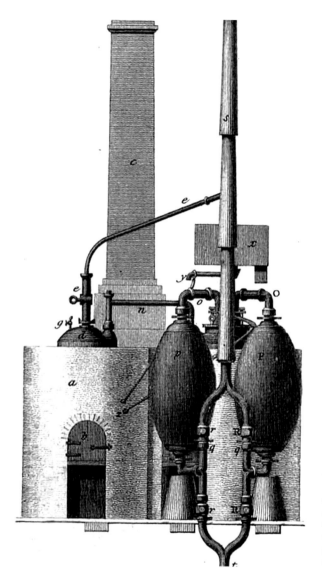

A DESCRIPTION

OF THE

DRAUGHT OF THE ENGINE,

FOR RAISING WATER BY FIRE.

THE

MANNER OF WORKING THE ENGINE.

Savery's machine had no pistons and the only moving parts were the taps. The functionality relied on raising steam in the boiler and creating a vacuum in the working vessel when the steam condensed. Pressure generated created need for running repairs on soldered joints and among its working limitations was that it couldn't really operate more than 30ft above the water it was aiming to clear.

Crockern Tor, site of the Tinners' Parliament.

PART TWO: GOING UNDERGROUND
THE AGE OF THE GENTLEMEN TINNER

The exhaustion of Dartmoor tin had been a gradual process, not just over the previous two or three hundred years, but over the previous two or three millennia. In pre-Conquest times, before written records began, the impact of that decline is difficult to plot, but the world had moved on since then, or at least the rest of the world had moved on, Plympton itself was struggling and the local authorities were determined to do something about it.

In the election of Members of Parliament, on 25 July 1702, the Mayor and Aldermen of Plympton decided to make a number of gentlemen from Exeter, and other places outside the precincts of the borough, free burgesses of Plympton, in order that they might exclude Richard Hele from being elected a burgess in Parliament.

Their reasoning was thus: *'Plympton was anciently a town of good trade and commerce, but being of late years much fallen and decayed, the Mayor and Alderman could think of no better expedient to promote and revive a trade in Plympton than to invite some gentlemen of the City of Exeter into their society, thereby to gain a good correspondence in that opulent and trading city.'* (quoted in Brooking Rowe)

One gentleman called in to support this move was former Plympton yarn-maker Andrew David. David claimed that the Exeter men were great traders in the manufacture of wool and the hope was that by making them freemen of Plympton there would be some advantage to the town in terms of the recovery of trade.

Unfortunately, when pressed *'to name such of them as were considerable traders in the woollen manufacture he was able to name one only – Thomas Jefferies.'*

Not surprisingly the election result was hotly contested. It was claimed that men had been made freemen when they shouldn't have been, that certain sons of freemen were denied a vote, while others were given a vote when they hadn't yet turned 21 and further that money had changed hands. Indeed it appears that the scale of the alleged bribes varied greatly according to who was trying to buy whose vote.

Sums changing hands in some instances were as little as a crown (five shillings) or a guinea (one pound and one shilling) to upwards of five pounds. Offers of clearing debts were made and in one instance Mary Fresey claimed that about a week before the election Mrs Aldwin sent for her and pressed her to persuade her husband to vote for the sitting members and said she would give her five pounds and allow her a year's rent in one of her houses.

To resolve one or two of these issues it should have been possible simply to look out the Records in the Town Chest. Unfortunately the relevant documents appeared to have gone missing, and so it was necessary to consult some of the town 'antients'. At a subsequent inquiry it was decided that the election of Richard Edgcumbe should stand, but that Thomas Jervoise was duly not elected (his 46 votes had included that of the Mayor John Tozer and the aforementioned Exeter man, Thomas Jefferies), and that Richard Hele, who had only polled 41 votes, should nevertheless serve in his stead. It should of course be noted that less than 100 men, all over 21, were entitled to vote, so that it was relatively easy to influence outcomes.

It was a practice that went on all over the country. However, given that it was no longer the powerful place it had been, and given that its population had remained somewhat static, Plympton was rapidly becoming a classic rotten borough. Reform of the political system was still over a century away and matters didn't come to a head until the 1830s, by which time Devonport, which barely existed in 1702, had grown to be the largest town west of Bristol, with a population in excess of 23,000 – and yet it had no representation in Parliament, while Plympton, with less than 1,000 citizens had two MPs. The situation was clearly untenable, something would have to change at some point.

Meanwhile, to return to the early 1700s, we find that the aforementioned Richard Hele was not re-elected in 1705, but Richard Edgcumbe was, indeed he was to serve the town for 35 years, until he was elevated to the House of Lords on becoming Lord Edgcumbe.

Left: *George Treby's father, Sir George Treby had been MP for Plympton before him, from 1677-81 and from 1689-92 . Treby Senior had also been speaker of the House of Commons. Becoming quite powerful within the Government, Treby managed the 1727 elections in the west of England, for the Government, but on the accession of George III found some of his power base removed. However in 1730 he returned to office as Master of the Household. Ten years later he was transferred to the Treasury where he remained until 1742, when he was removed in the wake of Walpole's downfall. He died a few weeks later aged 57.*

His son, also Richard Edgcumbe, succeeded him in the Commons.

For much of that time George Treby was the town's second MP, certainly until 1727 when Treby was successfully elected MP for Plympton, and for Dartmouth ... and for Plymouth.

Just as Treby had succeeded his father, so his son, another George, succeeded him in the House of Commons, once again representing Plympton.

Throughout this period the quantity of tin being produced in the area fell dramatically. After 1718 the amount fell below 10,000 thousand weight for the first time in 40 years, thereafter that figure was exceeded but once, in 1728.

Concomitantly, the coinage duties for Devon as a whole dropped below £10 a year while the Cornish revenues remained consistently, with one or two exceptions, above £6,000.

By 1730 there were only two blowing-mills left in Devon, one at Sheepstor and the other in Plympton itself – they are thought to have been the last smelting-mills on the Moors to have used a blast furnace. Other neighbouring blowing houses, like those at Hook Lake on the Erme and Har Tor on the Meavy, had long since fallen into disuse.

With little in the way of tin mining activity to legislate for, the need to convene became somewhat superfluous, and, in 1786, the Devon Court met for the last time at Crockern Tor.

Such was the lack of activity generally that 1786 also saw an attempt on the part of one rather optimistic prospector to claim the whole of Dartmoor, all 50,000 acres of it, as being included in a pair of bounds.

Meanwhile, across the Tamar, towards the end of the eighteenth century, a sudden rise in the trade in tin to the Indies saved the Cornish stannaries at least from a *'severe depression'* (Lewis), but the situation generally was not great.

Nor was industry locally helped by the state of Dartmoor's highways and byways. Another document produced in 1786 was that prepared by the Duchy surveyor, William Simpson, who, when reporting on the prospects for developing mining and farming on Dartmoor reported that *'within the last 20 years there were only three or four very blind roads across the whole, insomuch that going over the moor in winter was always considered not only as an arduous but really dangerous undertaking.'* To further illustrate his point, Simpson added: *'the many lives lost in such attempts is too notorious to be doubted.'* (from *A Survey of the Forest of Dartmore belonging to His Royal Highness the Prince of Wales*, a manuscript in Exeter Record Office)

In the early days of the industry, when tin-streaming predominated, tin was taken downstream to ports from whence it could be shipped and the need for cross-country roads was less vital. Nevertheless, the cross-country moorland routes in mining areas were better than those elsewhere in the county:

'The very earliest surviving Devon roads are on Dartmoor, dating from around 1750 – but 1750 BC rather than AD! They have survived on Dartmoor because the higher land has been so little used in subsequent centuries. Some of our existing country lanes lanes will have originated in the Neolithic or the Bronze Age.' (Paul White: *The South West Highway Atlas for 1675*)

The situation was similar in Cornwall, where early mining activity undoubtedly necessitated the creation of early thoroughfares. Perhaps this explains why, in 1699, Cornwall was the first major county in England (Rutland was earlier) to be mapped accurately – one inch to a mile – Joel Gascoyne being the man who undertook the task.

Clearly, the existing network impacted on the Romans who by and large didn't feel the need to make roads to this part of the world.

'Any Roman business further west (of Exeter) would have taken to the sea and rivers, or used the ancient trackways as the natives did.' (White)

Furthermore, the Romans didn't really need to march armies down here as they had already forged amicable trading relationships with those areas accessed by sea.

It has been estimated that when the Romans left the South West, around 410 AD, *'Devon had a main road network that might have comprised about 700 miles of unpaved trackway and about 50 miles of paved road.'* (Michael Hawkins *Devon Roads* 1988)

One of the earliest routes was perhaps the route that ran east from

Plympton via Ivybridge, South Brent, Staverton, Newton Abbot and crossing the Exe at Starcross, or west via Crownhill and crossing the Tamar by ferry to Saltash.

New routes appeared during the Middle Ages, but wheeled transport was rarely seen outside London and most goods were carried by packhorse … and most travel was done on foot.

As William Marshall commented in 1796, with reference to *'the roads of West Devonshire less than half a century ago: Speaking with little if any latitude, there was not, then, a wheel carriage in the district.'*

He added: *'Nor fortunately for the necks of travellers, any horse but those which were natives of the county.'*

Local horses, visitors were happy to acknowledge, seemed to know their way around better than their own expensive charges. Dartmoor ponies and the long lost Cornish 'Goonhillies' were even more sure footed and none, one suspects, were shod.

Marshall, incidentally, was writing in his account of *'The Rural Economy of the West of England'* and it is certainly interesting to reflect on the state of our roads before the introduction of the turnpikes.

For the most part small, self-sufficient, local communities were not particularly bothered about the state of the roads around them. Land locked market towns maybe, but ports and coastal towns were serviced by sea transport.

It was the Catholic Church who, even more so than the Crown, had a vested interest in getting from A to B. Established by St Augustine in the sixth century, the Church of Rome had, as we have already seen, by the time of the Norman Conquest become immensely rich and powerful.

'Religious houses, such as at Buckfast, Tavistock, Plympton and Buckland, owned vast estates and established, or re-established roads for the supervision and upkeep of their scattered properties.' (Hawkins)

Abbot's Way is one of the best examples, stretching from Cross Furzes via the fords at Buckland, Red Lake, Erme Pits and Plym, to a point north of Gutter Tor.

Such routes were traditionally marked with stone crosses and as the scale of the commercial operations increased, along with the profits enjoyed by the church, so the churchmen sought to improve and enhance the connectivity.

Again, as we have already noted, the Church is thought to have owned around a quarter of all of England by this time, and Devon was no exception. Thus it was the Church not the Crown that was chiefly responsible for the construction of most of our Medieval bridges.

'The Church regarded this as a sacred duty complementary to the building of churches and cathedrals. The builders of the churches, the master masons and their subordinate masons, would have built the bridges, as can

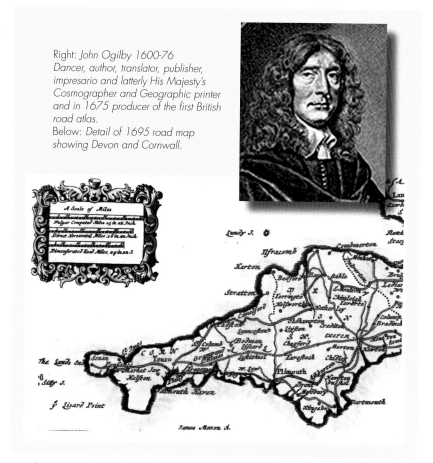

Right: *John Ogilby 1600-76 Dancer, author, translator, publisher, impresario and latterly His Majesty's Cosmographer and Geographic printer and in 1675 producer of the first British road atlas.*
Below: *Detail of 1695 road map showing Devon and Cornwall.*

be seen in the similarity of details between the bridges and the churches of the period,' observes Hawkins, before going on to reference *'chamfered voussoirs, multiple-arch orders and arch ribs'* on a handful of local bridges. Many of which had a chapel or chantry either on the structure, or somewhere nearby.

It's also worth noting that, at a time when few if any questioned the existence of God, and of Heaven and Hell, the clergy's ability to grant indulgences to those who contributed to such projects, helped elicit valuable extra funding from those who could afford it.

It seems clear that Henry VIII was aware that his Dissolution of the Monasteries would profoundly affect this situation and so we have his 1530 Statute of Bridges which set the tone for the next 350 years or so.

Celia Fiennes (1662-1741) is said to be the first woman ever to have visited every county in England. She travelled extensively between 1684 and 1703 and then intermittently until about 1712. At that time the idea of travelling for its own sake was still pretty novel, especially for a woman on her own, albeit latterly she was accompanied by one or two servants.

Her travel memoir was not published in her lifetime, having essentially been written purely for family reading. It wasn't until 1812 that extracts began to appear in print.

The Act required counties henceforth to be responsible for their own bridges, and in order to provide a basis for funding such work the Act introduced a levy on the all the inhabitants of a particular county or borough – a gesture that essentially gave us the first building block of our present rating system.

Needless to say the new legislation wasn't universally popular. Neither was the subsequent Statute of Highways that was passed in 1555 and which required churchwardens to appoint an (unpaid) overseer of highways each year from their parish. This overseer was, in theory at least, empowered to compel fellow parishioners to each contribute the equivalent of four days' (later increased to six) labour each year, also unpaid, in order to carry out any work to the highways that the overseer deemed necessary.

Cromwell's Commonwealth abolished this 'Statute Labour' in 1654 and replaced it with more rates, but it was reintroduced following the Restoration of Charles II in 1662.

Such is not to say that the Crown entirely washed their hands of all responsibility:

'There were the royal roads on which travellers were under the sovereign's protection. They were termed the King's Highway and anyone attacking travellers on these roads could be fined 100 shillings, a large sum that reflected the importance the State attached to ensuring the safe passage of traders ... All other roads were termed the Common Highway and the State made no provision for maintaining them nor did it recognise that any maintenance was necessary.' (Hawkins)

As the pace of life inevitably required quicker and more efficient communication networks so the demands on the road network increased. In 1635 the King's Post – the system of horsemen riding in relays, post-haste with messages of government – was opened to the general public, if they could afford to pay. One can imagine how easily this arrangement could have broken down if any one horse and rider had fallen foul of a hole in the road, or a highwayman.

It was some centuries since the Statute of Winchester (1285) had decreed, amongst other things, that the highways between towns should be widened and that within 200ft of the road there should be no bush, tree or ditch in which someone might hide with a view to ambushing travellers.

Roads in Devon and Cornwall were a long way from that ideal. Back in 1459 landowners John Gifford and John Vyall had been required to repair the route between 'Ley Mill and Lewood' which was *'deep in mud on both sides and overhung by hedges on both sides to the damage of the King's lieges.'*

One is left to assume that the aforementioned gentlemen owned the land on either side of the road. Hawkins goes on to state that *'Devon's deep lanes were formed as a result of this system of maintenance by owners of adjoining land. As the roads got muddier, the landowner would scrape off the mud and pitch it on the side, and, as time went by, the road became lower and the sides higher.'*

A delightful first-hand account of the situation in the late-seventeenth century is provided by the celebrated spinster, Celia Fiennes, then aged 33. In 1695 she described leaving the stannary town of Ashburton (*'a poor little town – bad is the best inn'*), and heading for Plymouth: *'Here the roads contract and ye lanes are exceeding narrow, and so cover'd up you can see little about; an army might be marching undiscover'd by any body, for when you are on those heights that shews a vast country about, you cannot see one road.'*

The army reference is interesting as Miss Fiennes was the daughter of a colonel who'd fought for the Parliamentarians during the Civil War.

'The wayes now become so difficult that one could scarcely pass by each other, even ye single horses, and so dirty in many places, and just

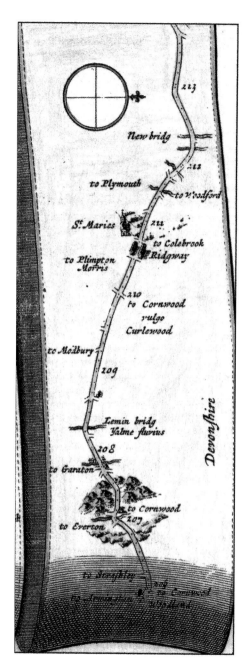

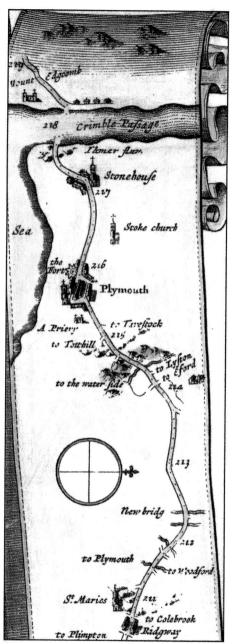

Prior to Ogilby's efforts, maps of English counties made little or no reference to highways or byways, only to various principal seats of the landed gentry, towns, villages and, significantly, rivers.

There was also, pre-Ogilby, no general agreement on measurement. There were Roman miles – literally milia passum – 1,000 paces (1,680 yards) long miles (2,428 yards), local miles (variable) and the shorter occasional mile of 1,760 yards.

The latter was the one adopted by Ogilby and this then became the standard measurement.

The strip opposite, divided here in two, is one of 100 strips that Ogilby's team produced for his 1675 Britannia Atlas.

His brief had been to 'depict the Post Roads for conveying letters to and from London' although it has been claimed by one conspiracy theorist – Terry Jones – to have been produced to facilitate a Catholic take-over of England.

Whatever their purpose, Ogilby's maps were subsequently used as the basis for a number of guides to English roads for the next 100 years.

a track for one horses feet,' furthermore she noted, 'the banks on either side are so near, were they not well secured and mended with stones stuck close like a drye wall everywhere when they discover the banks to breake and molder down, which else would be in danger of swallowing up the way.'

Given that everything then was transported on horseback this remarkable woman was at a loss to see how any commerce was possible. The poor packhorses, she noted, were fitted out with hooks, like yokes on their back, each side rising to a good height with receptacles carrying either wood, furse, lime, coal, corn, hay or straw – she didn't mention stone or ore.

'I cannot see, how two such horses can pass by each other, and yet these are the road that are all hereabouts. Some little corners may jut out that one may a little get of the way of each other, but this is but seldom.'

A couple of miles out of Plymouth Miss Fiennes arrived at the river Plym, 'just by a little town all built of stone … the tiling is all flat which with the lime it's cemented, makes it look white like snow and in the sun, shining on the slate, it glisters.'

Crossing the Plym at Plymbridge our diarist then goes on to state how the Plym 'increases and is a fine broad stream' that 'falls into the sea at Plymouth.'

TURNPIKE GATE.
Drawn by Henry Alken.

Turnpike Trusts were set up so that individuals or individual organisations could create new, or improve existing roads and charge people for using them. A large pole or pike was typically extended across the road until a fee was paid at which point the pole would be swung around to clear the way.

Turnpikes were not universally welcomed as some objected to paying to travel roads that they had previously been using for free. There were serious protests, but overall the state of the nation's roads were greatly enhanced, making possible faster connections between all parts of the realm, and, with wheeled transport now feasible, it meant that more people could travel more easily. It also meant that bigger and heavier items could now be moved around the country more readily.

'There is a depth of water for ships of the first rate to ride … Its great sea is dangerous by reason of the several points of land between which the sea runs up a great way, and there are several little islands also which bear the several tides hard one against the other.'

Several little islands? Clearly Plymouth Sound still looked rather like an archipelago less than 400 years ago!

Further upstream the rivers and tidal creeks may have been silting up, but Plymouth itself still had a fine deep water harbour and the King's new dock, Plymouth Dock, on the edge of the Hamoaze, where the anchorages were deeper still, was growing apace. What's more successive lighthouses on the Eddystone Reef had made the approach to Plymouth Sound safer than it had ever been, so activity on the seaward side had never been greater. It was the landward approaches that desperately needed attention.

It was a national problem and Turnpikes were seen as the solution, however Devon was slow to pick up on Turnpikes. By 1750 more than 400 trusts had been set up around the country, but none in this county.

Stonehouse had the first, in 1751 but it oversaw just a four-mile stretch. Two years later the Exeter Turnpike Trust was established and this took account of all the main roads leading out of Exeter, with a combined mileage of around 150 miles.

Also by 1753, lobbying had begun for a Great West Road, from Plymouth to Falmouth and four years later the Plymouth East Trust was founded covering the route between Gasking Gate, the north eastern gate to Plymouth, and Brent Bridge. The new road was completed in 1758. Prior to that the primary route to London from Plymouth was via Tavistock and Okehampton.

In the first year that the new road was open, John Bignell, of the Prince George Inn on the corner of Stillman Street and Vauxhall Street, ran a weekly travelling coach to Exeter … it took 12 hours!

Accessibility was improving all round and all the time. A bridge linking Stonehouse and Plymouth Dock was opened in 1769, the architect responsible was John Smeaton, who had recently completed the latest lighthouse on the Eddystone Reef. The men who had been empowered by Act of Parliament to build the bridge – and collect the halfpenny tolls for its usage – were George Earl of Mount Edgcumbe and Sir John St Aubyn. The former owned most of East and West Stonehouse, the latter most of Plymouth Dock.

It was an increasingly familiar pattern, it was the landed gentry that had the wealth and the power now, not so much the Church.

In 1791 the western exit from Plymouth Dock (known as Devonport from 1824), across the Tamar, was improved by the introduction of regularised ferry crossings between Dock and Torpoint. Previously the principal crossing had been between Cremyll (West Stonehouse) and Devil's Point, on the East Stonehouse peninsula. The men sanctioned to facilitate the new service, and ultimately profit handsomely from it, were the aforementioned George, Earl of Edgcumbe, and Reginald Carew Pole, whose family estate included much of the surrounding land on the Cornish side, as well as Torpoint Field itself (the hub of the new development area). Carew Pole was also one of the major employers in the area.

Further improvements to the eastern exit from the Three Towns came later when Lord Boringdon (who had moved the family seat from Boringdon) had a carriage drive created from Longbridge at Marsh Mills to his house at Saltram. This had the effect of keeping the tides out of the Plympton marshes. Plympton St Mary had long since been inaccessible by water and now the marshes that had been formed became drier.

Meanwhile, on the western banks of the Plym, Lord Boringdon promoted the Plymouth Embankment Company, which enclosed the Laira marshes – the creek had once run up to the bottom of Lipson Hill. With the earlier improvements it was now possible to create a new smooth and flat eastern exit from Plymouth avoiding the steep Lipson Hill route.

William Payne's painting of Stonehouse Bridge and Mount Edgcumbe, c1786.

By the time of George III's Jubilee in 1810 the town had an entirely new route from Bretonside to the Embankment. It was a major improvement. It's interesting to note that Lord Boringdon entertained George III, his wife and three eldest daughters, at Saltram, in 1789.

Such were the repercussions of all this development and improvement that in 1797 Richard Rosdew, whom Henry Woollcombe described as a financier, and who provided stamps and post-horses, was able to erect Beechwood House, Cornwood, out of his spoils.

London, incidentally, was now reachable within two days.

The new road from Bretonside also inspired the Earl of Morley (the son of Lord Boringdon) to create a new crossing of the Plym at the southern end of the new embankment. The earl was the existing proprietor of the ferry between Cattedown and Oreston and although the idea of a bridge had first been mooted in 1807, it wasn't until 1827, on 14 July, that the idea became a reality. The Duchess of Clarence, the late George III's daughter-in-law, opened the engineering masterpiece, one of Britain's earliest iron bridges. Designed by the young James

Meadows Rendel, the supporting stonework came from the Earl of Morley's quarries, and the £10,000 required to fund the project came from his purse.

Clearly Morley was rich, well-connected and had an appetite for enterprise. Writing in 1819, Henry Woollcombe, a local solicitor and Plymouth's first serious chronicler, described how Plymouth was dead by 1750 and only began to wake up with the accession of George III. The area's revival – for the economic gloom was cast over Dock, Stonehouse, Plymouth and Plympton – was built around a number of key elements: Crown investment – new barrack blocks in Dock, the Naval Hospital and Royal Marine Barracks at Stonehouse, the Military Hospital in Stoke Damerell, and the boom to the economy generated by the long wars with France; the improved landward links with the outside world and *'the discovery by the country gentry that they could make money out of the developing town.'* (Crispin Gill: *Plymouth A New History* 1993)

Foremost among them was the Parker family – headed by Lord Boringdon, elevated, in 1815, to become the Earl of Morley.

Henry Worsley's view of Lord Morley's new bridge over the Laira c1829.

Eighteenth century view of the Longbridge at Plympton.

Lord Boringdon it was, incidentally, who originated the idea of founding the Plymouth Chamber of Commerce in 1815.

Of course, it is apparent that one element that was not contributing to the area's improved economic position was mining, but while that was true east of the Tamar, on the other side of that great river, in Cornwall, mining was providing the landed gentry with plenty of rich pickings.

The early 1700s had seen the great refinements to Savery's primitive fire-engine pumping process. Having successfully patented his ideas, it meant that fellow Devonian, Thomas Newcomen, from Dartmouth, had to work with Savery to produce his atmospheric engine. Taking elements of the Frenchman Denis Papin's work, Newcomen produced a comparatively successful coal-fired steam machine for raising water out of mines and Wheal Vor, near Helston, was among the first mines to deploy a Newcomen machine. (With its own smelting works, this mine incidentally flourished spectacularly and, when Henry Woollcombe visited it in 1816, it was employing nearly 800 people – miners, carriers, smiths, carpenters, boys and girls and had, at that time an annual tin production worth £40,000).

Through a series of six lifts of ten fathoms it was now possible to pump to a depth of around 60 fathoms. Further refinements introduced on the back of James Watt's external steam condenser led to greater efficiencies, and required less coal, thereby massively increasing their viability and popularity.

'By 1778 there were over 60 fire engines in Cornwall and Devon,' wrote Peter Herring recently, adding that most of these were in Cornwall. Further improvements borne out of the contributions of the locomotive engineer from Camborne, Richard Trevithick, put Cornwall very much at the forefront of mining across Europe and, at the same time, at the vanguard of the Industrial Revolution.

Indeed Henry Woollcombe recounts in his diaries a telling encounter with Richard Trevithick on a coach to London in 1815. Trevithick was on his way to South America to install in the silver mines there, the pumping-engines that had proved so successful in the tin mines of Cornwall. The Spanish agent, who had come to the Westcountry to secure Trevithick's services, was on the coach with them.

'Trevithick was full of optimism about his prospects in South America, believing that much of the profits from the silver mines would be spent on the purchase of British manufactures to the benefit of trade on both sides.' (Woollcombe, summarised by J Stevens)

Woollcombe's brother, George was then the incumbent of Hemerdon House and the estate had long since been of interest to the mining community. After what was doubtless two to three thousand years of tin-streaming Hemerdon was still being worked throughout the eighteenth century, for tin, and at the end of that century we find Captain Samuel Terrell there as mine captain.

Captain Ward was working Hemerdon Ball in 1799 and Wheal Woollcombe, perhaps better known as East Bottle Hill, was being worked in the early-1800s.

The original Manor of Hemerdon had been split in 1687 when a significant part of the estate had been sold to Thomas Hurrell, through whose family it was later conveyed, in 1719, to George Parker of Boringdon. However, by the beginning of the nineteenth century, George Woollcombe bought the said moiety and re-united the two parts.

Meanwhile, the Parker family, who had inherited Boringdon through marriage back in 1587, had quietly been developing their grand residence at Saltram, hence all the improvements they had sponsored around it. They too were considering their options in respect of what lay beneath their land.

On 25 March 1806 part of Boringdon Park was leased, for a period of 21 years, by Lord Boringdon, to a consortium of five gentlemen adventurers in search of metalliferous minerals, specifically, copper.

Above left: *Joshua Reynold's portrait of Thomas Woollcombe and Right, Reynolds portrait of John Parker (1734-88)*
Below: *The former Parker residence of Boringdon Hall. Engraved in 1809 by William Wolnoth, from a drawing by JR Thompson.*

20 October 1814

My Lord

According to your Lordships request I have inspected Boringdon Park Mine

I find the Lode is poor and but small in the present end of their workings however from the appearance of the Lode nearer the Shaft I think I am justified in saying it deserves trial — to effect it I would recommend the present Shaft to be sunk (^there is 1½ fathoms deeper than it now is) all 20 fathoms, or otherwise to sink a new underlayer to the South to meet the Lode at that depth or nearly — And afterwards to drive 20 fathoms on the Lode East and 20 west or otherwise 40 fathoms in all the way most likely to be productive — By going to the extent above mentioned there will be sufficient light thrown on the subject to enable to form judgment for future proceedings — however I think it will be fair to leave them to work as they please after the above is done — but it should be examined and attended to — to see they do it in a manner agreeable to the Mining System —

As to the means they wish to have recourse to to clear the Mine of water is a matter perhaps may rest with themselves — however I should ... the ... will erect a small Engine to work by Steam — and to do what is recommended — and likewise for driving 10 or 20 fathoms East in the Edit which I likewise would recommend in order to prove the Lode further to hill if there is anything gone down to induce a further prosecution of the level East at 20 fathoms deep after the length is driven according to the proceeding part of this report

I am My Lord
your most Obt and
humble servant
W J Brenton

Mining Materials, Slate, and Timber.

13/6

TO BE SOLD, by Public Auction on Friday the 23d instant, by 10 o'clock in the Forenoon, at Boringdon Park Mine, in the Parish of Plympton Saint Mary, in the County of Devon, a variety of valuable

MINING MATERIALS,

Comprising a Water Wheel, about 23 feet in diameter, Cast Iron and Wood Pumps, &c. &c.

Also, on the same day by two o'clock in the Afternoon, at Cann Quarry, in Plympton Saint Mary, aforesaid, a large quantity of

Rags, Half-Rags, & Paviers.

And on TUESDAY, the 27th instant, by 10 o'clock in the Forenoon, at Turnchapel Dock-Yard, near Plymouth, a considerable quantity of valuable

OAK TIMBER,

The thick stuff and plank of great lengths and breadths, and the whole very convertible for ship-building.

The Mining Materials and Slate may be seen three days before the sale, on application to WILLIAM PORE, at the Cottage, Plymbridge; and the Timber, during the same period, by applying to Mr. PARKER, at Turnchapel Dock-yard aforesaid.

WILLIAM PARKHOUSE, AUCTIONEER.

Mernfield, July 10, 1824.

1814 Report to Lord Morley on Boringdon Park Mine with, inset, 1824 press advertisement giving details of sale of Mining Materials from Boringdon Park Mine.

NINETEENTH CENTURY MINING – A DRAINING EXPERIENCE

Boringdon Park Mine

The five gentlemen who sought to exploit Boringdon Park were William Warren, of Plympton St Mary; William Joll, merchant; Richard Stear, boot and shoemaker; John Hoar, tobacconist and James Budd, gentleman, all of Stoke Damerell. Like so many other ventures in the area this was no new mining exercise, their remit was to continue and extend an existing adit.

It is not clear how successful the endeavour was in the beginning, but there were indications that all was not well and in 1814 John Parker, or Lord Morley as he was now known, commissioned a report on the state of the mine. On 20 October he received the following:

'According to your Lordship's requests I have inspected Boringdon Park Mine.

'I find the lode is poor and but small in the present end of their workings, however from the appearance of the lode nearer the shaft I think I am satisfied in saying it deserves trial – to effect it I would recommend the present shaft to be sunk in all 20 fathoms, that is 10 fathoms deeper than it now is, or otherwise to sink a new underlayer to the south to meet the lode at that depth or nearby –and afterwards to drive 20 fathoms on the lode east and 20 west or otherwise 40 fathoms in all the way most likely to be productive.

'By going to the extent above mentioned there will be sufficient light thrown on the subject to enable to firm judgment for future proceedings – however I think it will be fair to leave them to work as they please after the above is done, but it should be examined and attended to, to see they do it in a manner agreeable to the mining system.

'As to the means they wish to have recourse to clear the mine of water is a matter perhaps may rest with themselves.'

The writer, Brenton, then went on to repeat his earlier recommendations before signing off.

Tantalisingly we don't know whether Brenton's advice was followed, or if it was even sound, however on 30 January 1822, with five years still to run on the lease, John Hoar died. In November it emerged that Ann Hoar, the deceased's wife, was 'desirous of taking a new lease of the mine ... she having a prospect of making up a respectable company.'

The wording is interesting, particularly in light of the fact that the 'several other adventurers mentioned on the (original) lease,' were described as 'having left the kingdom.'

One wonders why they all chose to leave. Clearly there was felt to be value in the enterprise and in 1820 a certain Captain Remfry sought permission to work a lode there. Perhaps he was part of the respectable company Mrs Hoar was referring to, perhaps not, either way the attempts to make a go of Boringdon Park Mine were not going well and in January 1823, Mrs Hoar wrote to the Right Honourable John, Earl of Morley and surrendered the lease.

The following year, 18 years after the enterprise had been entered into, an advertisement was posted in the local press for the sale of the mine materials.

There was still interest in Boringdon Park, but it was to be another ten years before anyone could be persuaded to invest again.

Thus it was in 1834 that a new company of investors, headed up by Captain Bray, began a fresh assault on the riches below grass.

Armed with one of William West's 30-inch rotary steam engines purchased from the foundry in Hayle they set to work.

Again it appears that the venture was short lived and by the beginning of January 1835 there looks to have been a change in personnel and the new mine captain was Joseph Malachy.

Curiously enough the 45-year-old Malachy, a Callington man who also had an involvement with Wheal Brothers and Wheal Sidney, had, just a year earlier, been released from Fleet Prison, having served time for bankruptcy. However, the chances are that his fellow venturers were unaware of that situation, although perhaps not the Devonport Solicitor he was working with, James Husband, with whom he had been dealing for a number of years.

On 4 January 1835 Husband wrote to Lord Morley from London requesting information about the mine and to ask how deep the mine was, what the returns to date had been, and why the work had stopped and for how long.

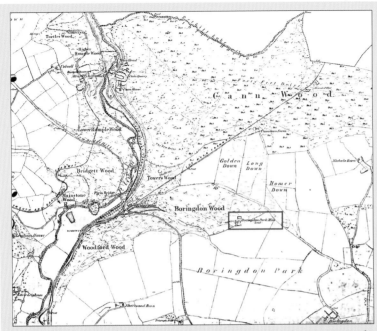

In it's last flurry of activity, 1852-55 Boringdon Consols yielded almost 150 tons of lead and over 7,500 ozs of silver, however the percentage of metal to ore fell away year by year: 1852, 75%; 1853, 45.5 %; 1854, peak year of production, 46% and 1855, 20%

The Miners' Bank of Truro had its origins in 1759 and was formally constituted in 1771 by a consortium of seven men: Francis Bassett, John Rogers, Humphrey Mackworth-Praed, Sir William Lemon, James Willyams, John Lubbock and John Furley. Initially it catered primarily for the mining industry but before long had expanded into other areas. Although it went through a number of incarnations it survived until the end of the nineteenth century. It was by no means the only Cornish bank to produce its own banknotes.

Husband also said that he had *'no doubt this mine will be brought out in good style.*

'I have had,' he added, *'a meeting with some of the Guardian Insurance Office Directors, this morning with a view to bringing her out as a company and I think the Directorship will be filled up by first rate capitalists.'*

Significantly the solicitor also asked *'whether your Lordship will extend the sett as to quantity of ground provided the company should desire to increase their outlay.'*

In September Husband received a letter from James Yolland, of Merafield, on behalf of Lord Morley, agreeing terms, and, on 5 November, a 21-year lease was signed.

At this stage it is unclear whether work had restarted or not, but quite possibly not, because, seven weeks later, Husband wrote to Yolland again asking much the same questions as before. The information was requested he says, because he wanted to be able to draw up a prospectus.

It further transpired that Husband had arranged with *'Mr Budge and Captain Williams to meet you (Yolland) on Friday 1 January … to decide on the best offer for building Engine House etc.'*

A few days later a printed notice appeared *'Boringdon Park Mine – Public Setting.'*

A week later Husband wrote again from Norfolk Street, on the Strand, suggesting that *'Boringdon Park Mine will cut quite a figure'* and that *'Malachy is most sanguine about her.'* He also said that Mr Budge had spoken to a miner who had worked there previously and clearly that encounter had given the Directors of the Boringdon Park Mining Company every reason to be optimistic.

In addition to Malachy and Husband it would appear that the other directors, as of 1 February 1836, were: William Copland of Parliament Street, Westminster; John Labouchere of Birchin Lane, London; John Martin of Lombard Street, London; Rowland Mitchell of Lime Street, London, and James Tulloch of Montague Place, Middlesex.

One wonders how many of these London gentlemen ever ventured this far west, and what further due diligence they undertook before agreeing to fund Malachy and Husband's enterprise to the tune of £2,500 (around £300,000 in today's terms).

Certainly William Copland did, for he died here, at Whiddon's Royal Hotel, in George Street, Plymouth, in November 1836. A Director of the Guardian Assurance Company, Copland was just 38 and interestingly enough his father had died just two years earlier and one can't help but speculate that he might have invested some inheritance monies in the Boringdon Park Mine venture.

Whatever his circumstances, the other directors wrote to Lord Morley in the summer of 1837 requesting an extension to the sett *'150 fathoms north* of Bottle Hill north lode and westward as far as the land of your lordship extends towards the river and 400 fathoms south of the Boringdon Park main lode.'

A few weeks later the Earl commissioned inspection reports from Captain William Williams and Captain Bray.

Clearly all was not well, Malachy had written the previous year to say that the mine would not be profitable 'for want of power in the machinery at 50 fathoms below the surface,' and somewhere along the line William Millett Thomas, who had first seen the mine over 20 years earlier, and who, according to The Miners' Bank of Truro, had been working various mines in the country 'with effect', had become involved.

Sadly for the investors, his engagement appears to have had little effect here. On 16 October 1837 the directors wrote to Mr Yolland on the subject of his shares in the company and used the missive as an opportunity to complain about the main protagonists of the project – Husband and Malachy:

'Mr Husband's conduct has been such that the Directors wish in future only to hold correspondence with him through solicitors. As to Mr Malachy, I am now investigating the affairs of the Wheal Brothers Company and the result will prove whether he is or not entitled to that confidence I have been led by Mr Husband, to bestow in him.'

The Wheal Brothers enterprise, as it transpires, had also landed Malachy in hot water and he and his father, Robert, who were the original leaseholders of that mine, found themselves in court in June 1836 countering claims that Joseph had sold a substantial interest in the mine without informing all shareholders. In 1838 Malachy was declared bankrupt again, nevertheless the following year he was in court again, defending an action, this time a petition brought by a former employee of another Cornish mine that Malachy had been engaged with as purser. It was around this time that he eventually fell out with his Devonport solicitor James Husband. But then he seemed to fall out with a number of people and for one reason or another Malachy was in court in 1839, 1840 and 1841.

In 1845, however, aged just 56, he was killed in an accident at the Linares Mine in Spain. The incident was reported widely in the press:

'Mr. Joseph Malachi [sic] the well-known mining captain, who made much money in working the silver ore in the neighbourhood of the Tamar, and selling the shares thereof, has been killed in Spain, by a fall in the mine, which he was employed to superintend. His life had been one series of ups and downs; he was suddenly wealthy, and suddenly the reverse.'

At one of the high points, he looked to buy 'the beautiful seat of Sir Salisbury Trelawney MP – Harewood House' but before long he was back in a position of having to sell everything. As if to emphasize the dangers not only to the pocket, but also to life and limb it's interesting to note that Malachy's father, Robert, also died at a mine, the Brothers' mine, at Calstock, in 1840 – he was 76.

Meanwhile, back at Boringdon Park, there was still thought to be potential in the enterprise and early in 1838 Captain WIlliams who had now inspected the mine three times and was managing the project in place of Malachy (who had been dismissed for non-payment of shares) recommended that his nervous fellow investors needed to extend the sett and give the scheme another eight months at least.

It would appear that in April, at an AGM held in the City of London Tavern, in Bishopsgate Street, Williams' pleas were sufficiently persuasive to keep the operation going. But only for eight months, for on 27 December 1838 the board decided that enough was enough: no one was keen to invest more capital and so a unanimous decision was taken to close the mine.

And yet there was still a feeling that with the right equipment the mine could still be profitable … and so it was that in 1849 the site was looked at again.

On Wednesday 4 December 1850 a general meeting of adventurers was held in Tavistock. Thomas Nicholls was in the chair and 51-year-old, Calstock-born, Jehu Hitchins was appointed chief manager and superintendent.

The meeting was told that 'fifteen years since a party wrought this property, and one of their trials was the driving of an adit … on the course of a lode for a distance of about 200 fathoms and which point there was met with a large slide (flookan) crossing the level, shortly after which the mine was abandoned. The present party resumed the driving of this adit level on the course of the lode, east of the said slide and having extended the drivings about 30 fathoms beyond the lode has been improving gradually every fathom since in appearance. In the present end the lode is four feet wide composed of silver lead and mundic principally and altogether it may be termed good dressing work.'

Once again a lease was negotiated with Lord Morley (for 21 years at one fifteenth dues) and it was noted that 'ore shipment will be cheap by means of the Plymouth and Dartmoor Railway which passes through the western portion of the sett.' The waterborne route commenced from a quay on the Laira.

The following November saw the adventurers visit the mine and inspect the new machine – a 40-inch engine from Harvey's of Hayle – and 'express great satisfaction in the manner in which it was working.'

At a dinner in the Globe Hotel in Bedford Street, Plymouth, that evening, JH Murchison, who was in the chair, was pleased to be able to report that they had already had to pay dues to Lord Morley, as 10 tons of lead

Globe Hotel, Bedford Street, Plymouth.

ore had already been sold for more than £200 and there were several tons more on the floors ready for market. All of it had so far been raised from just 10 fathoms below the surface and it was anticipated that by the beginning of the new year they would be digging some 15 fathoms below the adit *'after which the returns will probably be considerable and remunerative.*

'These adventures are considered to be safe investments,' he affirmed. The Earl of Morley, who was one of the adventurers this time around, as well as being the landowner, had intended to be present but was *'unavoidably prevented from being so.'* However, his agent, George Pridham, was there, as were Hitchins, Thomas Nicholls, and Captain Capel Coape, but *'David Halket, an insurance broker and ship owner from London, and a number of London shareholders were unable to make it.'* The following year, 1852, saw work continue in confident fashion as Boringdon Park and East Boringdon were amalgamated as Boringdon Consols. *'The united returns'* it was claimed, *'will in future be considerable, while the expenditure will be much diminished.'* The man in overall charge was now 29-year-old Captain William Godden from Calstock. Married with four children and a young mining clerk and assayer living under the rented roof of Boringdon Park Cottage – along with two serving-maids, Godden was on a basic salary of eight guineas per month *'... until returns justify a dividend.'* Murchison, as secretary of the mine, was on a slightly lesser wage of six guineas, *'including rent and office expenses except printing and stationery,'* while the new purser and clerk on site was Joseph Malachy. With a wage of five guineas per month, Joseph was the son of the earlier Joseph Malachy and was living as a lodger in Plympton St Mary. Among the adventurers at that time we find Messrs Halket, Hall, Locock Webb, Coape and Murray, all of whom were asked for a call of five

shillings on their shares at the October 1852 meeting.

Although now boasting the best equipment yet to work the site – the new flat-rod system enabled work to be carried out at new depths on Murchison's Engine Shaft, Hitchins, and Annie's Engine Shaft – the yields were still below what had been hoped for. Nevertheless, the chairman gave his best thanks to Captain Godden *'for his energy and zeal in the interests of the company.'*

Clearly it was pleasing to be able to report that there was a balance on the books in favour of the mine, with estimated assets over liabilities clocking in at over £500, but there was still a need to put a call of six shillings out on all shares to keep the venture moving forward.

Less than a week after the Christmas of 1852 it was estimated that *'15 tons of best quality and 18 tons of second quality ore will be ready for sale in about six weeks, and 65 tons of mundic are at present ready for sale.'* The note of optimism carried on: *'When the ore ground, already discovered, is laid open in the lower levels, now nearly arrived at, there is not the least doubt these will be profitable and remunerative mines.'*

The following September a further call of 10 shillings per share was made. The total receipts were up significantly, to over £15,000, but expenditure was up too, to over £14,000, but still there was the belief that *'the mines will become profitable when developed a little further.'* But not quite yet, and in the meantime *'the shareholders deserve the greatest credit for the spirited manner in which they have conducted the works, and it is to be hoped they will realise the expectations which they are so well justified in entertaining from the character and productiveness of the lode hitherto.'* But come December 1853 the message was much the same *'with prospects of soon paying dividends.'*

Nor did the story change in 1854. Mundic – arsenical pyrite – was the main produce and the price was rising, but it wasn't high yield material. Captain Godden tried to remain upbeat but he noted that *'going West, the ground is much the same as last reported, being very wet and troublesome.'*

In October 1854, at a special meeting of the shareholders, it was agreed to appoint James Wolferstan as manager and purser of the mines and two months later he reported that the lode in the present end *'was looking much better than usual, and was now yielding very fine rocks of lead, of greatly improved quality.'*

Wolferstan had a track record from Bedford United and other mines and his opinions were valued. One such was that he thought that there was a probability that *'an abundance of copper ore will be found underneath the eastern shaft'.*

Earlier that December Captain Godden had stated that the stopes to the east of the rise were *'promising to be the best bit of ground we've got.'*

At that point the shares were deemed to be worth around £1.10s.0d each and once again there appeared to be the promise of better times ahead. But there weren't.

The record yields achieved in 1854 – 135 tons of lead – were not to be repeated, and although over 2,000 ounces of silver were processed from the lead ore in 1855, there was *'a good deal of dissatisfaction felt at the manner in which this mine has been managed; objection being taken at the waste of money incurred in paying an inspecting agent –12 guineas a month – a sum never heard of in the best of Cornish mines.'*

The feelings of unease were exacerbated by the bankruptcy of one of the adventurers, David Halket. Back in 1852 Halket, it appears, was in possession of £25,000 *'a great portion of which, consisted of property of very precarious value – but the greater part of it had since vanished.'*

Halket it seems was no stranger to financial difficulties, or ingenious bookkeeping, and had become an enthusiastic, although perhaps not overly diligent, speculator in the railways and mining ventures. As well as the Boringdon venture it seems he also had shares in the Calstock United Mines.

By 1855 his debts had risen to over £15,000 and his assets had fallen to barely £3,000.

At a meeting of the Boringdon Consols shareholders in London in May the 397 shares that Halket held in the enterprise were *'absolutely forfeited.'* To make matters worse there was a further 9 shillings owed on each of those shares.

Notwithstanding these difficulties, work carried on at the mines and the following month Captain Jehu Hitchins reported that *'for a long time he had not seen a lode he liked better.*

'Everything combines to impress a favourable opinion, and I feel perfectly justified in recommending a spirited prosecution of another level.'

He added: *'The surface works are generally well laid out, and all machinery and plant in good order.'*

Which was probably just as well, because a little over 18 months later, on Monday 16 February 1857 the whole lot was put up for sale.

The site closed again after just eight years and in December 1859 the Mining Journal reported that *'the closure was caused through lack of monies rather than impoverishment of lodes, and there is every possibility that it may open again.'*

It didn't.

In May 1865 Richard Moore, of Dalston, Middlesex, was granted a licence for working for oxide of iron from ochre clay at Boringdon Park. There were no rights to work any metallic ores and there were clauses to *'ensure competent working and to protect the environment – no pollution of streams etc.'*

Moore was also given permission to erect drying and other sheds, machinery and appliances and to use and divert such adits, drifts, waters, leats and to use such buildings and erections as are now thereon … except the dwelling house, outbuildings and appurtenances now occupied by Mr William Harris.

The then Earl of Morley, Albert Edmund Parker, was due to receive one shilling for every ton that was sold.

It's not clear if his lordship ever received a shilling however, as we have no record of any sales. Furthermore, on 26 May 1869, a notice was pinned to the door of the mine buildings in Boringdon Park, it read:

'To the executors, administrators and assigns of Richard Moore, deceased. Notice of failure on the part of the tenant to work the ochre mine.'

The following month the Earl's steward received a letter from RA Harvey of Chacewater on behalf of RW Harvey, requesting a further response to his earlier missive regarding the mine which the writer states *'I think it belonged to a Mr Moore, or he was manager … and who has been dead for some time.'*

But was he? Owen Baker's research suggests that Moore was maybe still around in 1869 as a sett was granted to a Richard Moore, by the Earl of Morley, in 1873 to work for iron ore at Mount Batten.

'Moore's signature at the bottom of this sett being very weak and shaky but not dissimilar to that at the bottom of the Boringdon Ochre Lease of 1865.'

Whatever Moore's circumstance, there appears to have been no further action at Boringdon Consols.

Details of the sale of machinery at Boringdon Consols. As can be seen from the other advertisements it was not an isolated or unusual occurrence.

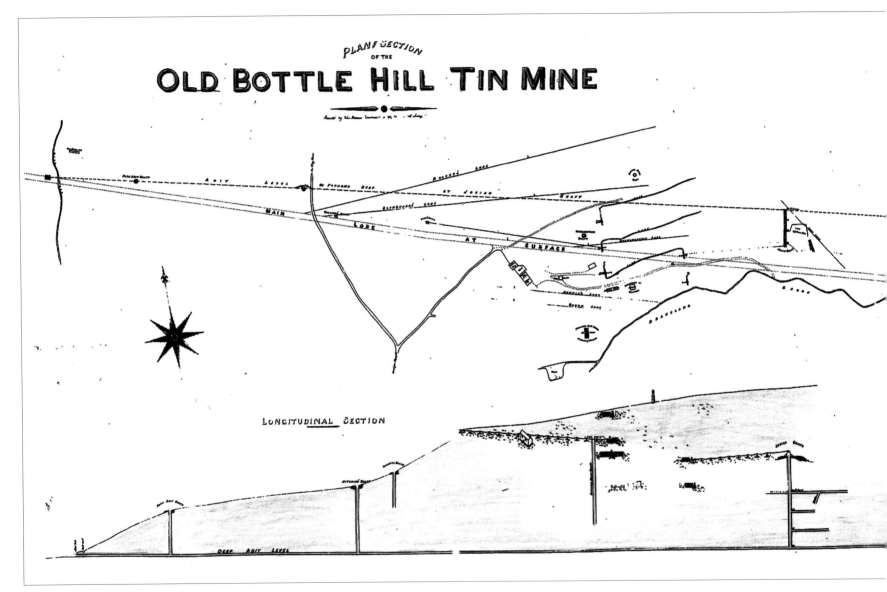

Surface plan and section of Old Bottle Hill Tin Mine

Bottle Hill

Just as Boringdon Park had been worked long before we have detailed production figures and anything in the way of documentary evidence, so too had many of the other setts in the neighbourhood, including, as we have already seen, Bottle Hill and Drakeland.

Work was revived on this site in 1808 and interestingly enough it appears that water was brought to the site from the Plym, via a leat starting near Ditsworthy Warren. Not a great deal more is known of this venture, until the story is picked up again in 1811 when Jehu Hitchins senior, formed the Bottle Hill Tin & Copper Company.

Two years later, armed with a 21-year licence from Reverend Richard Strode, they began their quest to dig and search for tin, copper, lead and *all other metals and minerals throughout all those parts ... of those two tenements called Bottle Hill and Drakeland ... that is to say commencing from the tail of the adit in Drakeland one hundred fathoms to the south west from thence in a straight line to Crownhill Down Lane, leaving Bottle Hill Carn to the south west then bounded by the said lane to Crownhill Down and by the boundary hedges of Bottle Hill and Drakeland estates round to the tail of the said adit with permission also to work on the south copper lode down to the river in Newnham Park for the purpose of bringing up the adit but not to work on the right or left of the said road west of Crownhill Down ...*

'... liberty to divert and turn ... watercourses and cut any channels for conducting ... the same in, through or over any part of the lands lying with the limits of the sett ... doing no injury to the paper mills of the said Richard Strode called Shaugh paper mills or to the tenant thereof in respect to the water now commonly used for driving the said paper mills.'

Hitchins' partners in this enterprise appear to have been Thomas Saunders, Thomas Gregory, John Vickry Bridgman, his sister Ann Bridgman and mother Susan (Mr Vickry Bridgman senior having died in 1815).

Between them they bought some 60 shares at a first call of £25 (around £2,200 in today's terms) a share, thereby raising a capital fund of £1,500. The following year, 1815, a further call of £10 a share was made, but it seems that Saunders failed to pay on one share.

The situation was further compounded when 35-year-old Vickry Bridgman, a Tavistock scrivener, was declared bankrupt in 1817 and then when a further call of £10 a share was made, Messrs Gregory and Saunders were again less than forthcoming. It was, presumably, no surprise therefore when Jehu Hitchins filed a petition against them in the Stannary Court at Ashburton.

The Lord Warden of the Stannaries at that time was the Right Honourable Francis Charles Seymour, Earl of Dartmouth and he found in favour of

Hitchins and in the subsequent ruling the defendants were ordered to pay £60 plus costs, and to have their shares sold. Quite how solvent the mine was at this stage is unclear but over £740 worth of copper had already been sent out.

Production continued into the 1820s with 40 tons of copper ore being sold to RJ Trevill in 1822 and a further 50 tons to the Birmingham Mining and Copper Company in 1823. The Midlands by then were very much at the heart of the country's metal based industries and in 1825-6 a further 103 tons of copper ore was sent thither from Bottle Hill.

Meanwhile a rather more modest quantity of tin – just over eight tons – was despatched to the then newly refurbished Ailsboro (Eylesbarrow) stamping mills at Sheepstor. Said to be the first reverberatory smelting house in the county, it was erected by the proprietors of Elysebarrow tin mine in the 1820s.

By this time the Reverend Richard Strode had gone to meet his maker and his wife, Admonition and his son, George, were in receipt of the customary one-sixteenth dues, rather than the apparently generous one-tenth dues his father had originally negotiated.

Nevertheless, one suspects, with the mine consistently producing some sort of yield, the Strode camp were relatively happy with the Bottle Hill enterprise, not so though, his neighbour George Woollcombe who in the summer of 1825 filed a complaint against Captain Nicholas Vesey, then residing at Drakeland, and local blacksmith John Hall – and others – for trespassing on his land and diverting a stream of water to the mine at Bottle Hill.

The land in question was Trowlesworthy Warren which Woollcombe claimed *'cannot be included in any pretended grant or charter of the Duchy of Cornwall by King Edward III and the Prince of Wales, my title to Trowlesworthy being under a Royal Grant from Baldwin, Earl of Devon ... being previous to the reign of Edward III.'*

Woollcombe's solicitors – Woollcombe and Jago – argued that the Stannary Laws did not apply to Trowlesworthy Warren as it wasn't part, nor had it ever been part of the Duke of Cornwall's possessions.

It transpires that water had long been brought to the Bottle Hill site via a leat fed by a brook about two miles from the mine, a leat, that was partly dug through Strode land and partly through the lands of others *'who have never interrupted the miners in the use of the leat, nor demanded any recompense or acknowledgement for the enjoyment of it.'*

The problem appears to have arisen as a consequence of the exceedingly dry summer of 1825 – across the country ten men and 16 horses died in July on account of the heat – and a stream, which had until then *'proved sufficient for the purposes of the mine, failed.'* Consequently all operations in the mine ceased and Nicholas Fezzy, *'the chief resident superintending agent of the mine, employed some of the miners to clear up an old leat, for the purposes of obtaining an additional supply of water.'*

A map, accompanying the response to Woollcombe and Jago, evidenced a hundred such water channels still remaining, *'indicating their having been used for carrying water to tin works.'*

The first leat referred to above would seem to be one that was fed from the Tory, near Tolchmoor Bridge, while the more recent and controversial one was sourced from the Plym.

In the end the plaintiff, Nicholls, the warrener, was awarded damages of £100 for the trespass, a surprisingly substantial sum, perhaps, under the circumstances. Certainly these were difficult times at Bottle Hill and when the summer of 1826 turned out to be every bit as hot and dry as the previous year, the sett and some of the machinery were offered for sale.

In an attempt to reposition the mine operation, a new company was formed. Jehu Hitchins was still very much involved, and in 1828 production figures show that there were now greater quantities of tin, rather than copper, being *'brought to grass'* at Bottle Hill.

Over the next seven years almost all of the tin produced, over 350 tons, was shifted across to Crowndale Smelting House where the Devon Tin Smelting Company had earlier been set up on the edge of the mine.

After 1835, however, that arrangement ceased and for the next few years the output went to a variety of smelting houses: Batten & Co; Bolitho; Calenick; Angarrack; Trethellen, Trelysick …

Meanwhile, copper extraction recommenced: 13 tons in 1831; 38 tons in 1832; 220 tons in 1833; peaking in 1834 with a recorded output of over 550 tons – all of it destined for Messrs Vivian & Sons. Although they were based at Hafod, in the lower Swansea valley, Vivian & Sons had been set up by a 50-year-old Cornishman John Vivian at the dawn of the nineteenth century and by this time the operation was being run by his second son, John Henry Vivian.

Mainly producing ingots and copper sheets, the copper supplies they were getting from Bottle Hill tailed off after 1834, the next three years seeing yields of just 143, 51, and 73 tons respectively.

Meanwhile, tin production over the same period fell to just 144 tons.

The situation precipitated another restructuring in 1834 as George Strode drew up a new lease with Jehu Hitchins. This time Jehu Hitchins the elder, now 63, and the younger, 35, were part of the new arrangement, along with John Vigus, who like Hitchins snr was a mining agent based in Tavistock – Hitchins was based in West Street, Vigus in Exeter Street. Their remit now covered around 110 acres of Bottle Hill and Drakeland, parcels of which were in the occupation of Henry Maddock, William

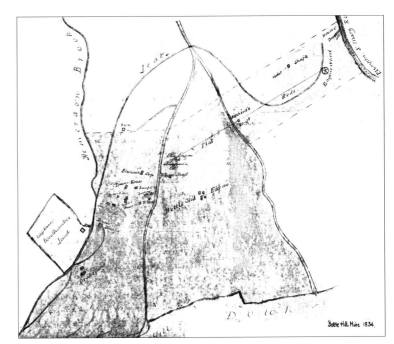

Bottle Hill Mine, 1834

Andrews and others. Clearly this was a mix of old and new in more ways than one as the current consortium had *'license and authority to erect such engines and machinery and build … such houses, mills and other edifices (except smelting houses). (No) burning houses shall be erected at a greater distance than 100 yards from the present burning house (without the written consent of George Strode).'*

Interestingly enough Strode stipulated that his one-fifteenth dues could be paid in smelted metal or money *'according to the desire of the grantor.'*

The Adventurers also agreed to *'constantly and bona fide cause (the mine) to be worked … with as many able men as can conveniently work the same …*

'… also deposit all deads, halvans, and refuse stuff in such places … as shall be least prejudicial to the surface … and to future working and mining of said limits.'

Hitchins was, without doubt, a very experienced mine operator, but no matter how much experience anyone had in the industry the potential for incidents and accidents, on top of the difficulties of trying to predict what route to take to follow a lode and how rich the seam might be in the first place, were infinite.

In September 1836 WJ Henwood had written to him from Penzance concerned that any tin ore lost in conveyance by sea should be paid for by Jehu (or his heirs or assigns) to the tune of *'one shilling and sixpence three farthings for every one hundred and twelve pounds weight of white or metallic tin contained in such tin ore.'* Henwood suggested that a bond of £50 should be ample to cover it.

Four months later tragedy struck when a young lad named Mattock, who worked on the Bottle Hill operation, was killed by falling into one of the shafts of the mine. A newspaper report noted that *'he was literally dashed to pieces'.*

One can't help but wonder whether the boy was the son of the aforementioned Henry Maddock (the misspelling of surnames in newspapers is nothing new) the farmer whose land the mine encroached upon. Whether it was or not, Maddock himself had cause to complain when he lost a sheep that fell down a mineshaft. He also lost two lambs that were killed by the engine rod. Nor did his grievances end there as, since September 1836, he claimed that one field of about two acres and his garden, had been totally destroyed in the sinking of Strode's shaft by the miners. He pressed for compensation – he was looking for £12.5.0d (£12.25 or around £1,200 in today's terms).

With few health and safety practices in place these were dangerous times, but then life itself was generally more hazardous.

Just how different so many aspects of everyday living were back then is vividly illustrated by the tale of another Bottle Hill employee, James Jeffery, a few years earlier:

On Saturday 14 February 1829, Jeffery had gone to the Devonshire Inn on the Ridgeway, to collect his monthly wages. It was mid-afternoon and according to usual practice one of the miners had taken on a set of work for six and, having been paid by the clerk of the mine, the six had gone to the inn to divide the money.

After a while Jeffery, who was from Buckfastleigh, some 16 miles away, and who was described as *'an old man near 60,'* announced that he was going to set out for his home town, whereupon his fellow miners, according to one of them, John Clemow, persuaded him to stay a little longer.

When he did eventually move to leave the pub, a couple of strangers, Thomas Helston, of Cornwall, and William Trethrew, from Devonport, who had been sitting within earshot in the pub kitchen much of that time, asked Jeffery if he knew where they might get a job of work, they being *'very poor and almost broken down'.*

The witness then said that Jeffery asked the men if they were going up or down the country and they answered by asking *'if there was not a man going to Buckfastleigh, he answered yes, to which they replied that they were going to Buckfastleigh, and witness (Clemow) said they would be company for one another'.*

As they left the pub Helston, the taller man – he was 5'8" or 5'9" – had a

shovel with him while the short one, Trethrew, had a bundle of tools under his arm. Both Clemow and Jeffery (who had been paid £1.9.2d) had spent a shilling each in the Devonshire and both were deemed to have been perfectly sober.

On leaving the Devonshire Jeffery called in at the Post House just beyond the Ridgeway – the George Inn. There was a waggon outside and it would seem that Jeffery was enquiring as to when there might next be a waggon heading towards Buckfastleigh.

Whatever the reply, according to William Webb, the ostler at the George Inn, Jeffery started walking off on the toll road in the direction of his home town. Meanwhile, two men dressed like Helston and Trethrew came up to the ostler and, claiming to be very poor, asked if they could be given *'leave to sleep in the hay loft'.*

The ostler agreed and they went off to the hay loft and weren't seen again until morning. At that time it was about eight o'clock in the evening.

Before long, about a mile and a half out of Plympton Jeffery encountered Helston and Trethrew again: *'So you are walking on,'* he said quizzically, but received no answer.

As he drew level with them the two separated, the one to the left the other to the right and as he came between them Helston put his left hand to the shovel he was carrying on his shoulder and struck Jeffery on his head. Jeffery's arm, raised in defence, taking part of the blow. The attack knocked Jeffery's hat off and bending down to retrieve it he was dealt another strike which rendered him senseless.

Devonshire Inn, Ridgeway, where the miners went to divide their earrnings.

Later that evening news reached ostler Webb, at the George, that a man had been knocked down and robbed, furthermore he had come to his senses and said that he had been assaulted by two men, *'a tall man and a short man, one of whom had a shovel.'*

On hearing this Helston said that yes, he did have a shovel, *'but God forbid I should knock any man down or injure him with such a thing as this.'*

Another witness, Edward Hicks, a labourer, was called and he said he was in Sandiford's blacksmith's shop that night, and he saw two men pass on towards Ivy Bridge, about a mile this side of the town, *'and it being a moonlit night he could see one of them had a spade or shovel on his shoulder.'*

Meanwhile, it transpired that the man who discovered Jeffery lying by the roadside was John Burch, who was driving the Subscription Coach to Plymouth. Burch halted his horses to avoid the body that was lying insensible in the wheel rut.

Burch *'desired his passenger to come down and observe that the coach had not touched the body, the wheel having swerved off, two feet seven inches from it. He heard footsteps and called out, a man named Mead came to his assistance, in whose care he left Jeffery while he drove to the Ridgway for medical assistance.'*

James Mead, was a local wheelwright and he managed to bundle Jeffery on to his cart, on top of some straw and take him to his lodgings in Colebrook. Mead measured the wheel of Burch's coach and concluded that there was no possibility of it being responsible for Jeffery being knocked down. Furthermore, it transpired that no other coach had driven that road since the mail had passed down, before Jeffery had set out – an indication of how busy the main route into Plympton was in those days! While Jeffery was still on the wheelwright's cart he was examined by James Osmond, a local surgeon who had been summoned by Burch the coach driver. Jeffery was then still 'insensible' and the surgeon found a wound *'6 or 7 inches in length, the scalp divided nearly to the pericranium, as if by a blow of blunt instrument, such as a stone or poker; the wound on the right side of the head was upon the parietal bone about four inches in length.'*

Next on the scene was Dr Butter, the well-known Plymouth physician, who inspected the victim with regard to the likelihood of the wounds inflicted leading to the latter's demise, or to the chances of him being able to speak coherently on recovering his senses.

Having been revived by a cordial, Jeffery, however, was able to give a description of his assailants and that Sunday morning Constable Lister found Helston and Trethrew sitting on a bank. The constable informed the two men that he was apprehending them for highway robbery and they returned with him quite willingly.

Early 1900s view of the George Inn, Ridgeway, Plympton

The two protested their innocence and claimed they had been in the hayloft all night, however, as the ostler noted, it would have been quite possible to leave and return to the loft unseen as long as they avoided the toll road. The two said that they been working for the parish for a shilling a day three days in the week, but that they found it hard to manage on that amount. Trethrew, who had three shillings and sixpence about his person, claimed that he had suggested to his overseer that he went away to find work and that the overseer had given him seven shillings, to assist and that he and his companion were on their way to Kingsbridge where they had heard that there was work to be obtained.

Judge Oxenham at the Exeter Assizes summed up the evidence, *'going over the circumstances as they bore upon the facts, & after a consideration of ten minutes the Jury returned a verdict of Guilty of an attempt to murder against both prisoners.*

'The names of the prisoners being called, the Judge put on the familiar insignia of the law, and proceeded to pass the dreadful sentence on the prisoners. He said they had been convicted upon testimony that would leave no doubt upon the minds of any one as to their guilt; and such was the frequency of crimes of the nature of which they had been found guilty, that it was necessary for the security of the public, that an example should be made.'

The Judge added that *'he was very sorry to see two men at their time of life in such a situation, and for such a crime; the unfortunate old man upon whom they had perpetrated their violence, should have rather been an object of their care and sympathy. He could give them no hopes of* mercy, and strongly recommended them to use the short period of life which remained to them here in preparation for that awful change they must shortly undergo.

'The sentence of law was passed upon them and they were removed from the Dock, attesting their innocence in the strongest manner.'

The report concluded with a graphic description of the two men: 'Helston, a very thin-faced man with compressed lips and rigid features, is 58 years of age,' while Trethew (the spelling was inconsistent in the article, furthermore he was referred to as Trethur in another newspaper and Trethru in yet another), 'is a short, set grown man, bald over his head, and is 46 years of age.'

'They will be executed on Friday week.'

And so it was that on the morning of Thursday 9 April 1829 the two men, both still protesting their innocence, were hanged in Exeter Gaol. Somewhat bizarrely it was reported in the *Dublin Morning Register*, that just before the execution, 'a silly woman applied at the prison gate for a piece of the rope with which either of the malefactors should be hanged (this was to act as a charm against the effects of some disease); and another for permission to rub the neck of some child afflicted with the King's evil with the hand of one of them after the execution.'

The newspaper piece was headed 'Gross Superstition' and the reporter noted that 'Mr Cole, the governor, had properly left orders that such applicants should have a decided negative.'

Beliefs and superstitions were wide and varied back then, as indeed were accounts of incidents. Reporting a week after the assault, the *Exeter and Plymouth Gazette* had Jeffery well and truly murdered, but clearly he was in Exeter to give evidence five weeks after his alleged demise.

A further insight into early nineteenth-century life around Bottle Hill is provided by the list of rules and regulations that were posted around the mine.

From it we understand that men worked a basic eight-hour day, which sounds eminently reasonable, but it was clear that those eight hours and the timing of them was non-negotiable.

The unacceptability of drunkenness is similarly understandable, as indeed is fighting, while the ruling on game hunting is logical as such wasn't written into the agreement with Strode.

Where the regulations perhaps strike us as rather more draconian than those we would expect today are those concerning the Sabbath.

Early nineteenth century rules and regulations relating to Bottle Hill Mine.

'That if any man, boy, or maid, belonging to this Mine, should be found in a public house on a Sunday drinking (except on business) any intoxicating liquors; he, she, or they, may at once be discharged, and all the money belonging to them in their present contract be forfeited to the Adventurers.'
The swearing fine is also something that the modern workplace might find challenging, but possibly no bad thing. However, the compulsion vested upon all employees to attend some place of Divine Worship every Lord's Day, on paying of what would today be at least a £5 fine or dismissal, certainly belongs to a different era.

As indeed does the thinking behind the final ruling, that, in effect, suggests that if any of the company directors is injured *'in property or about the Mine'* by the neglect of any man, then said employees wages will be docked accordingly.

Frustratingly it's not obvious what precise period of the Bottle Hill Mine's activities the rules and regulations relate to, but one suspects the sentiments held good for most of the nineteenth century.

Certainly the Bottle Hill Mine was one that stopped and started more than most. Little is known of the late 1830s revival, although there is record of over 100 tons of black tin from Bottle Hill being sold 'by ticket' in 1837. However, it would appear that times were hard once more and in June 1839 the Adventurers resolved to appoint Captain Richard Williams to succeed Captain M Hitchins, on a salary of eight guineas a month.

Meanwhile, the mine's purser, another of the Hitchins clan, Josiah, *'intimated to the meeting that in reference to the present state of the finances of the mine, he thought it right to reduce his salary one half from the end of the present month.*

'Not surprisingly his offer was accepted although the Adventurers did express the hope that 'the affairs of the mine will speedily be improved as to enable them to restore his full salary.'

The meeting also hoped that Mr Strode would grant a new sett at the present rate of dues, in consideration of the present outlay and loss of the Adventurers. It was further hoped that Mr Strode might contribute to the *'expenses of erecting a residence for the Captain in which there may be a counting house for the meeting of the Adventurers and the transacting of the business of the mine.'*

What happened next is not entirely clear. In September 1841 mine captain Williams, in conjunction with John Coryton Roberts and Thomas Sanders, signed a twelve-month agreement over the use of part of the Bottle Hill site and part of Woollcombe's land with George Strode. However, two years later, in September 1843, we find the Bottle Hill Mine had been put on the market, through Bridgman and Scobell solicitors of Tavistock. It would appear that there were no takers.

Equally it would seem that there was little activity on site and on 19 January 1846 an agent for George Strode, Charles Bewes, solicitor, publicly affixed a note on the door of the Bottle Hill Mine counting house.

By this time both Jehu Hitchins senior and John Vigus, had died and the notice stated that as there had been *'failures and breaches of the covenants and conditions ... and especially ... as there has not been for a considerable time a searching or working of the lodes ... I the said George Strode do intend to avoid (void?) the licences and thorities aforesaid ...'*

An identical notice was posted again by Bewes on 2 February 1847 and on 4 June, presumably having heard nothing from the Adventurers, Strode retook possession of Bottle Hill Mine.

Once again there appears to have been a reassessment of the mine and it's potential and statements were sought from former employees, and from Captain Williams as to its future viability.

On 16 February 1850 a prospectus was published in the *Mining Journal, Railway and Commercial Gazette* – the very title of the periodical an indication of the new world that was being created by the Industrial Revolution and the new opportunities that existed therein.

For the first time we find Bottle Hill Mine being described as being *'2 miles from the Plympton Station of the South Devon Railway'*, and not surprisingly either as the railway had only just reached this far west 18 months earlier with the first goods train leaving Plympton Station in September 1848 (incidentally, it wasn't until April the following year that the Iron Horse reached Millbay and Plymouth).

As it happened not even the railway was without problems. In June 1849 an engine – Goliath – on passing through Plympton, pulling seven heavily laden trucks, was about to climb Hemerdon Bank, when its boiler blew. The explosion was heard miles away, the engine was thrown 30 yards, the stoker, Evans, who was married with two children, was killed, while the driver, Thompson, who was married with six children, *'was lifted high in the air, and thrown into a garden several yards from the line.*

'He was taken insensible and conveyed to the Plymouth Inn, where he was promptly waited upon by Mr Square and Dr Soltau, a surgeon and physician of this town, who happened to be passing at the time.'

The carriage conductor, Lavers and Mr Cross, the clerk at the goods station in the town, were *'knocked about from one end of the carriage to the other, escaped unhurt'*. The engine was completely destroyed and all but two of the trucks and the carriage, were thrown off the line, *'and injured in several places'*.

A post script to the story, which appeared in the *Taunton Courier*, reported that the driver was much better and, for the benefit of anyone who might have been left apprehensive about rail travel: *'we are informed that the burst of a locomotive engine boiler is a most unusual occurrence, only three instances of such an accident being on record'*.

But to return to the Bottle Hill saga, the prospectus went on to provide an illuminating account of the story so far: *'The sett is very extensive, being about 1 mile in length on the course of the lodes east and west, of which there are six in number, and about half a mile from north to south. The north part of this sett is composed of granite, of a character congenial for mineral deposits – the old workings being in killas, or clay-slate stratum, with a great cross-course and several small ones, running north and south.'* Some rather interesting financial figures followed which suggested that the *'late adventurers'* had recently spent £12,000 on a deep adit to drain the mine, and *'an engine shaft sunk 110 fathoms from surface, giving 60 fathoms of back above the deep adit level. A great portion of this ground could be taken away at a tribute of 10s to 12s in the £1, within one month from the re commencement of operations which would very considerably assist the cost of the mine.'*

Having said, that the authors made it clear that *'In order that the workings should be fairly and regularly prosecuted, it is necessary that a steam engine should be erected, which will prevent any delays at any season – it having been ascertained that in very dry summers and severe winters, operations have been suspended nearly three months in the year, but it is considered that the engine would not be required more than two months, on an average, during the year.'*

Interestingly at this point we read that *'The expense of this steam-power having been taken into consideration by the lord, he liberally reduced the dues to 1-20th.'*

Clearly our local landowner was keen for the work to continue, and not surprisingly so, as he was not in real danger of losing money, unless he were to join the adventurers himself, which was currently unlikely as despite the claims to the contrary it did not seem that the operation had been that profitable in recent years for its investors.

'It will be seen,' carried on the prospectus, *'from the following reports, that this mine was abandoned by the late adventurers at the very time when good returns of tin were being made, but the waterwheel having broken down, and the machinery generally not being in a fit state to work the mine, and the tin market being at that time very depressed, many of the shareholders declined to expend money in the erection of any new machinery.*

'Tin and copper ores were sold during the last workings of the mine to an amount exceeding £100,000, which is sufficient to prove the character of the sett.' Indeed, but was that true? The records that survive make that seem a little over generous, although it is likely that at least that much or more was invested by successive groups of adventurers.

Offset against that was the fact the prospectus writer was claiming that *'there is now left in the bottom of the 50 fathom level a large quantity of*

tin-stuff already broken, with tram road, waggon, miners' tools, and the bottom of a 14-inch plunger, which, with the counting-house, agent's house, material house, smiths' shop, and burning-house at surface, cannot be taken at a less value than £1,000.' Presumably this was payable to the landlord, the previous adventurers having walked away from the operation. The ask of potential new adventurers was set at 1,024 shares, at £4 per share, with a deposit of £1 to be paid on each share.

Applications for shares could be made to a variety of gentlemen, John Metherell a sharebroker of Tavistock; Thomas Dunn, also of Tavistock; John Hamlyn, mining agent from Drake's Walls (sic), Calstock; John Williams of the Roseland Foundry in Liskeard; Messrs Watson and Cuell of Cornhill, London and George Trickett, Post Office Chambers, Plymouth. The bankers for the new concern were the Devon and Cornwall Banking Company who had branches in Plymouth and Tavistock.

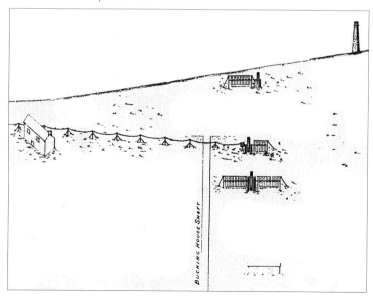

Top: *Plympton Station soon after opening in 1848.*
Bottom: *Detail showing bucking house shaft and stamps for crushing the ore.*

101

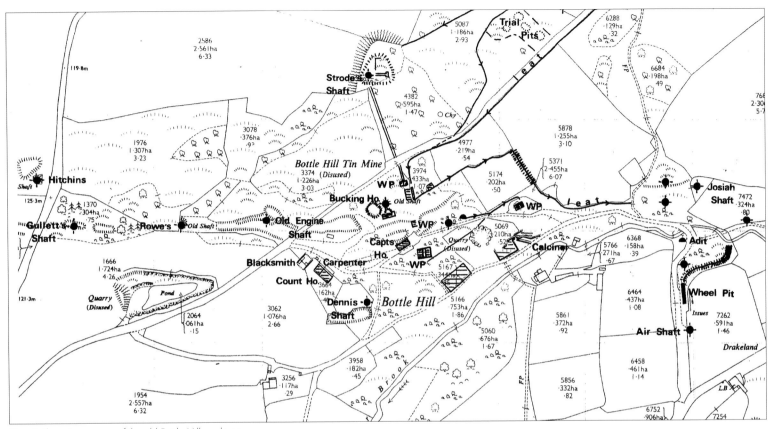

Twentieth century survey of the old Bottle Hill workings.

As part of the hard sell of the prospectus, the page in the *Gazette* also featured a report from Captain Richard Williams, *'an agent in the former workings of Bottle Hill Mine.'*

The report was filed from Plympton on 6 December 1849 and after outlining the possibilities he felt there were on site, Williams concluded his report by stating that he was of the opinion that *'any company with sufficient capital, combined with good management, would, in due time, find this a good and profitable undertaking; as in taking a geological view of the mine and its neighbourhood, the observer is at once struck with its very peculiar mining features; and, as a proof of its productive nature, it is only sufficient to know the amount of tin and copper produced – principally from one lode – amounting to more than £100,000 worth, by modern miners, without referring to the ancients, who mined extensively here.'* How far back, one wonders, could one go and still refer to 'modern miners'? Even during the really productive period 1828 to 1839 it would appear that the combined revenues for tin and copper sold were around £30,000 and it seems unlikely that a combined total of over £70,000 was brought to ground in the earlier 1808-28 period and in the ultimately aborted 1840s workings.

Nevertheless, there were clearly those who were keen to keep Bottle Hill operational and others who reported in support of this latest attempt to revive the mine included James Eddy who had worked at Bottle Hill for 13 years and spoke about *'a good tinny lode'.*

'I believe Bottle Hill to be one of the best tin and copper mines in the west of England, if put to work and properly managed.'

William Barrett's testimonial was that he had worked on the mine for 20 years and was there when the mine was stopped: 'At the time we knocked off working we were raising good quantities of tin, most of which was taken from Fizze's shaft.

'I should think the lode would be worth nearly £50 a fathom,' he added.

Meanwhile, Charles Blanchard, who'd worked there 35 years, and his colleague John Farley, were cited in a missive dated 1 January 1850 and sent from Hemerdon. These two old hands were of the view that there was plenty more tin to be taken from the sett and they too went into detail about the various lodes and claimed even greater revenues.

'During the last workings there was nearly £120,000 worth of tin and copper returned,' they averred and should the reader, 'or any other person, desire further information, we are willing to afford all we know about it.'

And why wouldn't they, after all, as experienced miners who were now a little long in the tooth, the idea of employment on their doorstep would have been preferable to having to move, or travel to find work.

The appeal worked, and on Tuesday 9 July 1850, 'We resumed operations here by placing men to close the deep adit collar of the old engine shaft and making all necessary preparations for our new future workings, as no time may be lost in preparing for the erection of the engines.' Hopkins was the mining engineer and Reede, the purser.

In January 1851 a new 21-year lease was signed between George Strode and the aforementioned Thomas Dunn, George Trickett and a Plymouth builder, William Conway.

The landowner conceded his dues down to 1/20th, but included the proviso that if there was another termination then he should have the right to purchase, 'at a realistic price, all the engines, machinery etc., remaining on the mine.'

As we have already noted, however, work was underway from the previous summer, and although we have no production figures for 1851 we know, from an unfortunate incident, that there were men at work down under, as, in the last week of July, William Farley while working with explosives in a Bottle Hill shaft, was killed.

Having lit the fuse to an explosive train, Farley was anxious to find out why the said fuse was 'hanging fire', and had gone back to find out whereupon, as the newspaper account of the incident put it: 'A cloud of smoke, accompanied by the disruption of a quantity of the stone was discovered to be attended with the death of the unfortunate man.'

Any cloud cast by this awful incident appears to have disappeared the following April, when, on the 27th of that month and 'in the presence of a large number of the gentry and inhabitants of the neighbourhood' the long wished for 50-inch cylinder pumping engine was set to work on the site.

The new machine was obtained from the Russell Street Foundry of 56-year-old local engineer John Mare and it seems to have had an immediate impact. In August 1852 an extraordinary general meeting at the mine heard Captain Dunn present a 'very favourable report.'

There were at that time, evidently, two waterwheels working on the site alongside 36 stamp heads, with tin enough in stock to justify double that number.

At the bottom of the 50 fathom level they had six men working on a 5ft wide lode, worth, it was said, between £20 and £30 per fathom.

However, reading between the lines one wonders how well things were really going and to what extent the figures were being talked up by the mine Captain.

Press reports indicated in October 1852 that 'the works were progressing very satisfactorily' and in December that 'the appearances have improved very considerably of late, and the most prosperous results may be expected'.

In February 1853 readers were informed that there was a 'large quantity of tin stuff now broken at the bottom of the mine, which can be at once brought to the surface' while in June it was noted that a 'nine-inch branch of copper ore had been cut of first rate quality.'

More investment was needed, however, and in February 1854, following the reading of Captain James Wolferstan's report, Robert Barnett chairing a meeting of the Adventurers made a call of 10 shillings a share. A week or two earlier, company secretary, 57-year-old, German-born Gustavus Kieckhoefer issued notices in the press appealing to all Scripholders in the Bottle Hill Mine, to take their scrips (chitties, or credit notes) to his office in Threadneedle Street, by 28 February or forfeit the right to redeem such scrips in the undertaking.

The undertaking was still underachieving and yet, in May 1854, Captain Wolferstan reported once again that the prospect continued to improve 'and there was every reason to expect that the returns would shortly meet the expenditure ... in fact the running cost of the mine was now met.'

In July a further call of 2/6d, was made and, in October, Wolferstan 'reported that everything at surface had been put into the most complete and efficient state.' He added that 'The future cost would, therefore, be much less than heretofore and although he sincerely deplored the loss they had hitherto sustained, he could conscientiously recommend them to do otherwise than persevere.'

Concerns were raised at the January meeting of 1855 and Captain Wolferstan was asked to provide answers to a variety of telling questions by the next meeting, scheduled for four days' time. Amongst other things the adventurers were anxious to know if the present monthly sale of six tons of tin could be sustained over the coming months and what the value of the ore in the ground between the 100 and 112 fathoms mark might be.

His responses must have gone some way to allaying their worst fears and at a meeting in April he provided further encouragement by stating that the tract of ground that they were now about to enter *'had never been worked'* and they *'could not but expect, on reaching the main part of the lode, that they should meet with good results.'*

But it wasn't to be, and on 18 February 1856, five years and one month after they had received their grant from George Strode, William Conway, Thomas Dunn and George Trickett, each parted with five shillings and surrendered the sett.

Soon afterwards the machinery and materials of the mine were offered for sale – by auction. However, the absolute sale of materials was evidently postponed, from time to time, with a view to *'assist or promote the re-granting of the sett to other adventurers who may be disposed to work it.'*

Undoubtedly there was potential in Bottle Hill Mine, the problem was that no one had really made a success of it and it was hard to imagine that there might be another band of hopefuls willing to take it on. But there was – and in the August of that same year, Hugh Ebrington Croker, a 35-year-old gentleman sharebroker, George Keen, iron founder, and Matthew Loam, engineer, signed a new arrangement with the landowner, George Strode.

A year later Croker, now styling himself Purser and Chief Agent of Bottle Hill, signed a further agreement, this time to secure an additional water course from the river Cad, via the Lee Moor Clayworks (aka the Lee Moor Porcelain Clay Company) and here represented by William Phillips, manager of the same.

The land in question was part of Edmund Earl of Morley's estate, but at that time the clay works had more water than they needed and so a leat was used to create a supply to work the engines and machinery at Bottle Hill … at a rent of £3.10s per month.

Later that year a press report noted that eleven tons of black tin had just been sold out of Bottle Hill.

'We are glad to see this old mine doing so well, and we are told the tributers are getting from £8 to £10 per month.' A tributer here being a miner who is paid a portion of the ore or its value. Generally tributers worked in gangs and would have a certain part of the lode or a tribute pitch on which to work.

Over the next few years a lot of tin was 'brought to ground', but again, not quite enough. Between April 1859 and November 1862 George Sidney Strode received almost £444 as his 1/18 cut, which meant that the total value of the tin – and copper –raised, was of the order of £8,000 or around £1million in today's terms. But it still wasn't profitable. What is more the landlord was starting to encounter a marked reluctance to settle dues promptly.

Through his solicitor, Bewes, an increasingly impatient series of letters were sent to the Bottle Hill site and in January 1863 a distraint was issued on behalf of George Sidney Strode (27-year-old George Sidney Strode had succeeded his father, George, on the latter's death, at the age of 77, in 1857).

In order to obtain the money owed him Strode claimed *'all the minerals, machinery, engines, mining materials and implements within the limits of Bottle Hill Mine … for the sum of £293.11s.11d.'*

By this time it appears that Jehu Hitchins junior had become secretary and manager of the mine, with Captain Eddy the resident man in charge.

In 1872 Jehu junior wrote to George junior, via Bewes the solicitor, requesting an early renewal of the 21-year lease their fathers had agreed 16 years earlier. It seems as though, one way or another the mine was 'in work' continuously from 1850 to 1876, at least that is what John Farley's testimony, provided in 1879 and relating to a water rights dispute, suggests.

Farley had been under-captain of Bottle Hill and his account is an interesting one as it was no doubt typical of the time and it gives us another insight into the Bottle Hill enterprise and to how a miner had to move around to earn a living.

A Plympton boy, he moved into the Hemerdon area around 1817 and went to work on Bottle Hill Mine, aged 19 in 1823:

'I worked on the mine about 20 years on and off under the Hitchins Company, during that time the mine was generally in work. In 1845 I went to work at the Devon Consols, worked there not many months, but still lived at Hemerdon Ball. I next worked on the granite works at Torycombe in the neighbourhood for a few months. Then at Keaton Moor, Ivybridge, for a very short time. Then I came back to Whiteworks, close to Bottle Hill, then back to Devon Consols again in September 1847. Next went to Yalland in Roborough Down (January 1848) remained till August 1848 – then to Karrier Whiteworks on Dartmoor, then to Hillsborough till the latter part of 1849, the Wembury, but only there seven weeks. Yalland again then to Wheal Sydney on Newnham property in May 1850 and remained there to 1865 or 1866 with the exception of a few weeks on Bottle Hill Mine. In 1865 or 1866 Wheal Sydney knocked and I then went to East Bottle Hill Mine for a few weeks, then to Wheal Mary Hutchings and remained there 13 years, leaving in November 1878.'

'During all this time I lived in the same house at Hemerdon Ball, which I have occupied about 40 years and before that I lived some 15 years in Hemerdon Manor House.'

During all that time, moreover, John Farley and his wife Elizabeth, who was a few years his senior, raised a family of eleven children, eight of them boys, most of them becoming miners and one of them, William, being the

No. of Schedule	ROAD, STREET, &c. and No. or NAME of HOUSE	HOUSES	NAME and Surname of each Person	RELATION to Head of Family	CON-DITION	AGE of Males	Females	Rank, Profession, or OCCUPATION	WHERE BORN	Whether Deaf-and-Dumb / Blind / Imbecile or Idiot / Lunatic
9	Bottle Hill	1	James L. Farley	Head	Mar	34		Tin Miner	Devon, Plympton St Mary	
	Do		Anne Do	Wife	Mar		33		Do Do	
			Eliza Jane Do	Daur			11	Scholar	Do Do	
			William H. Do	Son		7		Do	Do Do	
			George Do	Son		4		Do	Do Do	
10	Do	1	Joseph Eddy	Head	Mar	64		Tin Miner	Cornwall, Gwinnap	
			Anne Do	Wife	Mar		64		Do Do	
			Sally Bickle	Visitor	Mar		32	Shipwright Wife	Devon, Bradworthy	
			Emily Bickle	Do			1		Do Charles, Plymouth	
			Georgina Johnson	Do	Unm		21	Dressmaker	Do Sidwell, Exeter	
11	Do	1	Elias Cane	Head	Mar	50		Tin Miner	Do Plympton St Mary	
			Margaret Do	Wife	Mar		42		Do Tavistock	
			William Do	Son		12		Tin Miner	Do Plympton St Mary	
			Emma Do	Daur			10	Scholar	Do Do	
			Elias Do	Son		8		Do	Do Do	
			Margaret Do	Daur			5	Do	Do Do	
			Thomas Do	Son		3		Do	Do Do	
12	Drake Land	1	George Gully	Head	Mar	52		Tin Miner		
			Anne Do	Wife	Mar		48		Do Cornwall	
			John C. Do	Son	Unm	20		Tin Miner	Do Plympton St Mary	
			William H. Do	Son		12		Scholar	Do Do	
			Maria Do	Daur			10	Do	Do Do	
			Charles Do	Son		6		Do	Do Do	
			William Cose	Boarder	Widr	75		Retired Farmer	Do South Huish	

1871 census return for four Bottle Hill properties, showing the number of miners then living there.

unfortunate victim of a fatal accident, referred to previously, while working at Bottle Hill.

It is also worth bearing in mind that the chances are that John Farley walked to all of these sites he worked on. Undoubtedly, therefore he would have known the countryside well and his testimony about the local leats would have been as valuable as anyone's.

Essentially the dispute was about how long certain leats had been running, who had created them, who had used them and who, in certain circumstances, had rendered them either unsuitable for pot water – for domestic use – or cattle water – to serve the livestock – after the water had been used to wash ore or power the wheels of local industry.

As was the way of the world back then, several of Farley's children lived close by and it was perhaps no great surprise to find, in 1881, his eldest son, John William Farley of Hemerdon Ball, negotiating with George Strode's daughter, Dorothea Georgiana Admonition Strode, a twelve-month contract to work a sett at Bottle Hill. Dorothea's brother George Sydney had died, without issue, aged just 44, seven years earlier, and so the estate now passed to her, along with the dues on the mining activities thereon.

In 1881 John William Farley, working in conjunction with a neighbour, Thomas Gray, was looking to make trials for minerals – tin, copper, lead and silver, within a clearly defined section of the Bottle Hill site, with a view to claiming a 21-year lease on a sett, on similar terms to the sett granted to Frederick Louis Wilkins and William Jackson May the previous year. Figures suggest that less than two tons of tin were raised across 1881-82 by just a handful of men, a couple underground and a couple working on the surface, and, although Farley and Gray sought a three month extension in 1882 to their investigations, the enterprise appears to have come to a halt.

In 1886 the 'Old Bottle Hill' site was visited by Thomas Provis, who reported to the Strode solicitors at their Manor Office in Stonehouse, on the perceived viability of continuing to work the land. But nothing further was done until Bottle Hill was worked for arsenic, at the end of the century and arsenic it appears is what interested Wilkins and May, who in March 1880 leased the combined setts of Bottle Hill and Wheal Mary Hutchings. Indeed, a *Mining Journal* report of 1877 suggests that '*the Mary Hutchings company had acquired the 12 arsenic kilns at Bottle Hill three years earlier and had lengthened their stacks by 10 feet.*'

Between them the kilns at Bottle Hill had yielded over 13 tons of arsenic in 1874-75 and nationally there had been a growing demand for the product across the nineteenth century, but before we take a look at that, what of the other contemporary enterprises in the area?

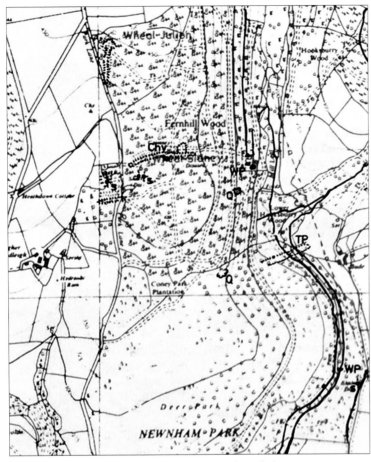

Above Wheal Julian and Wheal Sidney (latter also shown below)

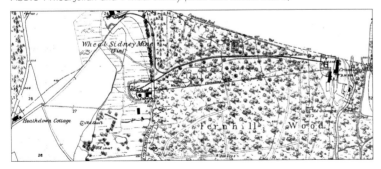

Wheal Sidney and Wheal Julian

Located in Fernhill Wood and the adjoining fields, it is clear that there had been work carried out here for hundreds of years, but most of it of the 'ancient' type – simple streaming and shallow working – although by the late-seventeenth century workings had reached depths of around 13 to 18 fathoms.

Lyson's *Magna Britannia* references 1795 as a late-eighteenth century date of activity, but there is no further evidence of working here until Captain Hitchins was granted a lease in 1836.

Jehu Hitchins had, by then, been involved with the Bottle Hill Mine for 25 years, and now, aged 65, one can but wonder as to what his motives were. His sons were also miners and would become active in the area, but according to the *Mining Journal* 'no mining of consequence' was undertaken here until a new lease was agreed with Messrs Eddy & Croker fourteen years later, in 1850.

The Eddys were another mining family and James Eddy had also worked on Bottle Hill, as indeed would the aforementioned gentleman sharebroker Hugh Croker. Together Eddy and Croker (and later Wood) formed a cost book company, the shares of which were held by a number of investors from Plymouth, Salisbury and London.

The mine consisted of three shafts: Old Engine, New Engine and Williams, which were sunk to depths of 46, 60 and 15 fathoms respectively. Over twelve years or so of production around 360 tons of black tin were brought to ground along with a little arsenic.

Tin prices fluctuated considerably over that time, from a peak of £84 per ton, to as little as £63. Somewhat frustratingly the best year of production, 1859, which saw some 78 tons of tin mined, was a year where the price dropped below £70, when the years either side saw returns of over £80 per ton.

All in all, the mine would appear to have been cost effective, total sales over that time amounting to around £25,000 with the paid up calls on shares only just tipping the scales at £10,000.

On the face of it, good returns for the investors, and reasonable employment for anywhere between 40 and 80 people.

However, following that post-1859 price drop, which also saw a drop in output, the earlier investors in this adventure handed the lease over to a new consortium, Henry Philemon Ewer, William Woodlands and Hingston Lindon, the latter a Plymouth man, the former both Salisbury residents.

Henry Philemon Ewer, 48, was a successful auctioneer, councillor, Justice of the Peace, and a senior partner in the firm Ewer & Winstanley, who were regularly charged with selling the assets and estates of bankrupt individuals to obtain the best results for creditors. William Woodlands, 50, was a currier, employing a number of men and, like Ewer, an upstanding member of the Salisbury community, indeed he had recently (1859-60) served as Mayor of Salisbury.

Hingston Lindon, meanwhile, although a seemingly successful Plymouth merchant who also had an interest in Wheal Mary Hutchings, was, for some reason, about to disappear – almost without trace – from local life. His involvement here didn't augur well for the future.

As it transpired, 1862 saw very little ore raised, less than seven tons, but by October a new 56-inch pumping-engine house had been built at the New Engine shaft and activity increased once more.

But not for long.

The returns for 1863 were, by and large, reasonable. There was no material sold in April, July and September but otherwise the Mine Captain, William Edwards, appeared upbeat, at least as far as the shareholders were concerned and work continued throughout 1864.

A meeting held in Salisbury, in May, resolved that all shares on which calls were outstanding should be forfeited and the purser, Charles Norton, reported that there were now 1245 such shares. Reporting to the board that same week, Edwards noted that the lode in the End East was hard but he imagined this to be a temporary situation. He also mentioned that recent hot and dry weather had seen water supplies become scarce and consequently it had been difficult to stamp the ore. *'We are now calcining the tin we have stamped, which will be ready for market in about a fortnight'.*

In October Edwards, together with James Seccombe, reported that End West had recently much improved and it was expected that there would be further improvement before the next meeting. However come the following month Hingston Lindon had disappeared.

So too, seemingly, had the prospect of profits in the short term.

At the first meeting of the new year, 25 January 1865, the minutes noted that *'in consequence of the Mine not looking as well as as at the former Meeting, the Committee, for the satisfaction of the Adventurers, resolved to procure the Report of Captain Gregory, of Drakewalls, on the present state of the Mine, which report was this day read.'*

This timely 'second opinion' sealed the mine's fate and it was duly resolved that *'all work not paying its own cost be suspended for the present time, and that the work in future be confined to the drivage of the 46'.*

It was also resolved that a further call on shares be made of 1/6d per share.

For the record, Captain Edwards' report was a little less bullish than usual, although he did speak of one lode presenting *'a kindly appearance for improvements'* and elsewhere reporting of another lode that if it were to be

found productive at our deep level *'we may fairly anticipate great success'.* Thomas Gregory's report however, although not without a degree of optimism, was even more sanguine:

'There are now some 4 or 5 pitches working in the back of and below the 46 fathom level East of diagonal shaft, but without some early discovery it appears the present returns of tin cannot be kept up very long.

'I regret not being able to furnish you with a better Report on the present occasion, but I consider there are fair chances for improvements in the Eastern ground.'

But it was all too little and too late. Work had already stopped.

In February 1865 tin to the value of £151 was sold, but that would appear to be material already raised and ready for market.

On the first day of January 1866 Thomas Pearse, Clerk to Messrs Bewes & Boger, Strode's solicitors, affixed a notice to Counting House door at Wheal Sidney. Countersigned by John Farley *'being a Captain to the late Wheal Sidney Mining Company'* it certified that *'no workings whatever have been carried on within the limits since the twelfth day of December last'.* It was thus a prelude to repossession.

By this time the sett seems to have included the northern openwork – Wheal Julian – which had been worked separately until 1860.

Wheal Julian had been worked on a relatively small scale since 1855 and an idea of that scale can be gleaned from the machinery that was advertised for sale at the close of operations: a 24ft diameter waterwheel; 12 heads of stamps and an 18-inch rotary steam engine.

Thereafter there was very little activity here. The Wheal Sidney sett was taken on by the Wheal Mary Hutchings operation in 1870 and a licence was acquired to use the calciner and a little bit of driving was done on the deep adit.

Henry Miners was listed as mine manager at the time, Alf Broad the secretary and the aforementioned John Farley, chief agent.

A decade later a detailed and rather optimistic report was made of the mine by 31-year-old Thomas Provis, secretary of the Mining Institute of Cornwall, who, the previous year, had been out to South America to report on mines in Chile and Peru.

Jamaican-born British citizen, Alfred Melhado was the one who evidently commissioned the report from the well-travelled Provis but the sett wasn't taken up, which was perhaps just as well.

Melhado, a 66-year-old financial agent, at that time living in Barnes with his wife, Sarah, and five of his six adult and unmarried children (aged between 20 and 32), was himself well-travelled. His wife, Sarah, was also Jamaican-born, while two of his five daughters had been born in Melbourne, Australia.

Working in 1858 as the manager of the Cambrian Assurance Company

Farley's letter acknowledging pinning of no workings notice dated 1 Jan 1866.

(which at one point boasted capital of £100,000) he was declared bankrupt at Canterbury Assizes, with debts of over £4,000 and no assets. Ten years later, in Bishopsgate, he was in court again, this time with debts of around £15,000 and 'no statement with regard to assets'. In May 1874 Melhado found himself in the Old Bailey on a charge of fraudulently transferring a client's shares into one of his daughters' account. On a tenuous technicality he was dealt with rather leniently, and directed to be imprisoned for one day and then discharged.

A chancer with a colourful CV, who would stand little chance in a modern world with internet access to information, he clearly kept bouncing back from a variety of self-inflicted setbacks. Nevertheless, it's not clear how he and his son, Howard, came to have an interest in Wheal Sidney.

In December 1881, armed with Provis' report, Alfred Melhado wrote to Strode's solicitors stating that before he was prepared to incur any further expense 'I must ask you to let me have a decisive answer to my application for the above sett [Wheal Sidney]. I find I shall have to get plans made and some three or four reports from mining engineers, in addition to Mr Provis' all of which requires more money. I am prepared to take a licence in the first instance, the lease to follow or to take the latter at once as you may decide upon.'

The following year there was correspondence relating to a draft sett, with a 21-year lease, 1/18th dues with an annual rent for the first year of £20, increasing to £30 in the second year, £40 in the third before settling at £50 for the remainder of the term.

But the sett wasn't taken up and a year later Melhado was declared bankrupt again!

At the end of the 1880s a new lease was granted to Messrs Pocock, Vosper & Manley, but little, if any work was undertaken.

26 October 1864, call of 1/6d on shares of Wheal Sidney

Wheal Mary Hutchings

As we have already noted this mine, earlier known as Lobb, Lobb Beame, or Muchells Beam, located on either side of the Smallhanger stream, had been worked for hundreds or perhaps thousands of years and may have been exploited earlier in the nineteenth century had it not been a little too close to the Strode's game reserves for his lordship's sensibilities. Certainly that was the apparent reason given for the abandonment of the adit on what was deemed to be a 'promising lode' in 1818.

Consequently it wasn't until there had been a significant amount of underground workings in the immediate, surrounding area that the sett was eventually opened up. Thus, in August 1854, three London-based adventurers signed a 21-year lease with George Strode on a sett of lands at Hemerdon (later known as Wheal Mary Hutchings). The document was backdated to Christmas 1853 so presumably some investigative work had already been carried out.

George Strode's dues were set at 1/15th indicating perhaps that there was a good deal of optimism surrounding the potential yields that were anticipated.

The three gentlemen in question were Francis Pegler of Lime Street, London, John Cunliffe Pickersgill of 4 Wanford Court, London, and George Moffatt of Eaton Square. Moffatt at that time was the sitting Liberal MP for Ashburton, having served the Dartmouth constituency prior to that, between 1845 and 1852, he was also the then owner of Goodrich Court, a neo-gothic castle in Herefordshire, built 25 years earlier by Sir Samuel Rush Meyrick. Pickersgill, meanwhile, was a successful London banker.

Quite what these gentlemen knew of the mine they were buying into is not known.

However, not much more is known about what happened, if anything, on the site over the next few years, as in March and April 1857, Strode's agent, 39-year-old Charles Bewes, posted notices on the gate of Cob Field, requiring that 'within 14 days six able men should be set to work, and thenceforth, constantly employed for six calendar months in sinking the deepest shafts or driving the deepest adits within the said limits.'

Clearly that requirement was not met and on 30 June 1858, George Strode junior (his father having died the previous year), gave notice to the three gentlemen of his intention 'to avail myself of such failure to avoid all the Licenses and Authorities' that had been granted four years earlier. On 20 October the following year, 1858, a notice appeared in the Plymouth Mail stating the licences granted to Messrs Moffatt, Pegler & Pickersgill had become 'absolutely forfeited.'

Born John Cunliffe Pickersgill (1819) to John Pickersgill, and Sophia Pickersgill (née Cunliffe), he assumed the name Cunliffe as a second surname in 1867, after inheriting the estate of an aunt of that name.

In 1869, a by-election was held in the Bewdley constituency, after the victory of Richard Atwood Glass in the 1868 general election was declared void. Pickersgill-Cunliffe was elected in the by-election, only for his victory to also be declared void on petition later that year, in favour of Augustus Anson.

Pickersgill-Cunliffe served as an MP for only six weeks, from 11 March until 30 April 1869.[2]

On 22 September 1873 Pickersgill-Cunliffe was struck by a train at Caterham Junction (Purley) railway station, near his home in Coulsdon, Surrey. He died two weeks later, on 6 October 1873, at Guy's Hospital in London. An inquest recorded a verdict of accidental death.

Tin ingots and tin straws. Wheal Mary Hutchings was one of the mines supplying cassiterite ore to the Tamar Smelting Works at Weir Quay on the River Tamar. Pic. Tommy Hatwell.

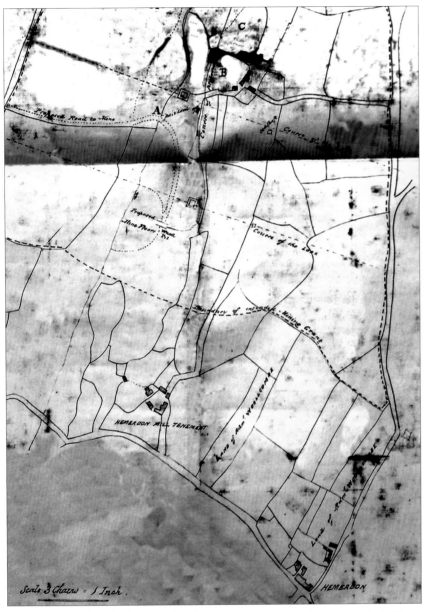

1880 plan of Wheal Mary Hutchings showing the course of the lodes, extent of the intended mining grant and the proposed new road.

Clearly anxious that the grass didn't grow too long on the operation, new Adventurers were granted the mining sett of lands at Hemerdon on 9 November 1861. Once again the new licence was for a term of 21 years, *'from Michaelmas 1861'.*

The new band of speculators appear to have been all local men, and doubtless therefore more cognisant of what they were taking on. The three main figures were William Edwards, mining agent of Plympton St Mary, and John Wills Stephens and the aforementioned Hingston Lindon both *'gentlemen of Plymouth'.*

The arrangement they signed up to was almost identical to the one their predecessors on this sett had agreed on seven years earlier: dues to be paid at least once in every three months, rendered in minerals, duly dressed and made merchantable; a quarterly statement of quantities; payment of all parochial, parliamentary and other rates, taxes etc: to work the mines with *'as many able men as can conveniently work the same and with such engines and machinery … best calculated to produce the greatest returns.'*

There were also clauses about not destroying existing shaft, levels, winzes, adits or other workings and furthermore that *'at the ending of the term … as the property of the landowner, the landowner shall take whatever he wants on the basis that he pay to the miners such a price as the same would reasonably be worth if sold or dismantled'.*

There was also an understanding that *'as little damage as possible be done to the land … and … property within or adjacent … Except for necessary air shafts and these not to exceed two in number and whilst so placed as to be sufficient for the miners purposes to be placed in such situations as shall least prejudice the value or appearance of Hemerdon estate.'*

The document also required the miners to keep all *'shafts, excavations, attel heaps and machinery constantly fenced, either with a hedge properly planted, or a wall of masonry'* and to keep all the watercourse, leats and streams, sufficiently bridged and with proper catch pits, which *'should be emptied from time to time so as to prevent the deposit of sand and other refuse stuff on the river.'*

In the event of any part of the site being rendered permanently useless, compensation was to be paid at the rate of £80 per acre for meadow land and £60 for arable ground. The landowner also reserved the right for his agents to inspect, measure, dial and map the workings.' Finally there was a long *'conditions of forfeiture clause'*, and, of course, it was hoped that this would not need to be invoked this time. Curiously enough, the landlord's dues were set at a slightly more modest 1/18th this time, with a rental figure of just five shillings in the first year, and thereafter a minimum of £20 a year – to be set against any payment of dues.

And so it was that George Sidney Strode and Messrs Edwards, Stephens & Lindon committed themselves to the next phase of mining activity on this parcel of Hemerdon.

Not surprisingly, perhaps there appears to have been no mineral extraction on site that year. Disappointingly, however, there seems to have been no ore brought to grass here in 1862 either.

The following year there was some activity as the enterprise was formally reconstituted as the Wheal Mary Hutchings Mining Company – the company being formed on 27 May 1863.

The name, incidentally, came from George Stode's wife Mary Hutchings Medlycott, the two had married, five years earlier, in Somerset.

In August at the first quarterly meeting of the new concern a balance of £112.17s was reported. William Edwards was the purser and manager of the mine and a year – September 1864 – later his statement of accounts showed that *'after payment of all expenses during the previous quarter there was a comparatively modest credit balance of £46.'*

A call of 2/- per share was made.

By this time it appears that the 40-year-old Hingston Lindon had disappeared. The son of a Borough Magistrate and successful local merchant, Joseph Lindon, Hingston's last transaction with his solicitors was, according to Thomas Wolferstan, in late December 1863. Wolferstan was evidently well acquainted with Lindon but had no idea where he had gone. Curiously enough it would seem that Lindon never was a shareholder of Wheal Mary Hutchings and had no interest in the company. Furthermore, in 1868 when some Plymouth property in which Lindon did have a share was being sold, advertisements were placed in Plymouth and London newspapers calling for interested parties, but Lindon hadn't come forward.

It was a mystery at the time and one now only partially solved by the discovery that Lindon left Plymouth for Liverpool where, in 1866 he married a local girl, a soldier's daughter, Jane Foulkes, 13 years his junior. The couple remained in Liverpool, where Lindon, who had taken on the family business in Finewell Street, Plymouth, reinvented himself as a commercial clerk and went on to sire at least six children with his new wife. He died in the Wirral in 1894.

Meanwhile, at the December 1864 shareholder's meeting in Plympton, accounts showed that there was a credit balance of £48. But still no prospect of a dividend, instead a further call of a shilling per share.

Things appear to have picked up as the new year dawned and in February 1865 Edwards, a former lead miner from Cornwall, announced that he had *'just dialled the ground and found that we have about 11 fathoms further to drive to intersect the great copper lode, unless any material change should take place in the underlay.'*

Edwards, whose son, John, was also a miner, lived on the Ridgeway, Plympton with his wife and seven children, and was most optimistic about the future of the Wheal Mary Hutchings.

However, the bottom line remained the same and in September the credit balance was much the same, down slightly to £43. A call of four shillings per share was made, primarily it seems to enable the erection of new machinery.

For once the optimism appeared to be well founded and at the March 1866 meeting the credit balance had significantly improved to a figure of £120, a figure that had almost doubled by the time the shareholders next convened in June.

Nevertheless, another call of three shillings on shares was made to enable the installation of yet more new machinery.

By September the balance in favour of the mine had risen to £269, but still there was another 3/- call on shares. The rising balance was not maintained for long, however, and perhaps as a consequence of falling figures there was some tension behind the scenes as John Stephens, the shareholder who hadn't disappeared, was taken to court by the man who claimed to have acted as the mine accountant for the last four years, Richard Lisle, of Church Street, Stoke.

Lisle maintained that he was in the employ of Stephens, a well-known local wine merchant, as well as purser of Wheal Mary Hutchings, and that Stephens had agreed to pay him £1 per month for work relating to the mine. The court reporter of the *Western Morning News* recorded that Lisle stated that after four years *'a little unpleasantness occurred, and the plaintiff left, and claimed £48 for the work he had done in the mine.'*

Stephens denied making any agreement with Lisle and said that Lisle did the work in his own private time, which he had no occasion to do. Whereupon a Mr King, who was Stephen's business manager, said that he had seen Lisle in the office during dinner hours, *'doing anything but his work'.*

The claim was rejected by the court. Meanwhile, back at the mine, things were looking up again and credit balance was back up around £250 and five tons of tin were sold to the Truro Tin Company.

Interestingly enough, around this time Captain Edwards inspected the Wheal Jane Mine near Truro for the shareholders there. These mines had recently gone through something of a depression, nevertheless, Edwards had advised his friends to hold onto their shares, which they did, *'and those shares have recently risen from £2 to £40'.* (*WMN* 6 December 1867)

Back on this side of the Tamar, in 1867 the mine here was merged with Wheal Sidney and the combination became known as Wheal Mary Hutchings United.

The amalgamation led to an improved yield and additional investment. A mining report in May of 1868 noted that in the course of the three previous months two circular buddles had been erected, along with 12 additional heads of stamps and a new 50ft by 6ft waterwheel that had been christened Medlycott – that being Mrs Strode's maiden name – her father was Sir WIlliam Coles Medlycott.

This large waterwheel now powered the operations at the mine and in 1869 the quantity of tin raised reached a new peak of just over 60 tons and at the September meeting that year a dividend of five shillings a share was announced. At last a local mine that was providing a return for its investors. For once, one imagines, everyone was happy, especially Miss Dorothea Strode who received an income that year of £223 (around £26,000) as her cut of the proceeds.

As the 1870s dawned there was a great deal of optimism in the air, however in November there was a bitter blow as the mine manager, Captain William Edwards, suddenly died.

Although just 49, Edwards had been a mine manager for over 20 years. An announcement in the *West Briton and Cornwall Advertiser* in November – he died on the 15th – described him as *'one to whom the miners owe so much for opening out the mine deposits of the neighbourhood in which he resided, and through whose industry the tin mines in Plympton have been worked so successfully.'*

It went on: *'To show his untiring perseverance and assiduity, it may be stated he actually took the sole charge of five mines at one time — Ashburton United, Wheal Emma, Brookwood, Huntingdon, and Wheal Sidney, and conducted the workings with satisfaction to all. Since then, for the last seven years, he has been manager of Wheal Mary Hutchings, the only mine here that has paid dividends, and Hemerdon United, which he has placed in such good working order that it must be eventually a great benefit to the shareholders.'*

Clearly Captain Edwards has left Wheal Mary Hutchings in good shape and at the meeting in September the following year a further, and even greater dividend, of 7/6d per share was declared for the previous quarter. The last quarter of the year was just as welcome, with 16 tons of tin being sold at a peak price of £90 per ton. The total amount of metal brought to grass may not have been as much as in 1868 and 1869 but the price paid for it yielded record receipts of over £5,000 for the first time (£5,719).

The mine was a veritable hive of activity, over 100 personnel were now working on Wheal Mary Hutchings, bringing a financial boost to the area not seen locally before in any of their lifetimes.

The output of the mine now was second only to that of East Wheal Russell, near Gunnislake. For the county, the following year, 1872 would see it produce half of Devon's entire tin output over a 12-month period.

In Truro that summer, one month's produce, a little over five tons, was sold for over £93 a ton – which, observed one local press report, *'is encouraging and speaks well for the mine'.*

But then the bubble burst. It perhaps didn't help that having lost Captain Edwards, Wheal Mary Hutchings also lost, in December 1872, one of its principal directors, the farmer from Bere Ferrers who had become a very successful Wine Merchant and businessman, 62-year-old John Wills Stephens.

As Hingston Lindon had to all intents and purposes disappeared, this situation paved the way for a change of personnel at the top and the three who stepped into the breech were William Hussey Bloomfield Kempe, a 'gentleman' from Bellevue, Brent, Edward Betteley, an accountant from Plymouth, and William Jackson May, a local auctioneer.

Just how much of an issue the transfer of power was, is impossible now to tell. The late Mr Stephens had been no stranger to controversy and court cases. Furthermore it wasn't immediately obvious that the proverbial writing was already on the wall. However, a report in the *Royal Cornwall Gazette*, dated 26 July 1873, may have inadvertently jinxed the mine when it stated that:

'At the present time Wheal Mary Hutchings stands at the head of the tin producing mines of Devon, and bids fair ere long to compete with the foremost in Cornwall. The caunter lode is opening up very rich at various points. The new south lode is also rich in the bottom sinking, and the main lode is looking splendid, and generally the various points and ends have a most healthy appearance. The mine, indeed, promises to early become the Great Wheal Vor of Devon.'

It didn't.

Production faltered and ten days before Christmas a new Limited Company was formed with two local mine agents, Henry Miners and Thomas Horswill each investing heavily, along with William Gillow, a medical man from Torquay.

Other principal investors and signatories to the new company were Samuel Heard of the Dock Hotel, Henry Dyer, a Royal Naval Paymaster, Charles Gibson, a share dealer, and fellow mining agent, the aforementioned John Farley from Hemerdon Ball.

The total output for 1873 had been a little under half of what it had been the previous year, however, come the summer of 1874, the situation rather than improve, had worsened further. There were barely a dozen men and a couple of boys working underground or on the site. Thomas Richards was asked to make a report on the state of affairs there.

It didn't make comfortable reading.

After describing the different workings he felt obliged to observe that having no underground working plan of the mine, *'it is difficult to say, with any nicety, where the end is driving … and to work a mine without regular dialling plans, is too much like going to sea at midnight without compass:- the Lord should insist on such plans being kept, because I presume you have a covenant to that effect in your sett or lease.'*

Richards' report gave his audience a very detailed account of what could be observed and at what depths and at what rate:

'The 32 end is driving east by one man and one boy, and this end ought to be prosecuted by six men to get under the tin ground driving through in the upper level.'

In another location, *'about 172 fathoms east of the Engine Shaft at the adit level a crosscut is driven South 57 fathoms and East on the South lode, containing tin ore and the lode for 2ft wide has a promising appearance and likely to be productive when wrought.'*

…and so on.

Comprehensive and compelling, Richards was also realistic about current conditions and the prospects for upping the levels of activity.

'Respecting the development, there have been low prices of tin ore for the last 6 months and it has paralysed the best energies of many mine managers.

'I believe the manager in this mine bought a large interest in this Adventure about 17 months ago [that would have been shortly after the death of Captain Edwards] when tin was high, and from want of capital to carry out the mine vigorously he has failed to explore sufficiently, which has led to the idea that the mine is poor, when the fact is the drivages in the different levels have not kept pace with the "reserves" taken away and the great point is what to do in future.

'I consider your manager deserving all the lenity that prudence can dictate because the price of tin ore sold at the smelting house having dropped from £90 in April 1872 to £46 per ton in April 1874. '

The sudden fall must have tried many a mine very severely in the two counties and a large number have had to succombe [sic].

'Perhaps it may be argued that [the price of] tin was unusually high in 1872, still I do think we have a right to expect the average price … for tin ore … during the last 20 years and that is £70 per ton for average quality.

'When that time arrives I consider Wheal Mary Hutchings is worthy of spirited development.

'Regarding the mine as an Adventure … the quantity of tin ore sold since Feb 1866 … ought to be considered large returns for the depth wrought, say 22 fathoms, because the 32 fm and 42 fm ends have not been extended E & W to prove the tin ground. The mine being drained by water power that goes over the pumping wheel, afterwards falls upon the stamping wheel so that consumption of coal is very trifling.'

[No. 206.]

Certificate of Incorporation

OF THE

WHEAL MARY HUTCHINGS MINING COMPANY, LIMITED.

I hereby certify that the WHEAL MARY HUTCHINGS MINING COMPANY, LIMITED, is this day Incorporated under the Companies' Act, 1862, and that this Company is LIMITED.

Given under my hand at Truro, this Twenty Sixth day of December, One Thousand Eight Hundred and Seventy Three.

FREDERICK MARSHALL,

Fee, £9 15.

s. 18.

Assistant Registrar of Joint Stock Companies, formed for working Mines within the jurisdiction of the Court of the Vice-Warden of the Stannaries.

Certificate of Incorporation for Wheal Mary Hutchings Mining Co. Ltd. 1873.

Captain Edwards' early demise may have had a greater impact than was apparent from the bottom line figures, but then again should he have been the one who better mapped the mine in the first place?

Whatever the principal reason for the present difficulties, and clearly the price of tin was a prime contender, Richards ended his report on an upbeat note:

'The situation of the mine being the south-west of the Dartmoor granite range and in the parallel of Bottle Hill Mine, it being in a clay slate formation traversed by Greenstone, there is much to argue in favour of it being a tin district worthy of greater exploration that it has hitherto received.'

The new manager was a Cornishman, Henry Miners, who, in 1871, we find living as a lodger with his predecessor's wife Eliza Edwards, in their house on Plympton Ridgeway. Ten years earlier he'd been living in Falmouth, with his wife Mary and their daughter, also Mary, and his widowed mother-in-law Clovina Chynoweth. By the time he arrived at Hemerdon, Henry Miners was then in his late thirties and it would appear that Captain Edwards' son, William, who was also living under the same roof, was one of the limited number of personnel still employed at Wheal Mary Hutchings.

But that number was dwindling all the time and despite a name change in December 1873 – to the Wheal Mary Hutchings Mining Co. – a move presumably accompanied by some further investment, the facility continued to struggle.

On 19 August 1876 a brief report in the *Royal Cornwall Gazette* read:

'Wheal Mary Hutchings which held out such bright prospects of success when we visited her 12 months ago, now presents a very different aspect, and we fear will soon have to follow the example of her neighbour Bottle Hill. Captain Miners of Pool is manager and the working staff about a score, compared to the hundred or more at work a year ago.'

The following year the 12 arsenic kilns that had been erected by the Bottle Hill 'Adventurers' were acquired by Wheal Mary Hutchings and their stacks, most of which appear to have been no longer standing, were extended by 10ft (3m). Thenceforth work at Wheal Mary Hutchings was focussed on the production of arsenic and a calcining works was erected in 1878 and come September that year arsenic was being sourced from the rich mundic or main lode for 230m at the 20m level.

But all was not well and following an Extraordinary General Meeting in November the decision was taken to wind the company up. The move was widely reported and on 29 November 1878 the *Carlisle Journal* noted that the Wheal Mary Hutchings Mining Co. had issued a winding up notice, as had the General Iron Screw Colliery Company Litd., the Alexandra Wall Co Ltd., Woolwich, and the Hull & County Bank Limited.

Wheal Mary Hutchings Mining Company, Limited.

Notice of Extraordinary General Meeting.

NOTICE IS HEREBY GIVEN that an EXTRAORDINARY GENERAL MEETING of the WHEAL MARY HUTCHINGS MINING COMPANY, LIMITED, will be held at the Offices of the Company, "Morning News" Chambers, Plymouth, on *Thursday* the *14th November* day of ~~October~~, 1878, at *3 p.m.*, to take into consideration the present position and prospects of the Company, and the propriety of Winding up the same; and if deemed advisable, to pass an Extraordinary Resolution to Wind up the Company voluntarily, in pursuance of the provisions of the Companies' Act, 1862.

Dated the *5th November* th day of ~~October~~, 1878.

(By order of the Directors,)

THOMAS HORSWILL,

SECRETARY.

Notice of Extraordinary General Meeting for Wheal Mary Hutchings November 1878

Nationally, this was a time when 'Adventurers' were investing in a wide variety of schemes and enterprises, many of which, almost inevitably failed. Certainly around the mines of Plympton successful ventures were thin on the ground and invariably short lived. However, Plympton was by no means unique in this respect, furthermore, it appears that a relatively consistent pattern of ultimate failure did not appear to deter those with monies to invest.

A week or so after the Liquidation was announced a notice appeared in the local press informing readers that local auctioneer, WJ May, was about to 'Sell by Auction, at Chubbs Hotel in Old Town Street, Plymouth, the whole of the Valuable MACHINERY, PLANT, Newly erected Arsenical Works, and lease of the Wheal Mary Hutching Mining Company, Limited, (in Liquidation), in the parish of Plympton, St Mary, Devon.'

The notice continued: 'The Mine produces large quantities of rich Arsenical Mundic and Tin, and being worked exclusively by Water Power, offers a splendid opportunity for Investment.'

There may have been some justification for this claim, after all, the available figures for 1878 suggest that over 170 tons of arsenic had been produced, which undoubtedly compared well with the 84 tons that had been retrieved in total during the three previous years. However, tin production was at a 12-year low with less than a ton of black tin being brought to grass across the whole of 1878, which was less than one-hundreth of what had been mined at the beginning of the decade.

Overall the output would appear not to have been nearly enough to support the 16 people employed underground, along with the 18 ground staff and the wear and tear on the site and machinery itself. The latter something potential investors were welcome to see for themselves. 'Inventory of Machinery and Plant may be seen, and orders to inspect the Mine obtained on application to the Auctioneer, or of THOMAS HORSWILL, Liquidator, Morning News Chambers, Plymouth. Dated Russell House, Liskeard, December 9th 1878.'

The auction was scheduled for Thursday 9 January 1879 at 3pm. Quite what happened on that day is unclear, but in April 1879 the ailing concern appears to have been bought by the Plympton Mining and Arsenical Company.

To all intents and purposes this was doubtless a new concern with, it seems, one or two familiar faces still sniffing around in the hope of a healthy profit.

Reading between the lines, or at least looking to extrapolate the sequence of events from subsequent court cases, it would appear that the Liquidator, Thomas Horswill, offered Wheal Mary Hutchings to Frederick Louis Wilkins, a civil engineer from Tavistock, for £1,000.

Mr Wilkins, apparently, did not have £1,000 to invest and so agreed to invest jointly with a Mr May, each putting £500 into the adventure. Coincidentally, this Mr May was the very same William Jackson May who was charged with selling the site at the January auction and who, like Wilkins had also had an interest in the Bottle Hill Mine.

Curiously enough Henry Miners was also still involved, as was a certain Thomas Horswill, mining secretary.

In March 1880, however, Horswill agreed to sell 'the goodwill of the mine and the mining materials and machinery thereon', to Wilkins and May 'and their co-adventurers 'with a view to the better enabling of further prosecuting mining operations'.

Miss Strode agreed and on 25 March 1880 a new 21-year lease was signed.

The document appears to be identical to that dated 9 November 1861, except that on the duplicate copy the option of erecting a burning-house on part of Crownhill Down or Bottle Hill appears to have been withdrawn as 'Crownhill Down' is pencilled through. There was, however, also mention of the tramway and the use of a burning-house.

In the event it was barely a year before everything went pear-shaped once again. Wilkins found himself in court being chased in the courts in London, by Mr WB Stephens, for £150. That was in the summer of 1881.

The following May Wilkins sold all his rights in the mine to May for £25.

Then, in November 1882, we find Strode's solicitors Boger & Bewes writing to say that they had nothing from May to substantiate any claim against his estate and that he, presumably Strode, would rather put up with the loss than 'mix myself up in the affairs of Captain Miners and Mr Wilkins'.

Later that winter the auctioneer May was declared bankrupt, Isaac Latimer and a host of local notables were listed as creditors, and Miners was in court being chased for around £4,475, the lion's share of which, over £3,000, had been advanced, as an unsecured sum, by Mr R Arnold of, Bank House, Chipping Sodbury.

There were a number of other creditors, but their claims, although not insubstantial – the solicitor CV Bridgman was chasing £115, and his firm, Messrs. Square, Bridgman, and Bond a similar sum – were certainly dwarfed by Arnold's potential loss.

Miners, then living at 3 Hemerdon Villas, Plympton, was apparently looking to declare himself bankrupt, but it was felt that he had shares not just in Wheal Mary Hutchings, that might still have some value, but also he had a few shares elsewhere, including Cornwall Great Consols Mine.

In the event, the creditors resolved to wind up the estate in liquidation and apply for the debtor's bankruptcy to be annulled.

That was in December 1882. The following year, Henry Miners died. The cause of death is not known, but Miners was just 51-years-old.

In the meantime there had been a related case in the Chancery Division of the High Court of Justice, where it emerged that Horswill's sale to Wilkins and Miners had been at an inflated price but both had sold their shares on to the benefit of themselves and not those shareholders who had lost out in the liquidation process.

It was all rather complicated and somewhat corrupt.

In April 1883 London solicitors Snell, Son & Greenip, wrote to Miss Strode's solicitor stating that the leases and plant were to be offered for sale as a going concern, but, they said, *'we do not believe anyone will purchase with the intention of working'* and accordingly hoped that, under the unfortunate circumstances Miss Strode might be prepared to accept *'say, a moiety of the sum payable to her'*.

As anticipated, it appears that no offer was forthcoming and Wheal Mary Hutchings Mine was officially struck off the register in 1884.

For the next ten years little mention was made of the mine … until March 1894 when Air Shaft collapsed, taking with it a significant section – around 50ft by 30ft – of Great Field, Windwhistle, and a part of the hedge on Galva Road.

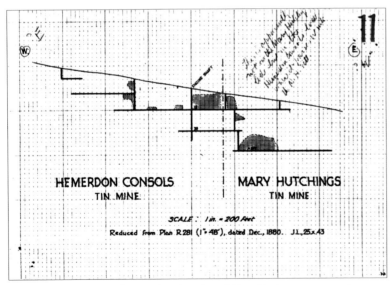

Above: Cross section of Hemerdon Consols and Mary Hutchings tin mines, showing levels and stoped out areas. Right: Prospectus for British Arsenic Mines, Limited.

The List of Subscriptions for the Preference Shares will be opened on Monday, 6th July, and closed on or before Tuesday, 7th July, at 4 o'clock for Town, and on Wednesday, July 8th, for the Country.

The Chairman of the Company, for the satisfaction of the Board, on the 30th of May last, paid a personal visit to the Mines, accompanied by an expert, and had samples taken under his own supervision; these were sent under his seal to Messrs. Johnson, Matthey and Co. for assay, whose Certificates are embodied in the Prospectus.

THE

BRITISH ARSENIC MINES, LIMITED.

DEVONSHIRE, ENGLAND.

Incorporated under the Companies Acts, 1862 to 1895.

CAPITAL £50,000.

Divided into 30,000 Ten per Cent. Cumulative Preference Shares and 20,000 Ordinary Shares of £1 each.

PAYABLE 2/6 on Application, 2/6 on Allotment, 5/- One Month after Allotment, and the Balance, as required, in Calls of not exceeding 5/- each, and at intervals of not less than One Month.

ISSUE OF 29,000 10% CUMULATIVE PREFERENCE SHARES,

Which will rank both for Capital and Dividend before the Ordinary Shares of the Company; after which, when the Ordinary Shares have also received 10% Dividend, the surplus profit will be equally divided between the Preference and Ordinary Shares.

The whole of the Ordinary Shares will be issued as fully paid, and be taken by the Vendors as part payment of the purchase price.

DIRECTORS.

G. PITT-LEWIS, Q.C., Paper Buildings, Temple, *Chairman.*
The Right Hon. LORD WATERPARK, Doveridge, Derby.
Alderman A. J. HAWKES, Brighton, Director of West Australian Loan and General Finance Corporation, Limited.
JOHN L. MATTHEWS, Director Lydenburg Minerals Exploring Company, Limited.
(And a Director to be nominated by the Vendors after Allotment).

BANKERS.

BROWN, JANSON & CO., 32, Abchurch Lane, E.C.

SOLICITORS.

ASHLEY, LUMBY & MICHAEL, 23, Birchin Lane, E.C.

BROKERS.

C. J. ALLEN & SON, 2, Cowper's Court, Cornhill, London, E.C.

CONSULTING ENGINEER.

THOMAS COLLINGWOOD KITTO, M.E.

AUDITORS.

TRIBE, CLARKE, PAINTER & Co., Chartered Accountants, 19, Coleman Street, E.C.
And at Bristol and Swansea.

SECRETARY AND OFFICES.

HENRY HAYDON, 16, Union Court, Old Broad Street, E.C.

PROSPECTUS.

THIS Company is formed to acquire the Leases and Mining Rights, for a period of 21 years, with the option of renewal, of three Arsenic Mines, known as Bottle Hill, Wheal Mary Hutchings and Wheal Sydney.

East Bottle Hill (Wheal Woollcombe)

Joseph Eddy was born in Guinap (Gwennap), Cornwall, in the second decade of the nineteenth century. Perhaps it's no surprise that this son of what was at that time described as the *'richest square mile in the Old World'*, on account of the copper and tin that lay below the surface there, should, in time, have ended up in Plympton, with interests in Bottle Hill and East Bottle Hill Mines.

East Bottle Hill – also known as Wheal Woollcombe – had been worked for hundreds of years, but there appears to have been little activity there in the nineteenth century until the 1860s. By this time Eddy and his wife Ann were living alongside miner and mining agent, James Farley and his wife, also Ann, at Bottle Hill. The Farleys appear to have been a fairly typical, substantial Victoria family, while Joseph and Ann appear to have had no children.

In the summer of 1863, following a favourable report from Thomas Gregory, the mine captain at the major Drakewalls Mine, Gunnislake, there was a concerted effort to restart mining at East Bottle Hill.

Gregory had said that he had *'every confidence that a valuable mine will be opened for a small outlay, and that few mines present such indications of early success'*.

By late September we learned from the newly appointed East Bottle Hill Mine Captain, Joseph Eddy, that they had cut through the elvan – the layer of quartz-porphyry – and hoped to see the first lode cut in the next few days.

With the value of shares gradually increasing, further impetus to the project was given when John Gifford (a descendant perhaps of the fifteenth century landowner of the same name in the area) in a very detailed account, reported that, in regard to East Bottle Hill, *'there can but be one opinion, that the geological indications are such as to justify a vigorous prosecution of the mine.'* (November 1863)

That same month, Captain Hancock of Liskeard inspected the mine and took samples of the lode, samples that were assayed by three men: Mr Bawden of Liskeard, Mr George of Liskeard, and James Harvey of Tavistock and each one reported very favourably on the copper content of the lode. Come December, Captain Eddy reported that the lode was looking better and that he hoped to *'be able to speak even more favourably in a few days'*.

The mine captain rhetoric was familiar, and one wonders to what extent they were speaking on behalf of investors, or potential investors, or the men under their command, in part to drive them on, in part to just keep them in gainful employment.

In September 1864 Richard Williams, then the Mine Captain at Wheal Sidney and a well-known figure around the Plympton mines, added his voice to East Bottle Hill champions:

'From my experience of the district and neighbourhood of the mine, extending over period of 25 years, I can safely say that, so far opened, there has been nothing like it for richness and importance discovered for many years at so shallow part, and the strength and richness of the tin are sufficient, in my opinion, to show that it is the outcrop of a magnificent deposit of ore.'

Captain Williams went into a good deal of detail, and noted that a call of £300 had recently been made but he did *'not hesitate to say that if the course of tin discovered continues– and there is no evidence to the contrary – no further call will be required.*

'There is,' he added, *'a fair chance of opening a good copper mine in addition to the tin actually discovered.'*

He concluded by saying: *'In my opinion you may with confidence recommend the property to any of your friends desiring investment.'*

A week or so later, we read in the *Western Daily Mercury* that the *'tin lode still improves'* and that *'from the present appearance there is not the slightest doubt'* of East Bottle Hill yielding first class dividends, *'with a very moderate outlay to erect machinery for stamping purposes … which can be done by water power.*

'Many tons of tin stuff of first rate quality are drawn to the surface now waiting the erection of machinery to bring it to market.'

The following summer, despite all the fine words suggesting otherwise, a further, but modest call of one shilling per share was made on the mine. Clearly there were encouraging signs and the value of the shares appears to have been on the increase in the early part of 1867. Nevertheless, in May a further call of a shilling was made on shares, but that same month at the mine's AGM investors were told that *'the stamps and dressing floors were in full work and that in nine days to a fortnight's time two or three tons of ore would be sampled.'*

The year also witnessed the installation of a 60ft waterwheel to work the crushing-stamps and to raise the ore.

Although no detailed figures are readily available, the situation cannot have been too gloomy as by June 1869 a mine meeting was informed that there was a balance of assets over liabilities of over £98; nevertheless, there was a further call on shares of 1/6d – payable on or before 10 June.

Around this time there appears to have been some 16 or so people working on the mine and an item in the *Cornish Telegraph* noted that *'the tin lodes at East Bottle Hill are improving in depth and new machinery is about to be erected'*.

The new machinery, it would appear, came courtesy of fresh investment. In the early part of 1870 a new company was created – The East Bottle Hill Mining Company (Limited) and a new indenture of a 20-year lease was dated 1 December 1870, with dues to the trustees of the late Admiral Woollcombe and Major Strode to be paid at 1-20th *as soon as a steam engine is erected*.

The company evidently was looking at a capital investment figure of £30,000 to be generated by 6,000 shares at £5 each. The directors of the new company were all from outside the South West: James Johnson, of Belmont House, Starbuck, Harrowgate, William Ward, of West Hill, Hull; 53-year-old George Dawes proprietor of the Milton and Elsecar Iron Works, near Barnsley (it employed nearly 1,000 men): John Perrott of St Anne's Hill, Cork and 49-year-old silk-manufacturer Edward Newton Carr, of Plymouth Grove, Manchester.

Captain Eddy again provided the necessary spiel: *'We have commenced to sink on the main lode of Bottle Hill'* this was the so-called Champion lode that crossed the sett and which Eddy explained had already, on its own, returned something like £2,000,000 in ores.

'A battery of 48 heads of stamps would crush 50 tons of tin ore a day, and with 1.5 per cent produce would yield 15 tons of tin per month, value £1,200 or £14,000 per annum, but after opening up the lodes you will by the returns double the amount; therefore allow me to say an engine should be put up that would work 72 heads of stamps. You have seven lodes already discovered. I know of no mine in the two counties possessing anything like the advantages of East Bottle Hill. It will soon be a good paying dividend mine.'

A report carried in various papers including the *Dublin Evening Telegraph* suggested that *'upwards of 5,000 shares are already subscribed for. The share list will close in a few days.'*

A post script to the piece informed readers that the latest assays for the mine had been made by Messrs. Johnson, Matthey & Co., assayers to the Bank of England and gave an average of 10.5 per cent for tin and 29.5 per cent for copper ... in other words seven times the basis on which Captain Eddy estimates profitable returns from.

Small wonder that new shareholders were keen to come on board and invest.

On 25 April 1871 Thomas Gregory, who had already reported on the mine and had long been involved with Bottle Hill Mine itself, spoke very optimistically about the need for *'a good battery of steam-stamps ... to enable you to work a large quantity of tinstone at all seasons of the year, and bring the mine into a good and profitable state.'*

In June there was further hyperbole from Henry Jones who also used the Bottle Hill statistics to excite investors in East Bottle Hill, although it is nowhere apparent where he got his figures from, as there appears to be no documentation to support them.

'As regards the productiveness of your Champion lode, I may just state that I have known 70 tons of tin sent off at one sale from Bottle Hill. No person can have a better idea of the remarkably riches of this lode then when I state that as proof of it there was sold annually from 150 to 250 tons of tin, and from 2000 to 3000 tons of rich copper ores.'

He continued: *'Tin averaged at that time [40 years earlier] about £45 per ton [it was now, 1871 – £80], and the copper £10 to £12 per ton.*

'You have, besides the Champion lode of this district, several other tin lodes each passing though your mine from 450 to 550 fathoms in length. I do not think there is a property in the two counties of Devon and Cornwall which has such great prospects before it. From the great facilities that East Bottle Hill possesses it can be developed to a result equal to the old mine, or indeed to any mine that is working at present in Devon or Cornwall.'

Another local tinner, 55-year-old Nicholas Fezzey, was equally gushing about the potential of the East Bottle Hill section of the Champion lode. *'I have broken some good tin therefrom that will pay well to work on tribute; this lode averages from 3 to 4 feet wide, and by driving 15 fathoms further you will get into the granite, which has never failed in producing rich tin.*

'From this end to the surface would be in height about 25 fathoms in whole ground, which would give some thousands of tons of mineral ground to take away at small cost.'

Fezzey was originally from Lydford, but had been living locally since the beginning of the 1850s. His wife, Ann, had borne them at least eight children, with birthplaces indicating that the family had moved around the county presumably chasing work. When the family relocated to Plympton in 1850 the eldest three boys were all described as tin miners. William, then 21 had been born in the parish, but brothers John, 19, and James, 15, were born in South Moulton and Bickleigh respectively, while Thomas, 9, Caroline, 7 and Lavinia 5, were all delivered into the world a little further afield in Buckland Monachorum.

In an age when the majority of the population were not particularly mobile, mining could be an inconsistent master and clearly there were good reasons for miners to want to stay put and work in their local area, than be forever in a position where they had to up sticks and start again.

Mine Captain Joseph Eddy was no exception and his monthly reports are couched in familiar terms of ambition and aspiration – viz the following extracts: January 12: *"The lode is improving both in size and quality. The tributers' tin would have been ready for market before this, but the late frost stopped all dressing; however if the weather proves favourable, I hope to have a sampling in a week or nine days from this time.'*

Hemerdon the Woollcombe family residence. It stands in park-like grounds approached by two long carriage drives. From the tennis ground a very fine view is commanded of the surrounding country, including Laira, Plymouth and the Harbour. The estate covers an area of about 800 acres. Trowlesworthy, an estate of some 500 acres, is also in the possession of Mr Woollcombe and has been in the Woollcombe family for about 400 years.

March 21: 'Good progress is being made ... I look forward to good deposits of tin being met with at the junction of killas and granite, which is in this mine as favourable situated as can be desired. I hope to send you more particulars in a few days.'

April 26: 'Our progress has been very encouraging ... I am confident ere long of communicating news of valuable discoveries as we have eight lodes, and the granite and killas intersect our mine most favourably. The 60ft water wheel and stamps are in excellent order.'

May 3: 'We are driving towards the junction of killas and granite with all speed, where I have not the least doubt good deposits of ore will be met with.'

May 24: 'We have proved the South Lode for 570 fathoms in length, and judging from the trials made on the lode for this distance we may fairly calculate that we have a first rate piece of mineral ground.

North Tin Lode ... good work for tin, and the ground easy for working, men getting good wages at 32s6d per fathom.'

Investors may have been getting a little nervous by this stage, however, and Eddy started to file weekly feedback.

June 8: 'I am glad to report that a good improvement has taken place here last week. We find lode greatly improving as we near the granite.'

June 15: 'We have overdriven this in the cross-cut plainly showing a less dip on the south lode than on the north tin lode. We may consider this all in favour of the lode. In the first place, the lode when cut will be worked at much less cost; secondly experience gives me to expect it more productive.'

June 29: 'We have sunk a trial shaft near our eastern boundary. and proved the great champion lode of the country for nearly 400 fathoms ...'

September 13: 'On Saturday last we cut through a branch about 4in wide and broke some good stones of tin from it; this branch is dropping into the lode, and when the droppers carry tin we have every reason to expect to find the south lode good when cut. All other operations are going on favourably.'

September 21: We have no figures of income being generated at this stage, but Eddy, when talking about the South Cross Cut said that they were driving *'by four men, at £4.10s per fathom.'* The new shaft, sinking on Bottle Hill main lode, *'is still dry, consequently the men are making good progress.'*

September 28: *'I have just come up from underground and I am glad to inform you that there is a good improvement in the lode in deep adit level east, now turning out rich work for tin … our different other points are producing their average quantity of tinstuff. Our stamps go to work tomorrow and shall make good returns of tin, and judging from appearances we shall continue to do so.'*

October 5: *'The new shaft progresses favourably … Our 60ft wheel is at work, and the tinstuff stamped out well. Next week I hope to report fully on the patent steam-stamps being tested at the manufactory as to the work coming from them.'*

October 12: *'The north tin lode continues its size (2ft wide) and is producing rich quality ore … we hope shortly to report the cutting of the south lode at a depth of 40 fathoms and from indications I have every reason to expect a good bunch of ore.'*

October 19: *'We now have plenty of water and our stamps in full work and yielding satisfactorily.'*

October 26: *'I have just come up from underground. We have great improvement in the north tin lode east. Champion lode has further improved, being a good lode at only 1.5 fathoms from the surface. The south cross cut men come up from underground are near the lode; the ground is changing favourably. I will send full particulars by post.'*

November 9: *'We have continued sinking the shaft under the adit level, and have sunk this last week by 7ft. The shaft sinking is by six men, price per fathom for sinking £4 … we are now clearing out the foundation for our new steam stamps. The engineer is now on the mine. He tells me that he shall fix and complete his work in a month from this time.'*

November 16: *'The north tin lode is opening up well. South Cross cut: the ground much improved, and now being driven for 40s per fathom. We are passing through branches of solid mundic. Seeing the change in the ground, and that so sudden, and being near the lode, my opinion is the lode when cut will be found large and rich for tin.'*

On 8 December the East Bottle Hill Mining Company had its first general meeting of shareholders. James Johnson, the man from Harrogate, chaired the meeting. The attendees heard that the new steam stamp machine would be going to work later that week on a 'rich pile of tinstuff'.

'Mr Hutton (of Messrs Hutton & McDonald, engineers, Leeds) said that he saw no reason to prevent the engine doing full work, which would save considerable cost of the old stamps.'

Meanwhile, the agent, presumably Joseph Eddy, said that there was no lack of lode stuff, which would last many years to take away at large profits.

With the accounts showing a bank balance of £1,233.10s2d and capital uncalled to date of £5,912, everything looked rosy. Indeed Mr Johnson stated that *'he and his friends were perfectly satisfied that they had a most valuable property'*.

Less than two weeks later Eddy reported that *'the old water stamps had run 50 tons of tinstuff through, which gave 32 cwts of tin, or 70lbs to the ton of stuff, which proves the lode beyond a doubt'*.

Certainly it sounds as though everything was fine and dandy. However, the much hoped for rich seams and impressive profits proved ever elusive. In May 1872 over four tons of black tin was sold by the East Bottle Hill Mine Company to Daubuz of Truro – a respectable quantity, but barely one sixth of the output from Great Wheal Vor that month.

In October, Captain Eddy noted that *'the lode in the whim shaft was now 18 inches wide and of a most promising character, and producing tin … but not to value'*. He added *'The ground in the south cross cut driving towards Old Bottle Hill main lode is now much easier for working. I think we are nearly through the hard bar of ground and if so we may soon expect to cut the lode.'*

Patience on the part of the Adventurers was doubtless starting to wear a little thin, everything seemed to be almost there, but not quite yet.

Heavy rains in December made the mine captain's job even more difficult as work was inevitably suspended in the whim shaft.

'A few days of dry weather will set us all right again', he wrote, early in the early part of the month but a week or so later there was still a lot of water around.

The weather, however, was by no means the only challenge facing the East Bottle Hill board.

The steam stamp-machine it seems, while it may have worked well in trials in Leeds, was a singular failure by the time it had travelled 300 miles or so south. In April 1873 Messrs Hutton & McDonald took the East Bottle Hill Mining Company to court on the grounds of breach of contract. They were chasing the sum of £240.12s (around £26,000) that being the balance outstanding on the machine they had supplied. Meanwhile, the Mining Company were counter claiming for the £212 .10s that they had already paid for a machine that they claimed was *'a total failure'*.

'Messrs Hutton & McDonald submitted that the defendants gave them definite instructions as to the construction of the machine, that they made it accordingly, that when tested before it left Leeds with ore sent from the mine it worked well in the expressed opinion of the company's agent, and that their responsibility was then at an end. The company, to the contrary,

contended that the machine did not do its work well, but when tried at the mine proved a thorough failure, and broke down.'

The case was heard by a special jury at the Yorkshire Spring Assizes and they found in favour of the Leeds firm on both accounts.

This was, it would appear, the final straw for the Adventurers and three months later notices appeared in the press announcing the voluntary liquidation of the East Bottle Hill Mining Company (Limited).

'Notice is hereby given that the Creditors of the above named Company are required to send the particulars of their claims together with their Names and Addresses, on or before the 10 day of August next, to Jehu Hitchins, of St Michael's House, St Michael's Abbey, Cornhill, in the City of London.'

A familiar figure on the local mining scene, Hitchins was the mine secretary, here as he was elsewhere in the neighbourhood.

Within a month of that August deadline a further notice appeared in the press inviting tenders for the job of removing the 60ft wheels and stamps at the mine, dismantling the same and re-erecting it all 'in a substantial and workmanlike manner' at the works of the East Vitifer Tin Mining Company (Limited) in the parish of North Bovey.

And so we had yet another unhappy ending to a chapter in the colourful story of nineteenth-century mining in the area. Although there was still room for a postscript.

In March 1875, the York Herald – remember the principal adventurers in this endeavour were Yorkshire based – printed notice of a call of 14 shillings a share being made by the East Bottle Hill Mining Company (Limited) the monies to be made payable by 6 April.

Remember that at that much happier first AGM a few years earlier it had been noted that there was almost £6,000 of uncalled capital – well now it seems the creditors were requiring that whatever sum was still uncalled should now be raised to settle debts.

Did it happen? Perhaps not, writing to the London Daily News nearly four years later, in January 1879 'A Subscriber' wrote: 'Sir, Hundreds of companies have within the last ten years gone into liquidation. Liquidators have been appointed, and the unfortunate shareholders have never afterwards heard anything more of the funds, nor any accounts of the winding up, nor any returns of money from the liquidators.

'The following are a few of the companies in which I was interested, and everything in connection with them seems to have sunk into a dead repose, except that the liquidators have called upon the shareholders for the full amount of their shares: The Braganza Gold Mining Company, East Bottle Hill Mining Company, Great Western Silver Mining Company, Duchy Great Consols Lead Mining Company, Canadian Native Oil Company, and several others.

'When liquidators are appointed by the Courts is it their duty to collect all the money from the shareholders and never render any account to them nor pay them back anything from the assets?'

Whatever happened in this particular instance in September 1883, East Bottle Hill was one of dozens of local companies that were struck off the Joint Stock Companies Register and declared dissolved.

However questions remain: were Eddy and his team about to hit the Champion lode, was he genuinely hopeful of East Bottle Hill yielding great profits for the out of town adventurers or was it, in part at least, a ploy to keep local miners in work?

1874 notice of sale of East Bottle Mine.

S. Baring Gould

THE KEENLY LODE

Old Uncle Pengerric a Captain was,
A dowser shrewd was he;
Who feathered his nest from the keenly lode
That ruined you and me.

The Captain was traversing Brandy Moor,
With hazel twig in hand,
The hazel twisted and turned about
And brought him to a stand.

CHORUS. Oh! the keenly lode, the keenly lode
Of balls the best, my boys;
Old Uncle Pengerric very well know'd
How to feather his nest, my boys.

Old Uncle Pengerric so big did brag
Of ore in Brandy Ball,
"Come fork out your money my Christian friends,
Your fortunes treble all!'

Now Uncle was reckoned a preacher stout,
A burning and shining light.
The people all said, "What he has in head
Will surely turn out right!'

CHORUS. Oh! the keenly lode, &c.

The Company floated, the Shares up paid,
The gold came flowing in.
He set up a whim, and began to sink
For the keenly lode of tin.

He had not burrowed but five foot six
'Ere he came to a buried hoss.
Said Uncle Pengerric, "No fault of mine,
Tho't turn out some one's loss!'

CHORUS. Oh! the keenly lode, &c.

The shaft descended, but ne'er a grain
Of ore was brought to ground.
And presently Uncle Pengerric too,
Was not in Cornwall found.

But wherever he goes, and whenever he talks,
He says:- "The rod told true,
It brought to me luck, but it turn'd and struck
At nought but an old horse-shoe."

CHORUS. Oh! the keenly lode, &c.

This ballad was collected and adapted by the Reverend Sabine Baring Gould (1834-1924), below is his account of the story. The ballad perfectly captures an all too common occurrence in the world of mining – then and now.

'Mr Bussell and I spent a week in 1894 at the Lugger Inn, Fowey, collecting songs. We met there one day an old miner, who asked us if we knew "The Keenly Lode," and on our saying that we did not, he gave us a long song on mining, that, however, lacked point. I have therefore re-composed the song. The air is that employed for " The Crocodile", an extravagant ballad, which has been published by Miss Broadwood in her County Songs. Her tune is practically the same as ours, but there are some differences. "The Crocodile" is a very popular ballad among old song-men, but no one would care to sing it in a drawing-room or at a concert, because it is vastly silly.
"A Keenly Lode" is a lode that promises well. A "Ball" is a mine in Cornish. In Cornwall every old man is termed "Uncle".

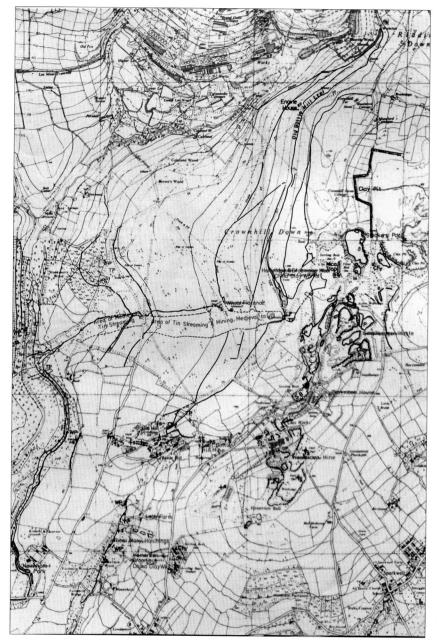

Wheal Florence
(see also Crownhill Down)

Situated on open moorland, on the north side of some ancient stream works on this part of Crownhill Down, about a third of a mile east of the Plympton-Lee Moor road, this mine appears not to have been an enterprise funded by some profit-hungry adventurers, rather a more traditional venture undertaken by a group of working miners.

Undoubtedly there were plenty such men in the area, and one can easily imagine that at a time when there may have been little other work in the neighbourhood, talk may have turned to where such a band of men might find enough tin to provide a living without the requirement for expensive investment in machinery.

Thus it was that in 1846 a number of men 'resumed the work of the ancients' and opened Wheal Albert – so named because the Lord Warden of the Stannaries at that time was Prince Albert, the Prince Consort, and husband of Queen Victoria.

Several rich branches of tin were discovered and in June a shaft was sunk to a depth of around six fathoms. Drained by a whim, the platform of which could be seen until relatively recently. The water was drawn by a 20ft waterwheel, with a 12ft wheel driving three heads of stamps.

The captain of the mine reported that *'most of the ore may be washed without stamping at all, the ground being a soft decomposed granite and china clay'*.

There are no recorded returns available and it would appear that within 18 months the miners had holed into the 'old men's workings' and the sett was abandoned.

In 1859 the sett was worked once more. Rechristened Wheal Florence, the activity again appears to have been focussed around an ancient tinwork, perhaps that was known as *'Bovewoode alias Bowwoode Beame'* and had been last referenced back in 1582.

With seemingly no shareholders to appease it appears that Wheal Florence was *'only slightly worked'* and there is little further reference to it, although somewhat intriguingly there is record of one pound being paid on 13 May 1871, the sum representing *'rent received under mining licence'*.

Mines of the Plympton orefield including Wheal Florence, that now sits below the Drakelands mine waste facility.

Hemerdon Consols

In 1854 John Henry Murchison published an interesting and much-quoted tome *British Mines Considered as a Means of Investment; With Particulars of the Principal Dividend and Progressive Mines in England and Wales*. Described in the *Mining World* as *'the Beau Brummel of secretaries … attired in the latest fashion'*, 30-year-old Jamaican-born Murchison was very much a dandy of the underworld who came to have interests in a number of mines up and down the country. The eldest son of a Scottish slave-owning doctor in Jamaica, Murchison had written his book at a time when a lot of gentlemen were looking to invest riches accrued off the back of the Industrial Revolution and his tome purported to be a guide to those mines around the country that might be worth a punt.

Now it just so happened that Hemerdon Consols had come on the radar at the very time that he was compiling information for the book, and when he was already acting as the secretary of neighbouring Boringdon Park Mine.

'Situate near Plympton, Devon, and in the neighbourhood of Bottle Hill, Wheal Sydney, and Boringdon Consols Mines. The lode is an unusually productive and promising one, for the comparatively limited stage of development yet arrived at, and the works are being carried out in a very spirited and energetic manner, under the management of Mr James Wolferstan [he was appointed in November 1853], *of the South Tamar, and other mines, and most satisfactory results are anticipated in less time, than it generally occupies to bring a young mine into a profitable state.'*

As was his wont, the author then went into some detail about the mine and what was already on site: *'A new 33in. double acting steam engine has just been erected by Mr West, the engineer, and in a few days the stamps will be at work.'* At the general meeting held on 11 August, 1854, Mr. Wolferstan reported as follows, *'The shaft is now sunk 14 fathoms from surface; and, as there is but little water in it, and the ground is moderately easy, I hope to get down to a depth of 20 fathoms, when we shall commence driving. This drivage will leave a high back, and lay open ground that will yield good supplies of Tin-work for the stamps. I was at the mine on Tuesday, and the men were then breaking finer rocks of Tin than any I had hitherto seen. The branch of Tin is about 10 inches wide, nearly solid, and free from mundic, so that it will not require burning. Should the lode prove to be equally good in driving on it, we shall very quickly return sufficient Tin to cover the whole of the outlay; and I see no reason to doubt this favourable result.'*

'The shaft is now down about 23 fathoms, and the lode is still yielding good work for tin. The stamps are to be set to work at the end of November, and it is expected that a good parcel of tin will shortly afterwards be sent to market.'

The narrative then included a further report from the mine manager, James Wolferstan, presented to the general meeting on the 8 November that year. *'I have the satisfaction of informing you that our machinery is nearly completed; the steam engine has been tried and proved to be perfect. The stamps axle is fixed, together with the frames and lifters. There is yet some work to do in getting the floors ready, and in bringing home the water, but I trust we shall be able to have all in readiness by the next pay day, when I hope that you and some members of the Committee, with other shareholders, will favour us with your presence.*

'The shaft is down about 23 fms. from surface, and we have now commenced to drive east and west on the course of the lode. The ground is favourable for driving, and will enable us to lay open rather rapidly good tribute pitches, that will keep, we trust, the stamps well occupied. The lode is not large at present, but is improving in this respect in depth, and the quality of the tin is good, and will no doubt realise a high price. The usual buildings have been erected, and consist of carpenters' and smiths' shops, with an account house over the former. I trust that due regard has been paid to economy as well as to efficiency, and that the whole will meet the approval of any deputation that may inspect it.

'The time occupied in the erection of the machinery has been much less than under the peculiar circumstances of the times could well have been expected, and I have the pleasure to say that the whole of the work is sound and good.'

Murchison concluded his review of Hemerdon Consols by noting that 'the present price of the shares is about 15s to 17s.6d per share, and may be considered a very advantageous investment, at anything about that price. 'The office,' he added, 'is at 38 Threadneedle Street.'

What Murchison neglected to point out in his overly enthusiastic assessment of Hemerdon Consols, was that he was the Company Secretary, and one wonders how his account might have read, had he produced his book two years later. It's interesting too to look at the share price he quoted as in May 1854, at a Hemerdon Consols general meeting, held in Murchison's own offices, accounts showed a balance of £650 (cash in hand) not withstanding which a call of 7/6d was made on each share.

By August although there was now a cash balance showing of nearly £900, there were calls in arrears of £448 and a further call of 2/6d was made, as it was again at the November meeting, by which time the cash-in-hand balance had dropped to £167.

In February 1855, presumably in an effort to address the problem mentioned by Wolferstan of *'bringing in the water'*, the adventurers of Hemerdon Consols cut a leat through the lands of George Strode on Hemerdon Ball.

The landowner was clearly not happy and paperwork changed hands concerning the valuation of compensation to be paid, there was also an agreement that as and when the leat *'at any future period shall be given up, the mining Company shall pay to George Strode, Esq. such a sum of money as will pay for filling in the leat and renewing the land to its original state'*.

In March 1855, with the war in the Crimea still raging – which was presumably the *'peculiar circumstances of the time'* that Murchison referred to (the Manager, Agents, and Men employed at Hemerdon Consols had just contributed £5.3s.3d to the Royal Commission of the Patriotic Fund to help widows and orphans who had lost breadwinners in the conflict, a similar amount was raised at Boringdon Consols and a little more, nearly £9 at Bottle Hill), Hemerdon Consols Mining Company sold four tons of tin. One ton was sold to Calenick Co. for £65, one to Trethellan for £64.10s, another to Daubuz for £4.7s.6d and the other to Bissoe's for £63.15s.

Five weeks later they sold another four tons, of similar quality tin to Trethellan and Calenick for a slightly lower figure of £63.2s.6d.

It appears to have been their final fling.

Come May, the *Morning Advertiser* reported that 764 forfeited shares in Hemerdon Tin Mine, on each of which £1.5s.6d had been paid, were being sold at between 2/6d and 7 shillings a share.

The following month, we read in the *London Daily News* that the number of forfeited shares for sale from Hemerdon Consols was up to 920. There was to be an auction at Garraway's Coffee House in Change Alley, Cornhill, London, on 27 June 1855 at 1pm precisely.

Mr TP Thomas, who had been instructed to make the sale, claimed that he had *'no hesitation in stating that they will be found to be speculations of more than ordinary promise. The shareholders are highly respectable and the local management is conducted by men of known practical experience and ability'*.

It was not good advice.

In 1856 it was reported that the mine was no longer working. Disputes with the other landowner and lessor, Admiral Woollcombe, were cited as the reason. It was reported in the *Mining Journal* that the mine had been running at a loss up to its closure with only £1,200 worth of tin being raised, against a capital outlay of *'some thousands of pounds'*.

At a Hemerdon Consols Mine meeting in March 1857 the accounts apparently showed a balance at the bankers of £10.12s.1d, with the balance of liabilities against the mine standing at £363.11s.1d. *'Resolutions were passed for abandoning the prosecution of the venture and directing the sale of the machinery and materials. Messrs Bayly, Britten, Adam, Murray & Martin, were appointed by the committee to wind up the affairs of the company. A vote of thanks to the chairman (John Bayly), terminated the proceedings.

The following year, in September (1858) an advertisement appeared in the local press: *'Mine to Let, Hemerdon Consols, within six miles of Plymouth and two of Plympton Station on the South Devon Railway. For Particulars apply to WJ Woollcombe, Solicitor, 13 Princess Square, Plymouth'*.

It's interesting to note that just a few weeks before that there had been great celebrations at Newnham, as Captain George Strode had celebrated his marriage to Miss Mary Hutchings Medlycott.

'The picturesque village of Ridgeway and "ancient borough" of Plympton were tastefully decorated … in compliment to the day.'

Around 70 sat down to dinner in a *'spacious and elegant marquee in Newnham Park'*. Among the many toasts was one to the tenantry on the Strode property, acknowledging that some tenants had been 50 or 60 years on the estate, with one, Manuel Maddick, enjoying some 70 years there.

Another local toast was to 'The Mining Interests' which was replied to by Captain Edwards of Wheal Sidney, who said that upwards of £24,000 (around £3 million today) had been expended on that mine, *'of which two-thirds was in labour alone, showing the great benefit of mining to the labouring classes'*.

Guests, incidentally included the Earl of Morley, Mr and Miss Woollcombe from Hemerdon House, Miss Treeby (Goodamoor), the Misses Coryton (Pentillie), the Misses Tolches (Ridgeway), G Soltau Esq. (Efford) and Miss Phillips (Ridgeway).

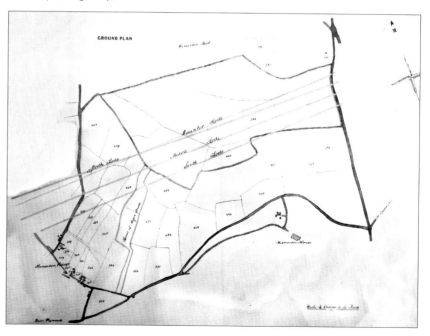

Map showing lodes of Hemerdon Consols in relation to Hemerdon Village (bottom left).

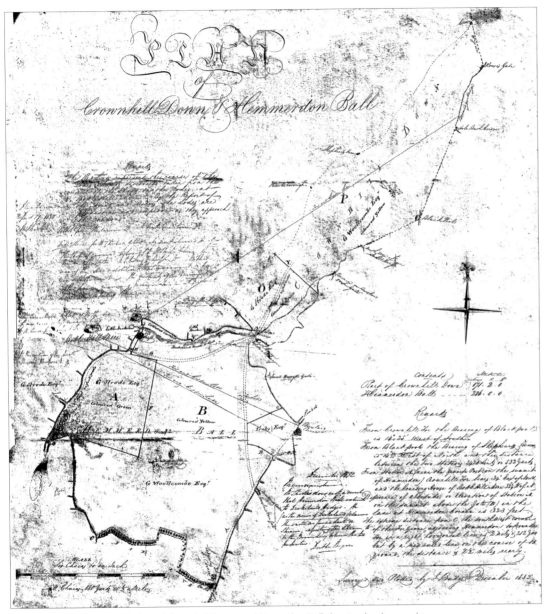

1832 plan of Crownhill Down and Hemerdon Ball showing land ownership.

Hemerdon Ball

The Plympton mines all sit in relatively close proximity to each other and so it is not surprising to see that over the course of the nineteenth century many of the same names crop up with regard to them.

As Bert Shorten put in his account of *Plympton's Metal Mines* (1985) *'in January, 1835 our old friends Messrs Hitchins senior and junior and Vigurs of Bottle Hill Mine, took out a grant which they held until August 1841'*.

In fact it seems that negotiations had begun three years earlier and the 21-year mining sett was originally agreed to start at Michelmas 1833.

Once again this site had, undoubtedly, been worked for centuries and written references take us back to the seventeenth century when we find it as *'Hamerton Ball, alias Great or East Hamerton Ball'*.

In October 1799 Captain Ward leased *'a sett, Hamerton Bowl mine, on behalf of a company of London gentlemen'*. However, we don't know what, if anything, happened with that enterprise.

Curiously there is an account of Worcester Regiment of Militia encamped on Hemerdon Ball during the winter of 1805, which would make it seem unlikely that there was any mining activity taking place there.

Certainly little appears to have happened with 'Hitchins and Vigurs' escapade either.

Although given licence to mine and search for tin and tin ore and all other metallic minerals within that parcel of ground called Hemerdon Ball (some 286 acres), it appears that they didn't go about their business *'with as many able men as can conveniently work the same ... according to the accustomed and improved methods of mining'*.

And so the clause *'if there be any failure or breach'* was invoked and notice of forfeiture on 11 August 1841.

The notice stated that *'there have been since the date of the indenture either no searching for working of the lodes* [which are shown on the plan opposite, drawn up by J Budge in December 1832] *or a searching and working of minerals only for a very short time and in an ineffectual manner and not with the number of men, nor with the engines and machinery nor by such methods on mining as are best calculated to procure the greatest returns and produce from the limits and in effect that the said limits have for a considerable time been wholly unwrought.'*

The situation seems to have been repeated the following decade when the holders of Wheal Mary Hutchings (Messrs Moffatt, Pickersgill and Pegler) obtained from George Strode permission to make a new channel through Hemerdon Ball, presumably to feed their other endeavour, an endeavour that they themselves forfeited in 1858.

Ten years later Miss Dorothea Strode was enjoying a somewhat better relationship with the new lessees of Hemerdon Ball, who had placed Henry Miners in charge of affairs there. From 1868 through to September 1874 at least, Miss Strode received over £340 in dues for Hemerdon Ball Consols and Hemerdon Clay Works. Secretary of the company was Truro-born, WHB (William Hussey Bloomfield) Kempe a retired wine merchant who was living in Lutton as a 39-year-old lodger at the time of the 1871 census. Married with four children, the youngest of whom, Lydia, had been born in Plymouth in 1867, Kempe was, according to Burt, Waite and Burnley (*Devon and Somerset Mines* 1984), the secretary at Hemerdon from 1872-75, having succeeded John Arnold who was in post in 1871. Again, quite what happened here in the 1870s is unclear: however, what we do know is that on 3 September 1878 Kempe was found dead, having drowned in the Thames at Woolwich.

In 1889 Joel Manley and Thomas Vosper, who had simultaneously taken a lease at Wheal Sidney, obtained a *'licence for trial within certain lands at Hemerdon'* from Miss Strode, although the term was twice extended – from 8 November 1890, to 8 August 1891 and then 8 December 1891 no further activity appears to have taken place over the next two decades. Not until interested parties started to act on a discovery made by the St Austell chemist and scientist, John Nicholls, in 1867 – Wolfram.

Nicholls had been successfully working the China Clay in the area since 1855. Prior to the nineteenth century the importance of china clay had not been understood, but its presence on Lee Moor, long known, hence the prevalence of names like White HIll, White Pit and White Works.

Nicholls shared his wolfram discovery with local mine captain, Richard Williams, and the two discussed the possibility of opening a mine but at that stage the significance of wolfram – iron tungstate – was by no means fully appreciated and the economics of extraction simply didn't work and so it was left, for the time being.

However, before we go on to look at what happened next at Hemerdon, let's take a look at some of the other mining adventures that took place within and around the modern Plymouth boundaries.

Wheal Harriet Sophia

Mentioned in the *Mining Journal* 1859/60, it sat on the northern edge of Boringdon Park Wood and was evidently named after the then 50 year-old wife of Edmund Parker second Earl of Morley, Harriet Sophia Coryton. Born, Harriet Sophia Parker, she was her husband's second cousin, he was her second husband, the first being William Coryton, of Pentillie Castle, in1834. William, however, died three years later and Harriet Sophia married Parker in 1842.
Curiously enough we know considerably more about her than we do about the copper mine that bore her name.

Harriet Sophia Parker (1809-97)
Painted in Rome in 1842 by Richard Buckner.

Wheal Reynard

Again, a little-known adventure one mile east of Hemerdon Ball, at Baccamore Pits.

There is evidence of tin working at Baccamore in the mid-seventeenth century and in 1846 a shallow adit was driven north for 70 fathoms, *'cutting first a copper, and then a tin lode'*, noted Bert Shorten.
He added: *'Samples showed good values at 10 fathoms below surface, and a level was extended for 20 fathoms'*. The venture was considered worthy of further development, but permission to exploit the find was refused by the owner of the adjoining land and the sett closed down. *'Although I have been unable to verify this, it is likely that more work was carried out at a later date.'*

The spelling of the name suggests this may have been on known hunting-ground, as reynard is the French for fox and Mr Reynard was a popular way of describing the bushy tailed creature in contemporary accounts of fox hunting.

Cann Mine

During the course of excavation work for the Cann Slate Quarry in the early 1820s a silver-lead lode was revealed at the side of the Plym. Initially known as the Canal Mine, it was worked briefly by William Petherick from St Blazey, but it seems that he conducted little more than exploratory work. Indeed it wasn't until it was reopened in 1829 by the well-known Cornish engineer Joseph Treffry that the mine was worked. (Treffry was actually born Joseph Austin in Plymouth in 1782 but when his uncle, William Esco Treffry of Fowey, died in 1808 he changed his name by deed poll).

By the time Joseph became interested in Canal Mine, he had become a prominent partner in Fowey Consols Mine at Tywardreath, then the most productive copper mine in Cornwall employing 1,680 personnel. In 1828 he drew up plans for a new safe harbour at Par and greatly improved the safety of that anchorage.

Here in the Plym Valley he oversaw the sinking of three shafts: one on the west of the canal, two on the east.

A small steam engine appears to have been deployed on the site along with a 22-ft waterwheel that provided the power for pumping, drawing and crushing.

In 1832 Charles Thomas, the then Captain of Dolcoath Mine in Camborne, inspected Cann Mine and reported that it lay in a slate formation that contained 'a little copper'.

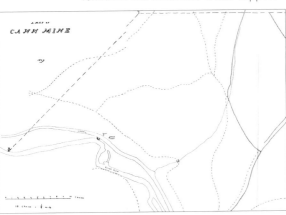

Above: Joseph Treffry, the celebrated Cornish engineer, born in Plymouth in 1782.
Left: Cann Mine, opened by Treffry in 1829 and listed as being derelict by 1859.

Crownhill Down

With all the advances in technology that took place in the nineteenth century it may seem a little odd that in the middle of it all a sett for streaming tin was granted to two mining agents, John Gifford of Bottle Hill Mine and Thomas Horswill. We have already encountered both gentlemen with regard to later mining activities in the area, but this is an interesting reversion to the way the old men of the moor worked.

The lease drawn up with George Strode gave the two miners '*license and authority by streaming or by superficial works in the nature of streaming and not by mining by shafts or levels*' to work Crownhill Down, or at least that portion known as 'The Pitts' and, significantly, for tin only.

The agreement, drawn up on 27 October 1855, was for '*three years from Michelmas last with the power of renewal for eighteen additional years*'. Dues were set at 1/12th, higher than usual presumably because the miners overheads were low, and an annual rent of £20, but not in the first year.

'*It shall not be lawful for the streamers to take up or divert any waters at any point above or within the distance of ten fathoms below the head or spring or course of the water now supplying Newnham mansion as potwater.*' There was also a proviso that should any pollution occur the sett would be forfeited.

'*All dirty and adulterated water unavoidably arising from any operations shall be confined to a sufficient channel so as not to escape but be conveyed without waste so that the whole thereof may ultimately pass by a launder of shute over the mill leat into the River Tory.*'

We have no idea of how successful this venture turned out to be, but in the event, the lease was surrendered on the 1 December 1856 just a year or so after it had been signed, and presumably before any significant amount of rent was due.

For the best part of 20 years all was quiet on the Down and then in February 1874, at a time when the industry was struggling, another Bottle Hill man, Joseph Eddy, together with John Peverall of Newcross, London, took a twelve month lease from George Strode, to explore the area with their workmen and agents '*to make trials for tin, copper, lead, silver, iron and clay by making shafts and adits on part of Crownhill Down and other lands adjoining*'. Rent was set at £20 for the year, but there was also to be compensation for any damages. Messrs Eddy and Peverall had, within that twelve-month period, the option to claim a sett.

They didn't. However, two years later Hugh Waldron Dallas, a 25-year-old mining engineer from Westminster, did.

Dallas, whose 58-year-old father, also called Hugh Waldron Dallas, was a successful colliery owner, and took a 21-year lease from Miss Strode '*for all mines of iron and iron ore and all other metals and minerals or iron under and throughout Crownhill Down, Little Fernhill and Coteland*'.

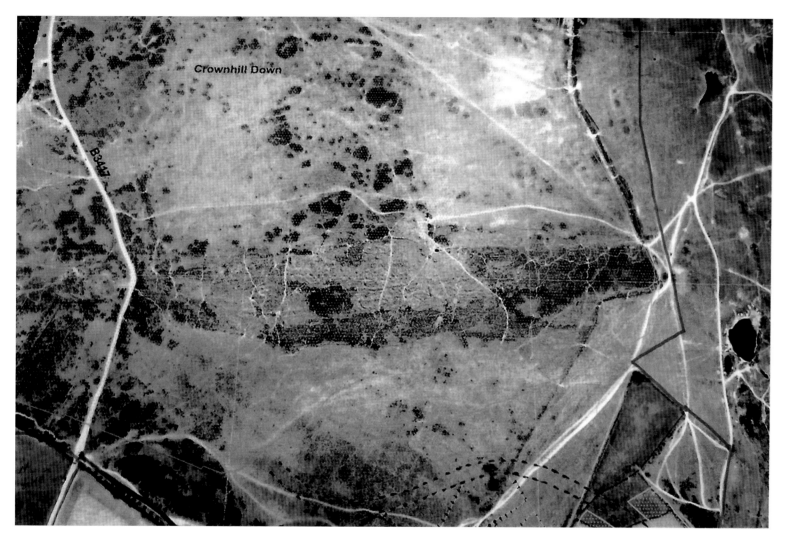

Above: Evidence of tin streaming on Crownhill Down, now covered by Wolfs' mine waste facility.

The lease stipulated that any building intended for any part of the estate of Little Fernhill or Coleland would need Miss Strode's approval. There was also an annual rental of £6 for the first year, rising to £10 thereafter and dues of a shilling per ton on all minerals of iron.

As was so often the case in such matters, there appears to have been very little subsequent activity, certainly nothing to suggest this arrangement ever bore fruit.

Mount Batten Iron Mine (Wheal Morley)

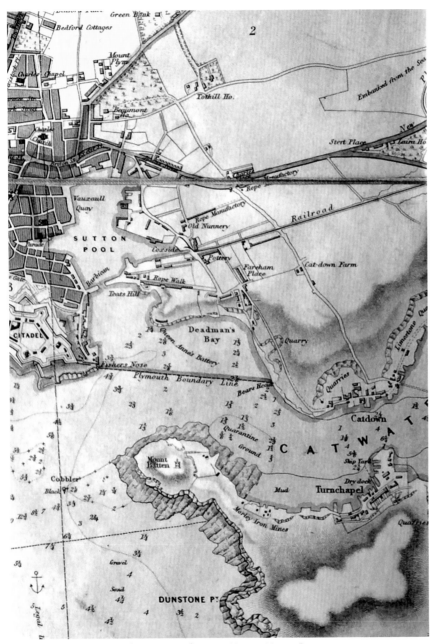

1841 map showing Morley Iron Mines, Mount Batten.

No account of nineteenth-century mining in the Plymouth area would be complete without reference to the iron mine ventures around the mouth of the Plym.

On 1 April 1839, perhaps not the most auspicious of days for launching a serious and expensive endeavour, William Conway of Plymouth secured from John, Earl of Morley, a six-month licence to dig for iron ore in Mount Batten field.

Not just iron in fact, but all *'metals and minerals save except fossils and lime stone of any kind … whatsoever.'*

On 1 August 1839, Lord Morley's agent, James Yolland, sent a written report to his master, to the effect that *'no iron has yet been shipped, and I know of no means of hastening it'*. However, true to the age of snail-mail as opposed to email, our man Yolland added a postscript: *'since writing the foregoing I have received a message that a cargo of iron ore is to be shipped.'*

And indeed it was, as a few days later some 56 tons of ore of *'very good appearance'* was shipped out bound for Neath in South Wales.

In February the following year Conway, together with Henry Trefusis Smith, and Joseph Giles, agreed to lease the Mount Batten field sett from Lord Morley for a 21-year period, along with a piece of land containing *'ruinous houses, quays, wharfs and beach at Mount Batten.'*

Henry Smith was a 46-year-old solicitor from Morice Town, Devonport and as he was signing up for this adventure and was also involved in the administration process of selling machinery from the Cornish Kellewerris Mine in the parish of Kea, and promoting the Godolphin Mines. A prominent figure in Morice Town, it's not clear what attracted him to the Mount Batten scheme but it appears not to have gone well. Two of their cargoes of ore were rejected by the South Wales smelting-houses, on the grounds that the cargoes *'being not ore but rubbish'*, and still in February 1840 we find John and Henry Trefusis Smith apparently facing bankruptcy charges.

Whatever the outcome, Smith clearly bounced back and was elected a councillor for Morice Town. In 1853 he turned down the Mayoralty of Devonport and in 1855 he served as Under-Sheriff to Carew Pole of Anthony in Cornwall.

Meanwhile, to return to Mount Batten, as if further complicate things, the first Earl of Morley, 68-year-old John Parker, died the following month, February 1840, and his 30-year-old son and heir, Edmund Parker (whose wife was Harriet Sophia – after whom, as we have seen, another mine was named) succeeded him.

It would appear that one of the conditions that Conway et al signed up to was making good any unnecessary pits or shafts (for the sake of local cattle) and this it seems proved prohibitively expensive when trying to make money from the mining operations there.

Another solicitor, J Elliot-Square, writing on 31 October 1840 to Edmund Parker requesting to be released from the covenant to remake the ground, and removing all the materials raised, and for permission to erect buildings. The material they were working with was evidently excellent material for making bricks and earthenware. Indeed, Conway was doubtless well aware of the suitability of the material as he had his own building company.

Having said that, Elliot-Square reported that *'this business … is … certainly the most slovenly that it has ever fallen to my lot to witness'*.

In January 1841 some 34 tons of stone and 87 tons of clay were shipped out of Wheal Morley and in February samples of iron pyrites were sent by Lord Morley to the Polytechnic Chemical School in London.

Having examined the stuff, W Maughan, the chemist tasked with the analysis, concluded that it was 41 parts sulphur, 48 iron, 4 silica, and 7 alumina. He wrote: *'I consider this a very superior and productive sulphur ore, but it is not an ore from which good iron can be advantageously obtained, sulphur ores not being worked for that metal.'*

Later that summer Lord Morley ventured out from Saltram to inspect the site himself: *'I went with Dr Buckland yesterday morning to see it, but I cannot quote him for any favourable report of it, so you may at once tell Mr Smith … he thought it a very poor speculation.'*

And, that, it seems, was that, although it wasn't until December 1844 that Messrs. Smith, Giles and Conway wrote to Lord Morley:

'We the lessees having long since ceased to exercise the license and authority granted … being desirous of abandoning the same … do hereby surrender unto the Earl of Morley the indenture etc.'

By the time we next hear of Wheal Morley, it is Edmund's son, Albert who is in charge, Edmund having died in August 1864. Edmund Parker had been very well connected, he was a Government Whip in the House of Lords for six years, Deputy Lieutenant of Devon and a Lord of the Bedchamber to Prince Albert – hence perhaps the choice of name for his own son.

Educated at Eton and Balliol College, Oxford, Albert Parker enjoyed a similarly illustrious status, a Lord-in-Waiting under Gladstone, he served as Under-Secretary of State for War for five years and had a brief spell as the First Commissioner of Works. Just 23 when he inherited the Earldom, it was in August 1873 that he granted the mine agent, Richard Moore, of Plymouth and North Bovey, a 21-year lease on portions of the Mount Batten estate.

1st Earl of Morley

Albert Edmund Parker, 3rd Earl of Morley

Richard Moore, described as a traveller in minerals, was not, however, a well man and he died, aged just 53, six months later, on the last day of January 1874.

His widow, Charlotte, 16 years his junior, attempted to auction the lease via Hussey & Sons at an auction at the Queens Hotel, Exeter, on Thursday 9 August 1877.

The auction was conducted by 52-year-old Edward Barlow Hussey, a former brewer, who had inherited the family business (established in 1777) on the death of his father five years earlier.

According to the account in the Western Daily Mercury two days later:

'Mr Hussey submitted the property in an elaborate speech. The property, he remarked, abutted on a quay belonging to the works, and there were rights over two other quays alongside of which vessels of 300 tons burden could load and consequently the whole could be worked at very small expense. Leaving the ironworks out of the question, and taking the simple production of limestone and clay (which was capable of producing the best bricks in the kingdom), the ochre (which was of good and usable quality) and the umber (which was also of good colouring capacity), he considered this property a wonderful piece of ground. Even the refuse was capable of being turned to account by vessels in search of ballast. It was close to one of the largest towns in the West of England, and one which was always increasing; so much so indeed that when he visited it

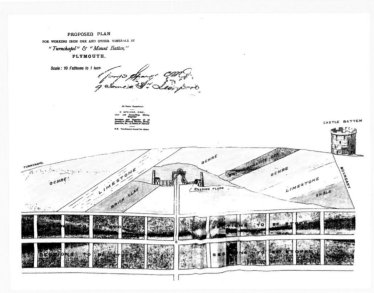

Captain Spargo's plan for Turnchapel and Mount Batten

from time to time he found parts of it so altered that he had to ask where he was. Therefore one scarcely needed to go out of the town to get rid of what could be raised from these works.'

The property was worth a fortune to anyone who would speculate, and was capable of making a profit of £2,000 a year.

Mr Huggins, Solicitor of Exeter, started the bidding at £2,500, upon which Mr Hussey said the Government valuation was £10,000.'

In the event no further bid was made *'and the property was bought in'*. Which presumably meant that Hussey & Sons were the new owners of the lease.

It would seem that they did little with it. In November 1880 Hussey wrote to Lord Morley's land steward, Samuel Newberry, asking if his lordship might be minded to renew the lease when it expired and if he would be prepared to drop the royalty on clay from a shilling to sixpence a ton. Four years later, this time with a partner in the enterprise, WD Mann of Torquay, he wrote again to Newberry asking for an extension to lease that was now 11 years in, *'as we now have an opportunity of the said property being worked in an energetic manner'*.

However, *'owing to the proposed extension of the railway to Turnchapel, and the effect that this might have on the value of his lands at Mount Batten, his Lordship was not disposed to change the terms or extend the period of the lease'*, wrote Owen Baker (manuscript papers).

As they stood, the terms of the leases were quite restrictive with regard to disturbing the land and *'an existing agreement between the landowner and Her Majesty's Principal Secretary of State for the War Department as to the continuance of ball practice on the whole of the said lands.'*

'Hussey and Mann decided to work the property on a large scale, hoping to obtain more favourable terms from Lord Morley. Baker adds, *'An increasingly vituperative series of correspondence ensued between 1884 and 1893, but Lord Morley remained unmoved and the last attempt at working iron at Mount Batten came to an end.'*

One wonders, however, if Lord Morley was better informed that his lessees gave him credit for. WD Mann, William Dodge Mann of Torquay, came to this venture as the secretary of the East Vitifer Mine at North Bovey. In it's day Vitifer had been a very profitable enterprise however, in the early 1870s, its glory days appeared to be on the wane. Just prior to his death, Vitifer had been managed by Richard Moore, who had taken on the original lease at Mount Batten, following his untimely demise a man already familiar to us from Hemerdon Ball and Wheal Mary Hutchings, took over at Vitifer – Henry Miners.

In April 1876, Mann, 69, describing himself as a share manager living in Torquay – the Vitifer office was in his home office – found himself defending charges of fraud against him at Bristol Assizes.

The plaintiff, Miss Alice Matthews who ran a girls' school in Torquay, claimed that Mann had sold her shares at an inflated price and had claimed that there was *'sufficient tin on the grass'* to pay each shareholder £5 and that the investment was *'as safe as the Bank of England'*. When asked if there was likely to be a call on shares, he allegedly replied, *'Yes but there will be no necessity for it, you will have a dividend very soon and it will not be long before you have the principal back as well'*.

Mann then reputedly added that he expected to be *'so rich from the profits that as there are only myself and my wife, and we don't require the money, I intend building alms houses and a church on the mine, and to give away the money for the glory of God.'*

The court had earlier expressed much mirth at the suggestion that Mann had ensured that the proceedings at the mine always opened with prayers and hymns, and at meetings he distributed tracts, and *'he thought it was said those religious performances would tend to the successful result of the mine – (laughter)'*.

It appeared that at Christmas 1875 £11,795 had been expended in the mine (Mann was on an income of £100 a year) and that the company with that expenditure actually succeeded in raising £700 worth of tin, but the wages, he was sorry to tell them, and other matters connected with the raising of the tin, had exceeded the £700 by £400, so that the cost of raising £700 worth of ore was £1,000'.

There had been £10,000 of capital investment, and *'out of the property of the mine the machinery would realise about £2,000 and there would be a deficit of over £8,000'.*

Miss Matthews had purchased 39 shares for £144.7s.6d in 1873, she had received no dividend and the shares could not now be sold for anything.

In his defence Mann denied most of the allegations and his solicitor offered Miss Mann £175 for the shares. After all the mine was still operating, although it was suggested that it would need at least another £5,000 or £6,000 of investment before it would become viable.

The jury were unable to reach a verdict and His Lordship 'expressed his regret, remarking that it would necessitate another trial'.

Perhaps a key element in the case was the then current story about Emma Mine in Utah, which was referenced during the proceedings. In the Spring of 1871 a couple of American businessmen, one of them a Senator, had attempted to make a significant amount of money by selling the 'worked out' previously profitable Emma Silver Mine to unsuspecting British investors. As it transpired, Vitifer remained in production until 1887, although it's not clear whether any real money was made apart from by the landowners, the miners, the solicitors and the auctioneers.

Oddly enough, Charles Maunder, who was the chief agent at East Vitifer in the late 1870s and throughout 1885-6, wrote in November 1886, on behalf of Hussey, to Lord Morley's land agent, asking again for renewal of the Mount Batten lease. *'I may add that I am just returned from Mr Baylys who has arranged for the new 21-year lease and added some more ground to make it a good sett.'*

However in his reply, Newberry noted that he had never met Maunder, and he would need to know the position of Moore's representatives. *'I might also add'*, he concluded, *'that since the lease referred to was granted and even since Mr Hussey's correspondence, circumstances have arisen which will require further consideration and necessarily require my bringing the subject before Lord Morley's notice before acquiescing in any such arrangement.'*

The Bayly lease was for land alongside Lord Morley's land and while it was argued that each on their own would struggle, the combined sett could be worked to everyone's gain.

Lord Morley was unmoved, however, after all it wasn't just about the railway. The Batten Breakwater had just been built, as had the Castle Inn, with a new slipway, so who knew exactly what the future had in store for Mount Batten. The idea of putting housing, for example, where there was mining activity going on, no matter how far underground, was not overly appealing.

An interesting observation on the situation was provided by William Kelly, ship-builder at Mount Batten Yard. Kelly had been sent the correspondence between Newberry and Messrs Hussey and Mann, by Lord Morley's man. On 8 August 1889 he replied as follows:

'You ask my opinion on the matter and I give it for what it may be worth, which I fear is not much as I am ignorant of mining matters. I have always heard that no one ever made these works pay; and seeing the awfully dilapidated condition of the whole of the buildings and premises and the tremendous outlay that would be required before commencing operations and also the cost of transporting the iron ore to a coal district and the comparatively low value of it when delivered there, I cannot see any prospect of its being made a paying concern.

My candid (private) opinion is that Mann is simply trying to get something for the remainder of his term in the lease of the property adjoining this.

I should also think that if there is any probability of the railway coming this way the railway company would strongly object to the place being undermined.

Of course it would make no difference to me as long as the ground was safe for shipbuilding purposes.'

Did Kelly's missive make any difference to the situation? Probably not, but doubtless it hardened the resolve of Lord Morley and despite Mann and Hussey obtaining new plans, the lease was never renewed.

Two views of the Castle Inn, Mount Batten

The heavily quarried Mount Batten at the mouth of the Plym.

Around this time major quarries lined both sides of the Plym. Yielding vast quantities of limestone most of it went on building Plymouth's rapidly expanding infrastructure, the creation of the massive, mile-long Breakwater in Plymouth Sound (1811-44) and the establishment of the 915-ft Batten Breakwater at the entrance to the Cattewater (1878-81).

It's interesting to note that the quarrying process was helped enormously around this time by the invention of one Alfred Bernhard Nobel – dynamite. For many years black gunpowder had been deployed for blasting rock, that and gun cotton. But Nobel's chance invention (one of hundreds he patented but the one that established his fame and principal fortune), made life much easier, although not necessarily less risky in the early days.

Nobel was not the only player in the field, however, and in October 1876 a Frenchman by the name of Camille Espir came down to Plymouth and, under the direction of Captain Julius Roberts RMA, carried out the first ever experiments with his 'new explosive' in the limestone quarries of Cattedown and Pomphlett.

M Espir's powder 'closely resembles in appearance mahogany sawdust', and Captain Roberts was charged with reporting to the War Department and the Board of Trade with regard to its efficacy.

Two years later, in April 1878, Captain Fairholm & Co. obtained permission to establish a factory for the manufacture of Monsieur Camille Espir's explosive powder made of sawdust (26%), sulphur (14%) and nitrate of soda (60%) at Hexton Quarry and Quay at Hooe.

Curiously enough M Espir of Notting Hill London, was declared bankrupt the following year, only to manage to have the bankruptcy annulled in October 1880.

Incidentally, Nobel having read a premature obituary condemning him for profiting from the sale of arms (he also owned the Bofors company among others, some of which are still trading today) decided to bequeath the bulk of his fortune to the establishment of prizes for academic, cultural and scientific advances.

Pomphlett Ochre Works

Mount Batten wasn't the only short-lived mining enterprise on Lord Morley's land on the eastern banks of the lower reaches of the Plym, there was also a sett *'for working iron, iron ore and all other metallic minerals and fossils (except limestones)'* granted to George and Glinn Pridham on 1 January 1873.

At that time when what was left of the local tin industry had started to falter, the Pridhams, a father and son team of solicitors, George was 68 and Glinn (Glinn was his mother's maiden name) somewhat unusually took on a lease that gave them rights to *'dig adits, lay tramways and ship ores, but not to disturb the surface of ground hitherto undisturbed by quarrying'*. The dues to Lord Morley were straight forward, 9d a ton on iron ores up to 5,000 tons, a shilling per ton for any quantity above that, and one-eighteenth on all other produce.

With no available figures on what if anything was actually dug out of the site, there is an intriguing note from George Pridham to Morley's agent Samuel Newberry. Written on 23 August 1875, two and a half years after the original agreement, Pridham says that: *'Pomphlett Ochre Works are to be visited tomorrow by a friend, with the view of making an offer for purchase of the concern ... He will of course want to know the terms of the holding and probably will object as regards the (Culm) yards it is only from year to year.'*

In October 1876 Pridham senior wrote again to Newberry following a meeting of the two of them.

'At our interview of 2 October two things were established as facts – viz:
1). That the lessee of the Quarries has no right to anything but limestone.
2). That the Lessee of the Ochre Works has no right to any limestone and the question then under discussion was how a large mass of ochreous matter (which was then called clay) now obstructing the access to limestone rock behind it should be dealt with.

'I have had a word with Mr Harvey on this question, who is perfectly willing that the quarry lessee shall remove and sell any required quantity of this clay on condition that some proportion of the proceeds of sales shall be receivable by him.'

Again we are not privy to any of the actual quantities involved, but what we do know is that less than three months later George Pridham was dead and the only other paperwork we have on the matter came in November 1883 when W Woollcombe replied to Newberry's request for two years' rent in respect of Pomphlett Stores. *'WIth regard to "dues" I think you will find no dues are payable unless the sett is being worked, which is not the case and has not been for several years.'*

Wheal Emily

Located at Wembury, Wheal Emily (named after the eldest daughter, and also wife, of the landowner, Charles Biggs Calmady) was described as a lead antimony mine that was operating in the 1840s, but perhaps not for long.

Henry Rook, a Devonport publican and brewer (he ran the Garden Inn in Garden Street, Morice Town), was purser of the mine, 'for a short time' prior to December 1848. We know that because it was mentioned in his court appearance that month when he was declared insolvent.

Clearly that didn't stop him running a licenced premises as in January he was sentenced to three months' imprisonment for obtaining malt on false pretences.

Wheal Emily appears to have closed down sometime in 1849, only to be revived later that year by a new body of shareholders, including Charles Calmady and a new mine captain, W Willcock. The new purser was a Mr R Sergeant and Henry Molyneux was secretary.

As with the first foray of the adventurers of Wheal Emily it's not clear how successful or otherwise the new personnel were in terms of extracting valuable minerals (boulangerite was also found there – the ores are complex mineralogically comprising of lead and antimony) from the mine, but a clue may be found in the case Captain Willcock brought against Calmady for non payment of wages in December 1851.

In the course of the case it emerged that Willcock had bought his shares in June 1850 and sometime between then and December 1851 he had sold his interest to Mrs Mary Parnell. Calmady, meanwhile, had evidently not paid up the amount of his calls and the Court of the Queen's Bench found in favour of the Mine Captain.

One wonders if the wedding of Calmady's third daughter, Honora, to Lieutenant John Augustus Boyd, in May 1850, had any bearing on his lordship's finances.

It's not clear who the other shareholders were, but it seems there were a number of Londoners involved and the November 1850 meeting had been held in Finsbury.

There is a suggestion that the mine was still operating in the early part of 1852, but certainly no record after that.

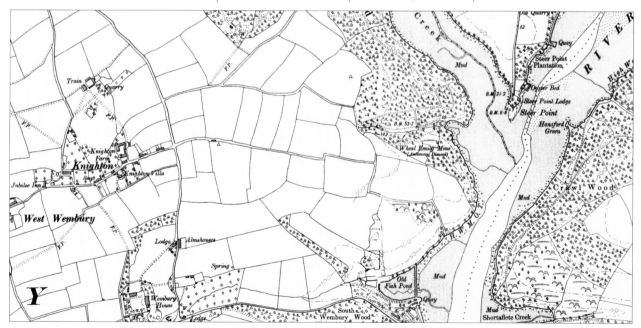

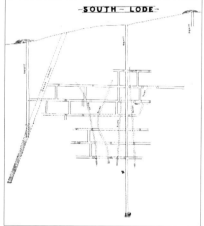

Top: *Charles Calmady's daughters Laura Ann (aged 2) and Emily (aged 4), on the right in 1823.* Left: *Wheal Emily, to the west of that point where the Cofflete Creek meets the River Yealm.* Above: *Part of Emily's shaft layout.*

Wheal Whitleigh

Map c.1850s with Owen Baker marking Wheal Gennys, Wheal Langmaid and the enigmatic Wheal Southway.

Clearly the geology of the wider Plymouth area points to potential underground riches in a number of places. One area that perhaps doesn't seem to have been on anyone's radar however was Whitleigh ... at least not until the 1840s. Much of the research referred to already with regard to this area during nineteenth century was the fruit of many years of research by life-long mining enthusiast and academic, Owen Baker and rather than attempt to rework his notes on the attempts to develop Tamerton Foliot as a mining district here, in full, is Owen's account of what happened:

In the mid 1840s plans were produced by the Plymouth and Tavistock Turnpike Trust for a branch road from Knackersknowle (now Crownhill) to Tamerton, and in March 1848 tenders for its construction were invited. The works, which involved an extensive cutting at Whitleigh Hill were scheduled for completion by the end of that year, but owing to persistent bad weather and the contractors' refusal to use any sort of machinery, operations were only half completed by March 1849. To make matters worse, Edmund Gennys of Whitleigh Hall, the owner of the land, filed an unsuccessful suit in chancery against the Turnpike Trust alleging improper purchase of the land, and by November, a stormy meeting of the Trust heard, that owing to unfortunate circumstances the cutting had been dug in slightly the wrong place, necessitating a much deeper excavation than originally intended and an additional expenditure of £700.

Another unexpected feature of the work was the discovery in the cutting, of North-South veins of blue clay (flookan) containing silver-lead ores, a discovery of which, bearing in mind the successful lead mines then working at nearby Bere Alston, speculators were quick to take advantage.

In December 1849 mining setts were granted over a wide area to the north and south of the cutting and two mining companies – named Wheal Gennys (sometimes called Guinness) and Langmead (or Langmaid) both after their respective landowners – were formed; mining operations beginning in January and March 1850 respectively. By February all the shares in the mines were not only taken, but in demand at a premium and by the time the road was opened in May, the *Mining Journal* could say that *'both mines were being commenced with vigour'*.

At Wheal Langmaid on the north, a shaft was being sunk and made secure for whim and footway and a level being driven on the lodes from near to the stream. The Wheal Gennys company was far more ambitious and by June was erecting a 36" pumping engine, count house and carpenters' and blacksmiths' shops. By July, the Adventurers were able to dine in the spacious count house to celebrate the starting of the new engine in its unusual flat-roofed house. By this time the engine shaft was 19 fathoms deep but the whole mine could be drained by the engine working only for an hour in the mornings and evenings. Continued operations revealed a wide lode of clay, impregnated with lead and by October several tons of ore were at the surface.

Work also continued at Wheal Langmaid, the shaft being sunk to a depth of 17 fathoms, and a horse whim installed, while in December 1850, a meeting of the adventurers, held at Tamerton, approved the erection of a 20-ft waterwheel to facilitate the drainage of the mine.

Throughout 1851 both mines continued operations. Wheal Gennys engine shaft reaching a depth of 52 fathoms, with levels driven north and south at 22, 32 and 42 fathoms. Between July and November £204.4s.4d worth of lead was sold by the mine, but this was not sufficient to pay costs.

Early in 1853 disaster struck when the Gennys engine shaft collapsed owing to the soft nature of the ground; fortunately no miners were underground at the time. This was the end of Wheal Gennys, the Adventurers resolving early in May that it was inexpedient to continue further operations, and that the mine be at once abandoned.

The following month, after two years of virtually unproductive effort, Wheal Langmaid was also abandoned and offered for sale.

Despite its untimely end, prospects at Wheal Gennys were sufficiently encouraging for a new company named Wheal Whitleigh to take up the option on the sett, together with all the machinery of the old company. Comprising 6,400 shares at 30s each, 7/8ths of which were taken up, the new company had adequate capital to begin the unproductive task of clearing the clogged shaft and levels.

By June 1853 the mine was cleared of debris, the work of extending the bottom (52 fm) level had begun, and some ore was already at the surface awaiting the installation of a crusher. The ore stockpile had grown to 30 tons by November, but the very large proportion of clay which it contained caused problems, as more water was needed to clean the ores than was being pumped from the mine. The difficulty was eventually overcome by water being pumped back again from the dressing-floors for re-use.

The underground workings of Wheal Whitleigh were extended throughout 1854 and 1855 to a depth of 82 fathoms, and a horizontal extent of at least 50 fathoms. The lode, of great size, impregnated throughout with lead, always promising to cut rich but never fulfilling its promise, yielded a regular but small output of lead. About 100 tons of dressed ore was produced during the two years, but nothing like enough to pay costs, and, on 5 December 1855, the mine, machinery, including the 36" engine, and the account house furniture was sold piecemeal by auction.

For several years the mineral potential of the area lay dormant, until the final attempt at putting Tamerton on the mining map was made by yet another company – Devonshire Silver Lead, which began operations on the old Whitleigh sett on 13 April 1859, by driving an adit south on the course of the lode.

Reports issued by this company were always very optimistic. For instance in October 1859 Captain Hodge reported, 'We have a splendid lode the size of which is as yet unknown. The depth of the hill is about six fathoms and towards the bottom it is full of lead.'

In November a meeting of the shareholders held at the Golden Lion Hotel, Plymouth, heard that since the commencement of work 97 fathoms of ground had been laid open, by means of an adit and crosscut, surface pitting and a trial shaft. These works it was claimed, had revealed two well-defined lodes 12 fathoms apart. Reports of the mine published weekly in the *Mining Journal* are confused and contradictory when examined in

detail, but it would appear that future hopes for the venture were placed on driving a cross cut from the poor eastern lode to the main or western lode which was expected to be much richer. The crosscut was driven on a newly discovered east-west lode carrying particles of copper, sulphurmundic, zinc blende and a little silver lead, but nothing in economic quantities. High hopes were held out for a rich shoot of ore at the junction of the two lodes, but when this was cut in March 1860, the long-awaited main lode, although 12 feet wide, was composed mainly of clay with some spots of lead.

Hope began to fade as levels were driven on the lode without signs of any improvement. Captain Hodge vainly attempted to keep the Adventurers cheerful by reporting in April *'a more promising lode cannot be seen but still poor for lead. I am expecting an improvement every day.'*

Whitleigh Hall, home of Edmund Bastard Henn Gennys, High Sheriff of Devon. Edmund's wife Ann, cut the first turf of Wheal Gennys on Wednesday 9 January 1850.

Said to have been an early seventeenth-century property in the late nineteenth century Whitleigh Hall was described as 'standing on a park-like lawn with ornamental pleasure grounds' commanding 'one of the finest views in the West of England'. Edmund did not survive much beyond the failure of the mine, he died in April 1869, aged just 64. His eldest son, also, Edmund, died aged 36 just four years later and the property was taken on by the second son, John Croad Henn Gennys. The house was demolished in 1949 and the grounds became part of the post-war Whitleigh estate.

Hope sprang eternal, Mr Peet, the mine secretary, had at that meeting in the Golden Lion, offered to forgo any remuneration for his previous five months work, such was his conviction and when Mr Codd, who was the mine purser and who chaired that meeting brought matters to a conclusion that November, 'a large increase in the number of shareholders took place' and 'a general determination was expressed to prosecute the adventure on a sound and honourable basis'.

Maybe so, but in less than four months the project closed and nothing more was heard of Devonshire Silver Lead.

The Tamerton mining operations had lasted off and on for almost exactly a decade. By 1866 the count house buildings of Wheal Whitleigh were converted and renamed Zoar Cottages which survived well into the twentieth century, when they were demolished for the construction of the Whitleigh housing estate.

It was a sorry saga, and one that was all too familiar. Various mine captains, Hodge, Robins, Clymo, Puckey, Wolferstan, Bennett, Phillips, Goss, had spoken in glowing terms of the potential of the mines, especially Wheal Gennys, but there is no indication that after the initial euphoria surrounding the opening of the mine that that glow ever carried over to the shareholders, despite being regularly regaled with reports suggesting that. With hindsight it was doubtless obvious to many from the outset that these mines would never make any real money.

James Dymond of Devonport was the first purser at Wheal Gennys, from January 1850 through to September 1852. The grant of the sett had been made to Captain William Clymo, along with a Mr Kitto and William West (an experienced mining engineer) and around £400 had been lodged with the bankers for security against any damage. 'The amount of calls paid up by the adventurers was £4,096. We proceeded to work the mine as efficiently as possible. The amount received for the sale of the ore when the company were at work was £730.6s9d. The calls paid up and the amount the ores realised were applied to the working of the mine. There was a return of £452.12s.6d to the shareholders. That was upon the winding up of the whole affair and sale of materials. That leaves a loss to the shareholders of £4,373'. Dymond was speaking at a hearing to determine not just the value of the mines but the value of the land. Henn Gennys was looking to maximise the worth of the land because, in 1862, he was being forced to surrender a large chunk of the estate in order to facilitate the construction of the ring of forts the Government were looking to erect in a defensive ring around Plymouth, Devonport and Stonehouse. Dymond's gloomy figures were exactly in line with the views of Captain James Richards, who also gave testimony to the hearing:

'I have made an inspection of this property of Mr Gennys, with a view to ascertain its value in mining speculation. I don't think it's worth anything as a mining speculation. I first inspected it in 1854 ... I have inspected it twice since, and the examinations I made then confirm my previous opinion.'

William West took over as purser and his view was that the mine had not paid one-tenth of its cost and his successor, Polkinghorne, who took over in January 1854, right through to its close, said that in that time Mr Gennys and his family were shareholders.

'The mine did not pay its working expenses. It was arranged, after fruitless endeavours to make the mine pay, that the whole affair should be wound up. I was secretary as well as purser. From April, 1853, to the close of my office, the amount expended on the mine was £7,855.5s.0d. The sum of £1,774 7s 3d was realised by the sale of ore. All this was lost with the exception of £405 9s 1d which was returned to the shareholders at the winding up of the concern, and £13 12s 4d which remained in hand; The former amount was returned to the shareholders in the shape of a dividend in bankruptcy at the rate of 1s thruppence h'appenny per share, on 6,276 shares.'

It appeared now that none of the mine captains had a good word to say about it, indeed Captain Grose, who succeeded Captain Phillips in September 1854, as resident agent and remained until November 1856, agreed: 'In my judgement the mine was fairly tried. I do not think it is worth working. I drew up a report recommending the shareholders to wind up the affair. In doing so I threw myself out of employment, and threw myself entirely on the world. I thought it my duty to make that report', he added, 'and upon that report the affair was wound up.' (Grose incidentally at that time, in 1862, was manager of the Cargoll Mines in Cornwall and had been engaged in lead mines since he was a boy).

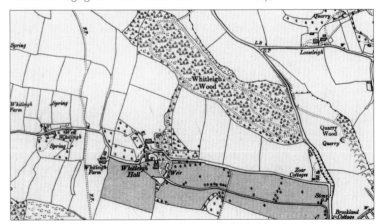

Whitleigh Hall with Zoar Cottages on the site of Wheal Gennys

Efford Lodes

Although we have no evidence of mining in Efford, we do have an interesting reference to the potential for mineral mining there. The situation arose in 1864, when, like Edmund Gennys at Whitleigh, Erving Clark at Efford Manor was faced with negotiating compensation of parts of his estate to be *'taken absolutely and kept free from buildings and other obstructions'*, when the Government, or rather the Secretary of State for the War Department, was clearing the way for the aforementioned ring of forts around the Three Towns.

Clark was to be paid £10,000 in compensation for *'all buildings, easements, rights'* with the vendor to be *'discharged of all estates rights and interests whatsoever except as regards the metallic minerals with the said lands.'*

As regards those *'metallic minerals,* Clark claimed to reserve the liberty of working and mining the same by the unrestricted use of all proper and usual means and appliances at all time … or failing this reservation the vendors shall be paid in addition to the sum mentioned above (£10,725) the value of such metallic minerals to them in their capacity of owners of the land containing such minerals – such value if not otherwise agreed upon to be determined by arbitration.'

There was more: *'The reasonable costs and charges of the Vendors solicitors and surveyors (including therein the valuation and sale of the metallic minerals, hereinafter referred to are to be wholly paid by the Government.'*

It was not the first time that Clark had been obliged to deal with alterations to his estate – it had happened in 1809 when the Embankment had been created and again a few years after that with the laying down of the Plymouth and Dartmoor horse-drawn railway and then again in the 1840s when the South Devon Railway steamed through his holdings.

In 1868 (by which time Clark senior had passed on – he died aged 72 in 1866) a second conveyance was made in Clark's favour, as an additional purchase was paid by the War Department which included the mineral rights. However none of the schedules to the plan give any indication of mining activity and unfortunately we appear to have no record of any mining engineer's assessment of the potential of the lodes shown

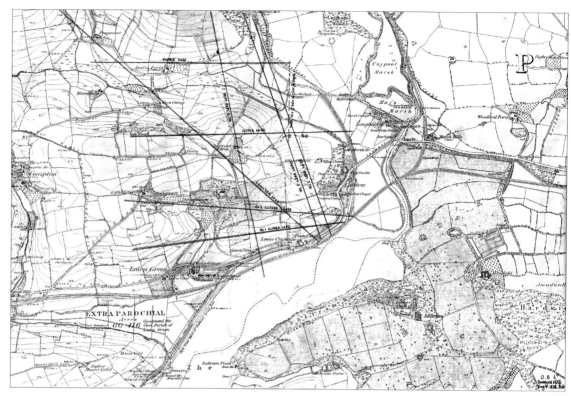

Reference: *The lands coloured yellow are those comprised in Mr Erving Clark's first contract with the War Department. Those coloured blue in his second contract. Those tinted yellow (in outline) Mr Erving Clark's remaining lands. The lands coloured green are those comprised in Mr Henry Clark's sale to the War Department. Those tinted green in outline Mr Henry Clark's remaining lands. The plan shows the typical E-W orientation of tin and copper lodes, with N-S lead lodes.*
NB: *Henry Clark was the only surviving son of Erving Clark senior and his wife Laetitia Annie Treby, the daughter of Paul Treby Treby of Goodamoor and Plympton House. Henry's brother, Erving Frederick, died in 1850 aged 27.*

on the map. Given the experience of the other mines in the immediate area, it surely could not have been an overly optimistic one from a profit perspective. The principal persons who stood to gain being the solicitors, surveyors and those in receipt of rents and dues – the landowners, unless, of course, they were sufficiently convinced of the merits of their minerals to invest their own money in such a project, which, as we have seen, many of them were.

DEVON,

Wheal Lopes, Tin and Copper Mine, with the Materials,

NEAR JUMP, FOR SALE.

To be Sold by Auction,

ON THURSDAY the 13th day of February next, on the Premises, by Eleven o'clock in the Forenoon, all that TIN and COPPER MINE, called

WHEAL LOPES,

Situate in the Parish of Bickleigh, in the County of Devon, within four miles of Lophill Quay, and five from Plymouth and Dock; together with all the Materials belonging to the said Mine, with the right of the present Adventurers therein.

The Materials consist of a Water Wheel thirty feet in diameter and three feet over the breast, Stamping Mills, Whim, Capstan and Shears, 25 fathoms of Wood and Iron Pumps, Rods, Ladders, &c.; together with a quantity of Mining and Smiths' Tools, &c. &c.

For a view of the same, apply to THOMAS TREWEEK, at Jump, near Plymouth.

WILLIAM MARTIN,

Auctioneer, Tavistock.

N. B.—A Deposit of £20 per Cent. to be paid on the day of Sale.

Dated 8th Feb. 1823.

Wheal Lopes

Overall it appears that most of the mining executed locally in the nineteenth century was on private land, land, moreover, that was in the hands of just a few wealthy landowners: the Parkers, the Strodes, the Woollcombes, the Calmadys, the Henn Gennys ... and the Lopes family.

A fair bit of the mining activity that we've looked at already was outside the boundaries of nineteenth-century Plymouth, much of it still is, but there can be little doubt that before the end of the present century most of it will be within the confines of a larger city. Efford and Laira were nineteenth-century additions, Tamerton, Plympton and Plymstock, twentieth-century acquisitions, and who knows what the future holds for Roborough, Newnham and Hemerdon? However, for the purposes of this review of local mining, it is certainly worth including a number of peripheral sites. Described as being five miles from Plymouth in 1823, Wheal Lopes was evidently first worked in 'modern' times in the late eighteenth century.

At a hearing in 1870, talking about water rights and mining activity over the years, Mr Millward acting for the Lopes estate, produced *'a bundle of mining setts, commencing in 1793'*, while Rolf von Arx, writing in *British Mining* No.48 in 1993, suggests the first lease for Wheal Lopes was granted in 1760.

While that is doubtless possible in some respects, it is unlikely that it would have been known by that name at the time as it wasn't until 1798 that the Jamaican-born Manasseh Masseh Lopes acquired Maristow House and made it his family seat.

How successful the mining operations were there is less than clear.

However, there is reference in October 1816 to *'Two 42nd shares in that Valuable Mine, called Wheal Lopes, in the Parish of Bickley (sic)'*, being sold by public auction on Friday 18th of that month in the Lopes's Arms, Jump, near Plymouth.

With no further clues to it's value we find, a little over six years later, that the Wheal Lopes Tin and Copper Mine itself was up for sale, with all the material and machinery along with it.

In February 1837 when the Shaugh Iron Mines were being advertised as an investment far and wide, one of the points made in the sales pitch was that there were *'indications of a Copper Lode, supposed to cross the Lode of the Wheal Lopes Copper Mine in the adjoining Sett'*.

Was Wheal Lopes actually open at that time? Again it's difficult to determine, however in the summer of 1844 we find a future Mayor of Plymouth, Alfred Rooker, handling the sale of *'Ten Shares in the Wheal Lopes Plymouth & Devonport Mining Company, affording at present a very fair prospect of prosperous adventure.'*

According to von Arx *'some ore was raised but the proceeds could not cover the costs and, in addition, the price of copper had fallen considerably'*. He adds: *'Serious financial difficulties set in – at least partly caused by mismanagement'*.

In 1846 Lopes granted another Sett which became known as Wheal Franco, Horrabridge, (Franco was the surname of Lopes' nephew who had inherited the estate on the death of his uncle in 1831, and who had subsequently changed his name to Lopes). Wheal Franco was, according to the report of the 1870 hearing, abandoned in 1862 and the materials were sold off.

The date here suggesting that this may have been related to Wheal Lopes, because it was in August 1862 that John Vosper, auctioneer of Tavistock, was instructed to offer *'Valuable Mine Materials for Sale, at Wheal Lopes'*. Given that Mr Vosper was recommending the materials, which were indeed extensive, confidently, *'as they have been placed on the Mine within the last 3 years, regardless of expense, a great portion of them being new'*, one suspects that this was incarnation of the mine that arose in December 1859, when, with some existing plant evidently still standing on the site, the Wheal Lopes Copper, Tin & Zinc Mining Company Limited, came into being.

The directors at this stage were William C Buller, of Lincoln's Inn and Pound, Tavistock; Theophilus Clive of Hampton Court; Charles H Daw of Tavistock; James Mitchell of Grosvenor Square, London and Thomas Nicholls of Tavistock. The capital for the 'new' concern was £10,000 in £1 shares, and the secretary of the company was W S Trotter, whose offices were at No.1 Great Winchester Street, London – although it seems he was soon superseded by Samuel Cardozo of Old Broad Street in the City of London.

It would appear that, as so often with these ventures, there was a high degree of optimism on the part of this new band of adventurers.

The prospectus noted that the Mine was formerly worked by the *'Plymouth and Dartmoor Company who were raising considerable quantities of Copper, when a lack of ability to invest and an untimely drop in the price of Copper deterred them from advancing further capital to develop the Mine in depth.'*

Captain James Phillips (of the undoubtedly successful Bedford United Mines at Tavistock) had described the lodes in glowing terms and assured the investors that he knew of *'no property better worth the attention of the Capitalist than Wheal Lopes'*.

But it was an all too familiar refrain and followed by an equally familiar scenario whereby the whole lot was put up for sale less than three years later.

However, the saga didn't end there. Three years after that, in August 1865, there was a new name, a new team of adventurers and everything was up and running again.

This time the nominal capital sum had doubled to over £20,000, the share price had risen dramatically to £20 a share with a caveat to the effect that *'it is not expected that more than £12 per share will ever be required to be called up.'*

The new mine manager was Captain Joseph Richards (the manager at Hawkmoor and agent at Devon Great Consols), and in a move that marked a shift in the balance of power to Lancashire, the Directors were: J Catterell Harvey, from Stoke-on-Trent, EA Ledgard, from Ashton-under-Lyne, both of them bankers; E Harvey Wadge, of Stradbrook Hall and Middle Temple, London; Lee Leowenstein, of St Ann's Square, Manchester; WH Williams, of Rook Street, Manchester and Campbell M Thomas of Messrs C & CM Thomas of Redruth and Manchester. The bankers for the new concern were the Devon & Cornwall Bank and the new name that they were trading under – Devon Wheal Lopes Mining Company (Limited), Copper, Tin, Lead, & Blende.

The new secretary was one Robert Charles Clifton, of 3 Clarence Street, Manchester.

In a bid to attract shareholders the net was thrown far and wide and prospectuses/advertorials were published in papers the length and breadth of the British Isles.

For anyone who may have heard rumours of previous escapades with regard to Wheal Lopes the text was full of explanations and excuses: *'The mine was in work for several years on the "cost book" principle, but only partially developed. The discoveries however, fully proved it to be a most valuable property, which only required a more vigorous development to open up riches equal to those for which Devon is so celebrated.'*

It continued: *'Another company who recently attempted to resume the works with insufficient means were obliged to abandon them, after having got no further than the purchase and erection of the very excellent machinery since bought up, by and now in possession of the present Company.*

'At the time of its suspension, the Mine was undergoing a phase which has characterised most of the richest Mines of Devon and Cornwall; that is to say, the Company were unable to find the further capital required, and the Works were consequently abandoned at a moment when success was evidently within reach.

'It is a remarkable fact that most of our richest Mines have been similarly abandoned for a period; and amongst numberless others, the following:– '

There followed a list of 19 mines, including Devon Great Consols, Carn Brea and Wheal Bassett.

Our scribe then went on to say: *'Many of which, still paying high dividends, were given up by the first and even the second and third parties who worked them, leaving to others, who were fortunate enough in taking them up, the realisation of enormous profits in dividends, exceeding at* the present time six millions sterling. It is the conviction of all mining men conversant with the facts, that this Property will be another to the list, a circumstance which appears to be the more certain from the conclusive results of the last Company's operations, for Copper of excellent quality was raised and sold, clearly showing the lodes to be Copper bearing. *'Another most striking evidence of the value of the veins is the fact that the water in the deeper levels was so highly mineralised with Copper, that returns of a high produce were made by precipitation and it is computed that important returns will be made from this inexpensive and simple source.'*

At this point you might perhaps have expected the sale pitch to end but there was more: *'One of the most important features of this Company, and which has led to its being formed, is the existence of an extensive deposit of Blende (Zinc), which, until recently, was a worthless Mineral, but now of great value. The recent modification in fact, in the present value of Blende affords every assurance that this Mine can be worked with very large profit to present investors from this Mineral alone (to say nothing of the splendid prospects as regards its Copper deposits), it being estimated that £20,000 worth stands in one level alone, which can be immediately taken away the moment the Mine is drained.'*

The account, which bears recording here, then went into detail about the scale of the previous workings: *'The operations during the last working were extensive and well planned; sinking was carried on to a considerable extent, the main engine shaft being down 60 fms, and the eastern shaft to 82 fms: three other shafts were also sunk. All the necessary levels were driven, and galleries made in different parts of the Mine; excavations were also made, which are now suitable to the application of new machinery, and a large sum was spent in tunnelling for a water course, by means of which a constant supply of water may be maintained at all seasons, which prevents the necessity of extensive steam power: all these workings are available, and it is estimated to constitute a clear saving of outlay to the present Company of at least £30,000.*

'All the necessary buildings are erected, comprising excellent Carpenter's Shop, Smiths' Shop, small office, sump room, and Pitman's House.

'When fresh "ore ground" is reached in depth, as well as large deposits of Copper ore by extending the deeper levels, the Shareholders will possess a very valuable dividend-paying Mine.'

It all sounded so perfect, everything was already in place, most of it had already been paid for, what could possibly go wrong?

Well it transpires that everything wasn't quite as described, despite the above appearing in newspapers here there and everywhere it seems that fake news, false information and fraudulent operators are not just a modern-day phenomenon. The chairman of the new venture, Edwin Harvey

Wadge, who appears to have sometime used his brother's name, Erwin Harvey Wadge, as an alias, was not quite all he appeared to be, and he had 'form' – as did his father, an auctioneer and mine agent, who had been declared bankrupt in 1855.

Cornish born, Edwin Harvey Wadge was one of five children born to Edward Wadge, who, for reasons best known to himself gave all five of his children Christian names beginning with 'E' including Edward, Edmund, Edwin and Erwin … his daughter was called Emma. An articled clerk who would later claim *'I was bred to the law, and a member – I fear a very degenerate one – of the Honourable Society of the Middle Temple'*, Edwin appears to have made a fortune in his early twenties.

Having supposedly realised an immense fortune being a large proprietor of 'English Mines', he moved to Ireland in the early 1860s and set up *The Irish Industrial Magazine* and a flax factory in the Dublin area. He made a grand promise to regenerate Ireland by developing it's mineral resources. *'His entertainments were in a style of splendour almost unparalleled as he became a millionaire. His house was furnished in the most costly manner, and his taste was the theme of general admiration. He had in his cellar a quantity of the choicest vintages, which he declared to be 100 years old. Marley, the fine old family seat the La Touches, was in the Landed Estates Court, and Mr. Harvey Wadge was declared the purchaser, making a deposit of £12,000 in part payment.*

'In the meantime there were mysterious whispers in commercial circles that all was not right' … and the whisperers were right.

An early indication had come in 1859 when Erwin had become a principal shareholder in the West Ashburton Mine (originally known as East Hazel Mine). Irregularities in the accounts manifested themselves the following summer and Erwin and Edwin Harvey Wadge evidently *'seized the books and carried them off'* (*Exeter and Plymouth Gazette* 12 April 1861) and the following day the *Western Times* covered the story under the headline: *'The Mine Rigging Case'*. *'Fine copper lodes'* had been found according to the promoters of the mine. *'Copper lodes or loads of copper'*, asked the judge to the amusement of the court, while the reporter noted that *'gross swindling may be perpetrated under the form of mine speculations'*.

How right they were and that is precisely what Edwin Harvey Wadge seems to have spent much of his life doing, save when he was behind bars, which he was on a regular basis.

On 2 January 1866 we find him chairing a meeting of the Devon Wheal Lopes Mining Company in Manchester. Some 59 shareholders were in attendance. Some difficult questions were fielded by Wadge, and the usual eternally optimistic Mine Captain's report from Joseph Richards appears to have mollified even the most sceptical.

Later that same month Wadge was in the chair again, this time in St Austell for an Emergency General Meeting of the South Cornwall Mining Company at the White Hart Hotel.

Here, again in the face of unease from certain shareholders, Wadge stage-managed an extraordinary gathering with support for the already ailing venture coming from all corners. Captain John Martin (of Wheal Bunny) with some 47 years' experience, claimed the venture was *'a dead certainty, and I believe that every £100 put into it will come out £1,000'.* Mr Alexander Miller, of Sale near Manchester who was by his own admission *'a cautious Scotchman sceptical about mines'* said that Mr Harvey Harvey of Manchester made him change his mind. As for Mr Harvey Wadge *'a clearer headed or smarter man of business and withal a more perfect gentleman it has never been my lot to come across. I have met several clear headed men in my time, but they were generally slow, I have met no end of smart men, but they generally wanted ballast; and I have met few real gentlemen (and no gentleman can come up to a real Scotch gentleman) but I have never in 40 years' experience met the three qualities combined in a man who could make 100,000 in three years'.* *'Mr Harvey Wadge',* he averred, *'is a good classical scholar and an able geologist, his only fault is that he is not a Scotchman (sic).'* He added: *'I am quite satisfied we are now in a safe concern, with thoroughly sound and honest management.'*

SOUTH CORNWALL MINING COMPANY LIMITED.—Divided into 2,000 shares of £20 each, £5 payable on application and £5 on allotment.

DIRECTORS.

E. Harvey Wadge. Esq., F.G.S., Stradbrook Hall, chairman of the Devon Wheal Lopes.
W. H. Williams. Esq., Manchester, director of the Devon Wheal Lopes.
Harold Evans, Esq., Edge Vale, Liverpool.
Henry J. Harvey, Esq., Church-street, Liverpool.
Osmond Rhodes, Esq., Potter Newton, near Leeds.
Frederick Rooke, Esq., Southirlee Crescent, Bedminster.

Messrs. Harvey and Co. are requested by the Secretary to announce that the SHARE LIST will be CLOSED on the 20th instant. Intending applicants, therefore, are recommended to send in their applications without delay, or they may otherwise be too late to secure allotments, which cannot be guaranteed.

Messrs. H. and Co. once more take the opportunity of recommending the shares of this company, as offering a good sound investment, which will prove immensely profitable to those who embark in it.

Forms of application may be obtained of Messrs. Harvey and Co.

One of the many sham companies created over a 50-year-period by perhaps one of the most prolific conmen ever to come out of Cornwall, Edwin Harvey Wadge.

But they really weren't and there was a clue as to why in the answer given to one concerned shareholder, Mr R Scott of Newcastle, who wanted to know why shares in the Mine were not quoted in the Mining Exchange in London.

Harvey Wadge said it was a matter of mines not shares, while his relative, Mr Harvey Harvey claimed 'no love of the mining market for he feared it had done grievous harm to sound mining enterprises, indeed the statistics of the results of market and broker-controlled mines in that county was most disastrous'.

In July 1866, with mining matters heating up at home, Wadge suddenly ceased publishing his *Irish Industrial Magazine*, after just a few issues. Apologising to subscribers, the press announcement read that 'there can be no question that he will best serve the cause of Irish industry by bringing about an active expenditure of capital in developing its various and magnificent resources'.

Indeed in one issue of the magazine readers were informed of mines in Ireland lying dormant that contained 'banks of wealth'. The writer, presumably Wadge himself, taking pains to point out the then recent revival of Botallack St Just Mine that had yielded great rewards for its Royal patrons.

In October that year he wound up his City of Dublin Flax Spinning Company and then he left Ireland. On the boat across to Holyhead he was involved in a skirmish with the MP for Athlone, Denis Rearden. Wadge alleged that the 49-year-old Auctioneer and Estate Agent assaulted him on the ferry and again at Euston Station, however, as Wadge had 'bought' so much land, furniture and other material goods without apparently paying for them, one can but wonder at what actually provoked the fracas.

Meanwhile, the Cornish venture continued to drain certain individuals of money, Wadge apparently including himself in that group. But then in July of the following year our man was in court in Manchester as the secretary of Wheal Lopes. Robert Clifton, a partner in crime, was charged with embezzling £1,450 from shareholders. However despite tales of forged documents, fake directors and other fraudulent activity, there were apparently no prosecutions, at least not on that occasion.

Mention was also made of the apparently loss-making West Great St George Mining Company that had also been started by Clifton & Wadge. Two months later at an Extraordinary General Meeting of Devon Wheal Lopes in Bristol, it was all over, or at least the running of the mine was over, as George Rogers chaired a meeting that resolved to wind the company up – voluntarily. That was after it had 'been proved to the satisfaction of the Company that this Company cannot be carried on in a profitable manner'.

It was also resolved that any application to the Court would be made to the Court of Chancery, and not to the Stannaries Court (Wadge would attempt to use the protection of the Stannary Court on more than one occasion, although generally without ever registering with them).

Frederick Rooke was appointed liquidator and Charles Taddy, was the solicitor in charge. Meanwhile, John Vosper was, once again, given the job, the following January, of auctioning the Mine Sett and all the Plant, Machinery and Materials.

There was no hint that our Mr Harvey Wadge was in attendance, indeed he appears to have kept a very low profile with rumours of sorties to the Continent (he claimed to have had offices in Paris in 1867), and to Canada, where it was hinted that 'he had got into trouble for having exercised his financial abilities in a manner that was not only not appreciated, but warmly resented by the plain, simple minded colonists'.

Returning to England in the Spring of 1870 and looking to start businesses up in London and Glasgow, again as a mining agent, but this time calling himself Henry C Gray, he started up the North Caradon Mining Company, with a mine in Cornwall that was said to already be in successful operation. The company, which had Thomas Gibson and Gray (Wadge) as brokers, was backed by 7,500 shares of £2 each and 'there was every reason to expect immense profits'.

This time Wadge did not even bother to go through with the tedious business of actually acquiring a mine and equipment, but he did issue a printed prospectus along with 'lithographed forms, purporting to be reports from mining captains and surveyors employed at the mine'.

Having apprehended two of Wadge's co-conspirators – Wadge managed to slip away, again – Inspector Shandley of Scotland Yard headed down to Cornwall to inspect the North Caradon Mine at Rilla Mills. There he found that the so-called mine was 'a small piece of land attached to a farm heaped up with ferns and rubbish.

'Witnesses stated that the nature of the soil was entirely opposed to the successful carrying on of mining operations, and nothing had been done there for years.' (*Belfast News-Letter* 3 December 1873)

Gibson was sentenced at the time but it wasn't until another three years had elapsed that the long arm of the law managed to catch up with Wadge himself, and in a court in Manchester he was sentenced by Baron Pollock to five years' penal servitude at Spike Island.

Some years later Wadge re-emerged as Captain Archer (another family name), a mining agent with offices in Bristol trading under the name of Bishop, Earle & Company of Bristol, London and Plymouth.

This company was said to have a working mine in Callington, Cornwall Great Consols (formerly known as South Kithill Mining Company) with £20,000 capital.

'A prospectus was got out, in which the mine was described as having paid enormous dividends, and as being a source of great wealth if properly worked.' The capital was subscribed, but the mine produced nothing in the shape of dividend. At length certain shareholders got suspicious, and made inquiries. It was found that the whole affair was a swindle. Wadge was arrested in India, and brought to Bristol on a charge of fraud. The inquiry lasted several days and the most extraordinary revelations were made. It appears however that only £300 worth of tin was ever extracted and the wealthy syndicate was made up of Wadge's clerks, and office boys, some of whom figured as 'holders of many thousands of pounds worth of shares.' (Western Daily Press 18 August 1882)

It transpired, incidentally, that Wadge had also worked his deceptive financial magic in India, 'he boasted that whilst he was in custody he had made £20,000 at that game, and that he did not mind another five years for that'.

Somehow he slipped the authorities once more, only to be arrested in New York the following year, on a charge of forgery.

A couple of bankruptcy charges in the early 1890s suggest that he was still attempting to deceive all and sundry and in 1898 we find Wadge purporting to manage the White Cleave Iron Mine, and WR Coulton's Kilbury Lode.

There were yet other episodes to follow, and on 29 September 1904 The Cornishman reported thus:

'It is said that attention is now being given again to the Perranzabuloe and Luxulyan tin fields. Wheal Crigg, in the former, will be worked by a London syndicate with a capital of £5,000 and Wheal Viou in the former and Trescoll in the latter are amalgamated to be worked by another syndicate of the same city, with a capital of £11,000. Mr E Harvey Archer Wadge the managing director, will, it is understood, reside at Perranporth.'

And the following year, on 24 August 1905 the same paper printed the following: 'Mr. E. Harvey Archer Wadge, a mining engineer, at present residing at St. Austell, has communicated the following very interesting facts to the Press concerning the resuscitation of the well known Wheal Eliza and Buckler's Tin Mines which have been closed down for many years. He says: "I have succeeded in getting wealthy syndicate, who have never given their attention to Cornish mining to put £300,000, without issuing prospectus or the public for subscriptions, to rework and further develop the well-known Wheal Eliza and Buckler's Tin Mines, and to work and develop adjacent valuable tin and other mineral property in the parish of St. Austell, one of the best districts in the county. A compact area of 1,200 acres or there about, the riches of lodes have been abundantly proved existing records and recent prospecting. It is beyond dispute that these mines and properties have a great prospective value. When their abandoned ends are resumed, the lodes at deeper levels opened out, and other immediately parallel lodes almost intact to the surface are uncovered and developed, their great worth will be discovered to vastly increase the reserves already existing. The estimated returns are between 80 and 100 tons black tin per month, ensuring dividend of £30,000 per annum to be made".'

With newspapers apparently making little or no effort to check such 'facts', but very much taking these press handouts at face value, it requires no great effort to see how simple it was for Wadge (who died in Plymouth in 1909) to lure people into his schemes. With the telephone still a novelty and the internet understandably not within anyone's intellectual grasp of what the future might hold, it was ridiculously easy to obtain substantial early investment off the back of a web of lies and false statements and then plead bad luck, 'the lode was spent after all', or just disappear with the initial wave of investment and hope that no-one would find you. Even so it is remarkable how similar Wadge's scams were and one can't help but think that he wasn't the only well-dressed, well-spoken rogue operating at that time or in that field.

Indeed, one doesn't have to look far at all to find another rogue, even though this one certainly didn't need to misbehave to get his hands on a fortune.

Wadge's Wheal Lopes scam was conducted, as we have seen on land that had been bought by Manasseh Masseh Lopes, a member of a wealthy family of Portuguese Jews, who when he arrived in Devon became interested in becoming an MP. At that time Jews, and a number of other Christian denominations, were prohibited from entering Parliament, and so, in 1802 Lopes converted to the Church of England and later that year entered the House of Commons as the Tory member for New Romney, he later (1807) represented Evesham and (1812) Barnstaple and bought control of both seats for Westbury.

Westbury was a burgage borough where the right to vote went with the ownership of certain properties and Lopes acquired all but two of them, hence he could 'elect' whoever he chose, and in 1814 he chose his nephew and heir Ralph Franco.

Sir Manasseh Masseh Lopes (1755-1831) bought Maristow in 1798 and was created a baronet in 1805. He was appointed High Sheriff of Devon in 1810. He was described as 'not a bad minded man ... only something of a miser, which those lovers of the root of evil nearly all are, who acquire large fortunes by attention to small sums'.

Franco sat until 1819 but in that year Sir Manasseh was apprehended for bribing voters in two separate constituencies – it was a common enough practice at the time but reformers were looking for a scapegoat and as a foreign Jew, Lopes was the ideal candidate to complain about.

In his own Barnstaple constituency he was alleged to have spent £3000 on bribes (that's around a whopping £250,000 in today's terms but trifling when you consider that his worth then was around £75 million and his Devon estates encompassed over 30,000 acres). His election was declared void. Meanwhile, in Grampound, proceedings under criminal law saw him convicted, fined £10,000 and jailed for two years.

The sentence was remitted in September 1820, and he subsequently re-entered Parliament for one of his fail-safe seats in Westbury. However, as a result of the scandal, the notoriously corrupt borough of Grampound was deprived of its right to return MPs.

Reform, fortunately was on its way and eventually came in 1832, however Sir Manasseh had died the previous year and his nephew Ralph became the 2nd Baronet of Maristow. Ralph also spent many years in Parliament, but it is with his son, Sir Massey Lopes, that we pick up on the local mining story.

Educated at Winchester and Oxford, he was appointed High Sheriff of Devon in 1857 and elected MP for Devonshire South in 1868. In May 1870, Sir Massey was involved in a lengthy arbitration appeal at the Globe Hotel, Plymouth, to assess the amount of compensation he might expect as a result of giving up certain water rights and Wheal Lopes was mentioned. Determined to *'show that it was a very constant occurrence that long abandoned mines had been reworked profitably'* he had Captains Haswell, Horswill and Geddon give supporting evidence.

Lopes's QC then *'put in a bundle of leases of mining setts commencing in 1793 and ending in 1868'*, the implication clearly being that this was a potentially profitable endeavour, which patently it wasn't!

Mention was also made of Shaugh Iron Mine, which was also on Lopes land.

Massey Lopes cartoon from Vanity Fair

Shaugh Iron Mines

Described in 1838 as *'being very valuable and inexhaustible'* a 50% stake in the Shaugh Iron Mines was being sold in the spring of that year by Public Auction at the King's Arms Hotel, at Briton Side.

The press advertisement for the event informed readers that the works had been undertaken over the last four years by Messrs Langdon & Paddon and had been *'progressive, successful, and uninterrupted and confined to an immense lode of Haematite Iron Ore, averaging 6 feet in width by an open cutting already driven to 90 fathoms in from the side of the hill, at a depth of 30 fathoms from the surface of the Lode, intermixed with Plumbago, and being of the Argillaceous description upward of 20,000 tons may be raised annually with great facility, and at small expense.'*

And if that didn't make the prospect attractive enough in its own right, it was further claimed that *'there are also indications of a COPPER LODE, supposed to cross the Lode of the Wheal Lopes Copper Mine, in the adjoining sett'*.

Furthermore, it was noted that not only could the mines be worked without machinery and were well regarded by the Iron Masters in Wales, but the neighbouring *'Port of Plymouth possesses peculiar advantages as a place of shipment and the contiguous Railways essentially reduce the expense of transit'*.

Thomas Henwood was the Mine Captain, and the Devonport solicitors were James & Henry Smith, who, as we have seen already, were based in Morice Town, had an interest in Lord Morley's Iron Mines and were in danger of being declared bankrupt in 1840, a situation from which they later appear to have fully recovered. Meanwhile, London solicitors were named as Keddell & Baker and the Plymouth legal matters were dealt with by John Kelly (whose company was one of the original elements of the current Wolferstans practice and who had then recently served Plymouth as its Mayor).

The interesting bit of this story, however, is that while all of the above sounded strong and healthy, the aforementioned co-adventurers in this enterprise, the iron ore merchants William Langdon, John Paddon and Henry John Paddon had had their partnership dissolved the previous spring, and had apparently gone bust, which hardly suggests a successful, valuable and inexhaustible operation.

Doubtless this was what prompted the sale of such a sizeable share of the business, indeed the whole lot had been put up for sale in August 1837 and clearly this had not been fully effected, although at that stage William Langdon, of East Stonehouse, was listed as someone from whom particulars were available.

THE SHAUGH IRON MINES,
NEAR PLYMOUTH.

To be Peremptorily SOLD by Public Auction, by Mr. JAMES SKARDON, at the KING'S ARMS HOTEL, Briton Side, Plymouth, on WEDNESDAY the 11th day of April next, at Twelve o'Clock,—the MOIETY HALF-PART, or SHARE, of and in all those very valuable and

INEXHAUSTIBLE IRON MINES,

Known as the SHAUGH IRON MINES, situated in the Parish of Shaugh, about 7 miles from Plymouth, on the Lands of SIR RALPH LOPES, Bart., with the like share of and in the *Railways, Waggons, Tools, Implements, and Materials*
BELONGING THERETO.

The Works, which have been carried on for the last Four Years, by Messrs. LANGDON and PADDONS, have been progressive, successful, and uninterrupted, confined to an immense Lode of HÆMATITE IRON ORE, averaging 6 feet in width by an OPEN CUTTING already driven 90 fathoms in from the side of the Hill, at a depth of 30 fathoms from the surface of the Lode, intermixed with Plumbago, and being of the Argillaceous description, upwards of 20,000 Tons may be raised annually with great facility, and at a small expense.

There are also indications of a COPPER LODE, supposed to cross the Lode of the Wheal Lopes Copper Mine, in the adjoining Sett.

From the localities of the Mines, the Works can be prosecuted without the assistance of Machinery. The Ores bear a high character with the Iron Masters in Wales. The Port of Plymouth possesses peculiar advantages as a place of shipment, and the contiguous Railways essentially reduce the expence of transit.

In short, with a very moderate Capital, these Mines, which are deemed nearly inexhaustible, will be found to require only intelligence and attention to open a most prolific source of wealth.

The present Sett extends over a space of about 125 Acres, in a Country abounding with rich veins of Copper, Tin, and Iron Ore, and is held for the remainder of a Term of 21 years from Michaelmas 1835, subject to the Dues of 1-12th; but on the road being made through Bickleigh Vale, Sir Ralph Lopes has agreed to extend the limits of the Sett to about 25 Acres in addition.

Captain THOMAS HENWOOD at the Mines will show the same, and Printed Particulars with Plans of the Sett and Conditions of Sale, and all further particulars may be obtained on application (if by Letter to be Post-paid) to Messrs. KEDDELL and BAKER, Solicitors, 36, Fenchurch-street, London; Messrs. J. and H. T. SMITH, Solicitors, Devonport; or Mr. JOHN KELLY, Solicitor, Plymouth.
Dated, 24th March, 1838.

Above: Sale notice from 1838
Right: Ferro Ceramic Mine.

Information beyond this point is thin on the ground, perhaps there were no takers. However, some 30 years later, there was a substantial resurgence of the mine: H Gordon was credited as Chief Agent and the owner, John Brogden & Son – Brogden owned an Ironworks in Tondu, in South Wales.

Over a five year period the mine produced over 4,600 tons of iron ore, with exploratory work carried out looking for lead and copper. However, in 1873, changes in the industry saw the closure of a number of Welsh iron mines and in Plymouth where there had evidently been huge investment – many times more than £2,500 realised by the sale of the iron raised here – and the mine was closed, with Captain John Peacock managing what appears to have become a non-productive facility for a few years.

In July 1874, in a letter to Copplestone Radciffe, the then land agent for Lord Lopes, Captain Thomas Gregory wrote:

'I am assured by Old Miners who worked here many years since that the Mine was in good Ore at the bottom of the shaft B, but the then enormous prices paid for Carriage of the Ore together with the low price of the same was the principal Cause of suspension at that time & not for want of Ore.'

Having carried out various investigations across the site he stated that *'I cannot for a moment entertain an opinion that the Ore is exhausted & the Mine worked out.*

'I have no doubt the Lodes [yet to be thoroughly investigated] will be found of Equal Value which will Yield a large & profitable output of Ore, for a long time to come.'

Standard mine captain speak perhaps, certainly we'd seen it before from the man who came from a line of experienced miners. His reports previously referred on Bottle Hill, East Bottle Hill and Wheal Sidney and Julian were often peppered with a large dose of optimism. But here, even if it was entirely well founded, Gregory's confidence was not picked up with any relish by new Adventurers.

In 1879 authority to 'mine and search' for iron was granted in a lease to a new venture, in a different location – the Ferro Ceramic Company. But there appears to have been no further significant activity here after that and the other endeavour didn't last for long either as the assets of what had become the Dewerstone Iron Mine were put up for sale in 1883, apparently again without a buyer as it was referred to as being 'disused' by 1886.

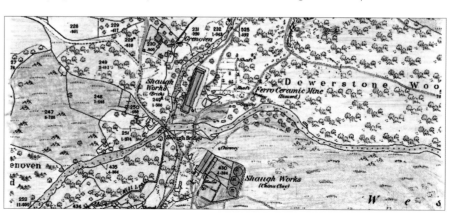

Tunnel Mine or Bickleigh Vale Phoenix

AN Important MINERAL DISCOVERY was made while cutting the tunnel of the South Devon and Tavistock Railway, in the lands belonging to Sir Massey Lopes, Bart., Bickleigh, Devon. It has excited some sensation, and led to very great competition among mining men and others to obtain the property. A lease has been obtained for 21 years; royalty 1-15th.

The BICKLEIGH VALE PHŒNIX COPPER and TIN MINING COMPANY (Limited).

To be divided into 7,500 shares of £2 each.

£1 per share to be paid upon allotment, whereof 10s. per share deposit to be paid at the Bankers'.

No Shareholder liable beyond the actual amount of his own share.

DIRECTORS.

George Cyprian Hacker, Esq., Aldermanbury, and 38, Grove-road, St. John's-wood.

William Thomas, Esq., Gresham-house, and Clifton Villa, Elm-grove, Peckham.

John Williams, Esq., Bedford Iron Works, Tavistock, and Dartmouth-park-road, Hampstead.

(With power to increase to six.)

AUDITOR—Henry Lloyd Morgan, Esq., 74, Cornhill.

BANKERS—Commercial Bank of London, Lothbury, City.

SECRETARY (pro tem,)—Robert Gallon, Esq.

Registered Offices—167 and 168, Gresham-house, Broad-street, City, London.

The Bickleigh-vale Phœnix Mine is brought before the public not as a speculative mining job, but as a fair prospective medium for investment, fully as remunerative as any of our first-class dividend paying mines in Cornwall or Devon.

The past year has been remarkable for mining progress and mining success; £336,973 was paid in dividends against £249,682 in 1858. The value of copper ores raised last year was £1,079,075, the quantity being 183,944 tons, and the average standard was as high as £133 6s., produce 6¾. Tin advanced from 12 to 15 per cent., and lead maintained a good average position. The mining interest has reaped a good harvest for their investments generally, as during the past year numerous mines have entered the dividend list, while many others have increased their dividends.

This valuable mineral property is situate in the parish of Bickleigh, Devon, about four miles from Plymouth, and extends 800 fathoms on the course of the lodes. The main copper lode, as opened at surface, is 12 feet wide, composed of a peculiarly fine gossan, and of quartz of a most favourable description. A fine tin lode is also opened at the mouth of the tunnel, from four to six feet wide, which, it is asserted, would of itself warrant the working of this grant, and with every prospect of a good dividend mine.

The stratum is a decomposed granite, similar to that of the rich Phœnix and South Caradon Copper Mines of Cornwall, and to the Devon Great Consols Copper Mine, as forming a junction of the granite and clay-slate or killas—mines remarkable for their great value as investments, and also as specimens of the extraordinary and lasting productiveness of the granite formation.

The vast Lopes estates included a number of mines, most of them fired up around the middle of the nineteenth century when the scramble to find new lodes, or to revisit old ones with new technology, was at its height. Among them were Lady Bertha Mine, East Lady Bertha, South Lady Bertha, Maristow Mine, Lopwell Mine and Wood Mine none of which would appear to have raised anything like enough material to even begin to pay for the work put into them. However, the Virtuous Lady mine, to the northwest of Buckland Monachorum raised around 30 tons of copper in the early 1870s and a couple of tons of tin.

Said to be named after the Virgin Queen, Elizabeth I, it had evidently been worked on an off for centuries.

Not so though Bickleigh Vale Phoenix. A little closer to Plymouth this adventure came off the back of 'an important mineral discovery made while cutting the tunnel of the South Devon and Tavistock Railway'.

As was now the standard practice advertisements were placed in newspapers all over the United Kingdom and 44-year-old George Cyprian Hacker was listed at the head of the board of directors.

In the press blurb published in January and February 1860, it was claimed that the venture was being brought before the public 'not as a speculative mining job, but as a fair prospective medium for investment, fully as remunerative as any of our first-class dividend paying mines in Cornwall or Devon'.

The account continued with a dazzling set of statistics, the like of which had undoubtedly fired up other mining interests around this time: 'The past year has been remarkable for mining progress and mining success; £336,973 was paid in dividends against £249,682 in 1858 …

'The mining interest has reaped a good harvest for their investments and generally, as during the past year, numerous mines have entered the dividend list, while many others have increased their dividends.'

The prospectus then went on to describe the various lodes, for copper, for tin and for iron, that Bickleigh Vale Phoenix had to tap into. And with the added convenience of the railway, which could hardly be nearer the mine itself, and the River Shaugh, which would supply the water power needed, then 'the limited capital will be ample for the effectual development of the mine'.

'The unusually large size of this lode, its perfect formation, the richness of the ore, together with the geological features of the surrounding district, continue to attract the attention of experienced mineralogists who have visited the spot and all concur in pronouncing this the most important discovery yet made in the county of Devon.'

There followed three brief reports from three experienced mine captains from which the key statements were, from John Hambly:
'There cannot be the least doubt of this being a very valuable property for mining purposes'.
Joseph Hodge: *'I think at no very distant date you will have a really good mine.'*
John Phillips: *'I do not hesitate to say that the copper lode in the tunnel, and also the north lode (tin) are two as fine lodes as I ever I have seen: and no doubt this will make a good lasting mine.'*
The reality, however, as ever, was never quite as rosy as the picture painted by these ever hopeful mining men. Again and again the question that arises, did they believe their own hype, or was it mainly to get a group of Adventurers to invest sufficient funds to keep them and their partners in grime in gainful employment?
Certainly, with regard to Bickleigh Vale Phoenix the promising honeymoon period was all too familiar and short-lived.
On 5 March 1860, a piece in the *London Daily News* read:
'A deputation consisting of two of the directors and managing director, visited this mine on Saturday and again on Monday last, February 27. They were accompanied by Captain Goss, formerly of Lady Bertha Mine and now of Virtuous Lady Mine, both mines on the Lopes property. By Captain John Hambly of Calstock and by Captain William Rowe of Treweatha Mine Liskeard. The reports of these three mining captains on the prospects and on the best and most economical mode of at once proceeding to cut the copper lode, when received will be printed and circulated among the shareholders. The directors are enabled to hold out to the shareholders the most encouraging prospects and to congratulate them on the most extraordinary indications rarely seen of the existence of copper, in fact on passing through the Bickleigh tunnel at about 60 yards from the south east entrance the granite is completely green with copper arising from the dripping of the water from the copper lode, which was cut during the construction of the tunnel may be seen.'
This green granite and heavily mineralised water was to prove extremely tantalising. In August 1860 Hambly reported that there must be a lode near their present workings *'to be letting out so much water'.*
In October: *'the men are getting on nicely, and I hope it will continue ... I have nothing new further to communicate.'*
In November: *'there is a little more water coming out than lately, showing there is some lode or branch before us. I hope soon to find it good.'*
May 1861: *'Our progress is now slow, but the ground is exactly such as I should expect to find near a large lode.'*
July 1861: *'I see no reason why we may not soon cut into what we much want to see – a course of copper ore.'*

As it transpired it appears that the shareholders did have a reason why – they were reluctant to keep spending money on a mine for which it seems there was never a detailed record of any ore brought to ground and sold. In fairness it is possible there were other serious issues affecting this particular adventure.
In the latter part of 1860, when the future was still looking bright for Bickleigh Vale Phoenix, the aforementioned George Cyprian Hacker, became involved in the promotion of another new enterprise – the Great Northern & Midland Coal Company. Across the country and across the whole of September, October, November and December space was taken in a number of newspaper to print an abridged version of the company prospectus. This was a more ambitious project than Bickleigh, as the directors were looking to raise £50,000 capital via 10,000 shares at £5 each. To be fair this wasn't an entirely new endeavour as it was *'established for the purposes of carrying on the extensive trade in the purchase and sale of Coals from Sunderland, South Yorkshire, and Derbyshire Collieries, hitherto carried on by the Great Northern Railway Company, which trade the Company are compelled to abandon on and after the 1st day of October 1860, in accordance with the terms of an injunction against the Company, granted by his Honour the Vice Chancellor Kindersley, on the 25th day of June, 1860, in the suit of "The Attorney General v the Great Northern Railway Company".'*
This time there were clearly demonstrable amounts of material involved, around 800,000 tons of coal a year. However, it would appear that the manager of the company, George Butcher, had been involved before, and that the directors were looking to purchase the goodwill of his business ... but, perhaps less obvious at the outset was the fact that Mr Butcher had twice been declared bankrupt.
What is more, over the course of the next twelve months, his behaviour and that of his fellow directors, including our man George Cyprian Hacker, was such that the company had gone bust again by December 1861.
Hacker and certain of his co-directors appear not to have behaved in an entirely honourable way with those investors purchasing shares and found themselves in trouble with the Lord Chancellor in the Court of Appeal.
A few years later, in 1865, he was declared bankrupt over a different business, and again in 1869, so it is perhaps no wonder that the Bickleigh Vale Phoenix undertaking seems to have fizzled out with little or no fanfare.
A successful draper with a number of employees at one stage, George Cyprian Hacker would appear to have been another overly ambitious Victorian entrepreneur who may not always have been all that he claimed to be. He may have been misled, or misguided, but more worryingly, especially for those who came to regret becoming involved with him, he may simply have been mischievous

The British Arsenic Mines

Before we leave the local nineteenth-century mining escapades, there is an interesting footnote to be told to the story of several of the Plympton mines, notably Bottle Hill, Wheal Mary Hutchings and Wheal Sydney. We have already alluded to it earlier, as it is a metalloid that is regularly to be found in areas rich in the metals we have been looking at so far – Arsenic. Certain of its qualities had been known about from time immemorial. In the Bronze Age it was often included in the mix to make the alloy harder, its use as a discreet poison led to it being known as the *'king of poisons'* or the *'poison of kings'*, but in the second half of the nineteenth century it found a widespread number of new uses – and so demand increased.

Victorian women started using it in combination with chalk and vinegar in an effort to make their complexion look more pale, so it was more obvious that they didn't work in the fields. It was used to adulterate certain foods in the pursuit of profit and wallpaper producers started using it in their dyes to make their pigments brighter and more colourful.

Thus, as the tin market started to falter in the 1870s and the demand for this celebrated metalloid increased, so Adventurers started to look for another vein of material they could dig out of the ground and sell.

Advertisements were taken out in papers across the United Kingdom, including the Western Times, London Evening Standard, Leeds Mercury, The Sketch, The Scotsman, *and* The Belfast Newsletter

But as with the tin, copper and iron enterprises, this was by no means any easier or any less plagued by intrigue and duplicity.

As we have already seen with the sorry story of Wheal Mary Hutchings, arsenic had become the main focus back in the 1870s but that never became the successful operation that had been anticipated – an all too familiar scenario – but, in 1896 with the *West Briton* on 28 May suggesting that *'Arsenic continues scarce, and a further advance on the present extremely high figures seems quite possible'* – The Economist was quoting figures of £24-£25 a ton, just a couple of weeks later – a new company was launched: The British Arsenic Mines Limited, a rather grand title given that the mines in question were all in Plympton!

As ever the prospectus ploughed a familiar furrow. Notices appeared on the front page of newspapers – in those days the front page was nothing but advertisements and public notices – the chairman of the Board of Directors announced that he had visited the mines, on 30 May, accompanied by an expert and samples had been taken under his own supervision and sent under his seal to Messrs Johnson, Matthey & Co., for assay, whose certificates are embodied in the prospectus.

With samples having been taken from Bottle Hill, Wheal Mary Hutchings, Wheal Sydney and the waste heaps of Bottle Hill Burrows and Mary Hutchings, all yielding between 11.5% and 25.5% arsenic, as well, in some cases native black tin, the prospects were deemed exceedingly good.

Captains William Gill and Henry Rodda estimated that there were around 65,800 tons of ore that could be brought to grass at the cost of six shillings per ton at Wheal Mary Hutchings, while at Wheal Sydney *'there is an enormous quantity of "debris" thrown away by the late workers, which we feel certain would pay handsomely to treat ... there cannot be less than 20,000 tons which can be treated at a cost of two shillings and sixpence per ton and will yield an almost immediate return'*.

Meanwhile, Captain John Farley was quoted as saying with regard to the Bottle Hill Sett that there were *'five or six well defined lodes throughout the entire length of the sett ... all pregnant with Arsenic, Tin and Copper'*. He added another refrain familiar through the years: *'I can with confidence recommend this property as one of the most promising in the West of England'*.

To the outsider it doubtless looked, in modern parlance, like a no-brainer, a get rich quick opportunity the like of which didn't come around that often. Perhaps that is how it struck the 50-year-old chairman, George Pitts-Lewis, the Honiton-born vicar's son, who had represented Barnstaple from 1885-1892 and who had become a member of the Queen's Council in the year he was first elected to the House of Commons.

Certainly he didn't have any of the hallmarks of a rogue trader and neither did his fellow director, 56-year-old Henry Anson Cavendish, the 4th Baron Waterpark, who was Deputy Lieutenant of Derbyshire County Council. Other directors included Alderman AJ Hawkes, who was also a director of the West Australian Loan and General Finance Corporation Limited, and John L Matthew, who also held a directorship of the Lydenburg Minerals Exploring Company.

It's not clear whether these gentlemen were also major shareholders of the newly formed British Arsenic Mines Company, but there was space for a fifth director to be nominated 'by the Vendors after Allotment'.

The capital of the company (incorporated under the Companies Act) was set at £50,000 divided into 30,000 10% Cumulative Preference Shares and 20,000 Ordinary Shares of £1 each payable: two shillings and sixpence on application, with a further half a crown on allotment and five shillings one month after allotment, and the balance as required.

We know that the company was theoretically granted a sett for Hemerdon and permission, also from Miss Dorothea Strode, to set up a burning house and tramway, but it appears that although amendments to the draft lease were made by both parties, the lease was never finally dated or signed.

It transpires that there was another company that still claimed to have an interest in the mines – the Beta Mining Syndicate. The situation was further complicated by the fact that there was unpaid rent outstanding on the mines, dating in the case of Wheal Sidney, back to 1888.

The British Arsenic Mines board anticipated that these leases would be renewable, and wrote to Strode's solicitors stating that they would not be in a position to allot shares, until that was agreed.

After months of correspondence between various sets of solicitors, in September 1896, Pitts-Lewis wrote to Bewes & Hellard, the Strode's lawyers, more or less suggesting that as the Beta Syndicate had held the leases for a number of years without actually doing much, then it might be an idea for the Strodes to look to his new company to actually get something done.

However, nothing appears to have been done and in October Pitts-Lewis again wrote to Strode's solicitors to say that 'under the circumstances my brother directors and I unanimously declined to proceed to allotment and' we have 'returned the subscriptions – having actually been obliged to find a portion of the money to do this out of our own pockets ... but this appeared preferable to lending ourselves to a transaction of the nature ... of which the facts I have told you enable you to judge.

'I repeat that having seen your client's property I think it is very valuable.'

Curiously enough, that was not quite the end of the matter. The next letter from Pitts-Lewis & Co. came via their London solicitors, Ashley, Lumby

& Michael, noting, with regret, the demise of the 73-year-old spinster, Dorothea Georgina Admonition Strode and enquiring whether her death would 'make any difference to the granting of leases'.

It appears that Pitts-Lewis had now tentatively put a new syndicate together, in which he and his partners proposed to join forces with a firm of merchants in London 'who have a very high reputation'.

The heir to the Newnham estates was Miss Strode's nephew, George Sydney Strode Lowe, a 35-year-old Army Captain, then living in Collingwood Villas, Stoke, just outside Plymouth. It appears that George, who soon afterwards changed his surname to Strode, wasn't minded to change the lease arrangements.

The lease of Wheal Sidney reverted to the Strode estate, John Stebbing and Eliza Ward having been left Thomas Vosper's interests in his will, but that was not enough to make a substantial difference to the situation and so it was that the much anticipated rush for Plympton arsenic didn't really get going this time around, leaving those in the area to perhaps breathe more easily!

The following year, incidentally, in December 1897, Lord Watermark's eldest son and heir Henry, died, aged 22, and in 1899 Lord Watermark became Chairman of Derbyshire County Council.

George Pitts-Lewis (1845-1906) English judge, Liberal MP for Barnstaple (1885-92), enthusiastic freemason, tricyclist and chairman of the British Arsenic Mines.

Refined arsenic crystals prior to crushing.

Originally, bronze had been created by mixing copper with arsenic. The poisonous element, however, created toxic fumes that led to metallurgists' early deaths. Tin was found to be more stable — and less lethal — but somewhat elusive, thus it was that for hundreds of years arsenic had been left in the lodes underground as there was no known industrial use for it and many of the mine dumps contained tons of waste arsenic.

PART THREE: TWENTIETH CENTURY – FOXED
HARD TIMES - INTRODUCING TUNGSTEN

It's one of life's quirks of fate, perhaps, that the next major adventure in the story of mining in the immediate Plymouth area was concentrated around a mineral that wasn't even on anyone's radar until the end of the eighteenth century, and wasn't mined in earnest until the middle of the nineteenth century when most of the mines in and around here were 'knacked'. Tungsten (tung sten, the former Swedish name for one of its principal ores – scheelite literally translated as heavy stone) is a rare metal that was identified as a new element in 1781 and first isolated as a metal two years later.

The major ores of this remarkably robust metal are wolframite (so named because of its wolf-like black and hairy appearance) and scheelite (named after the Swedish scientist Carl Scheele who was the man who published in 1781 that the mineral contained lime and a hitherto unknown acid – tungstic acid). The name wolfram itself is actually derived from two Latin words for 'wolf's foam', the notion being that the wolf devoured the tin. In the early days of processing tin ore, the 'foam' formed on the molten tin and reduced the tin recovery (the other two tungsten yielding minerals incidentally are ferberite and hubnerite).

Around the same time, a Spanish nobleman, Juan José de D'Elhuyar, researched the 'new' metal and concluded that it was an iron and manganese salt of a new acid and that wolfram contained the same acid as Scheele had found.

With the highest melting point of all elements so far discovered (3,422°C) it is almost twice as dense as lead and its modern usages include light bulb filaments, x-ray tubes, superalloys and radiation shielding. In the early twentieth century, however, it was its hardness and density that made it of great value in metal cutting and the creation of penetrative missiles – in other words it had enormous potential in the world of metal-based military hardware.

As it happens wolfram is generally found in areas associated with tin, however, in the early days, because it was deemed to have no real use, the presence of wolfram was considered a contaminant and tin concentrates would lose value per ton if it was found to contain even a low proportion of wolfram.

Processing such ore was very difficult as both wolfram and cassiterite have high specific gravities. If a vein was found underground, it would be left undisturbed and if found during processing it would be dumped along with other gangue (non-metallic) matter.

Given the conditions in which wolfram tended to be found it was no great surprise to find that the Gunnislake area of the Tamar Valley would come to be termed *'the cradle of tungsten processing development,'* as two processes were devised for extracting this the heaviest metal of heavy metals.

The first was the invention of a local man, Dr Robert Oxland, a chemist and metallurgist who lived at No.8 Portland Square (which stood on a site now subsumed under the University of Plymouth campus). The process was first introduced to Drakewalls Mine, Gunnislake where Oxland even paid for the soda used in the process

Oxland patented his manufacturing process, for extracting 'sodium tungstate' ('tungstate of soda'), tungstic acid, and the metal tungsten itself, in 1847. A decade later, this time with inestimable consequences, he followed up with a further new process, for producing the very hard alloy of tungsten steel.

The following year, 1858, we find the first mention of tungsten in the official mineral statistics, by which time the process had been introduced at Kit Hill. That same year tungstate of soda was sold by both Drakewalls and Kit Hill Mines. The process is described as follows by *Collings Mining Journal* of 1915:

'The process included the 'burnt whits' being buddled or tabled to get rid of silica or other light waste, mixed with soda-ash in the proportion of about 50% of wolfram present, heated to a considerable temperature in a reverberatory furnace for several hours, being stirred during the process, thus converting the wolfram into tungstate of soda.

'The mass is then thrown into lixiviating vats [vats into which the ore is placed to be washed with hot or cold water to extract the soluble mineral content], *the solution is drawn off into evaporating pans where the tungstate is crystallised out. The tin present can be separated after pulverisation.'*

Oxland's pioneering work in the field was earlier evidenced at the Great Exhibition of 1851 where he exhibited *'a case containing illustrations of tin ore containing wolfram, and of it being removed'.*

Such was Oxland's passion for his wolfram work that he evidently erected the machinery at Drakewalls at his own expense, and that he also provided the 'soda' for the process free of charge.

In 1861, in what was to prove a remarkably prescient suggestion, John Henry Pepper (*Playbook of Metals* p.491) spoke of Oxland's manufacture of the hardest steel (a tungsten alloy) *'which will bore through and file ordinary steel, so that, if England is to begin a course of experiments on the best armour for ships, Mr Oxland should be consulted on this most important question.'*

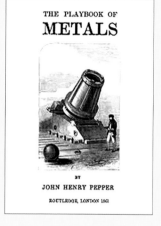

John Henry Pepper (1821-1900)

OXLAND'S EXPERIMENTS WITH TUNGSTEN. 491

like steel, and possesses considerable brilliancy. It possesses a remarkable hardness, and has lately been applied with success by Mr. Oxland, of Plymouth, in the manufacture of the hardest steel, which, it is said, will bore through and file ordinary steel, so that, if England is to begin a course of experiments on the best armour for ships, Mr. Oxland should be consulted on this most important question.

The specific gravity of tungsten is 17·6, and its equivalent 95. It forms with oxygen gas two combinations :—

Binoxide of tungsten . . . . . WO_2
Tungstic acid . . . . WO_3

Wolfram is obtained abundantly in Cornwall, and was formerly considered to be worthless; but since Oxland has discovered a mode of separating the tin, and is now likely to employ the tungstic acid, we may shortly expect to see the price of wolfram take a respectable position in the metallic market. Wolfram is a tungstate of iron, and consists of—

Tungstic acid . . . . 78·77
Protoxide of iron . . . . 18·32
Protoxide of manganese . . . . . 6·22
Silica . . . . 1·25

Robert Oxland, Plymouth chemist, whose tungsten processing was first used at Drakewalls Mine at Gunnislake. He had two patents from Queen Victoria, dated 1871 and 1875.

Pepper also hinted that *'since Oxland has discovered a mode for separating the tin and wolfram it is now likely that the price of wolfram should take a respectable position in the metal market'.*

However, Pepper's proposal appeared to fall on deaf ears, in England at least, and it was the Germans who steamed ahead in the game of mining technology and processing.

In summer of 1898 a licence was obtained from the Reverend George Woollcombe and operations were started on Hemerdon Ball, *'where several fine specimens* [of wolfram] *had been found in the stones on the hedges placed there when the land was reclaimed from the moor* (The Times, Saturday 21 April 1950).*'* However, little came of it all. The problem was that it became clear that the yield could not be more than three to five pounds per ton of material treated and this would not be viable unless a significant lodes could be identified.

Another attempt was made in 1907, when building stone was removed from a Hemerdon Ball quarry and a lower level was opened up to see if a lode could be found, but only a small pocket was discovered and it soon petered out.

Meanwhile, sometime around 1900, wolfram/tungsten processing was further improved by the use of 'magnetic separation'. An early manufacturer of equipment employing this process was the Luhrig Company from Germany: *'the company's chief designer, Dr Buss, had invented a new type of shaking table, the Buss Swinging Table* (Doug Westaway).*'*

Supported on 32 thin vertical wooden laths, arranged to provide a slight tossing motion to the ore as it was vibrated to and fro, it produced an efficient separation of the ore and waste material.

So confident was Dr Buss (whose process had already proved successful in Australian gold mines) that when dealing with the operators of the Gunnislake Clitters mine, he said that if the trial of his technology proved unsuccessful the Luhrig Company would remove his tables and replace

Dr Kuo Ching Li, born in the Hunan Province of China, in 1887, and a student at Imperial College, London before the First World War, Dr Li discovered and developed the first Tungsten deposits in China. Having invented the Li Process for tungsten carbide manufacture he established the Wah Change Trading Corporation in New York and went on to further enhance his reputation as a global authority on Tungsten, leading him to become known widely as the 'Tungsten King'. He died in 1961 a naturalised American citizen.

them with the original ones. He didn't need to worry.

On 2 January 1904 the latest edition of *Mining World* reported on the first AGM of Gunnislake Clitters with reference to the new process:

'We commenced negotiations with the view of purchasing a Wetherill electromagnetic separator. At the time we commenced negotiations the price asked was prohibitive, but a new separator was brought out which was of a much more satisfactory character and after inspection by our consulting engineer and our director Mr A Schiff we were able to obtain a separator which left us a satisfactory profit in treating our mixed concentrates.

'Initial difficulties have been overcome solving the treatment of these complex ores. We have been pioneers in the matter, we have now a plant which is practically second to none in the world and is the finest of its sort in Cornwall.'

Curiously enough it was around this time that our Germanic friends had acquired their own wolfram mine, in England, and the only one outside Devon and Cornwall to produce the mineral – the Carrock Mine in Cumbria.

This facility was a 'sole-producer' (i.e. only wolfram) as would be Castle-an-Dinas Mine in Cornwall later in the twentieth century.

First worked in 1854, the Cumbria wolfram mine was known as 'Carrock Mines Ltd' in 1902, and fell idle in 1905. It was then reopened the following year by two Germans, William Boss and Frederick Boehm, and began trading as Cumbrian Mining Co Ltd.

Inevitably, both gentlemen subsequently left when British relations with Germany deteriorated. By 1911 production had again ceased, only to re-commence as The Carrock Mining Syndicate under a group of steel manufacturers until operations again stopped in 1917.

In the meantime, back in the summer of 1913, a 26-year-old Chinese student, Kuo Ching Li, working under Cornish-born Professor Samuel Truscott at the Royal School of Mines, Imperial College, London, was assigned to look in more detail at the magnetic separation process then being used in the mines at Redruth.

'One day Professor Truscott inspected the separation room. He asked how I was progressing. I told him I had got quite a bit of wolfram out. As I presented my "production" to him I queried, "What will be done with the wolframite after it is recovered?"

'"Oh", Professor Truscott quickly replied, "We send this to the Germans who somehow or other know how to make use of this blooming stuff".

"At what prices"?, I asked.

"We are getting 8 to 10 shillings a unit," the Professor answered.

'This was about one year before World War One broke out and around the time that such British industries that were using tungsten were obtaining

around 90% of their mineral supplies from German companies that in turn were sourcing their raw material from Carrock and companies in Cornwall and Devon.'

KC Li picks up the narrative again: 'With the discovery that the Germans were effectively using tungsten in the manufacture of munitions the first tungsten rush began. The Ministry of Munitions sent representatives to Devon and Cornwall to stimulate the production from known sources of supply, and to induce the search for new deposits.

The first major discovery at Hemerdon was a lode averaging 26 inches in width on the outcrop which was followed through a quarry for a distance of 150 feet and assayed 0.97%- WO_3.

Terrell recorded that 'prospectors suspected that they had struck a stockwork deposit and sank a series of sampling pits in the kaolinised granite to determine the nature of the ore body.' Each sampling pit exposed a network of small quartz veins containing good wolframite values.

It appears that a shortage of industrial diamonds had led to the Germans deploying tungsten in their cutting dies thereby accelerating their ability to produce munitions at the very time the Allies thought they would be exhausting their stocks within six months in the event of a war.

It was back in 1867 that John Nicholls senior, a well-known chemical manufacturer and china clay merchant from St Austell, first identified the presence of wolfram at Hemerdon. However, as there was little demand for the mineral at that time and as Nicholls was clearly more interested in the clay deposit, there was no further action.

The following decade it appears that Nicholls' son, also called John, and then in his late-20s, discussed the possibility of attempting to do something with the deposit, with Richard Williams, a local mine captain with extensive experience around the Plympton mines, but again nothing came of it.

Indeed it wasn't until it had become obvious that the German military might was certainly not going to be silenced by Christmas 1914, or even Christmas 1915, that the perceived benefits of adding to our tungsten reserves resulted in further exploration of Hemerdon Ball.

Geologists now suggest that the granite deposit at Hemerdon is much older than that of the neighbouring igneous landmass that is Dartmoor, and the earlier melt doubtless accounts for the presence of this rare, heavy and hard mineral often associated with tin.

In the event it was one of the workmen from the neighbouring clayworks, Lawrence Macbean, who was credited with the tungsten discovery at Hemerdon in 1915. Macbean lived at Bottle Hill and, like his father, William, and elder brothers, John and James, worked at the china clay works that was run by the aforementioned John Nicholls junior, who lived at Galva House, close by. Nicholls was married, to Edith Woollcombe,

whose father was the Reverend George Ley Woollcombe and brother was George Arthur Ley Woollcombe – heir to the Hemerdon estate.

Indeed it was George Arthur who, in April 1916, agreed the draft lease for the new Hemerdon Mine sett, which included Strode land, with a new band of adventurers: engineer Ernest William Stedman, Reginald George Rodney and William Crosbie Hamilton, a retired surgeon, all of Plymouth. The draft appears to have been an adaptation of an earlier document for most of it is typescript and each time the phrase 'liberty, licence and authority to dig, mine, stream work and search for tin and tin ore, copper and copper ore, lead and lead ore and all other metals and metallic minerals (except Royal Metals),' appears, someone has hand written 'wolfram and other tungsten minerals' at the beginning of the list (Royal Metals, incidentally, refers to gold and silver).

Before long, however, a new board had taken on the lease, Stedman and Co., having sold their interest in the lease, for £15,000, in April 1917 (£3,500 cash and £11,500 in fully paid shares of £1 each). Styling themselves the Hemerdon Mines Ltd., the new company was officially registered in Edinburgh, but its operating office was in Glasgow.

The original directors were Messrs DD Binnie, a director of the Century Insurance Company, RA Murray, chartered accountant and a director of several large trust companies, Gilbert McPherson, General Manager for the Government of the largest shell-filling factory in Scotland and also Managing Director of Wheal Jewell and Mary Tavy Mines, and John Traill Cargill. The company had an authorised capital of £80,000 (around £5.5 million in today's terms), of which £76,000 was issued, fortified by a loan of £20,000 which was said to have been advanced by JT Cargill, who chaired the board.

John Traill Cargill was one of Scotland's wealthiest sons. His father had founded the Burmah Oil Company back in the 1870s and it had gone on to become one of the largest oil companies to be based in Britain.

Sir John Traill Cargill (1867-1954) went to Burma in his early 20s to work in the Rangoon office of his father's oil company. He succeeded his father in 1904 and remained in charge until 1943. He chaired Scottish Oils Ltd., from 1922-43.

He was created a baronet, of Glasgow, in 1920, and in addition to his chairmanship of Hemerdon Mines Ltd., he also served as a director of the Anglo-Sumatra Rubber Company, the Anglo-Persian Oil Company and the Assam Oil Company.

In the month that saw the end of the Great War, Cargill donated £20,000 to Glasgow University for the establishment of a Chair of Applied Physics – it was re-designated as Natural Philosophy in 1945.

JT had taken on this business on the death of his father in 1904 and had gone on to take an interest in other key industries of the day – he had become a director of the Anglo-Sumatra Rubber Company in 1916. Given his shrewd investments elsewhere, one can but wonder at Cargill's motives for investing in Hemerdon. Did he think there would be an ongoing government contract for the mineral? Did he see a healthy long-term future for tungsten or was he doing his bit for the war effort, given that the government resources were already stretched?

Gilbert McPherson was clearly the vital link. Well connected in Scotland and in the local mining community, he, Binnie and Murray had already come together as directors of The British Tungsten Mines Ltd.

Lawrence Macbean (right) with George Bayram, an engineer who worked at Hemerdon in the early days. Both men are sporting their Masonic aprons, Ernest Terrell was also involved with the Masons briefly.

Ernest Terrell was a keen local cricketer and here we see him with Ilsington Wanderers Cricket Club c.1909. Back row: Herbert Harris, Tom Ball, Ronald Harris, Ike Sanders, Sydney Grose. Middle row: Ernest Terrell, Sydney Wills, Harry Harris (Capt.), W Roberts, J Webb. Front Charlie Wills, Norman Grose.

The company had been set up in the summer of 1916 with offices at 176 West George Street, Glasgow, the adjacent premises to those of Murray's accountancy firm out of which Hemerdon Mines would operate. Incidentally as well as McPherson, the other major mining engineer-cum-director that British Tungsten had on their books was Ernest Terrell who had set the venture up in the first place.

Whatever Cargill's rationale for getting involved, it was inevitably something of a gamble, although Ernest Terrell, a man with some not inconsiderable experience in matters wolfram, had already made some very positive noises.

Six or seven weeks before Christmas 1916, having been charged with running the new enterprise, Terrell, produced his first report on the 300-acre sett. At that stage it looked as though the ground rent was to be £100 per annum which was to be merged into a royalty of 1/20th of the gross value of the mineral sold, with the potential to rise to 1/16th. The length of the term was set at 21 years – that is through to 1937.

Terrell, then aged 37, was every inch a mining man, from an established mining family, stretching back at least four generations to Samuel Terrell who was the mine captain at Drakewalls back in the 1790s. His father, Stephen, was a mine captain and tin dresser, while his grandfather, also Stephen, was a copper miner from Redruth. His brothers, Fred and Stephen, also opted for careers in mining, and at one point, around the turn of the nineteenth/twentieth centuries, all three brothers were working at Gunnislake Clitters mine.

Ernest's wife, Emma, similarly came from a solid mining family, curiously enough by the name of Nicholls – her father, James, was a copper miner, as were at least four of her eight younger brothers, James, Jonathan, George and Francis. Nine years before his arrival at Hemerdon, Ernest Terrell had become the mine manager at Stormsdown, near Ilsington, north of Ashburton and before that he had been assistant mine manager at the aforementioned Gunnislake Clitters Mine, where he gained valuable experience working with both tin and wolfram concentrations and more importantly, magnetic separation of complex tin and wolfram ores.

During the course of 1916 Terrell, as the managing director of British Tungsten Mines, designed and supervised the construction of an alluvial operation at Buttern Hill Mine on Bodmin Moor (on remote moorland between Davidstow airfield and Altarnun), he also visited the Hemerdon sett on several occasions, thoroughly examining the prospecting operations – some of which he reported *'have been done in accordance with my own suggestions in order to obtain as clear an idea as possible of the mineral value of the property'*.

After going into some detail about the quality of the mineral samples assayed, the apparent size of the lodes and the amount of useful material potentially on site he concluded that, in his opinion, *'the property affords an opportunity for a very profitable enterprise. The surface deposit is a most attractive feature on account of its extent, mineral value and low cost of treatment; also because production is assured as soon as the necessary plant and equipment is erected.*

'The (Hemerdon) Ball Lode offers more than a reasonable chance of a good lode mine and should be persevered with. The ore obtained from this lode can be conveniently treated through a plant dealing with the surface deposit.'

Earlier in the document Terrell had emphasised the notion of the ore *'being attacked by the open-work system. It is difficult to give a serviceable estimate of mineral output as this is governed not by the amount of material available, but by the scale on which it is decided to conduct operations. I have calculated, however, that with a unit treating one hundred tons per day by crushing with light gravity-stamps and concentrating the mineral by means of modern dressing machines, the total working costs, including power requirements and local supervision, will not exceed 9/6d per ton.'*

In a later document, that underpinned the formation of the Hemerdon Mines Company, in April 1917, Terrell, with McPherson, amended the figures slightly:

'The deposit so far as proved is estimated on a conservative basis to contain 1,300,000 tons of Tungsten and Tin bearing material.

'The mineral values contained in this Deposit as chemically assayed are valued at 37/6d per ton and the recoverable value with the latest appliances is estimated at 20/8d per ton and present prices of the products.

'Reducing the latter value to 15/- per ton to allow for fluctuation in price and other contingencies and estimating cost of working at 5/- per ton, the return from the property, allowing for expenses of administration is estimated as follows:

'Capital £40,000 output 100 tons per day DIVIDEND 26%
Capital £60,000 output 300 tons per day DIVIDEND 68%

'The present price of Tungsten is £190 per ton and of Oxide of Tin about £128. Should, however, the average price of both products fall to £100 per ton, the profit on an output of 300 tons per day would yield a dividend of 20% on a capital of £60,000.'

On this occasion there was no formal prospectus and no appeal to the public to encourage them to purchase shares. The Treasury, on behalf of the Government, doubtless anxious to get their hands on another supply of tungsten, granted consent to raise the capital without a general appeal. Clearly it was felt that the stats stacked up well enough and those shareholders that did come on board, clearly anticipated handsome rewards. The list was impressive and included Sir William Beardmore of Parkhead, Mr RAD Howie, coal master of Kilmarnock and London based but Scottish born Thomas Callendar of Callenders Cable and Construction Company (established in 1870, they patented vulcanised bitumen in 1881 and the company is still going today as Balfour Beatty).

Thus it was that Hemerdon Mines Limited came into being with no shortage of genuine backers. Gilbert McPherson was appointed managing director and Ernest Terrell, general manager. With every prospect of immediate investment, excellent returns and seemingly a degree of urgency because of the ongoing war, development wasn't as swift as it might have been.

Charles Barclay, a young local teenager visiting the site just a fortnight after his father had died, in April 1917, noted a number of men working on trial pits, but the only building on site at that time was *'a small wooden shanty to the east of the clump of firs (Hemerdon Ball) where tools and specimens were kept'*.

Twelve months' later work on what was to be *'the largest plant in the Western Counties'* was not complete. The roof was not finished and only one bit of machinery had been fixed in position. There were on the premises 50 head of Californian stamps for crushing, but although the foundations for them had been completed they were not yet in place. There was a similar situation regarding three gas engines.

The basic layout was fixed though, arranged across three terraces, the top one for crushing, the next for shaking tables and the third for slimes and separators, all with concrete floors.

Waggons from the china clay works were used to bring ore to the washer and stamps from the open pit..

Hemerdon Mine c.1919 showing the mill, powerhouse, and workshops. The mine office is in the foreground, the inclined tramway is on the left, the pump house on the right in the foreground – see site plan inset for further details

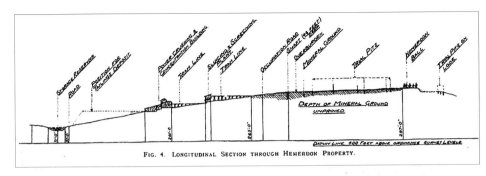

FIG. 4. LONGITUDINAL SECTION THROUGH HEMERDON PROPERTY.

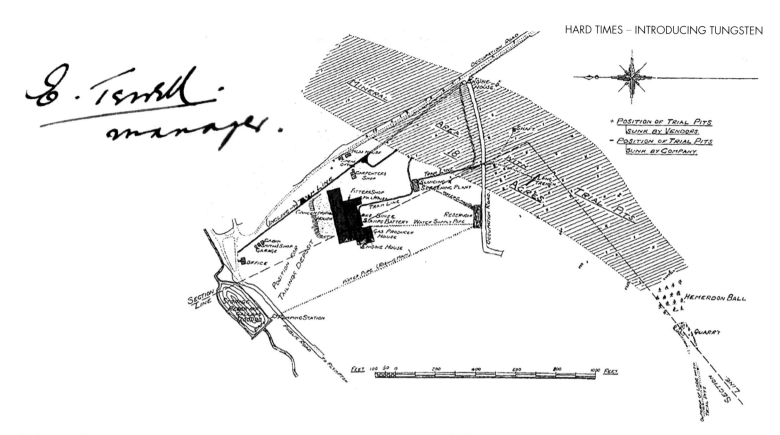

'At the bottom of the hill below the mill there is a steam ram pump driven by a portable engine for pumping water from the stream to the mill.'
At that point a dam was in the course of construction across the stream to form a reservoir that would ensure a constant supply of water.'

Charles Felix Barclay, remarkably enough, was barely 15 years old in 1918, but he possessed a real passion for mines in the area, making detailed plans of most of them over the next few years.

His notes on his visit that year to Hemerdon concluded with the observation that there was an office at the bottom of the site along with several huts, one for the men, another for assaying and another as a kind of office.

He also made mention of two Foden steam wagons which were used to bring the machinery up from Plympton Station. It was the intention to use these vehicles to take tin and tungsten concentrate from the mine to the station.

The fact that the country was at war throughout this period made the job of setting up the mine all the more difficult, as Terrell himself explained:

'The power station and mill house, mineral dressing department, carpenters' and fitters' workshops, and store form one compact set of buildings. It was intended to construct these of wood framing, covered with corrugated galvanised sheets,. The construction being undertaken during the war, the Government could not give permits for the use of galvanised iron sheets, and it was decided to adopt brick walls and use asbestos cement sheets for the roofs. A permit for the latter material was also refused, however. 'Eventually the roofs were constructed of 3/4in match-boarding, covered with ruberoid felt, and supported by lattice girders of pitch-pine resting on brickwork pillars. The buildings are lit throughout by electricity. The form of construction can be seen by reference to the cross-section (below left).'

When the war ended, in November 1918, there were still a few outstanding items on Terrell's plans – work on the last 10 head of stamps, slime-dressing machines and the delivery of a third gas engine – but it hadn't just been the sourcing of materials and machinery that had caused the mine manager headaches during the war.

'Throughout the period occupied in erecting the plant an extreme shortage of skilled and semi-skilled labour was experienced. When the first unit of the power and mill equipment was ready for service it was found impossible to obtain men capable of running it, notwithstanding the offers

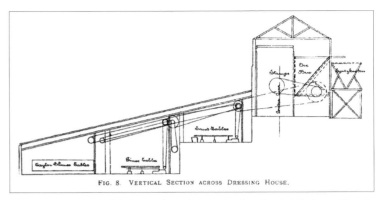

FIG. 8. VERTICAL SECTION ACROSS DRESSING HOUSE.

Above: *Cross section of the main plant, showing the three levels. Left: James Slime Tables and Sand-Middlings Pulverisers. Below: The open-cast pit, each stope, as they were called, had its own track, workers using pick and shovel would load waggons (from the china clay works) they were then taken to the wash plant. The wooden posts provided lighting to work the opencast at night.*

of good remuneration and appeals to the Ministry of Munitions and the Labour Exchanges.

'Not even one experienced gas-engine driver could be secured, although three were required for continuous running. The same remark applies to the stamp battery. General labourers were therefore requisitioned for service in the engine room and stamp mill, and girls proved the only class of labour available for the concentration plant.

'The results obtained under these circumstances were far from satisfactory, and with the full equipment nearing completion without any indication of an improvement in the labour position, the directors felt unjustified in continuing to expose such a costly plant to the constant risk of serious accident, beyond proving the value of the mineral deposit.

'Furthermore, in March, 1919, the Ministry of Munitions intimated that no wolfram parcels would be accepted by the Government after April 30.

'This was disappointing in view of the encouragement that the department bestowed on the enterprise and the promises given of a maintenance of the war-time price for a post-war period of two years. At the same time it was stated that the existing stocks of wolfram concentrate were considerable, and producers were advised to curtail, or, if possible, suspend production "in their own interests" until such stocks were reduced.'

Reading between the lines the mine manager's sense of frustration was manifest. Having been let down by the Government, Terrell felt that he and his fellow directors had no alternative and 'under the circumstances no other course was open but to cease work ...'

However, he clearly didn't see the matter as closed for he added 'except to erect the third gas engine and complete the mill plant, and then await the return of more favourable conditions.

'Milling was therefore suspended forthwith.'

Terrell's comprehensive and illuminating account of the happenings at Hemerdon were published in the February 1920 edition of the Mining Magazine and it's possible he thought that by providing a fulsome account of the situation he might attract other interested parties or simply put pressure on the authorities to find some other way of making the mine viable.

Certainly Terrell had had plenty of opportunity to assess and cost most of the elements that went into the process from extraction to finished product and in that regard it's worth repeating the end of the article in full.

'It is unfortunate,' he wrote, 'that a suspension of operations became necessary before it was possible to obtain figures indicating the actual working costs. As already stated, neither the power plant nor the stamp battery and concentrating equipment was then completed, and even the machinery in commission had not run its full trials necessary for the most advantageous adjustments to meet various conditions which only became evident in actual practice.

'Generally speaking, however, after allowing for an increase in the cost of labour and materials beyond the earlier anticipations, the experience gained indicates that the essential factors in connection with the proposition were recognised in advance and estimated with approximate accuracy.

'The clay in the ore gives considerable trouble if even a small proportion of it is permitted to pass into the washing and screening plant and finds its way into the ore-bin, the tendency being to cement the ore and prevent regular feeding of the battery. On this account it may be necessary to supplement the washing arrangements, but otherwise no abnormal difficulties of treatment are encountered.

'The cost of breaking the ore and tramming it an average distance of about 180 yards to the screening and rock-breaking plant is found to be 2s2d per ton.'

Although not in production Terrell was eager to understand more regarding the formation of the deposit and set about driving a prospecting tunnel which showed 'no perceptible increase in hardness of the ground to an additional 50ft of depth, and this is the principal factor likely to affect the above charge. Screening and rock breaking cost 43/4d per ton, exclusive of a continuous electric power supply of 16 to 18 hp. Tramming from the screen plant to the battery ore-bin costs 53/4d per ton, but as 28% of the ore is eliminated by the screens and washed down to the dressing plant, this charge, spread over the total quantity of ore treated is reduced to 4.14d per ton.

'The total cost of breaking, screening and delivering the ore to the stamp mill is therefore 2s10.39d plus about 1d for power per ton.'

Mill, brick construction with match boarding roof, making use of the hillside slope.

'In the stamp mill and concentration house the costs will certainly compare most favourably with those obtaining in West Country mining generally. The stamps give a duty of 6 tons per head per 224 hours, and as for each 6 tons passed through the stamp mill fully two tons are delivered through the screen, the full, through put capacity, in terms of 50 stamps, is 400 tons per 24 hours.

'From the experience gained in operating a section of the plant it has been found that at the stamp battery, for the full through-put and for each shift of eight hours, two men will be required in the ore-bins and three for the ore-feeders to ensure regular feeding, but this cost may be reduced and probably eliminated altogether with clearer washing of the ore. One stamp man can attend to 25 stamps.'

Terrell then went into more detail about the number of employees that would be needed on each shift, in the event of the full concentration plant to be working:

'1 foreman, 1 man attending 15 James tables treating sand from battery pulp, 1 man attending 15 James tables treating fines from battery pulp, 1 man attending 5 pulverisers and 5 James tables treating product from pulverisers, 1 man attending 3 Taylor tables treating slimes, 1 man cleaning out concentrates and attending Record tables treating screens ore, 3 men reconcentrating fines and slimes heads in two shifts.

'In the dressing house, in which work was carried on in one day-shift only, the largest output treated was in the last 4 weeks of operations, when 13 tons of wolfram and black tin were obtained from an average of 16.35 stamps working full time.

'One foreman dresser, 1 man with 3 lads dealt with the concentrates yielding this mineral, performing all the work entailed in drying, magnetically separating, and dressing the material handled.

'As it will be necessary to work continuously in the dressing house in 3 shifts when the entire stamp-mill is in commission, it can be taken that 12 persons will be required in this department.

'Two fitters, one smith and a carpenter are also necessary for general work in these trades.

A total of 61 can therefore deal with a through-put of 400 tons per day, from delivery of the ore at the bins to the recovery of the finished products.

'It is established that, working on a full scale, the overall operating charges, including local management, cannot exceed 8s per ton of ore at the present cost of labour and materials.

'The opportunity may later present itself for supplementing this article by giving a close analysis of working costs under the stated conditions. In the meantime, it is hoped that the wolfram mining industry will soon emerge from the dark cloud overshadowing it owing to foreign over-production, stimulated by the necessities of war, and consequent extraordinarily high prices.

'It is in the national interest to foster this industry by all reasonable means and not permit it to decay because of the existing abnormal conditions. Given a reasonable price and a market for the reception of its products, Hemerdon could quickly establish itself among the leading mines of the West of England.'

All in all Terrell estimated that £100,000 had been invested in the site since 1916, and in 1918 some £753.2s.2d worth of wolfram and tin had been sold. At the one-twentieth rate to the landowners, this meant a potential yield of £37.16s.11d. However, as Terrell was keen to point out to Woollcombe & Yonge, Strode's solicitors, as this was way below the £100 minimum agreed under the terms of the lease, no royalty was due. Terrell's missive was dated 21 January 1919 and in it he acknowledged that another consignment of nearly three tons had been sold, with another 'parcel of about 4 tons ready for despatch', but that wasn't the full story.

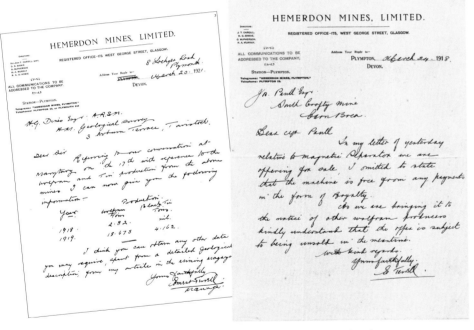

Left: Ernest Terrell's letter to HG Dines in March 1921 detailing the precise production figures from Hemerdon under his management. Right: Letter to Paull of South Crofty Mine regarding the sale of the Hemerdon magnetic separator in March 1918.

It wasn't far off though, for it was only five or six weeks later, on 4 March, that Terrell wrote again to Woollcombe & Yonge, with altogether less happy news:

'We beg to inform you that with deep regret and much reluctance, the directors of this Company are obliged to suspend operations at the Mine for the present:

'We have from the outset, experienced great difficulty in obtaining labour for our constructional work, but we have contrived to get this practically completed except for the installation of one Gas Engine. As soon as we commenced milling operations our difficulties were almost insuperable owing to the entire absence of the necessary skilled labour for running our Power Plant, Stamp Battery, and Dressing Machines.

'We have only ordinary general labourers in charge of our expensive and intricate Gas Engines, and the same class of labour is operating our Stamp Mill, with the result that we are in constant fear of a catastrophe with the Power Plant, while the maintenance charges in the Stamp Mill, and the loss of time due to inefficient handling is really appalling. We felt justified during the War in running the extraordinary risks entailed in view of the great national value of Wolfram, and for some time we retained hope that conditions might improve.

'As a matter of fact, however, we are now in a worse position than ever in regard to skilled labour, notwithstanding repeated appeals to and promises of assistance from the Employment Exchange. Advertisements in the local press have also failed to induce any of the men required to enter our Employ.

'The Directors now feel that they are no longer justified in taking such grave risks with the plant and at such abnormal maintenance charges, and have decided to suspend work until such time as an adequate supply of the skilled labour absolutely vital to efficient work is obtainable.

'The disappointment is all the greater as we are gradually working into the body of ore more representative of general mineral values than those in the areas we were obliged to first pass through. This you will understand from the fact that we are just selling well over ten tons of Tin and Wolfram, our last sale at the end of January being not quite five tons.'

From the figures that Terrell would send through to Henry George Dines in March 1920 it would appear that Hemerdon's total output was around 21.5 tons of wolfram and just over four tons of tin, scant return indeed for the massive amount of investment.

One can but wonder how the investors felt this time around, particularly as this had been in part an answer to the country's call to armaments and the Government, while not directly involved in the set up, had promised to purchase minerals from the company for at least two years after the cessation of hostilities.

As it transpired the Government, gave the Hemerdon Company all of a week's notice of the fact that they would no longer require wolfram from Plympton.

Their reasoning, apparently, was that there was a wolfram glut and they had also made a similar two-year, post-war pledge to China where 'very large deposits' of wolfram were made during wartime.

As Terrell subsequently explained to a group of fellow Rotarians when walking them around the mine in September 1921: The Government 'also became a prudent and alarmed Government, accelerated deliveries to the highest possible pitch.

'Had the war lasted, England's supplies of tungsten would have played a tremendous part in the engineering phase of it.

'When the war collapsed the Allies had such immense stocks of the precious reagent as are calculated to last for the next two years.

'And Hemerdon, with a mill capacity of 400 tons a day, had only just begun to deliver.'

When asked why the Government couldn't have broken with China instead, Mr Terrell said, dispassionately, 'I suppose the Government was bound in honour to China.'

It was doubtless something of a bitter pill for the shareholders, but Terrell remained relatively upbeat about the supply of this 'unique' mineral. Although the price had tumbled spectacularly from £190 to £30 per ton and everyone now appeared to have all they needed and more, he took the view that the supply would eventually be exhausted and that other scientific possibilities were yet to be found for the material.

'The use of tungsten is in its infancy,' he said, 'it comes from a group of metals the properties of which are very rare. It is the general opinion of metallurgists that there are far greater uses for it.'

While there may have been little or no demand for Hemerdon's wolfram at that time, the company found a ready market for the pulverised waste material – sand – that was the by product of the mineral extraction. Essentially it appears that almost 8,500 tons of matter was processed to achieve the 21.5 tons of wolfram and that created enough sand to generate 2,610 lorry-loads that was snapped up by Plympton coal merchant, William Willmott & Sons. But this wasn't worth anything like £30 a ton, more like two to three shillings per load.

Nevertheless, given that gravel and sand were reserved for those granting the leases, a letter arrived on Terrell's desk in March 1921 asking him to comment on the apparent irregularity. In the event, however, the view was taken to leave things as they were as 'it is unlikely that any other Company could be found just now to take over the Mine, as it clearly cannot be a paying proposition at the present price of wolfram.'

On 9 August 1921, Ernest Terrell, responding to the issue of sand sales, was anxious to point out to Strode's solicitors that, *'notwithstanding the discouraging outlook, the Directors have decided to incur the considerable expenditure necessary for a thorough overhaul of the three 280-hp Gas Engines and to give them a run under power, in pursuance of our policy of preserving the Machinery, in constant readiness for resumption of duty whenever the position warrants this course.'*

A commendable gesture when exercised by the owners for those reasons, but not so when, a couple of years later, in November 1923, two local lads, Leonard Hill, of Embankment Road and William Willmott of St Hilary Terrace, Plymouth, decided to start up an engine on site that had had its water jacket emptied. The incident had caused the paintwork to blister and the boys were summoned to the bench and ordered to pay £2, with a 10 shilling fine (around £30 today) and four shillings costs. One wonders if the William Willmott in question was the same William Willmott who was the eldest son of WF Willmott the coal and haulage contractor who had bought so much sand from Hemerdon – certainly he would probably have had some knowledge of the otherwise silent site.

Acting for the prosecution Mr Wolferstan conceded that the mine was in a state of suspended animation *'but it was hoped at some period to restart it and that therefore it was essential that it should be kept in good order.'*

Two years later, on 15 June 1925, we had reports from Gilbert McPherson, still on the books as the Managing Director, and Gilbert McPherson junior, along with Ernest Terrell, and a copy Terrell's *Mining Magazine* article, suggesting that perhaps the time had come to revive the mine.

'I feel strongly that the time has arrived for action seeing that Wolfram stocks are becoming depleted and that the position of the Tin market is satisfactory.'

Before outlining his latest proposals for the venture, McPherson spelt out in a little more detail the issues that hampered them in the first instance:

'a: Only part of the plant was in use – 20% of full capacity.

b: Only the poorest class of inexperienced ill-disciplined war labour was obtainable, even untrained women being employed on the concentration tables.

c: There was always a shortage even of this type of labour and a severe outbreak of influenza was a further handicap. [the 1918 influenza pandemic infected 500 million people around the world killing between 50-100 million]

Above: An early, pre-pneumatic tyre Willmott lorry, Right: James patent Ore Concentrating Tables were in use at Hemerdon and amongst those items put up for sale in 1928 when the Company went into liquidation.

d: The washing arrangements proved unsatisfactory and as the clay and fines were not all removed from the ore great trouble was experienced in stamping it.

e: The -1/8th sand product was not treated properly by the James dressing tables. Three Record tables were ordered, but only one was in use for a short time before the mill closed down.

f: Only a small part of the slimes plant was completed and used before closing down.

g: The mill ran for only short periods with continual stoppages and irregularities of flow and so was never tuned up to give the most efficient recovery.

h: Constructional work was being carried on alongside and among plant in operation.'

With those issues seemingly resolved and with McPherson's detailed proposals being put into place, he estimated healthy profits almost irrespective of price: his workings showed surpluses whether calculated at present prices or pre-war prices.

The key to rendering the operation viable was in automation of certain elements of the mine workings – more specifically the *'employment of a steam shovel in the quarry and the use of mechanical appliances to transport the ore to the washery and stamps ore bins instead of the old manual methods. It has been obvious,'* he averred, *'that if such methods of excavating and handling the ore could be introduced, a large reduction of working cost would be effected ...'*

The total capital required to effect this level of mechanization was, according to McPherson, £30,000 (£1.8 million in today's terms), made up of £17,000 of capital expenditure and £13,000 for working capital and expenses of new issue.

'This is,' he conceded, *'£10,000 more than the amount required to start on the old lines. Otherwise the schemes are not comparable as under the new scheme the present price of Wolfram is a profitable one, and the advantages which would result from such a substantial reduction in working cost are plain.'*

Plain and obvious to McPherson and Terrell maybe, but not to anyone else, the existing directors had apparently had enough and potential investors were unmoved by McPherson's logic.

Thus it was, that, barely eighteen months later, the decision was taken to put Hemerdon Mines Ltd into Liquidation.

It was a sad end to what could have been a major local endeavour. One can but speculate on how the Scottish investors viewed the whole sorry saga, and indeed to what extent McPherson and Terrell genuinely felt that this was an opportunity missed. Without the Great War perhaps the activity at Hemerdon would not have happened in the first place, and

HEMERDON MINES, LTD, (In Liquidation).—TENDERS, which are returnable before March 12th, 1928, are invited for the whole or part of the PLANT and EQUIPMENT of the Hemerdon Mines, near Plympton, Devon.

The equipment includes three large gas engines, with gas producer plant, air compressor, Californian stamps, pulverizers, James sand and slime tables, magnetic separators, and electric dynamos and generators.

Further particulars, permits for inspection, &c., may be obtained from Fox, Roy, and Co., Ltd., Prudential Chambers, Plymouth, Agents for J. Herbert Wilson, Esq.. C.A., Liquidator, 175, West George-street, Glasgow.

The highest or any tender not necessarily accepted.

perhaps the investment would have been more difficult to raise in the first place, however there was little doubt that the exigencies of war made the successful operation of the mine more difficult. One suspects that McPherson's description of the *'poorest class of inexperienced ill-disciplined war labour'* was the source of great frustration for the mine manager and doubtless the death, on 3 June 1918, of mine worker Francis Davis only added to the problems.

Davis, a former stoker at the local paper mill at Ivybridge, was 46 and married with three children, he was working at the Hemerdon site when a trench collapsed.

Nor could it have been easy when German prisoners of war were taken on to help bolster Hemerdon's workforce. Initially they were marched daily from their camp at Lee Mill, but then quarters were established for them at the mine, while a few lodged with local families. On some plans a spade working area is marked out as the 'German pit'. However, on Armistice Day – 11.11.1918 – it was reported that the German PoWs threw down their tools and shouted *'No more war, no more work!'* Language problems, attitude problems and who knows what other difficulties would have further hindered the production process.

That there was potential at the sett was in little doubt, that it was economically viable to exploit that potential was, as yet, for all of the reasons above, unproven. Terrell, however, remained convinced that one day the mine would re-open, but it was not to be something he would live to see as sadly he passed away on 20 June 1923.

(He had recovered after a week's illness from pneumonia, but then collapsed and died on the Saturday after his birthday. He had suffered from asthma for over seventeen years, which had prevented him serving in the Great War. He left £9,657 8s 3d, which he bequeathed to his wife and children, worth about £350,000 today.' Helen Wilson *Friends of the Tamar Valley Journal)*

Hemerdon shafted again

For fifteen years nothing happened of consequence at Hemerdon. Projects may have been mooted but action was there none, until, in the summer of 1936 the newly constituted Hemerdon Syndicate – a London-based enterprise – obtained the right to prospect the site, which according to press reports at the time *'belongs to a Cornish firm of mining engineers'*. Was this still McPherson holding out with a 21-year lease negotiated during the Great War?

Whatever the circumstances, the Hemerdon Syndicate appears to have been an offshoot of the British Metal Company which had mining interests all over the world and it was from all over the world that Germany – and France, Italy and Russia – began placing 'extraordinary' orders for tungsten concentrates. Indeed, according to the Tungsten Institute, *'Germany bought up virtually the entire world supply of off grade tungsten ores.*

'In a barter agreement with China, in 1936, Germany obtained directly about 45% of China's rich tungsten ores … as well as ores from Bolivia, Argentina, Peru, Mexico and even the United States.' (The Tungsten Institute, Washington DC 1955)

Hence this British initiative which saw Captain SP Higgings and DKF MacLachlan, supervise some 60, mainly local men, sinking three shafts all around the site, along with sampling pits.

Scottish-born Donald Kerr Fulton MacLachlan, was 43 and a very well-travelled mining engineer, and together with Higgings, he was working in a small corrugated iron office *'built under the shelter of a wall of one of the buildings erected when the mine was worked by German prisoners during the war.'* (WMN 6 July 1936)

MacLachlan is thought to have been staying in the Treby Arms at Sparkwell at the time, along with Higgings, and when the *Western Morning News* visited the Hemerdon site the experienced engineer offered the newspaper journalist an opportunity to join him in one of the newly dug shafts. The account gives us a fascinating insight into the working practices of the time.

'After climbing almost to the top of Hemerdon Ball to the clump of trees which crowns it, the first of the shafts was reached. At the top was a large windlass which hoists and lowers a two-way bucket system to bring the excavated material to the surface, while down the side of the same shaft run the ladders for the men.

'There are six of these ladders, and they alternate from one side of the shaft to the other, with a small platform at the top of each.

'As one descends, the buckets – one full, the other empty – go up and down beside the ladders. Also down this shaft runs a wooden ventilation shaft, through which air is blown from a hand-worked fan to clear away

the fumes from the workings after blasting operations have taken place. 'From the bottom of the shaft levels run out approximately North and South. These are not quite high enough for a man to walk along upright, and are about four feet wide. At intervals the roof is shored up with cross-beams and posts.

'The air at the bottom of the workings is surprisingly fresh, and as there is no fear of fire-damp the men are able to smoke and work by the light of naked acetylene lamps.

'At the moment picks and shovels are used, and long chisels to make the blasting holes, but it is hoped to get mechanical hand excavators before long.

'The blasting is done with the modern type of blasting powder, which has superseded the old method, extensively used by the Cornish and other miners, of black powder and quills. The forward progress in each level averages between 2ft. and 6ft. a day according to the hardness of the rock.

'At each face of the levels the seams of various minerals can be seen, quartz, china clay, tourmaline, and others. Occasionally there glistens in the light of the acetylene lamps a piece of coloured quartz, little pieces of amethyst, and grains of tungsten, and occasional larger pieces of tungsten ore reveal that the excavators may be approaching a large vein.'

The writer noted that the engineers hoped that the samples that were being taken would show that the workings would be worthy enough of excavation on a wider scale, and that other products of the workings would also be able to find a market.

Captain Higgings was not of the opinion, in the event of work being conducted on a grander scale, that any great increase in the workforce would be required, as most of the additional throughput could be managed by the deployment of mechanical means.

Towards the end of the summer Higgings and MacLachlan were advertising for a 'Merryweather or Portable Pump', but no staff in the short term. A year later a light tramway had been built, crushing-machines had been brought on site and Hemerdon was being run as a testing-plant.

By this time the mine was being run by 34-year-old Hugh Halton, a young, married, metallurgist from Croydon who had graduated from Imperial College, London, a decade or so earlier. There were now, according to Mr Halton, around 40 men being employed at Hemerdon, and some 6,000 tons of ore awaiting treatment.

Once again, however, it wasn't to be. The following year everything portable on site was put up for sale by the Glasgow accountants who were handling the winding up of the mine and eventually a sum of over £6,000 was handed over to the liquidators by a Plymouth firm. The Hemerdon Syndicate was officially wound up on 14 February 1939.

Sinking shafts with levels to sample ore body, 1936

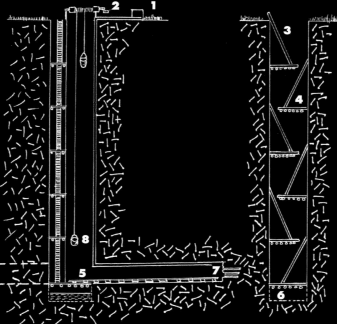

In the July 1936 Western Morning News report the journalist was taken underground. He refers to using a carbide cap lamp, as shown above and below. *Above:* Miner's felt tull impregnated with resin to make harder. *Below:* The thirties was also to see compressed card helmets with brackets to hold the cap lamp.

1: Hand-operated fan forcing air to the face area. 2: Hand windlass to raise and lower kibbles of ore and rock. 3: Ladder way, six individual ten-foot ladders. 4: Platforms. 5: Track laid to move ore trucks to base of shaft. 6: Possible sump to collect water from levels. 7: Hand drilling at face. 8: Kibble.

Above: Poll picks were in common use, just one sharp point and a hammer head. *Below:* Shovel, mallet, and pick. Holes were drilled by one miner, holding and twisting the borer whilst being driven by two miners with mallets taking alternate blows.

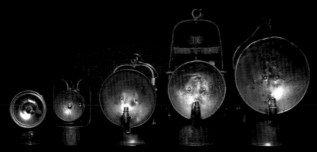

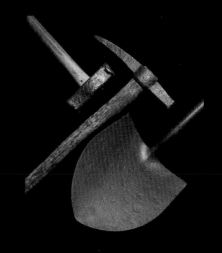

Carbide cap and hand lamps, manufactured by the Premier Engineering Works of Leeds. Cap lamps lasted for four hours, hand lamps, ten.

Photographs: Tommy Hatwell. Artefacts and line drawing: Keith Loze

War Brings A New Opening

All in all it appears that three shafts were sunk in that 1936/37 burst of activity, each to a depth of 60ft with over 1,200 ft of crosscuts made right across the site from the bottom of the shafts. Sampling of material was carried out every 10 or 20 feet and two substantial milling tests were made.

Overall the chemical tests indicated that there was 6.53 lbs/ton (less than 0.3%) of wolfram and black tin concentrates and the milling tests demonstrated that over half of the values (55%) of the chemical assays could be recovered by milling, so that meant that the figures achieved by the now defunct Hemerdon Syndicate were around 3.59 lbs per ton (0.16%) of mixed sales concentrates (wolfram and black tin).

Was it deemed uneconomical to progress at these values? Certainly the dark shadow of war was already casting something of gloom across Europe and the importance of this strategic mineral was not lost on those responsible for our munitions. Surely someone would be prepared to grasp the nettle?

Step forward 51-year-old Cornish quarry owner, Leonard Gregory Tom. On Wednesday 30 August 1939 under the auspices of the Three Towns Storage Ltd. of Menheniot – a company he had formed in Stonehouse, Plymouth, with his wife Ruth five years earlier – Tom informed the War Office that he proposed to re-open a wolfram mine near Plymouth and asked whether it would be in the national interest for the mine to be worked.

The Ministry of Supply wrote back the following Tuesday 5 September – just two days after the Prime Minister had informed the country that we were at war with Germany – stating that it was not feasible to encourage production of indigenous ores and referred the matter to the British Ferro Tungsten Association.

With their registered office at Clicker Tor, Menheniot, Tom's new venture, Hemerdon Wolfram Limited, signed the first of four 30-year-leases with mine lessors George Arthur Ley Woollcombe and George Sydney Strode Strode in July 1940, but back dated with effect from 29 September 1939. In the months that followed further leases were drawn up and Hemerdon Wolfram extended their hold over the wider site and established a 300-ton mill, which started processing raw material in early 1941. The company secretary, John Keast, the accountant, Louis Pengelly and the solicitor, Horace Visick of Nalder & Son, were all based in Truro (Gerald Nalder and Arthur Lyne were other partners who were variously listed as company secretaries).

The original directors were LG Tom, G Thatcher and CE Trestrail.

The operators were expecting to treat 300 tons every 24 hours and the men in charge were Edgar (CE) Trestrail, the consulting engineer, S A Glendinning, the mine manager, and John Partington, the mill superintendent.

Charles Edgar Trestrail was a 40-year-old mining engineer from Redruth. Married with one daughter, he had lost his two brothers in the Great War, Edward in Flanders in August 1917 and John, who died the following April in Catterick Military Hospital, and one suspects the only reason Edgar wasn't called up himself, was because his role as a mining engineer had protected status.

Meanwhile John 'Jack' Partington, officially appointed mill superintendent in November 1940, was a former star pupil of the School of Metalliferous Mining in Camborne. He was awarded his diploma in 1912 and on 1 September that same year was appointed as student instructor at the King Edward Training Mine with a salary of £50 per annum. Still only in his teens, Jack had then also assisted HP Berringer with evening classes for miners in practical chemistry.

Jack Partington with his wife Winifred (in the dark coat) and young children John and Elizabeth just prior to their arrival at Hemerdon. Right: Sir Thomas Kirke Rose Director of Mining Resources from the Ministry of Munitions during the Great War.

Over the next few years he was to be found working at East Pool mine as a research chemist and assayer.

In 1916 the Director of Mining Resources from The Ministry of Munitions and Sir Thomas Rose, Chief of the Research Committee and former assayer for the Royal Mint, made favourable comments on the usefulness of the research that Jack was conducting with Berringer, and in 1919 Jack filed a patent for the process that he and another colleague had been working on. In the twenties and thirties he built up valuable experience managing mines across Devon and Cornwall, coming to Hemerdon via the Bridford barytes mine at Christow, in the Teign Valley.

Thus it was that in January 1941, the tall, bespectacled, 47- year-old moved into Colonel Conram's rental property, Blacklands at Sparkwell, with his wife and two young children.

In the event, Jack's employment with Hemerdon Wolfram Ltd. turned out to be comparatively brief – as the war rolled inexorably on Hemerdon Wolfram Ltd was bought out by the Ministry of Supply. Happily for the Partington family, Jack's services were retained by the Government.

The Government had clearly been looking at Hemerdon for some time. Just six months into the war, in March 1940 a Non-Ferrous Metallic Ores Committee was appointed to advise the Ministry of Supply on the possibility of increasing home production of non-ferrous ores. The committee was chaired by Sir William Larke: Larke had distinguished himself working for the Ministry of Munitions during the Great War, later becoming the Director General of Raw Materials. He had been knighted in 1921 and in the 1930s he was appointed the first ever director of the newly constituted British Iron & Steel Foundation.

Sir William Larke 1875-1959
Went to Colfe's School, Lewisham, then Regent Street Polytechnic.
Larke undertook his engineering training with HF Joel & Co and joined Siemens Brothers & Co in Woolwich aged 20.
He received the OBE in 1917, and the CBE in 1920.
He was a member of many learned societies and a president of several of them.

Acting on the committee's behalf, Donald Gill, the Ministry's man in the field, was dispatched to find sources of wolfram. During the course of his investigations Gill arrived in Hemerdon on 15 May 1941. Over the next week or so he compiled a detailed assessment which he completed in Tavistock and followed up in July 1941 as a *'Secret and Confidential'* report to his employers suggesting a sampling programme to determine *'whether the average recovery value of the deposit is of the order of 7-10lbs of mixed concentrates per ton as determined by the late Ernest Terrell, or 4-5 lbs per ton as determined by the British (Non-Ferrous) Mining Corporation Ltd.,'* and as communicated to him verbally by Mr JC Allen. *'The weight of evidence at present seems to lean toward a higher figure than that of Mr Allen.'*

At that time the Hemerdon Wolfram enterprise was working to achieve a daily throughput of 300 tons of ore, but Gill saw no reason why there should not be a mill on site dealing with at least five times that amount – say 50,000 tons a month – which would yield 90-122 tons of wolfram concentrate and 36 tons of black tin concentrate, all at an operating cost *'for mining and processing could scarcely exceed four shillings and sixpence per ton'.*

This was an even better prospect than that anticipated by Hemerdon Wolfram themselves and reflected the obvious potential economies of scale. Hemerdon Wolfram were anticipating running costs of around 5/- per ton, for their 300-ton-per-24-hours operation.

Gill's enthusiasm at this point was reminiscent of the nineteenth-century mine captains who were looking for investment that in turn would lead, at the very least, to local employment, but these were different times, we were at war and tungsten could be an important ingredient in the war effort. However, his confidence was by no means unbounded and rather than just work from existing findings Gill posited the need to dig 10 or 12 pits to depths of 30ft and 60ft and work with fresh samples, samples which, he argued, would need to be taken to the Prince of Wales mine at Harrowbarrow, 18 miles away, to be tested, *'owing to the absence of suitable plant and probable water shortage in the late summer and autumn at Hemerdon.'*

In the meantime there would need to be a certain amount of modification to the Prince of Wales set up, something that Gill recommended should be done by Terrell, Davis & Toll *'for a fixed fee plus cost'* (the Terrell in question was one of Ernest's sons, while Toll was Reggie Toll a mining engineer from Bere Alston who formed a mining partnership with CF Barclay looking at mines thought to be worth reopening, mainly in the Tamar Valley).

Gill further felt that all the record keeping and plotting of the geology should be done by senior students from the Royal School of Mines. *'It will be possible to keep twelve men employed, of whom at least four should be 4th year men capable of taking charge of juniors.'*

SECRET & CONFIDENTIAL.

For internal circulation within the Ministry of Supply

NON-FERROUS MINERAL DEVELOPMENT CONTROL

(Ministry of Supply)

QUARTERLY REPORT NO. 2

This report covers the activities of the Control and of Non-Ferrous Minerals Development Ltd., during the period 1st August/31st October, 1942.

GENERAL: Mr. Thomas Pryor, M.Inst.M.M. (Past President) has been appointed Consulting Engineer to the Control in place of Mr. E.H. Clifford, who resigned this position due to ill health. The latter has, however, been able to continue to serve on the Advisory Committee.

Mr. G.F. Anderson has been appointed Assistant on the Control staff in London.

WOLFRAM

(a) Hemerdon: Constructional work on the new plant is now making satisfactory progress, but as stated in the last report, work has been delayed chiefly owing to shortage of labour and to other labour difficulties, such as absenteeism; in this case, however, the Ministry of Labour & National Service is taking energetic action. The target date for completion of the new plant is now fixed for June 1943.

During September and October the existing mill has been working on a three shift basis for the first time. About 5,100 tons of ore were treated during September, from which 5.5 tons of 65% of wolfram concentrates and 1.2 tons of 65% tin concentrates were produced. During October there have been several stoppages due to the need to carry out temporary repairs on some of the machinery, much of which is in bad condition; even so, the tonnage of ore treated was a record monthly figure of 6,087 dry tons from which about 6.7 tons of wolfram and 1.5 tons of tin concentrates were produced.

Above: *Ministry of Supply second quarterly report highlighting issues with Hemerdon.*
Right: *Seal of Hemerdon Wolfram Ltd., from the wartime lease.*

Obtaining human resources in wartime was always going to be something of a challenge, particularly if there was a need for specialist skills. Fortunately Gribble appeared to have a surplus of men at that time and had agreed to lend about nine men for the pit-sinking work at Hemerdon. As far as Gill's personal services were concerned, he made it quite clear that if the committee were keen to press ahead and in the absence of having an office, an assistant or a typist, he would have to be relieved of the need to visit London any more than necessary, and of making reports about any other properties for a few months.

He also said that he *'should be relieved entirely of the job of finding lodgings and daily transport for students, and for the labourers required at Hemerdon.*

'This is going to be a difficult and annoying job,' he said, and suggested that *'Dr RO Jones should be employed to undertake it and should be allowed the use of a car to do the job.'*

That last little aside, reminding us that the world was a slightly different place back then, as was a second little remark at the end of his argument for a clerk of some kind, to help deal with the significant amount of data that there would be to process and pay-sheets to calculate. *'I should,'* he volunteered, *'be willing to loan my own typewriters for office use'* ... no computers back then!

Over and above all the aforementioned concerns, there was also a need to: Improve the power supply at Hemerdon – and at Cligga (Perranporth – the other mine then being worked up by the Ministry); improve the water supply at Hemerdon (and for someone, Mr Rose or Mr Lavers perhaps study the clarification of the claywater), and to sort out flow-sheets of the processing at the mill *'to enable order for heavy machinery to be placed as soon as (a) it is decided to proceed, (b) the tonnage to be treated daily can be determined and (c) the mining method at Cligga can be outlined from sampling and geological study (by the metallurgist chosen to investigate the milling aspect).'*

Subject to all of the above being dealt with and the committee dealing with any of the companies that would become involved, Gill felt that the sampling could be done inside three months.

In the event the sampling did go ahead although throughout the time that work was being carried out, Hemerdon Wolfram continued to work towards operating their comparatively modest 300-ton a day processing plant.

It had been during June 1941 that some development work had been concentrated on ore from an earlier adit area, this had been termed 'haematite ore,' by Jack Partington. Jack had also made notes where he recorded that the wolfram obtained was *'a brownish colour probably hubnerite'*. In effect he was already doubting that the ore was wolfram.

This page: *various views of the Miner's Arms, inside and out.*

The story goes that Admiral George Woollcombe founded the Miner's Arms back in the early nineteenth century and it remained in the family until the wartime licensee, Ned Honey, pictured above with members of the local Home Guard unit, bought it from the estate in 1947.

The issue was further compounded by the need to make sure that whatever mineral was obtained, wolfram, black tin or whatever, it had to be as near pure as possible. In the case of tin, any trace of wolfram could be a problem, excess over 2% saw a 6d reduction for each 0.1%. There was also a commodity war risk to be paid and finally, if there was a difference exceeding 0.25% between the assays of the sellers on the one hand and the buyers on the other, then reference was made to an independent referee and the cost of that third-party evaluation was to be borne by the party whose assay figure was furthest from that of the referee.

Clearly it was in Jack Partington's interest to achieve the best possible separation of the material his plant was treating, and the situation was not lost on Donald Gill either.

On 10 December 1941 Gill, wrote, from 1 Taviton Street, London WC 1 to WCC (William) Rose, the secretary of the Non-Ferrous Ores Committee voicing his concerns over the purity of the wolfram from Hemerdon:

'Dear Rose,

'We have heard something about the limiting quantity of TIN allowable in wolfram concentrates for the manufacture of ferro-tungsten, but we have no official information on file regarding the allowable percentages of other possible deleterious components, for example SILICA, SULPHUR, ARSENIC, COPPER, IRON, TITANIUM, &c.

'Could you get a full specification of both the allowable and desirable limits for all these components, as well as any specification for physical properties of the concentrates (for example, mesh size).

'It would also be a help to know what the money penalties on deleterious components are.

'It is possible that a very small proportion of the Hemerdon wolfram, from the treatment of slimes, may have to be produced as a mixed concentrate with tin, for eventual separation by the sodium tungstate process.'

Clearly Gill was worried that a small degree of contamination may result in a substantial drop in price.

In the meantime, Jack Partington was just about to press the all systems go button back at Hemerdon and with Christmas 1941 and New Year's Day out of the way, full production, or the nearest they could get to it, began, under new management, on Saturday 3 January 1942.

That same day Gill wrote to the secretary of the Non Ferrous Ores Committee with some comments on a claim by a Mr Saunt that Hemerdon Wolfram had been capable operating at a profit. He suggested that the notion was based on the uncritical acceptance of Ernest Terrell's assessment at the end of the First World War. Having looked into the matter in more detail, Gill was now of the opinion that while Terrell doubtless did produce as much wolfram as he claimed, it is likely that he milled around twice the amount of ore than he claimed, and that therefore a truer picture would

be that his yields were around 4lbs per ton rather than the 7.6lbs he suggested.

Furthermore, Saunt's claim appeared to have been predicated on the notion that the existing Hemerdon plant could 'treat 300/400 tons in a day continuously throughout the year. *'I am quite sure,'* Gill attested, *'that the mill has never yet treated 300 tons in a day and it is certain that every summer, from May to October, it will be limited to a very small tonnage (less than 100 tons per day) owing to lack of water.*

'This arises from two facts: a) that Hemerdon Wolfram Ltd. have not developed any water supply and have to rely entirely on the Smallhangar brook, which has a small flow throughout the summer months on end, and b) they have made no provision whatever for clarifying their clay-laden water and using it over again.'

Saunt was clearly trying to get the best compensation deal from the Ministry of Supply in relation to the lease assignment and what might happen after the war. But these, and other reasons, not least of which was the likely post war price of wolfram, Gill thought that they would be well advised to simply take a lump sum in compensation for the risk the company took in starting the venture in the first place.

'It is quite possible,' he concluded, *'that Hemerdon might not have been considered by the Committee as a source of wolfram if the Company had not had the initiative to build their mill and begin production.'*

The Ministry of Supply had had the lease of the property assigned to them from Hemerdon Wolfram Ltd. and the plant was now being operated by Non Ferrous Minerals Development Ltd. on behalf of the Ministry of Supply. The new company had been created by the Treasury and was being operated as a private concern.

As it transpired, as Partington noted in his meticulous recordings of the activities of the mine, some 700 tons of wet ore were processed in that first week, during the course of 37.7 hours that the plant was running for, not quite the 300 tons every working day that was anticipated, but a start nonetheless, with 3.61 lbs of wolfram and tin concentrate being harvested on every ton processed.

Meanwhile, 200 miles east up the A38 and A303 to London, we find that same month that the Non Ferrous Metallic Ores Committee had just been reconstituted as the aforementioned Non Ferrous Mineral Development Control under Sir William Larke. Members of the original committee were asked to continue to act as an Advisory Committee to the Controller, with the addition of Mr Eastwood (Geological Survey) and Professor Ritson (Royal School of Mines). Andrew Pearson agreed to serve as Consulting Metallurgist.

Sparkwell Home Guard (from Pam James Book of Sparkwell) back row includes Kingwell, Oxenham, Westlage, George Lee, Alfred Lee, Stan Tall, anon, Bill Collings, Charlie Serpell, Leonard Gulley, Steve Hoskin, Joe Collings, Alf Collings, Harry Masters. Middle row: S Clemo, Harold Reed, Ned Honey, Bill Chapman, Tim Collings, Adrian Palmer, Stan Sandover, Bill Nicholson, Reg Short, Tom Matthews, Bob Phillips, George Townsend, Reg Serpell. Seated: Colonel Conran, Lt Wheeler, Major Bull. Front: Charlie Miller, Archie Phillips, Wilks, Les Mutton, Hunt, Reed, Ron Barker, Reg Lee, Ted Lardeaux. Pam James writes: 'The wolfram mine at Hemerdon was considered to be at risk from sabotage, so a contingent of men from the Sparkwell Company was always on duty to protect it.' The Sparkwell Company was part of the 15th Devon (Plympton) Battalion, and was commanded by Colonel WD Conran – the man who let out his Blacklands home to Jack Partington and his family.

Sparkwell Home Guard outside the Treby Arms 1940. Back: Ken Hurn, G Muttram, Bill Collings, Bill Collings snr., Basil Stephens, C Taylor, C Collings, Tom Williams, H Steele, Palmer, W Kitts, Risdon Rowe, G Mumford, Ned Honey, Tim Collings, Stan Bowden, G Townsend. Front: Dolphus Tallamy, Fred Pengelly, 'Kesyie' Collings, Wattie May, Alf Collings, N Nelder (on motorbike) and Stan Sandover.

Some of the men here worked at the Hemerdon plant, among the names we have in Partington's workforce list from 11 October 1943 are the three shift bosses: JH Hocking, A Amman, and Mr Curnow; ore bin-crushers, three on each shift, C Willcock, D Higman, H Churchward, S Clemo, E Osborne, J Tribble, E Easterbrook, JF Harris, SF Willcocks; surge bin-washers, one per shift: B Bull, H Willis and F Roberts; on crushers, cones and screens J Smith, J Mumford and SJ Northey; rolls and hardings required two men per shift: viz EJ Mudge and R Mumford, J Hammett and R Hodge, and W Willis and J Harris; JF Bulle, WJ Small and R Bawden were responsible for the dosing plant on each shift while the ropeways were dealt with by AJ and WH Collings, J Phillips, JH Hodges and WH Elford and Messrs J Turpin, WH Roberts, T Hard and Uren. Meanwhile, the day work men included R Saunders on the dosing plant, Sheriff on the ropeways, F Olver, E Hambly and H Lee on tailings disposal; G Lee, R Hardmill, and R Leeford on retreatment, B Tay, W Wilde, AH Phillips and E May on transport and H Turnbull, Kingdom and Neury in the garage. Other names we find recorded include foremen H Morgan, G Manly, A Newsome, labourers, E Heals, J Stancombe, F Wichell, J David, J Baskerville, F Clegg, N Wingett, WJ Shelby, C Liddicoat, A Bund, M Bookman, J Shilabeer, W Puckey and J Jennings.

Since the original foundation of the committee ten interim reports had been submitted to the Minister and recommendations made in respect of over 59 mining prospects had been sent to the RMD (Raw Materials Division). Having now had all that groundwork done the function of this body became more clearly defined as the *'development of the non-ferrous mineral resources of the country as required for war purposes'*. Although the ore body at Hemerdon may not have been thought by some experts to be that high value it did emerge from these early investigations as the project that the Non Ferrous Mineral Development Control were most prepared to invest in.

All in all there were three projects to emerge, at St Erth (alluvial tin, Cornwall), Nenthead (zinc, Cumbria) and Hemerdon (tungsten). The Nenthead adventure was looking like a £90,000 investment while the Hemerdon Wolfram was estimated to come in at around double that at £180,000 (that's over £8 million in today's terms).

With that degree of commitment one imagines that they were hoping for greater returns than Partington was to post across in 1942.

Across the next eight months Hemerdon Wolfram processed a little over 30,700 wet tons of ore across 34 weeks, at an average of 900 tons per week, confirming Gill's perception and suggesting either that the plant couldn't run for as many days of the week as was anticipated or that the plant couldn't be fed as well as had been hoped. In the event it was a combination of many different factors.

Partington divided them into two main categories – voluntary and involuntary.

The former included overloading the launders, the shutes, and the drains, which along with water shortages accounted for 129 hours of lost time. Loss of the power supply due to enemy action was responsible for a rather modest seven hours lost, however by far the largest unplanned cause of delay was wear and tear to the plant which accounted for a not inconsiderable 301 hours of involuntary down time.

The biggest offenders on the voluntary list were a short supply of ore, transport issues, weather and state of the roads. Other elements included the sand drain being blocked, a lack of petrol for the on-site vehicles, excavator breakdowns, ore shortages due to weather (including frost), sticking clay and holidays (a mere 16 hours).

Total stoppage time therefore topped 1,050 hours and represented, on those figures, a loss of over a third of the potential running time as throughout that time the plant had been on for a total of 1,895 hours, or, again on average 55.7 hours a week. In fairness, however, after the initial, inevitable teething troubles, when running time only exceeded that figure twice, the weekly running time only dipped below 55.7 hours three times in 18 weeks from May to the end of August.

However, even allowing for just a five-day working week with the machines in action 24 hours a day (120 hours in total), the highest total achieved was 83.7 hours.

Meanwhile, the average return of wolfram and tin concentrate per ton was 3.96lbs, a slight improvement on the figure of 3.59lbs (0.16%) achieved by their predecessors the Hemerdon Syndicate but overall relatively consistent with it.

Production throughout 1942 had been on behalf of the Ministry of Supply and during September and October that year and for the first time the Hemerdon Wolfram mill worked on a three-shift basis. Not surprisingly, more ore was treated with the October figure setting a record throughput of over 6,000 tons, but still there were stoppages as some of the machinery required emergency repairs.

The following year the Ministry formally took over the lease and a total compensation package was made to Hemerdon Wolfram of £51,166.13s.11d.

The official assignment of lease was made on 7 June 1943 by which time the site had been greatly developed in readiness for much higher levels of throughput.

The original date for full production – set at 2,000 tons of ore per day – had been planned for a start in March/April 1943 but work was initially delayed some six to eight weeks owing to a shortage of specialist labour – it was proving very difficult to get men to fill some of the subcontracting work, like electrical wiring and pipe laying.

In the event, having decided to increase the capacity of the mill from 2,000 to 3,000 tons per day it wasn't until October 1943 that the new plant was ready for a full test, with running time gradually being increased during November and December. In the meantime production at the original mill continued alongside the build programme, right through until 14 September 1943, with all staff transferring across to the new facility a week later to start work on 21 September.

Unsurprisingly perhaps, throughput at the new plant was restricted from the very beginning – on account of technical adjustments, delays in delivery of machinery, and poor quality materials being used in the construction, resulting in breakdowns … and that was without any personnel concerns. With a shortage of skilled labour, it was proving difficult to fully populate three eight-hour shifts, especially as many of those taken on at Hemerdon were elderly and unfit, while others were not fully trained. The transfer of labour from Mount Wellington Mine in Cornwall helped to some extent, but skilled men were still needed.

Contractors for the new plant eventually left the site in the early part of November, but by the end of December 1943 the mill was still only processing 1,700 tons per 24 hour shift.

Above: shift workers from Hemerdon: Florrie Mudge, Gwen Clemo, Doris Higman, Blanche Lee, Betty Mudge.

It's reckoned that around 40 women worked at Hemerdon during the war and Jack Partington recorded the names of many of them, including those who were working on the day that the new plant started on Monday 11 October 1943: Betty Mudge was the forewoman on the first shift, Miss Doris Taylor was on the hydrosizers, Miss Florrie Kitts and Miss K Nicholson were on the primary tables, Miss B Lee and Miss D Nicholson on the mids tables, Miss J Taylor on the jigs.

On the B Shift Miss A Mudge was forewoman, Miss Audrey Willcocks was on the hydrosizers, Miss V Phillips and J Penwell were on primaries, Miss V Exworthy and Miss E Exworthy were on mids, and Miss Hilda Brand was on jigs.

C Shift saw Miss M Lee as forewoman, Mrs Macy on hydrosizers, Mrs Carne and Miss J Simpson on primary tables, Miss Hambley, unusually with a male partner, Reg Lee, on mids (an accident waiting to happen as it transpired), Mrs J Alphey on jigs. Each shift, apart from 'C' (which had six women and 14 men) had seven women and twelve men.

The day work staff also numbered twenty and included five women: Mrs Joan Tucker, Mrs Thornington, Mrs Cohen, Miss Harmen and Miss J Collings, who accounted for most of the eight strong team on retreatments.

Other ladies whose names we have include Miss Tuckin, Mable Lee, M Murray, Muriel MacBean and Doreen Thornington.

It was not unusual to find several members of the same local family working on site on any one day.

Left: Unamed group of ladies, note the heavy duty rubber boots. Working conditions in places were very wet.

It was this model – a 17-RB machine – that Jack Partington monitored to calculate the exact cost per ton of extraction, taking into account the cost of replacing the bucket teeth.

The patented jig, designed to treat undersize material from the main revolving-screen, and the concentrates dressing plant had still to be completed, thereby restricting the plant capacity to just 2,000 tons per 24 hours. There were also still issues with the labour base and defective plant. Added to which there was a flu epidemic in December that *'seriously affected operations'*.

Mill Superintendent Partington was diligent in recording the detail of the disappointments with some of the machinery. The handful of swing shovel diggers on crawler tracks, produced by Ruston Bucyrus, (based in Lincoln, and at one time said to be the largest excavator manufacturer in the world) that were deployed in the open pit, were particularly problematic.

RB 16 arrived late and broke down during its first working session on site, RB 10, the first to arrive, broke down on the same day – 20 April 1943. The former was out of action for over a week and broke down again almost as soon as it went back into service. RB 10 had been on site almost a year already, while RB Bullgrader had been around since the beginning of 1942 levelling the site for new buildings.

RB 17, an excavator with a forward bucket, had teeth of ordinary tool steel but these had worn out in just over three weeks in May/June 1942. The teeth were replaced by Ruston that same June, but these too had worn out within the month, prompting Partington to factor in the cost of continually replacing digger teeth, both in terms of metal and man power, into his calculations for cost of finished material.

The Ministry of Supply were at this stage receiving regular reports on activities they were sponsoring around the country. Hemerdon was invariably at the top of the agenda and it's worth noting that Hemerdon was then also receiving material from other mines for processing, but they were small amounts. To quote from the report:

By the end of December 1943 Hemerdon had dealt with *'approximately 22,500 tons of ore, resulting in a production of between 15 and 20 tons of mixed tin and wolfram concentrates, averaging 59% WO3 and Sn [which equates to 0.09% recovery].'* By contrast: *'The total quantity of wolfram concentrates produced from concentrates received from small producers – among them Redmoor, Buttern Hill and Ashburton Mine – during the quarter was about 3.5 tons averaging 59.76% WO3.'*

A low tonnage, but the wolfram return percentage figure was remarkably consistent with the 59% obtained from the Hemerdon material itself. However, the issue here was the *'time and expense involved when only small quantities of material are dealt with, are out of proportion to the resulting production of wolfram.'* It was, therefore, felt that the arrangement should be reviewed.

Inevitably there were all sorts of issues that needed to be reviewed, not just in terms of the throughput of material and mineral yields from that material but also more mundane matters, like the putting up and taking down of blackout sheets, the need for rubber boots and clogs and the provision of basic first-aid on site.

Almost all of this appears to have been the responsibility of the highly qualified mining man Jack Partington. In a familiar, blue-covered, Challenge Duplicate Book (obtained from Thompsons the printers and stationers based in Tavistock Road, Plymouth), Jack recorded the names of all of the workforce at Hemerdon, what shifts they were on, what areas they worked in and what responsibilities they had.

In the summer of 1943, in the interests of keeping his workforce happy, Jack set up a Works Committee. Each section put up candidates, there was a male and female nomination from each shift, as well as candidates from the canteen, garage, maintenance department, new construction section and outside labour.

An indication of the sorts of issues that concerned the committee is obvious from the agenda of the August meeting that followed that election:

A suggestion for improvement in the procedure of paying out wages

A matter concerning tea provided at the canteen

Essential Works Order a clear understanding of it by members of the committee

No precedent created by NFMD dealing in considering case

Proposition re naming is concern of all Irishmen

Signed constitution of committee

Fire Prevention arrangements

List of Committee to be forwarded to M and NS

Doctor's Certificate in case of sickness

Air Raid Shelter

Co-opt an Irishman to attend meeting to hear explanations re their conditions of labour and objections on them to provide for sickness, etc.

One can but wonder, from this distance, at one or two of the items discussed in the mill offices on that last Friday in August 1943.

Earlier in the month Plymouth had experienced one of the worst bombing raids since the devastating blitz raids of March and April 1941; however, although they could not know it then, there would only be two more raids on Plymouth before the end of the war, in November 1943 and April 1944.

The issue of the Irishmen is less clear and although it's not obvious it would seem that M was CW Milner who was then managing the mine on behalf of NFMDC.

A possible problem concerning the provision of tea was perhaps no more complicated than the need to have someone on hand to do the job. Early in 1944, Mr Lyon, representing the canteen staff, had placed an advertisement locally looking for a *'male or female assistant for a small industrial canteen 48 hours weekly, night work one week in three.'*

Wartime shift at the Hemerdon Tungsten mine with Joan Tucker front row light top, Betty Mudge, second from right, front row, Florrie Mudge, middle row, third from left and Amy Underwood and Gwen Taylor, back row third and second from right respectively.

Back row: Arthur Baskerville, Marjorie Jones, Doris Taylor, Florrie Kitts, Gwen Taylor. Middle: Joan Tucker, Audrey Willcocks, Betty Mudge, George Lee, Blanche Lee. Front: Norman Lee.

Transport from Plymouth or Plympton provided, previous experience or recommendation. Apply Hemerdon Mine.'

Meanwhile, in October, another item on Partington's to do list had been to supply certain members of staff with rubber boots. Much of the processing in the mill involved a considerable amount of water and not all employees came equipped with their own boots, and even if they did, it would appear, quite reasonably, that they expected to have them repaired at the company's expense if they became damaged in the workplace. Blanche Lee would later recall working conditions that sometimes saw women working up to their knees in water.

Doreen Thorington was in her early twenties, when as a young newly wed (she was married in Sparkwell Church in June 1941) without any children, she was sent to work at Hemerdon: *'We had to wear overalls and boots,'* she later recalled for the *BBC WW2peopleswar:* *'It was a very wet job as most of the work entailed washing and grading the wolfram. I earned £2.0s.5d a week.*

'I left the wolfram and was sent to Coypool where the Americans were based.' Doreen had worked on the mids tables and hydrosizers with a couple of the Nicholson women – it was a time consuming and skilled job. It was not just rubber boots that were required either, in December 1943 Partington raised a note to stores to issue six pairs of clogs for use at the ropeways loading station.

The aerial ropeway, or blondin, was used to transport sand from the processing area to the large, v-shaped, sand dump.

Incidentally, one of the first acts of the works committee had been the setting up of a first-aid room and while we have no specific record of the doubtless many minor accidents that occurred on site, we do have a detailed report from Partington (to Milner) where he described an incident involving another member of the Lee family, Reg.

According to an eye-witness report, while working on the mids and tables on 'C' shift, Reg was explaining the operation of the table to Mrs Alphey, in the presence of Miss McBean (mids tables) and Miss Penwill (primary tables).

'Mrs Alphey noted that Mr Lee was standing on the edge of the jig and asked her to hold a spanner he had in his possession. He then extracted something from his pocket and reached over to grip the grease lubrication point in order to force grease into the bearing.

'Mrs Alphey was then aware of the fact that Lee had been caught in some part of the mechanism and was being rotated thereby.'

Partington explained to Milner that he hadn't found any evidence of Lee *'receiving instructions to lubricate or in any way attend to the machine by any person in authority.'*

Interestingly enough, Miss Lorna Penwill has a slightly different version

of the event. She says that on that night the staff canteen was hit by incendiary bombs.

'We were all in a panic to say the least; the Jerries had a direct hit on the canteen and it was well and truly alight. Reg, our boss, decided it would be best to turn off all the machinery. In doing so his arm became entangled in the machinery. We all rushed to his aid and he was really lucky he didn't lose his arm.'

Certainly there's no record of an enemy raid on Plymouth that night, and no record of any fire in the canteen to be found in Partington's diary. Whatever the circumstances, according to his brother, Tony, Reg received no compensation for the injury he sustained, and he never fully regained use of the said limb which he couldn't properly elevate. After the war he became a lorry driver collecting milk churns. Tony also recalls that his big brother had a mischievous streak as he can vividly remember Reg asking him if he'd *'like to go for a little ride'* and placing the four-year-old Tony in one of the buckets on the aerial ropeway, sending him on a journey of several hundred yards. *'I could only just peer out over the top of the bucket,'* recalls Tony.

The Lees were just one of several local families to supply a number of wartime employees to Hemerdon, there were also various Mumford, Collings, Phillips, Nicholson and Harris family members as well as a great many other local people among the hundred or so employees.

Hemerdon during the Second World War was a hive of activity. In addition to the fact that there were more people employed at the mine than ever before, there was also the rest camp that had been set up in Tin Wood, south of Sparkwell for Naval personnel in 1942. The facility was primarily for the rest and recuperation of survivors from ships that had been sunk by enemy action and consisted of around 20 Nissen huts for accommodation purposes, a NAAFI canteen, which doubled as a cinema (open to locals free of charge) and a dance hall. There was also a brick-built sick bay and morgue.

The number of servicemen in the area was ramped up considerably in 1943 with the arrival of American troops who were billeted in tents in the grounds of Hemerdon House. And there were servicemen *'from Poland, France, Australia and New Zealand'* (Pam James) among the many other nations represented in the area – as well as the *'turbanned soldiers of the Indian sub-continent,'* who were based in a camp near Chaddlewood House.

'Although these men, accompanied by their mules, were frequently encountered on local roads, they were rarely, if ever, seen at social functions. A half a century ago it was understandably difficult for the local population, many of whom had never before seen a coloured face, to accept a culture so very different from their own. Indeed many of the local

The gleaming white concrete-constructed mill, sprawling over the hillside below the open pit (top left). The tree lined Hemerdon Ball is top centre. The buildings, to the left of the main mill are the offices and long garage. The small building, centre front of the mill is the First Aid room. The square chimney, middle centre, is from the earlier china clay works. Far right lower buildings belong to Drakelands Farm. (Pic: British Geological Survey, detail)

Inside the mill showing the cast concrete construction with asbestos sheet cladding. The photograph shows several floors of machinery which were reliant on gravity and water. The middle floor Stokes Hydrosizers, producing a graded feed to the shaking tables. Final overflow from the classifiers would feed the slime tables. Pic: BGS 1945)

womenfolk were unreasonably afraid even to meet these soldiers along the road.' (Pam James – *The Book of Sparkwell with Hemerdon and Lee Mill*) And then there was the matter of the local encampment of Italian prisoners or war.

It is also worth noting that these areas then were still without electricity and life was very different. Furthermore, being very much on the outskirts of a city that was home to all four branches of the Armed Services, it was by no means unusual to see hundreds of Plymothians trekking out to fields and farms during the evening, to escape the possible perils of night-time bombing raids, not to mention those who took up semi-permanent accommodation in the form of caravans and huts in local fields.

It's hard now to imagine life under those circumstances, as far as life in the Hemerdon Mine was concerned, where fit young men of call-up age were conspicuous by their absence, we can glean more from Lorna Penwill's fascinating account in Pam James' book.

'I was on 'B' shift,' she recalls. 'Dick Sanders was the boss of our shift. He was a lovely man – he must have been in his sixties at that time. He was injured by a grenade in the First World War and suffered a leg injury. He would turn up for work on his motorbike and side car. He lived at Moorbridge, in the cottage by the railway line.

'Some of the girls working on 'B' shift were Muriel Macbean (from Bottle Hill), Violet Phillips (from Cornwood), and Molly Harris (from Spring Cottage, Hemerdon). There were a couple of girls from Padstow who lodged in Plympton and another couple of girls from Plympton as well. The men on 'B' shift were: Reg Lee (Drakelands), Jack Mumford (Galva Cottage) and Joe Bull (Sparkwell). We supplied our own bib and brace overalls.

'We mainly worked on what were called jigging tables. Men outside of the mill dug up quarry stones and materials with big machinery which was then loaded onto a conveyor belt system which took it up very high. It then dropped down into a cone crusher inside the mill.

'Every two hours we had to all shift around and take it in turns using the trap door. There was a knack to this – you could only let just the right amount of material through at once. If too much passed through the trap door it would certainly choke up the system and everything would have to be switched off and sorted out before starting up again.

'It was quite heart stopping to hear enormous pieces of stone travelling up the outside because you knew it would have to come crashing down inside the cone to be let through the trap door.

'Maybe once or twice during a shift we would encounter huge pieces of stone that just wouldn't come through the trap – everything had to stop and usually Jack Mumford would arrive with a group of men and have to break it up by hand until it was small enough to pass through the trap door.

'As material passed through the various stages of processing it became finer in texture. Waiting for its arrival the girls would be standing at the shacking tables. The tables would be vibrating and this action separated the minerals Water jets were used to wash the wolfram out of the sand and silt. A line of black shiny wolfram was called a seam.

'After this it ended up in a drying shed and was later bagged up. Muriel and Dick worked in the bagging shed which was a filthy job. They were issued with face masks but by the end of the shift they were completely black from head to foot. The only way we could tell which one was which was by Dick's little silver rimmed glasses.

'It was very hard work. Although the bags were not that big they were extremely heavy.

'The waste from the mill went out on another conveyor belt and filled giant mechanical buckets that went around on overhead cables. There were emptied out onto a tip in the field away from the mill – near to Hemerdon Ball Lane. Massive tips formed during the war years.'

Like the vast majority of the workforce however, Lorna Penwill wasn't to remain at the mill until the end of the war, on it's closure she went to work at the American Food and Clothing Depot at Coypool.

'Part of the task here was to press the uniforms when they had been laundered and send them back to the American troops. In other workshops girls would be sewing buttons on uniforms and doing all kinds of repairs and stitching. The girls would have the terrible job of taking all the personal belongings out of the uniforms of the soldiers that had been killed in the battle fields. Lockets, rings and photographs of their wives and girlfriends that they had carried all had to be listed and sent back to America to their families. It was a heartbreaking job just knowing these poor lads would never be going home.'

There was heartbreak ahead for the Partington family too. Just five days into the new year, 1944, Jack was forced to take time off work with eye problems. His diary entry notes that the mine was working a bit better, but he certainly wasn't. 'Milner called to see me, had general conversation re eye and mine. Offered car for visit to consultant.'

It transpired that Jack had a detached retina and the following day, Thursday 6 January, Jack rang up Milner to request the use of the car to visit Mr Burr, the specialist eye consultant in Plymouth.

In the event, James Cameron, the then resident mine geologist at Hemerdon, drove Jack to his appointment and with no further improvement in the situation Partington was admitted to the Royal Eye Hospital on 7 February where he was to spend the next four weeks.

'March 7 1944: Returned home today, not well, very chesty and weak.'

Reading between the lines Partington was to remain housebound for the next month or so:

Two cone crushers, which would have material from the jaw crusher, the sequence would then be: cone crusher, rod mill, classifier tables. Pic: British Geological Survey 1945)

181

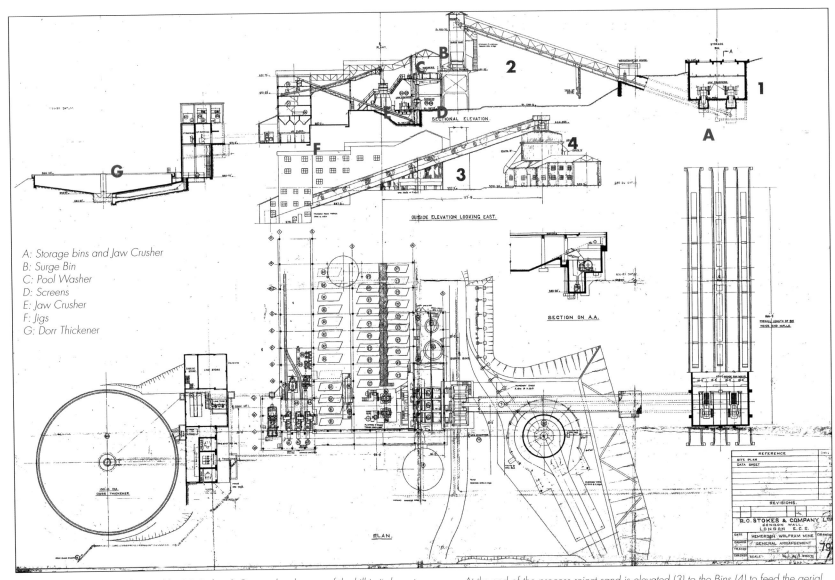

A: Storage bins and Jaw Crusher
B: Surge Bin
C: Pool Washer
D: Screens
E: Jaw Crusher
F: Jigs
G: Dorr Thickener

The Mill was designed by RO Stokes & Co., and makes use of the hill in its layout. Ore from storage bins (1) falls to the Jaw Crushers, then up the elevator (2), to start its journey through the mill, making use of gravity.

At the end of the process reject sand is elevated (3) to the Bins (4) to feed the aerial blondin where it is taken to the sand dump.

'April 12 1944: Discussed matters re my illness and prospects of returning to the mine ...
'May 5 1944: Acknowledged cheques from Hemerdon and salary in lieu of three months notice.
'May 31 1944: Went to top of Hemerdon this afternoon and dimly saw mine for 1st time for 6 months.'

It was a sorry end to an all too short a career for a man so dedicated to his work and for such a capable individual.

The sadness was all the greater when we read Jack's diary entry for 23 June 1944: *'Heard today that Hemerdon Mine is closing down. Most workers will be off tomorrow.'*

It was just two weeks or so after the Allies had successfully landed their forces on the beaches of Normandy. The tide of the war had turned dramatically, the end was in sight.

For Jack Partington it would have meant that he was out of that particular job anyway, sadly he was destined never to work again. On 30 August 1944 he received a letter from Gerald Nalder, one of the solicitors of his original employers on the Plympton site, Hemerdon Wolfram:

'I am writing to tell you how very grieved all the Shareholders of the Company were to hear that you had lost your eyesight, and I write to extend to you their very deep sympathy in your trouble.

'I send you enclosed cheque for £100 [around £4,500 today] on their behalf by the Liquidator of the Company which they will be glad if you will accept as a mark of appreciation of the services you rendered them whilst they were working on the Hemerdon Sett.'

Just over a year later, in December 1946, Jack Partington died at his rented home in Sparkwell. Colonel Conram, the owner of the property, was, recalls Jack's daughter, *'very kind to us, but we couldn't stay there forever and in 1949 we moved into a property in Thornhill Road, in Plymouth.'*

Meanwhile, back at Hemerdon, the site had fallen silent ... again.

The new mill had come into operation in late September 1943, and part of the earlier mill had been demolished. The new facility ran for little more than eight months, officially from 10 October 1943 to the 21 June 1944, equating to 256 days, during which time just over 200,000 tons of ore were quarried and treated yielding some 181 tons of mixed concentrate. Proportionately giving 42.61% of wolfram (1.38lbs per ton), and 11.86% of tin (0.366lbs per ton), recovery was only 48% of what was expected based on the original sampling, and the figures anticipated by Gill. This was blamed on the adjustments necessary to sections of the new mill, which would have cost about £25,000.

For the last five months of its operation the mill was a little more efficient and managed to process, on average, around 2,000 tons per 24 hours,

but given that the target was 3,000 tons it was disappointing. However, it was not altogether surprising, taking into account the fact that the running time of the plant was only 71% of what it could have been.

In a confidential report published on 26 February 1945 (which remained classified for the next 13 years) it was noted that:

a) *'The flowsheet of the mill is open to criticism in so far as it lacks the flexibility which is very necessary when dealing with an ore susceptible to wide variations in grade and type. Experience in the operations shewed that the slime/sand ratio in the ore as quarried could vary by as much as 100% quantitatively and by a wide range in physical characteristics thereby throwing an unexpected and unprovided for burden on the desliming arrangements within the plant. Furthermore, the assumption that a clean jig tailing could be discharged at the sizes provided proved too optimistic, and as no means were provided in the flow sheet for further reduction in size of these coarse tailings, a totally unwarranted loss of metallic values was the result.*

Again, although ample evidence was available through experience in the old mill to shew the troubles which had to be anticipated by the presence of balled clay in the jigging circuit, the methods adopted for the elimination of this 'bug bear' proved unsuccessful, and it is even possible that the type of rotary ore washers installed to some extent augmented rather than decreased this evil.

b) *Certain essential units of the plant were mechanically inadequately designed or constructed, and as a result running time was adversely affected and maintenance costs were excessive. As a natural corollary to these breakdowns and stoppages, extraction and ultimate recovery were influenced unfavourably.*

'The difficulties experienced in reclamation from the ore bin and the high maintenance costs on the scraper haulage unit have been discussed by both Messrs Milner & Goode, and some of these will remain inherent in the present system.'

Milner, who had, effectively, been managing the mine for Ministry of Supply, had, together with Goode, made a number of recommendations to his employers, recommendations endorsed by the author of the confidential document, although even with the improvements proposed the writer did not believe that the price of producing wolfram from Hemerdon could be achieved at a price below that *'indicated to RMD in a minute dated 16.3.44, namely 55/- per unit.'*

Furthermore, working on the basis that there was the cost of the plant to factor into the whole equation, the writer (for whom we have no name, could it have been Donald Gill again?) estimated that allowing for four years' worth of ore being present in the sett (2.5 million tons) then the true cost would be nearer 80/- per unit ... *'a cost only to be considered in a*

Far left: *View of Hemerdon opencast mine looking south west. The small windlass on the right sits above a 60-ft shaft.*

Left: *A close up of the workings – when operations stopped in June 1944 quarrying had exposed the ore body to a depth of around 20 ft.*

Below: *A wider view of the site showing the blondin, or aerial ropeway on the skyline to the right. Pix: BGS 1945 After both World Wars large quantities of sand were sold for new developments in the Plymouth area.*

wartime project, but unlikely to have any commercial interest or attraction.'
Therefore, concluded our anonymous author, in 'attempting to place a valuation on the Hemerdon investment it can only be approached from the political angle by assessing its value as:

a) a possible subsidised producer of a strategic reserve of wolfram for national use and/or

b) a possible source of employment, direct and indirect, for from 200 to 250 men over a period of four or five years.' [200 was said to be the size of the labour force in 1943/4, a figure that included 40 women.]

Certainly that was the bottom line once again when it came to assessing the operation of mines in the immediate area – the only people who made money out of the whole business were the workers and the middle men and not the investors. Indeed a report published a few years later by the Ministry of Fuel and Power noted that 'the cost of producing wolfram during the War was considerably higher than had been estimated. The average cost of wolfram, omitting the trial weeks at the beginning when the plant was 'running in' was approximately of the order of 190/- per unit.'

And even that was allowing for a credit in respect of the tin produced as a by product.

The question now was, what next to do?

'The question of the disposal of the Hemerdon plant or its continued retention on a care and maintenance basis is one which, in our view, must be considered in relation to the potential economic and strategic importance to the country of the mineral deposit.

'Our provisional opinion (which should be confirmed or otherwise by a detailed examination) is that with suitable modifications the existing plant is admirably fitted and equipped for long-term operation. It is the most modern plant of its kind in the country, and has a capacity about twelve times that of any other tin or wolfram plant in Devon and Cornwall. The Hemerdon project, though so far not proved to be economic, represents the first attempt in this country to work a low-grade ore body on a large scale and on modern lines.

'It would seem to us, therefore, that Hemerdon presents a strong argument for the outlay of capital with the object of proving the extension in depth and value of the mineral deposit. Without this essential information it is useless to consider the possible economic importance of the plant when an ore supply of, at the most, only 3-4 years' duration is at present known.

'We have considered various schemes of exploration drawn up by the Hemerdon Management, and while the final method selected could only be arrived at after careful study, it is probable that a series of exploratory

shafts and galleries would be most suitable (Terrell drove the adit level after World War I and James Cameron also suggested shafts with levels to help understand the deposit).

The cost might be as much as £50,000 and the work would take about two years to complete but this estimate should be verified by a more detailed examination. The cost of care and maintenance is about £3,000 per annum.'

Summing up, the authors of this report concluded that 'without plant modifications to improve recovery and efficiency of operation, as indicated above, it is unlikely that costs could be much reduced from the high figure attained during the War. We could only recommend that the plant be re-started as a temporary measure on the assumption that uneconomic production of wolfram is required for important strategic or national considerations in which cost is not the most important factor. Subject to this, we recommend that no further steps be taken at Hemerdon, either with a view to temporary operation or disposal of the plant, until further exploratory work has been undertaken.'

So although, to date the Hemerdon project had cost the Government a staggering £368,000 pounds (over £16 million in todays' terms) and there were ongoing annual maintenance costs of £3,000 (equivalent now to over £100,000 per annum), there was no immediate plan to pull the plug.

Shortly after Gill's report was published the Government's Mineral Development Committee began preparing a paper on the mineral resources of the country. It was published, after three years' deliberation and investigation, in July 1949.

Widely hoped by the mining community in Cornwall to contain proposals for nationalising mineral mining in the UK, the paper, which became known as the Westwood Committee report, advocated only the nationalisation of mineral rights. Nevertheless this was seen a positive move by the Cornish Mining Development Association as they had been advocating such a move for a long time.

Part of the committee's problem had been that generally there was little in the way of precise information about proven reserves of tin or wolfram … 'with the possible exception of Hemerdon'.

'Hemerdon,' the report conceded, 'might be an important exception, particularly in view of the large and modern treatment plant erected by the Ministry of Supply during the recent war, and because the deposit could be worked opencast on a large scale.'

In the event, however, nothing much happened following the publication of the report, at least not for a few more years.

Discovery lode in the quarry on Hemerdon Ball.

To Be Or Not To Be?

In November 1944 James Cameron, who had worked with Jack Partington as the geologist on site, began preparing a report on the issues raised during the time the mine had been working and how the geology of Hemerdon had impacted on the outputs achieved.

In 1951, Cameron, who had formerly been with HM Geological Survey & Museum and was now working as Chief Geologist for Companhia Portuguesa de Radium Ltda., produced a more thoroughly worked up version of his paper. Presented in January 1951, it was published in October, more than seven years after production at Hemerdon had ceased. The paper constituted the first in-depth analysis of the Hemerdon orebody which Cameron suggested *'extends north-east from the summit of the hill* [Hemerdon Ball] *for a distance of approximately 2,000 ft. by 450 ft. 'The orebody is a stockwork composed of granite traversed by quartz veins carrying the ore minerals (wolfram and cassiterite), and the granite between the quartz veins has been so thoroughly kaolinized that it is usually soft enough to be broken by hand. The clay varies in colour between white, yellow, brown, and red.'*

As it transpired it was this very variation that was to cause problems when it came to processing the material. As Cameron explained:
'The yellow-brown colour may be due to staining from peaty surface waters, while the red colour is due to staining from the oxidation of the specular iron ore veins. In the recovery of mill water by the 100-ft Dorr-Oliver thickener, using alkaline reagents and starch, it was found that clays of the different colour-types had very different flocculation [separation] and settlement properties. The yellow-brown clay, which was only slightly acid, flocculated and settled both rapidly and easily. The red clay was highly acid, extremely difficult to flocculate, and gave very slow settlement rates. At times the red clay caused a rise in the thickener bed and a mill shutdown, no matter how the chemical conditioning reagents were varied. 'Although a good deal of time was spent on the problem, numerous experiments in the use of chemical reagent being tried, the only practical solution arrived at was to mill small quantities of the red ore mixed with the yellow-brown type of ore. This practice,' noted Cameron, 'gave fairly satisfactory results and, as the red ore came mainly from the area of 'head', it was the same solution as for the leached wolfram problem.'
There were other problems too, one of the more serious being the overwhelming amount of clayey slimes being generated. Tests had indicated that around 25% of the ore would be 'slimes', but *'in large-scale practice, it was found that the material to be dealt with as 'slimes'*

reached 40% of the ore milled, thus imperilling the whole scheme for slimes storage.' Although Cameron added that *'alterations were in hand'* to deal with the matter, *'at the time of the mill close-down.'*

There was also an issue with small amounts of wolfram being broken *through* when crushed in quartz veins rather than being broken *from* the host quartz, leading to the loss of more wolfram than was anticipated into the tailings.

Clearly all of these concerns were matters that Cameron considered could be addressed and would have been, had the expanded operation run for more than the eight months that it did. He also felt that the orebody could be at least twice what had originally been anticipated thus potentially at least doubling the life of the mine. He also thought that the orebody might spread over a larger area than the sett as currently defined: *'During 1943, a preliminary attempt was made at sampling the north and south extensions of the orebody by a shallow pit sampling programme'* .... an *'encouraging area found, was near the eastern granite contact on the south side of the hill.'*

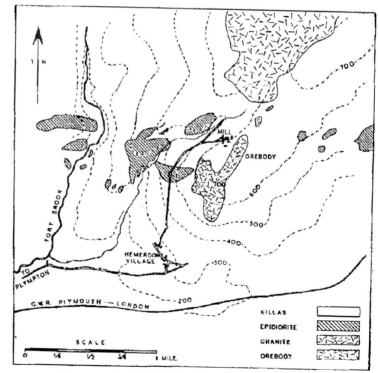

Fig. 1.—Geology of the area surrounding the Hemerdon orebody.

187

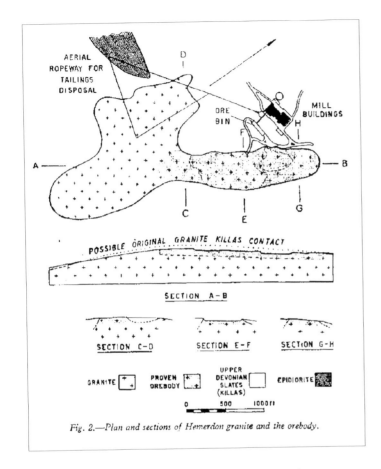

Fig. 2.—Plan and sections of Hemerdon granite and the orebody.

He added, '*The mineral is extremely friable and breaks down with great ease by mechanical action to a chocolate-red powder or slime.*'

Curiously enough, at the time Cameron's paper was published Britain was once again involved in theatre of war, this time in Korea.

The issue this time was that this particular military action impacted on the British supply chain for tungsten, which was then coming from the Far East, and so it prompted the powers that be to have another look at the potential of the mineral deposit at Hemerdon.

Indeed, on 9 April 1951 the Minister of Supply, George Strauss, informed the North Cornwall MP, Sir Harold Roper, that, confronted by the growing world scarcity of non-ferrous metals, the Government had decided to resume wolfram mining at Hemerdon. Although, according to the *Western Morning News*' report the following day: '*He himself gave no indication when workings were likely to begin or to what extent they would be undertaken, but it was stated that the mine would be reopened this year.*' [1951]

A week later the *Daily Express*, somewhat dramatically, reported that the mine was '*opening up to help Britain*'.

Perhaps one of Cameron's most significant observations however was on the nature of the wolfram found at Hemerdon. '*The mineral occurs in particles of all sizes up to bunches 5-6 in. in length. It is of a blue-black colour, with a bright shiny metallic lustre on cleavage faces. When broken across the cleavage it is a deep chocolate colour and its streak is also chocolate red.*'

He concluded that the '*proportion of the FeO molecule to MnO is approaching the ferberite end of the hubnreite-wolframite-ferberite series.*' In other words, as had been suggested before, the Hemerdon wolfram wasn't pure wolfram, indeed the pure samples assayed showed it to be 16.46% iron oxide, 7.44% manganese oxide, 1.27% tin oxide and 0.51 silicate minerals.

George Strauss (1901-93) served as Minister of Supply from 1947-51. First elected as an MP in 1929, he remained in the House of Commons, with just a short break in the early 1930s, until 1979.

Six months later there was little sign of any development however and the *News Chronicle* carried an account of the current state of affairs at the Plympton site:

'*Richard Saunders,*' wrote their reporter, is a '*55-year-old works foreman and has machinery and plant worth £1,000,000 under his care.*

'*The equipment is at Hemerdon, on the fringe of Dartmoor, where on a granite spur overlooking South Devon and the sea a giant mining concern lies idle.*

'*It is built over Britain's richest deposit of the rare mineral wolfram, vital to the rearmament drive.*

'*This is what Richard Saunders has on his mind.*

"*Not only do I have to keep the machinery in good condition, but also I have to look out for unauthorised visitors.*"

'*The present plant was constructed during the war, and it has been estimated there is enough crude ore there to last 70 years at an expenditure rate of 400 tons a day.*

'*But the mine was closed in 1945.*

'*Only Richard Saunders, in the mining business all his life, stayed on. He has looked after it ever since.*

'*On the windy moorland hillside in a building as big as 20 aeroplane hangars, the foreman-who-stayed was busy today tending his million pound charge.*

'*And the only sound was the moan of the wind and the quiet purr of electric motors as Richard started them up to keep the rust away.*

"*Rather lonely here," he said.*'

Meanwhile, the newspaper reporter reminded his readers that the Government had stated in the spring that the mine would be reopened this year.

'*An announcement will be made before very long*', a Ministry of Materials spokesman was quoted as saying.

In the event it wasn't until the following summer that there was any sign of extra activity at Hemerdon, and even then it wasn't exactly the long-anticipated reopening.

On 23 June 1952 the Ministry of Materials (the Mineral Development Commission was no longer acting under the aegis of the Ministry of Supply and we now had a Minister of Fuel and Power and a Ministry of Materials) appointed 64-year-old Professor John Ritson to advise '*on the steps to be taken to test the Hemerdon Wolfram and Cassiterite deposit near Plymouth*'. They also appointed Messrs. English Clays, Lovering Pochin & Co. Ltd to act as their managing agents.

The men from the ministry had clearly read the findings of the Westwood Committee and James Cameron's paper and charged Ritson with a three-stage plan for Hemerdon:

John Anthony Sydney Ritson DSO & Bar, OBE, MC (18 August 1887 – 16 October 1957)[1] was an English mines inspector and engineer who became professor of mining at Leeds University and at the Royal School of Mines, Imperial College, London. In his early life he was a rugby union player of note playing international rugby for both England and the British and Irish Lions, and was a member of the first ever English Grand Slam winning side. During the First World War he served in the Durham Light Infantry and later commanded a battalion of the Royal Scots.

1. Prove experimentally whether the adhering clay could be removed from the gravel and valuable minerals.
2. A small scale pilot plant trial of the laboratory conclusions.
3. A full scale run.

Reporting back to the ministry 18 months later, in December 1953, Ritson noted that '*Laboratory tests combined with your Agents' knowledge of the properties of china clay, soon showed that it was possible to remove the clay.*'

That was back in January. It transpired that they had been able to process '*newly mined material from the quarry at the rate of 100 tons per hour*' and that it had passed through the trommel leaving no apparent trace of adhering clay.

The investigation then moved to stage two and remarkably, in the absence of a new pilot plant, the existing plant at Hemerdon was cranked up again with plans for a single shift to work it.

This, reported Ritson, '*took longer than was anticipated because it was found, as was to be expected, the plant had deteriorated during its nine years' idleness and many deficiencies had to be made good.*'

Furthermore, as he added, '*Labour had to be collected and trained.* '*Thus it was not until 28 July that a pilot test was made.*'

The test lasted for eight and a half hours and during that time 545 tons of dry ore passed through the mill. Interestingly enough the test was supervised by CW Milner who had managed the mine during the War and who had been '*borrowed from his current employers*' specifically for this test.

Also present in a supervisory capacity, were Messrs Parker & Brown, from the agents appointed by the ministry, the former as Chief Chemist. Once again there were problems around getting experienced personnel for such a short experiment and Ritson explained that the *'temporary labour force included local men and students from Plymouth technical college.*

'Naturally,' he noted, *'it cannot be described as skilled owing to lack of practice, but it worked willingly and intelligently.'*

Acknowledging that there were still questions to be answered, the Professor went on to give his estimates on the cost of re-opening the plant, costs that included spending around £50,000 just to get the mill back into proper working order.

'This is in excess of what I suggested in August 1952,' he admitted, *'but I know more about the mill now.'*

All told, factoring in the cost of the existing plant, putting it right and acquiring the quarry, Ritson reckoned on a budget requirement of £380,000 with estimated running costs of £750 a day, £200 of which was wages for the 118 men needed for the smooth running of the operation. That being for a three-shift arrangement as it had been during the war, with at least 2,000 tons of material being through-put each day. As to the anticipated value of the tin and wolfram realised in that processing each day, he gave a figure of £1,156, which gave the plant a healthy surplus of a shade over £400 per day, which, in theory, would cover the cost of setting up within a few years. Furthermore, he had believed that there was sufficient ore to keep the mine going for at least seven years, maybe more: *'ore should be found at lower levels, but it has not yet been proved.'*

Ritson held back from actually advising the Minister to crack on with the re-opening of the mine; however, he did say that *'a decision has to be made as to whether the mine should be worked now and the wolfram stock-piled or whether the plant should be put on a care and maintenance basis ready for when wanted.*

'It must be realised,' he added, *'that a care and maintenance basis means probably a delay of 12 months before the plant will turn round properly and adequate staff obtained and trained.'*

He wasn't finished: *'I am also of the opinion if the existing plant stands idle for another lengthy period it will have so deteriorated as to be useless; only the shell of the building will be useful.'*

As to the cost of that care and maintenance, *'that will be heavy,'* he ventured, *'consisting of rates, wages and interest, in addition to the cost of material required for maintaining the property.'*

Nothing much was heard on the matter after that.

In 1956 December Earl Jowitt raised the subject of wolfram and Hemerdon in the House of Lords.

Not thinking he would find one of his fellow Peers familiar with the mineral, he appears to have been somewhat surprised when the then Earl of Morley addressed the House:

'My Lords, may I tell the noble and learned Earl that I was a director of the company at Hemerdon? We worked that mine for the Government, and it cost so much money that it was quite impossible to carry on.'

Earl Jowitt then mentioned the Westwood Committee Report, which by then was seven years old, although he referenced it as though it were hot news: *'They recommend,'* he said, *'that nothing be done there until further exploratory work has been undertaken.'*

Was he, therefore, unaware of Professor Ritson's report that had been produced in the meantime?

Certainly it didn't appear so, for he responded to the Earl of Morley by saying that *'the actual figures are given here'* (presumably he had a copy of the Committee report to hand).

'I am not saying that it is necessary that the Government should do it. If they could encourage somebody to take it on, I am sure that the noble Earl would not mind. I know that he is not one of the people who are going to take it on, but I am sure that he would not mind anybody else trying.'

To which Morley replied: *'I should be perfectly willing to take it on if there were any possibility of its paying.'*

Later in the debate Lord Mancroft spoke of other ways the Government might be able to support operations like Hemerdon, specifically mentioning tax 'holidays' – tax-free periods of working.

By this stage of the proceeding Ritson's findings had been mentioned: *'As the House now knows,'* said Lord Mancroft, *'fresh attempts have been made to overcome the existing technical difficulties. I am told that a new process has been developed and the venture now looks a good deal more attractive commercially. The Board of Trade are now negotiating the disposal of the assets to a commercial operator. We shall watch its future with interest.'*

Clearly, as far as the Government was concerned, the cost was too heavy.

In 1957 what was then the last working wolfram mine in England, at Castle-an-Dinas, near St Columb, was closed down.

Two years later the Government put Hemerdon's last remaining employee out of work as they sold the Hemerdon plant to one of the largest engineering and machinery firms in the country – the George Cohen 600 Group.

In 1959 in their in-house industry *600 Magazine*, they carried a piece making reference to the Hemerdon deposit and the strategic importance of tungsten: *'valuable in peace, but essential in war'*.

The article gave a very potted, somewhat casual, overview of the recent Hemerdon saga.

'In the last war, first the Germans and, later, the Allies used tungsten carbide for the cores of armour piercing shells. Indeed it has been said that these nearly gave Rommel the battle for North Africa – and later still, used by the Americans, stopped Rundstedt's tanks at the Battle of the Bulge.

'Before the war, much of the world's tungsten came from the Far East – notably China. With the entry of Japan, the Allies had to face the problem of finding their supplies elsewhere – and it really meant scraping the barrel with a vengeance.

'Before Hemerdon was in production however, the shortage of tungsten had largely been met in other ways. The plant was placed on a care-and-maintenance basis.

'The war ended. The Mineral Resources Committee advised that the plant should not be dispersed, but that further investigation of the ore deposit should be made to ascertain the nature and reserves of ore. Later, with the reduction of conventional armaments throughout the world, the strategic value of tungsten fell.

'But tungsten is still important – and may become more so – since the heat resistant qualities of its alloys are wanted for jet engines and rockets; but, unless greater commercial use is found for it, Hemerdon Ball is likely to remain undisturbed, as a lovely part of the lovely Devon landscape.

'Tungsten, however, still plays a big part in our lives. Without a tungsten-tipped tool, how can we put up that hook in the kitchen for the Missus?'

And then, following that unashamedly sexist remark, came the punchline: 'George Cohen Sons and Company Ltd., have now purchased this plant for disposal piecemeal. May they send you a catalogue?'

Clearly there were a number of enquiries and by April 1960, Percy Levy, a director of the George Coken 600 Group was able to tell the *Western Morning News* that, 'between half and three-fifths of the plant has been sold already.

'Much of it,' he added, 'will be used for quarrying and mining in Cornwall.'

Not everything, however, was sold as seen, and, after being felled, the great 160ft pylon from the blondin was broken up and sold as scrap. A number of the plant buildings remained, but there were no serious thoughts of maintenance.

The question now was, what did fate have in store for Hemerdon next?

The feed bin, right, with wire rope of the blondin to pylon to transport buckets of sand.

Any scrap iron? The giant Hemerdon pylon is broken up in 1960.

Above: Mrs. J. M. Hussell at the wheel of her Triumph TR3
Far Left: Mr. Russell Ham on the Hemerdon Mine track.
Left: Cover of the Plymouth Motor Club magazine with 'Sam' Crocker at the wheel at Hemerdon.

Making Inroads

In September 1958 a new challenge opened up for Hemerdon, as the Plymouth Motor Club secured permission to stage 'The Allen Trophy Driving Test' at Hemerdon Mine. Some 16 competitors took part in two runs of eight tests, driving on a variety of cambers and gradients. The main sports event was won by Mr GS Edwards driving a Dellow (a little like the MG Midget, these cars, manufactured by Ken Delingpole and Ron Lowe – hence the combined name – were in production between 1949 and 1956 and were largely intended for trials, rallies and hill-climbs), while Alan Penhale driving a Morris Minor, won the 'opposite class'.

There had been an earlier 'hill climb' assault on Hemerdon Mine by the club in the summer of 1955, conducted with the permission of ECLP (English Clays, Lovering Pochin Ltd.).

The venue proved to be popular with the club and in July 1961 it was reported to the club's committee that they had been given permission to use the mine 'whilst the Agents continued to negotiate the sale of lease of the site.'

Although health and safety precautions were somewhat in the infancy, Basil Tye of the RAC agreed to look over the mine site with a view to it being used as Hill Climb venue. The following summer, PMC's first Hemerdon Hill Climb was staged. Entry to the event was £1 but, it was reasoned, expenses were high, especially with regard to insurance.

Winners that year were Mike Lane in a modified Mini, Norman Brooks in his Austin Healey was second, while Sylvia McGregor won the Ladies Award in a Triumph TR2, with a time of 30 seconds, less than four seconds off the time of the fastest man.

The following year saw another event at Hemerdon and by 1964 the number of competitors rose to 59, John Grafton becoming the first to break the 24-second barrier. A number of cars cut the bottom bend very tightly and one observer commented that had he taken the bend any tighter he would have gone through the factory rather than around it. Meanwhile, the gorse bushes at the top of the course were said to have taken quite a clobbering.

An additional Hemerdon Climb was held later in the year and numbers were up again; however, the unofficial use of the course by go-karts was threatening to compromise the club's licence.

The 1966 climb was cancelled but the following year the RAC approved an extended climb at the site. This too proved popular and at their first meeting of the New Year, in February 1968 the question was asked whether the Club could gain full control of Hemerdon. However, club member and local garage proprietor, Ken Haskell informed the meeting that 'the mining company had the lease of the mine and that it was shortly to be renewed again ... there did not appear to be any hope that PMC could obtain it.'

The following year Hemerdon's managing agents, D Ward & Sons, wrote to the club stating that henceforth the key to the mine would be kept at their office and should be returned after each meeting. Curiously the club was also requested to 'dump one of the old cars lying around up there into the pit specified on the map.'

Despite this extra security provision a bath went missing from the site and PMC were blamed. The club agreed to respond by pointing out that 'they were not the only persons using the hill and could not be held responsible for others.'

In January 1971 the club's Anon Trial at Hemerdon was cancelled due to the icy conditions, but the popularity of the events continued and there was a discussion about allowing spectators, but the RAC said it would be expensive to 'enclose them'.

April 1972 witnessed a 'more than members' only' event as the band of the Royal Marines played, enlivening activities that included Chris Inch almost equalling the climb record.

Over the next couple of years the club were told that they would need to have an ambulance in attendance for future events, the club also experimented with polystyrene bales, rather than straw bales, but it was agreed that the former constituted a greater fire risk. Other issues included drivers going through Hemerdon Village too fast and a conspicuous lack of helpers for the Hill Climbs.

Most serious of all the issues, however, was the fact that in 1975 it was announced that drilling was about to start up again at the mine. That summer the club received a letter from Paul Williams to say that 'PMC would not be able to use Hemerdon again as several shafts had been reopened and it would be too dangerous ... however if the exploration work came to nothing, the club would be welcome back.'

So who was Paul Williams, and who was he working for?

Great Expectations

The next instalment of the Hemerdon saga began sometime around the time that Beatlemania was sweeping the country. William Augustus Richardson nicknamed Bully, was a 44-year-old former flight officer who had served with Coastal Command in the Royal Canadian Air Force during the Second World War. The father of seven children, his gravestone describes him as a *'Prospector and Promotor Extraordinair'*, although those who knew a little more about 'Bully' may have used other epithets.

Richardson first appears to have latched on to Hemerdon in 1963 but it wasn't until 1965 that the local press (*WMN* 5 April) started to flesh out stories of a 'Canadian concern' who were looking at the mine with a view to *'considering the possibility of reopening'*.

Having stumbled upon the Hemerdon story, Richardson started sending out feelers to see if he could get anyone interested in funding development of the under-exploited sett.

In December 1965 Richardson received a report from Bill Morgan, of Geo-Met Reactors of Ontario. Having reviewed the previous attempts to make the mine work, Morgan acknowledged the obvious potential of Hemerdon but recommended that before any serious investment was considered there should be:

'A detailed feasibility study of the deposit, followed by further investigation into the ore reserves and then metallurgical testing of bulk samples.'

On a more positive note, however, Morgan, who appears to have been the President and Metallurgist with Geo-Met, spoke of work Geo-Met had already done in the UK using the *'new Geo-Met hydrogen reduction-leaching technique'* prior to designing a mill and smelter.

Apart from suggesting that *'present-day practice and equipment could no doubt upgrade'* previous mineral recovery rates, Morgan's evaluation did little more than revisit the history of the mine.

Nevertheless, despite Morgan's clear caveats, a few weeks later Richardson, who was not without experience in the field, indeed he styled himself a 'prospector', claimed that Geo-Met Reactors had 4,000 dollars to invest and were confident of being able to get at least another $2,000. They were keen to set up a subsidiary company for tungsten carbide stud cores, near Hemerdon. Geo-Met also spoke of the possibility of loans from the British government and potential tax holidays.

Richardson signed an agreement with the landowners in February 1966, but there had been little activity, as yet, on site.

However, other companies contacted by Richardson also expressed a degree of enthusiasm for the proposal. *'We are interested in hearing more'*, wrote a representative of the huge WR Grace & Co., shipping and chemical company from New York, while the Ottawa-based Goldrum Mining enterprise were a little more circumspect, wondering if Richardson was after some sort of deal on Hemerdon.

However, despite some positive feedback, no-one had quite bitten the bullet and Richardson was prompted to send out a fresh wave of correspondence following the gentle reminder he had had, in May 1967, from (Humphrey) Woollcombe and (Mrs Grigg) Strode's solicitor, D Ward & Son, to renew his option on the sett.

Richardson appears to have significantly upped his endeavours over the next few weeks and before long he had received responses from General Electric, then the world's largest individual purchaser of tungsten, the Hecla Mining Co., of Idaho, Canadian Industrial Gas & Oil, the Hudson Bay Mining & Smelting Company, Sylvania Electric of Pennsylvannia, the American Smelting & Refining Co., the Howmet Corporation of New York, Kerr Addison Mines, Noranda Mines, Toronto, the Westing House Electric Corporation, and AMAX Exploration. There were doubtless many others he contacted who didn't feel the need to reply.

The nature of the responses he was getting suggested that he hadn't held back in his enthusiasm for the Hemerdon project and when he eventually replied to Ward & Son, he was full of seemingly unbridled optimism. His letter, marked 'Confidential' and dated Sunday 25 June 1967, is worth considering in full. Defying a number of the basic conventions of grammar and punctuation, Richardson opened with an introductory paragraph that sat above the main content of the letter:

RE: HEMERDON MINE

Minimum of 15,000 tons production a day – $500,000.00 annual royalties to Hemerdon Owners – – and buy up most of your allowable surrounding ground! "Timing is Everything in Mining – – Tungsten is Now Right!"

Drawing a line under that dramatic opening he continued: *'Deeply sorry I am late in answering your letter (of 8 May) - - I have been very busy.* He continued: *'As I now write you, I have a third of the mining world checking Hemerdon; This summer, all the mining world will know Hemerdon as of 1967.*

'Paul [the Paul in question was the very same, aforementioned, Paul Williams who, it transpired, was a partner of Ward & Son], *– by all means I will keep my Hemerdon option and lease for 40 years, but we are starting the largest base metal mine development in the United Kingdom on Hemerdon this year; please hold all interested surface buyers off Hemerdon and surrounding ground; your Hemerdon is about to make mining history*

CONFIDENTIAL

Richardson Mining Associates

810 TEMPLE BUILDING, 62 RICHMOND STREET WEST
TORONTO 1, CANADA
TEL. 364-3312 (AREA CODE 416) CABLE "FREEDOM"

Temp. Off. Tel. No. - EM. 4-3944

WM. A. RICHARDSON, *Prospector*
RES. TEL. 922-0397

JEAN CLAUDE LeROY, B.Sc., *Chief Geologist*
RES. TEL. 922-7980

Sunday, June 25, 1967.

Mr. Paul Williams, M.B.E.,
D. Ward & Son,
11, The Crescent,
Plymouth, (South Devon),
England.

CC: Mr. Cecil Venn, LL.B.,
Bond, Pearce, Eliott & Knape,
1, The Crescent,
Plymouth, England.

CC: Mrs. A.M.D. Grigg-Strode,
Newham Park,
Plympton, England.

CC: Mr. Humphrey Woolcombe,
Woolcombe & Yonge,
2 Queen Anne's Terrace,
Tavistock Road,
Plymouth, England.

CC: Mr. Ernest A. DuVernet, Q.C.,
DuVernet, Carruthers & Eastman,
121 Richmond St. West, Suite 602,
TORONTO 1, Ontario, Canada.

RE: HEMERDON MINE

Minimum of 15,000 tons production a day - $500,000.00 annual royalties to
Hemerdon Owners -- and buy up most of your allowable surrounding ground!
"Timing is Everything in Mining -- Tungsten is Now Right!"

Dear Paul:

Thank you for your attached letter of May 8th -- I have been very busy.
Deeply sorry I am late in answering your letter.

As I now write you, I have a third of the mining world checking Hemerdon;
This summer, all the mining world will know Hemerdon as of 1967.

Paul - by all means I will keep my Hemerdon option and lease for 40 years;
but we are starting the largest base metal mine development in the United Kingdom
on Hemerdon this year; please hold all interested surface buyers off Hemerdon and
surrounding ground; your Hemerdon is about to make mining history for many years
to come! Tungsten is currently making many new break-throughs in use and demand
volume; after the U.S. WO3 stockpile and Chinese tungsten (the handwriting is now
on the wall for the finish of both), Hemerdon will now be developed to be the WO3
supplier for all Europe, and part of the U.S.

Paul: - Hemerdon Ball and surrounding mineral rights are now the most
important ground in all the British Isles.

We will very soon have to arrange large dump rights in to the old pits of
adjoining China Clay works and large non-pollution water rights, and buy from you,
the much large surrounding mineral rights areas!

When I first saw Hemerdon some five years ago, I knew it could be made
into a great mine; -- but due to three, main problems, it was going to be a waiting
game in preparing the most modern text and correlation on the property. The
three main problems were:- (Mines are made, not found!)

One - Tungsten, though an important metal, had smaller volume uses, and
therefore, lesser markets in the world. -- In the last few years, there has been a
number of break-throughs for uses; and increased volume of tungsten in the world;
and shortage from Russia and China (see attached).

MINERAL EXPLORATION AND MINE DEVELOPMENT   ALASKA · IRELAND · WALES · EUROPE · CANADA · S AMERICA · ORIENT

... /2

The second problem was the "low-grade" of Hemerdon; - and the separation;
where the government only got around 55% in their war emergency operations. I
now have metallurgical groups that can get from 80% to 90% recovery with this type
of tungsten ore. As for low-grade, I think Hemerdon will definitely average out, at
worse -- 4 pounds WO3 to the ton; and nearly one pound tin -- - and if the tonnage
is large enough, -- anywhere from 15,000 to 30,000 tons a day; the diviso will make
Hemerdon a big profit maker. Climax Molybdenum (attached) of moly, a similar
metal, does 40,000 tons a day, at 11,000 feet, with water problems in Colorado, with
.19 moly - or just under 4 pounds. Moly is $1.80 --- WO3 is now $2.30 a pound.
Climax was in 1956 a 5 million share company. - 30,000 tons a day -- sold at $70.00
a share before amalgamating with American Metals. All large tonnage mines in
the world are "low grade". Initial costs are tremendous, but they are the big profit
makers. Nature doesn't create high "grade" in large tonnage.

Great Britain *now* imports some thirty million dollars worth of tungsten a year.
Hemerdon would have to produce 15,000 tons a day, to meet this market alone, - not
counting the European market, which could again double this figure.

Prime Minister Wilson and the British Parliament will now back most any
plan to see Hemerdon a success; i.e., proper mining tax incentive, and otherwise!
It will be a great help in the British Isles balance of payment efforts.

Paul - You being one of the main "and recent" ball carriers and "God Fathers"
of Hemerdon Ball; and now on through to production -- could be knighted for your
efficient efforts and foresight in keeping and bringing all ends together, for success
at Hemerdon!

The great, tungsten producer, China, has flooded the tungsten market in its
quarterly Canton Trade Fair through the years. Slowly, in the last two years, the
Chinese export of tungsten has been drying up; mainly since their mines are older
and deeper; and their own industrial expansion is absorbing most of their production.

The other part of this tungsten flooding threat was the U.S. government's
large stock pile, which has now proven a healthy stabilizer in letting out tungsten,
and holding the price, now around $2.15 + a pound, WO3. -- The U.S./G.S.A. stock-
pile has recently been working with the London Metal Market to stabilize the world
tungsten price! But this / can last only so long; Hemerdon is needed now!
supply

Attached is the beginning of some of the interested correspondence in Hemerdon
Ball.

Frank Nemec; *recently retired* the head of General Electric's Bulb & Metallurgical Division,
drove up to see me from Cleveland a few days ago -- he is the largest, individual
buyer of tungsten in the world! Many others have been coming by! -- Sylvania;
Westinghouse; A.S. & R.; International Nickel; Cerro Copper of N.Y.C. and Peru,
etc., etc.

Paul - Many thanks for getting the samples off to Paul Kavanagh of Kerr
Addison. -- Will be in very close touch!

With best wishes,

Bill

WAR:Diana

William A. Richardson

GEO-MET REACTORS LIMITED — 13 —

TABLE I

MAIN PRODUCING COUNTRIES OF THE WORLD

	1957	1958	1959	1960	1961	1962	1963
China	16,500	16,500	22,500	24,900	24,900	24,900	24,900
U.S.S.R.	8,300	8,300	9,900	10,500	11,000	11,600	12,100
South Korea	4,567	3,597	3,761	6,321	8,107	8,219	6,724
U.S.A.	5,520	3,788	3,649	7,325	8,245	8,429	5,657
North Korea	2,665	3,300	4,400	5,500	5,500	4,400	4,400
Bolivia	4,809	2,457	2,671	2,370	3,104	2,798	2,513
Australia	2,629	1,587	1,218	2,075	2,866	1,946	1,771
Portugal	4,756	2,109	2,478	3,189	3,274	2,754	1,635
Brazil	2,304	2,596	2,302	1,867	1,361	1,368	1,050
Japan	1,144	881	1,194	1,082	1,033	1,160	858
Burma	2,893	1,667	1,269	1,041	1,102	882	728
Peru	1,215	922	542	538	428	435	510
Sweden	557	660	768	311	345	386	385
Austria	140	146	152	243	317	320	246
S.W. Africa	298	64	2	154	190	184	239
Thailand	1,080	725	553	486	565	463	226
Congo, Republic of	1,914	1,479	1,038	634	642	408	223
Spain	1,319	1,301	854	1,030	1,192	777	160
Argentina	1,441	1,127	827	893	892	635	129
Others	3,989	2,238	1,563	1,780	2,302	1,231	198
TOTAL	68,000	55,500	61,200	72,200	77,400	73,300	64,700

Handwritten annotation on the table: HEMERDON BALL (by South Korea row); 6,000 (by 6,724)

Geo-Met's statistics on the world tungsten producers in 1964, with Richardson's projection of where Hemerdon could be in the grand scheme of things.

for many years to come! Tungsten is currently making many new break-throughs in use and demand volume; after the U.S. WO_3 stockpile and Chinese tungsten (the handwriting is now on the wall for the finish of both), Hemerdon will now be developed to the WO_3 supplier for all Europe, and part of the U.S.

'Paul : – Hemerdon Ball and surrounding mineral rights are now the most important ground in all the British Isles.

We will very soon have to arrange large dump rights in to the old pits of adjoining China Clay works and large non-pollution water rights, and buy from you the much large surrounding mineral rights areas [sic]!

'When I first saw Hemerdon some five years ago, I knew it could made into a great mine; – – but due to three, main problems, it was going to be a _waiting game_ in preparing the most modern text and correlation on the property. The three main problems were:– (_Mines are made_, not found!)'

Bearing all the hallmarks of a somewhat naïve, overgrown schoolboy, who hadn't quite passed all his exams but clearly thought he'd stumbled on a potential goldmine in the tungsten deposit at Hemerdon, Richardson carried on, his obvious excitement emphasised by an overuse of the exclamation mark!

'One – Tungsten, though an important metal, had smaller volume uses, and therefore, lesser markets in the world. – – In the last few years, there has been a number of break-throughs for uses; and increased volume of tungsten in the world; and shortage from Russia and China (see attached).

'The second problem was the "low-grade" of Hemerdon; – and the separation; where the government only got around 55% in their war emergency operations. I have now metallurgical groups that can get from 80% to 90% recovery with this type of tungsten ore. As for low-grade, I think that Hemerdon will definitely average out, at worse – – 4 pounds WO_3 to the ton; and nearly one pound tin – – – and if the tonnage is large enough, – – anywhere from 15,000 to 30,000 tons a day; the diviso will make Hemerdon a big profit maker. Climax Molybdenum (attached) or moly, a similar metal, does 40,000 tons a day, at 11,000 feet, with water problems in Colorado, with .19 moly – or just under 4 pounds. Moly is $1.80 – – – WO_3 is now $2.30 a pound. Climax was in 1956 a 5 million share company. – 30,00 tons a day – – sold at $70.00 a share before amalgamating with American Metals. All large tonnage mines in the world are "low grade". Initial costs are tremendous, but they are big profit makers. Nature doesn't create high "grade" in large tonnage!

'Great Britain now imports some thirty million dollars worth of tungsten a year, Hemerdon would have to produce 15,000 tons a day, to meet this figure alone, – not counting the European market, which could again double this figure.

'Prime Minister Wilson and the British Parliament will now back most any plan to see Hemerdon a success; i.e., proper mining tax incentive, and otherwise! It will be a great help in the British Isles balance of payments efforts.'

The Richardson hyperbole didn't end there either, he carried on, again addressing his target in an unusually direct manner:

'Paul – you being one of the main "and recent" ball carriers and "God Fathers" of Hemerdon Ball; and now on through to production – – could be knighted for your efficient efforts and foresight in keeping and bringing all ends together, for success at Hemerdon!'

Clearly our 'Bully' was one of those who believed that flattery would get him anywhere.

The rest of the letter was a little more prosaic: 'The great, tungsten producer, China, has flooded the tungsten market in its quarterly Canton Trade Fair through the years. Slowly, in the last two years, the Chinese export of tungsten has been drying up; mainly since their mines are older and deeper; and their own industrial expansion is absorbing most of their production.

'The other part of this tungsten flooding threat was the U.S. government's large stock pile, which has now proven a healthy stabilizer in letting out tungsten and holding the price, now around $2.15 + a pound, WO_3. – – The U.S./G.S.A. stockpile has recently been working with the London Metal Market to stabilize the world tungsten price! But this supply can only last so long; Hemerdon is needed now!'

Richardson concluded his missive with reference to some other attachments which took the form of 'some of the interested correspondence in Hemerdon Ball'.

'Frank Nemec; the recently retired head of General Electric's Bulb & Metallurgical Division drove up to see me from Cleveland [Richardson was writing from his office in the Big Temple Building in Toronto] a few days ago – – he is the largest individual buyer of tungsten in the world! Many others have been coming by! – – Sylvania; Westinghouse; A.S. & R.; International Nickel; Cerro Copper of N.Y.C. and Peru etc., etc.'

Writing long before the internet era Richardson, somewhat flamboyantly listed four other individuals that he had cc'd his letter to. The landowners Humphrey Woollcombe and Mrs AMD Griff-Strode, Cecil Venn, Bond Pearce solicitor, and Ernest A DuVernet, who appears to have been Richardson's lawyer in Toronto.

One imagines Richardson Mining Associates was not a particularly large organisation and that he either did not want, or could not afford a qualified secretary, although that might be a disservice to Diana who typed the letter. The real question though to what extent was Richardson exaggerating everything, or at the very least, being overly optimistic about what could be achieved at Hemerdon. It sounded rather like the sort of gushing prospectus that we had seen from various nineteenth-century Adventurers and written with a ringing endorsement from their onside Mine Captains. But was it justified?

In July 1967 Geo-Met, who certainly appeared to be the most interested of those parties Richardson had contacted, received a technical report that they had commissioned from Lamp Metals of London. The man who had actually carried out the report for Lamp was Dr GA Schnellman of the London-based geological and mining consultancy firm of Mackay and Schnellmann.

Schnellmann ran over the recent history of Hemerdon and contacted RO Stokes who had built the plant some 25 years earlier. Richardson had already forewarned the Stokes company of the potential that now seemed to exist in development here: 'Since we are about to get major underwriting on the property, we would be pleased to have our mining group approach your company for new work to be done on the Hemerdon Ball property particularly since your company is already familiar with the technical facts of the property.'

The latter in response now felt confident that using a "Stokes" Hydrosizer they would be able to improve on the separation process and save substantially on the floor space required and the number of tables and employees that would be required. Their best guestimate as to costs was £600,000 (over £10m in today's terms) for plant, erection, equipment and electrical wiring, with a further £54,000 for engineering costs.

As for the running costs, these were roughly rounded up to £50,000 per year, being primarily made up of wages £17,940,0s.0d. – the working assumption being three shifts per day for 52 weeks a year at £345 (just over £6,000 today) per week – plus £27,000 electricity running costs.

Four months later Geo-Met's Bill Morgan wrote to Bill Richardson with his report on the samples that Paul Kavanaugh had sent from Hemerdon. His conclusion was that by applying 'a sink float preconcentration to the vein type material, a very large increase of throughput through the mill', could be achieved and that 'this could result in substantial capital cost savings'.

It's interesting to note that having received the report from Schnellmann, that, unknown to Richardson, Morgan subsequently sanctioned its release to AMAX.

The following month, another Toronto-based geological engineer, Jack McOuat, produced a report on Hemerdon for his colleague Murray Watts. Like Schnellman, the 34-year-old McOuat, concluded that Hemerdon looked 'very attractive and should be followed up'.

It had been just five years earlier that McOuat had joined forces with Murray Watts (then 53 and an accomplished explorer and mining

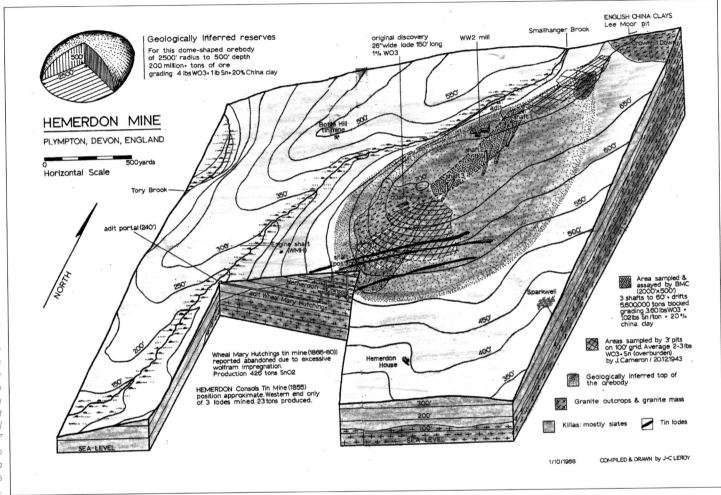

From Jean Claude Leroy's report on Hemerdon Mine 1971 highlighting first discovery lode in quarry on Hemerdon Ball, in the main open cast pit World War I adit level, 1936-37 three shafts with levels, 1943 area sampled by James Camerson.

Within the figure:

Geologically inferred reserves
For this dome-shaped orebody of 2500' radius to 500' depth 200 million+ tons of ore grading 4 lbs WO3+ 1 lb Sn+ 20% China clay

HEMERDON MINE

PLYMPTON, DEVON, ENGLAND

0   500yards
Horizontal Scale

NORTH

Tory Brook

adit portal (240')

Engine shaft (WMH)
shaft post?

Hemerdon Consols

adit Wheal Mary Hutchings

Wheal Mary Hutchings tin mine (1866-80)) reported abandoned due to excessive wolfram impregnation. Production 426 tons SnO2

HEMERDON Consols Tin Mine (1855) position approximate. Western end only of 3 lodes mined. 23 tons produced.

original discovery 26"wide lode 150' long 1% WO3

WW2 mill   Smallhanger Brook   ENGLISH CHINA CLAYS Lee Moor pit   Crownhill Down

adit   Shaft 1
Shaft 2
Shaft 3
quarry

Bottle Hill tin mine

Sparkwell

Hemerdon House

SEA LEVEL   SEA LEVEL

Area sampled & assayed by BMC (2000'x500') 3 shafts to 60' + drifts 5,600,000 tons blocked grading 3.60 lbs WO3 + 1.02 lbs Sn /ton + 20 % china clay

Areas sampled by 3' pits on 100' grid. Average 2-3 lbs WO3+ Sn (overburden) by J. Cameron / 20.12.1943

Geologically inferred top of the orebody

Granite outcrops & granite mass

Killas: mostly slates   Tin lodes

1/10/1968   COMPILED & DRAWN by J-C LEROY

engineer) and Arthur Griffis (a 50-year-old experienced mining man and specialist in mineral economics, who had already played a major part in the discovery of five iron ore deposits in Canada) to form WGM (Watts, Griffis, McOuat: the company that is still going today and is Canada's longest running independent firm of geological and mining consultants). McOuat also thought that the property was worth pursuing. He suggested that all the data from the 1937 and 1941 programmes should be obtained and studied for its usefulness, and in the event of that not being

possible, *'a property inspection, geological mapping and sampling of old openings should be undertaken'.*

McOuat's considered approach also included a *'study of the potential value of the china clay fraction'* and, *'as soon as any reliable or realistic grade and grade recovery figures are available, a preliminary feasibility study should be prepared, and particular care should be taken with regard to taxes, conservation laws, and overall UK government policy.'*

And then having satisfied all of the above, McOuat envisaged that *'a*

large diamond drilling programme should be undertaken.
'Results,' he noted, 'are potentially erratic and this must be carefully considered when laying out a drilling grid.'
Estimated costings of all of this? $10,000-$25,000 for the literature searches, property inspection, sampling mapping, metallurgical testing and evaluation, $250,000 ($1.9m today) for drilling and a further $250,000 for detailed metallurgical testing, flow sheet design and feasibility report. Thus Geo-Met's figures were coming in at a little over $500,000 (or around £170,000 based on the exchange rate in 1967) without the cost of any major plant itself. It was worth bearing in mind, however, that the last two figures were reckoned by McOuat to be minimum-spend figures not top end.
It would appear that both of these reports were commissioned by Geo-Met and that it wasn't Richardson himself who was funding these investigations. However, in December 1967, the man Richardson included on his headed notepaper as being his Chief Geologist, Jean Claude LeRoy, produced some detailed figures based on a reassessment of BMC's (British (Non-Ferrous) Metal Corporations) pre-War operation. The work, though, didn't really add much to the Hemerdon knowledge bank.
Straight after receiving LeRoy's report Richardson wrote to Mackay & Schnellman, only to be told by them that they were already acting on behalf of Lamp Metals, and therefore Geo-Met.
The following summer, LeRoy produced an 'Assessment of the Hemerdon Mine (Tungsten Mountain Mines Limited), Hemerdon Ball'. The aim of this paper was 'to evaluate several exploration methods, one of which would eventually be selected in the development work to be carried out at Hemerdon.
'As of date (30 July 1968), since no drilling of any sort is known to have been done on the property, and therefore the mechanical qualities of the rock to be investigated are largely unknown, it should be kept in mind that we are considering various cures without knowing the exact nature of the disease.'
However, LeRoy also felt that Hemerdon had plenty of merit and, as well as achieving better than ever recovery values of tungsten, 'could be producing half as much as the largest existing tin mine in the world. It would also be the largest tin producer in Europe and North America:
'The largest tin producer in Canada,' he added, is 'Cominco' which 'produces an average of 400 tons of tin per year' ... 'Considering they treat about 3 million tons of ore per year, it means a grade of about 1/6th of lb of tin per ton of ore.'
Meanwhile, 'the only producer in the US is AMAX' whose amount recovered is less than Cominco's, the implication being that Hemerdon was good for tungsten, tin, and to a lesser extent, china clay, while the

'commercial potential of <u>gravel and sand</u> from the operation remains to be investigated.'
The extensive use of underlining in the whole report smacked of the hand of Richardson, so perhaps this was another attempt to 'big up' the project rather than simply acknowledge the past in the present.
It is not clear that Richardson had any substantial funds of his own to invest, rather he was hoping to attract a company with major resources that he could somehow do a deal with, as he was the one with the lease.
In the meantime he continued to write to anyone he thought might be able to help his cause, including the then leader of the opposition, Harold Wilson, the Queen and, separately, her husband, the Duke of Edinburgh. From the former (in July 1968) he received a letter acknowledging receipt of his letter, and from the Queen's representative he received a missive stating that 'Her Majesty of course knows that The Duke of Edinburgh has replied to Mr Richardson's letter'.
Thus Prince Philip was the only one to commit to doing anything, and that didn't extend to much more than agreeing that there should be tax incentives for British mining initiatives:
'It didn't take many visits to Canadian mining enterprises for me to appreciate that their development had something to do with the system of taxation'.
The Duke added 'As you may well guess I am particularly interested in this problem because of the possibilities in the Duchy of Cornwall properties. I will certainly use your material to try again. As a first step I'm sending it to Sir Solly Zuckerman, Chairman of the Central Advisory Council for Science and Technology.
'I hope Pary's Mountain (another Richardson initiative) and Hemerdon are highly successful.'
There could be no denying that Richardson had raised awareness of Hemerdon, but as yet he appeared to have raised little in the way of hard cash and a big backer.
On 24 January 1969 Murray Watts let Richardson know that Hemerdon was still on his radar: 'I can confirm my interest in proceeding with the Hemerdon project, but as I stated before, I think we should get a good clear understanding before starting, so that no misunderstanding can arise at a later date. No mineral deposit anywhere is worth that to me. Live and let live, and stay away from big companies until you can make them pay the price, and don't ever get at their mercy. The only group that I've ever found I could trust was the Anglo-American group, who by coincidence is an African English Company.' He then added 'Newconex is completely untrustworthy.'
Richardson was still keeping his options open and on 6 and 7 March 1969 he met with Melville Robinson in Pittsburgh. Robinson was the

Director of Research & Development at the Dravo Corporation, then a major American shipbuilding concern who'd won awards for their output in the Second World War.

Having been enthused by Richardson at their meetings, Davro had undertaken *'the preliminary investigations and planning on this project at our own expense because the location and previous history of the Hemerdon deposits looked promising. In our detailed examinations over the past five months we have found nothing to discourage our early opinion regarding the commercial viability of the ore body and metallurgical situation.'*

Davro had reviewed First and Second World War material sent over by Geoffrey Cox, an international minerals and engineering consultant to the site, several times, and had corresponded with Ernest Lehmann a consulting geologist and conducted metallurgical tests of the ore in their labs.

'We estimate costs or proving out of the ore reserves together with sufficient amount of pilot plant processing to be around $3.9 and with no delays could be done in 14 -18 months the whole project in 26-30 months.'

Clearly Richardson was doing his best to get serious players to look at the property he had signed a lease for, but although several concerns had now looked at the site, or at least some of the existing paperwork on the site, no-one yet had committed to the project.

In the summer of 1969 LeRoy revised his earlier report on Hemerdon and claimed the value of tungsten was now $43m, to which could be added tin to the value of $7.5m, china clay worth $7.5 m and silica sand a further $1.5m. All in all he was postulating a post pay-out profit after the investment of $9m over four years and that *'under the most limiting physical conditions which could be only remotely possibly encountered'.*

However, not everyone agreed, and furthermore it was suspected that

Paul WIlliams MBE and land agent for Hemerdon, originally with D Ward & Son, and later Paul Williams & Partners. Long-suffering correspondent with Bill Richardson over the latter's various attempts to find someone to take the project on, but at the same time retain Richardson as a working partner.

LeRoy was extolling the virtues of a site he'd never actually seen with his own eyes.

In a memo dated 30 December 1969 David Seaton, of the Institute of Geological Sciences wrote stating that he believed that LeRoy's report had been written when he (LeRoy) had been employed by Richardson, who *'probably commissioned it primarily to attract financial interest'.*

Seaton noted how the author had ignored some of James Cameron's observations and appeared to have *'little appreciation of planning conditions in England'.*

How otherwise could he suggest that in terms of waste disposal *'Hemerdon is fortunately located at the edge of the unsettled Dartmoor granite mass'* and that *'as any traveller could testify, the English seem completely oblivious to the extensive disturbance of the land.'*

Seaton added that *'the report ignores a number of established facts which fail to support the author's thesis and would tend to give an erroneous impression to anyone unfamiliar with other literature on the subject.'*

Overall Seaton, and the others who had reviewed LeRoy's report, concluded that not enough work had been done to evaluate the mineral deposit at Hemerdon and, further, that as things stood it was wrong to put any commercial value on the china clay and sand that could be recovered at the mine.

Realistically the view was that the figures that could be achieved would reduce to *'about half the totals quoted.'*

Undaunted or oblivious, Richardson ploughed on. In January 1970 he received a letter from David Owen, saying although the mine did not fall within his constituency he would be happy to help as he was a local man, but he would need to have a better idea of what RIchardson wanted from him.

What Richardson really needed was help with the planning application for re-opening the mine and the major investor to bank-roll that work and the planning permission leading up to it. Outline planning for exploration work had been granted back in December, but the real challenge was the more detailed application for re-opening and the necessity to starting the exploratory drilling programme that would potentially justify that re-opening.

In April an increasingly agitated Paul Williams wrote to Richardson:

'I refer to my letter to you of 24 March concerning the application and now enclose herewith confirmation from Devon County Council that the Minister of Housing & Local Government has decided that this application should be referred to him and arrangements are to be made for a local inquiry. I must stress that it is imperative that as much information as possible is available.'

The Board of Trade, he added, *'expect you to take immediate steps to press on with the drilling programme as the Government will view with the*

greatest concern any unreasonable delay in opening up the Mine'.
However, Richardson had yet to have landed any big fish and was still floundering around in all directions looking for a bite.

That very month he had what appeared to be a promising letter from Fraser McVittie of the British-based Steetley Company who *'having examined the various and very full papers and reports on Hemerdon'* were of the opinion *'that the prospects for developing Hemerdon are generally good and the Steetley Company is still interested in considering participation in this project which has exciting and very large potential, in contrast with so many projects which in the end make very little contribution to profits. 'With our large cash flow, the size of the operation as such is not something which frightens us.'*

Doubtless that was music to Bill's ears, but notwithstanding their opening remarks, they had a number of reservations, not least of which was the disposal of sand *'likely to be a liability rather than an asset'* and china clay, the disposal of which *'could still pose a problem which neither price adjustments nor clay processing are likely to resolve ... the conclusion then is that the Hemerdon operation will have to depend on its metal values, which was the basis of Mr Leroy's examination but production costs may well be realised by the necessity for suitable disposal arrangements for clay and sand'.*

McVittie also raised the vexed question of outline planning, but went on to say that *'apart from these technical matters, we certainly need to explore at an early stage the possible nature of participation by Steetley in this venture and the contribution we can make to its success.'*

To that end there was a suggestion that Richardson should either meet with Steetley's John Bailey in Toronto, when he was on his way back from Australia, or venture over to Steetley's Head Office in Worksop whenever it might be convenient.

Richardson, doubtless hoping for a ringing endorsement from the Government-backed body, had written to Dr Joy in January and sent him a copy of LeRoy's updated report, the updating apparently being little more than the substitution of a new date on the old report rather than a re-evaluation of the subject matter.

Describing the document as being an 'excellent dossier', Dr Joy was manifestly confused as to what Richardson's rationale had been in sending the 'many enclosures' on Hemerdon:

'Frankly, I confess that it is not clear to me from your letter what action you would like us to take in regard to further developments.'

One suspects that Richardson had been hoping for some free analysis of the material raised at Hemerdon, but Joy sent back an up-to-date copy of the Laboratory brochure, presumably with a price list.

Paul Williams, acting for Ward and thus Richardson, had sent an advance payment to Joy in April and an interim report, conducted by the aforementioned K Beer of the Institute of Geological Sciences and R Benjamin of Warren Springs, was published that November. Although encouraging in respect of the greater recovery that might be obtainable through magnetic separation, the report recognised that more work needed to be done before a more definitive verdict could be arrived at. Benjamin and Beer, from the IGS, took samples away from the site in a Land Rover in April and it was made clear that with a major planning application looming the Board of Trade, and Warren Springs, were expecting Richardson to start drilling on site.

How long could he keep wheeling and dealing without actually arriving at a deal and still keep his plates spinning? On 14 July Paul Williams reported that he had had *'an unexpected visit yesterday from Geoffrey Cox [of Dravo] who had been in Cornwall and called into my office on the way back. He told me of his visit and meeting with you last month. In this connection I was sorry to learn that the Steetley Group had somewhat withdrawn from their position and discussing this with Geoffrey Cox it seems that the difficulty is that with the uncertainties of Hemerdon unless private financing can be found, which does seem difficult, no major company is going to put up a large sum of money initially.*

'Similarly from a financing point of view, it does not seem likely that a large amount of capital would be forthcoming but if taken in stages the capital commitments could be increased progressively as satisfactory drilling and assaying tests were carried out.

'It seems that Dravo could be involved in this way and might, I understand even undertake the venture themselves providing the initial costs and commitments were not too high. While I know you do not favour this method, if no-one will come forward and agree to an extensive drilling programme and feasibility study immediately, there does not seem to be any other way to get things moving in the near future. As of course you know – I have stressed this point many times – time is not on our side, as I feel it essential that some work must be in progress and some results produced to support the Planning Application at the Inquiry.'

Paul Williams letter was revealing in many ways as it set out quite clearly where Richardson's friendly Plymouth-based agent saw the current state of play:

'... if we were unsuccessful at the Inquiry and the Planning Application was refused, the chances of opening Hemerdon Mine in the future would be very slight indeed, since the waste disposal areas of Crownhill Down would in consequence of the refusal almost certainly be allocated to ECLP [English Clays Lovering Pochin & Co. Ltd., the main operating subsidiary of English China Clays Ltd.]

As you know, ECLP themselves are keen to operate Hemerdon Mine and if you would let me know your minimum terms, which I suggest should be progressive, I would put them to the Company and see if a settlement can be reached. This also applies of course to other companies who have shown interest. I feel that a progressive but properly protected form of contract is the most realistic way to obtain Planning Approval and the re-opening of the Mine.'

The Ward & Son surveyor cum land agent also made reference to the change of Government from Labour to Conservative suggesting that if there were to be grants available then the sooner they were applied for the better.

That summer it appears that any further Warren Springs analysis was put on hold for a while as they were awaiting payment from Richardson. A cheque, for $2,000 dated 31 August and signed by Richardson's admin assistant, Diana Schwartz, ensured its continuation.

Meanwhile, in September, it appeared that Steetley might still be interested

after all, but according to Williams' latest missive dated 8 September, it appeared that Richardson might have sorted someone else to finance the drilling, in which case there might still be interest from Steetley anyway, and Williams' recent dealings with them led him to believe that they were *'a most excellent firm and one with whom one could work to the mutual advantage of all parties'.*

But Williams also stressed the need to set up a separate company, and, with 'the revised Planning Application being submitted this week', the even more urgent need to start drilling on site. Williams also looked forward to receiving the findings of Warren Springs.

In the meantime a letter arrived at Ward & Son, marked for the attention of Mr Beaumont. It came from the manager of the mining and exploration department of Charter Consolidated, PCD Burnell, who it seems was now interested in getting involved in the Hemerdon project and wanted to know what the terms of any potential agreement might be.

But maybe Steetley were now on board too. John Bailey visited Bill, Dean Vaughan and Sheldon Swaye in Toronto on 5 and 6 November. From the correspondence that followed it would appear that Steetley were now a little clearer about Richardson's motives, and possibly lack of financial backing and while they were prepared to stay involved, it would need to be on their terms.

The most hopeful solution to me,' wrote Bailey, *'seems one in which we should undertake exploratory work for a given period. During this period we would do exploratory deep trenching, some deep drilling but only of modest extent, together with plant feasibility trials tapping the latest technology in the world metallurgical house. We feel that if you have the fullest confidence in Hemerdon, then there should be little question of such a programme jeopardising any further development if for some reason we find it necessary to withdraw, which we feel is not at all likely or we would not be pursuing Hemerdon. It would certainly get things moving, which we believe is very important at this time with impending planning appeals.'*

Furthermore, the two were also awaiting the results of the next report from the Ministry of Technology's Warren Spring Laboratory.

As the looming Planning Application served increasingly to focus the mind, the Warren Springs paper, 'The Primary Evaluation of the Separation of Hemerdon Ore' from DN Collins and his colleagues, Muller, Parsonage and Penhale, was signed off by Dr Joy on 5 November 1970.

Their concern wasn't so much with the amount of mineral deposit at Hemerdon but the amount that could successfully be recovered. Using the Ritson/Cameron work as their yardstick, their conclusion was that it largely depended on how good the recovery process could get, and how well the slimes could be managed. Richardson approved; however, he had still to get anyone to sign on the dotted line.

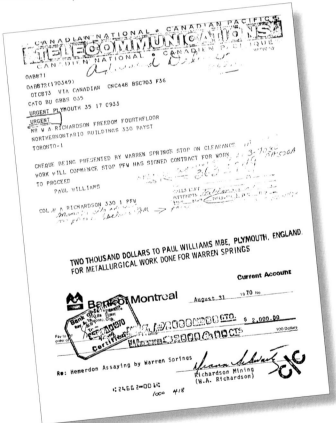

Furthermore, there was no indication from the report as to the potential value for any of the clay or sand residues, as pointed out to Dr Joy by Paul Williams. It seemed that the latter was still buying into Richardson's assertion that both elements were assets rather than liabilities.

It was now more than six years since Richardson had picked up the Hemerdon baton, and the question was how much longer could he hold on to it without drilling, setting up a pilot plant.

With just a few weeks of 1970 still to run, another letter arrived from Charters, this time it transpired that their representative John Kettel was visiting Plymouth with the intention of speaking to both Ward & Son and Richardson's solicitor about the terms of the lease.

Charters' view was that the long-term market for tungsten was good and further that a pilot plant processing one ton a day would be adequate for the first phase of investigation, although they added the proviso:

'You will appreciate that the above comments are given purely for your interest and we may vary our views after more detailed consideration.'

With both Charters and Steetley keen but still hedging their bets, Richardson met with Harry Fletcher in Toronto. Fletcher was the head of mineral procurement for British Oxygen and General Manager of Murex an offshoot of BOC. While not in a position to invest in the exploration of Hemerdon, Fletcher indicated, in a letter sent three days before Christmas 1970, that they would be able – upon the satisfactory completion of that stage – to *'contemplate providing finance for the exploitation of the deposit, in return for a substantial, though not necessarily controlling interest in the company so formed.'*

He also said that they would guarantee to take a sizeable offtake of the Wolfram and act as sole selling agent.

One way or another it looked like a new company, whoever ran it, was going to be the way forward

On the first day of the New Year Paul Williams wrote to Richardson to confirm just such an eventuality. Cecil Venn from Bond Pearce, had drawn up Articles of a new company – Hemerdon Tungsten Mines.

'He and another from his office will take one share each in the Company,' he wrote, adding, *'I felt that at this stage it would be as well if I was not included but remained as professional advisor.'*

Williams also reiterated the urgency with regard to commencing drilling operations, repeating a quote from other correspondence to the effect that *'delay could be fatal'*.

A few weeks later a notice appeared in the *Western Morning News*, under 'New Companies': Hemerdon Tungsten Mines Ltd. – Private company. Incorporated January 22, Capital £100 in £1 shares. Subscribers (each with 1 share): Cecil Venn and Richard G West, both of 1, The Crescent, Plymouth. First directors not named. Solicitors: Bond Pearce and Co. 1,

The Crescent Plymouth. Registered office: 1 The Crescent, Plymouth. However, despite the formation of this grandly named yet extremely modest company, very little happened in 1971. In June the local press reported that *'an eight-week inquiry to consider applications to re-open the Hemerdon Wolfram Mine will start at Exeter on September 21.'*

In the event, however, the application was withdrawn when it became obvious that substantially more information than was available would be required.

One can imagine the frustration of Paul Williams who had been gently badgering Richardson over the previous few years.

Remarkably, however, Richardson was not done yet, and in January 1972 he commissioned yet another report, this time from WJD Stone, the Vice-President of Magnetics International. Based in Quebec, William Stone was a graduate of the Camborne School of Mines and was then currently listed project developer and research director for Magnetics International. The report broke little in the way of new ground and interestingly enough, in a statement of non-interest at the end of the report, which was based on *'experience and certain investigations'* Stone averred that *'Magnetics International Group of Companies has no direct, indirect or anticipated interest in either WA Richardson & Associates or the property reported herein.'*

And yet, in the introduction to the report, it was stated that Magnetics International had been interested in the Hemerdon Tungsten deposit for *'a number of years'* and that a new piece of equipment that they had developed, the Jones High Intensity Wet Magnetic Separator, could be extremely useful to the operation. *'Each large unit can treat up to 120 tons per hour'* – *'Magnetics believed that the Jones Separator would provide such a process and hence discussed with W.A. Richardson & Associates the possibility of some joint venture.'*

Interest or no interest nothing of consequence appears to have happened as a result of the report

There was a certain amount of press speculation again towards the end of 1973, after Paul Williams had addressed a meeting of Sparkwell Parish Council.

He explained that Richardson Mining Associates had reopened a shaft originally sunk in 1936 and it had shown mineralisation to a depth of 60ft. The council was told that it was not intended to develop the mine to the south or south-west of Hemerdon Ball, and further that both the mineral owners and Mr Richardson, the lessee, were anxious that any development be carefully and conscientiously carried out.

Generally there appeared to be little mining-related activity taking place. There was, however, a fair bit of sport, as first the South West Rover Owners Club and then, from 1976 onwards, the Cornwall & Devon Land

Above: *Stand well back! The crowd watch Roger Stanstill's Land Rover as it squeezes between the markers at Hemerdon.*

Right: *Roger Stanstill and Norman Gay go through the gap.*

Left: *LDV 983: A Series I Land Rover owned and driven by Malcolm Kerns who was a motor tech with Turnbulls. This vehicle has recently been tracked down by Malcolm's two sons who have bought it with the intention of getting it back on the road again.*

Rover Owners' Club gained access to the site for a variety of arduous trials. In the meantime, in October 1975 and now under the auspices of the Department of Industry, the Warren Spring Labs tendered a proposal for yet another investigation for Hemerdon Mines Ltd. Their charges this time around: £330 for 10 assay samples, £320 per core, £1,900 per sample.

Richardson was still involved as, in June that year, Jay Howson, a young student from the other side of the Atlantic, came across to work on the Hemerdon site and in a letter he wrote to Richardson he described what was effectively a working holiday. It makes for fascinating reading and gives an interesting insight into the work that was being done … and the lack of budget supporting the enterprise!

Introduced to mine geologist Dr John Rottenbury, Jay found his accommodation to be a caravan, delivered to the site on Sunday 21 June. Working with John his first task was to remove the top off an old, 1918 adit, until it was safe to drain out the water. On inspection they discovered that the adit was in reasonable condition, with just two falls. There was also a shaft at the end of the adit, but that had been filled in.

Equipment was thin on the ground, John had his own geologist's hammer, pick, Devon spade and 30ft long rope, while the company had provided a shorthandled spade and a hand-digger with no handle.

After a week of work and inspecting existing shafts, all of which had been filled, they had a meeting with the newly arrived mining engineer, Jeff Cox. Jeff instantly displayed his 'versatility of dress by doing a quick change from his suit down to his underwear to examine a stope John and I had found. Luckily it was late at night and no-one saw us, for I think we would have attracted an audience.'

The next day 'we had an impressive summit talk with Colonel Paul Williams MBE, FRICS, Director of the Company, Jeff Cox, Director of the Company, David Clayton, engineer, John and myself.

'It was decided at this meeting that No.1 shaft or Northern Shaft, was to be opened and over the next two weeks we assembled a platform and tripod in order to get the garbage and dirt out of the shaft.

'The main beams were supplied by Mr Cobbold, while the winch that was to hoist the bucket came from an Ivybridge equipment company.

'As time went on the shaft grew deeper, different people came to work on the shaft, first David Clayton, then John Clutterbuck. Charles Cobbold came for two weeks. During the change over of personnel and for most of Charles' two-week stint we found the going was slow, because of two reasons.

'The first was that Jeff Cox had arranged a Geo-Physics study of the top bench (opencast). This involved 5 lines, 30 metres apart, with 10 holes in each line which were filled with cement, with a small piece of copper pipe in the middle. The grid pattern took us five days to complete and was done before No.1 Shaft was started.

'John Thomas, the surveyor, came to survey the grid and I got ordered to show him around it. This exercise took two days and believe me by that time I was having nightmares of gorse bushes attacking me. It didn't stop there, for, a week later the man that was to do the Geo-Physics study came and since I was the only other person that knew the grid pattern I had to show him around.'

Jay carried on to say that the other factor that slowed them down was the introduction of a 'train of students' brought in by Jeff Cox. 'They demanded expert instruction in the value and geological formation of the hill.

'Of course everyone knows that John Rottenbury knows Hemerdon like the palm of his hand so off he went as a tour guide and off we went for a rest to the pub, for the rest of the day.

'Last but not least, Thomas Williams appeared on the scene, remembered most of all, not for his physical labour, even though sometimes he even surprised himself with the fierceness with which he attacked his work, but for his composition of a song for the Hemerdon Mining & Smelting (UK) Ltd, which was appropriately named "The Hemerdon Blues".

'The last part of the job involved John, Tom, Tom Fahy and myself. While John, Tom and I finished digging the shaft, Tom Fahy used his bulldozer to come into the north part of the level plus make some cuttings around the top of the pit to help us find where the killas and the granite met.

'With the digging completed in all areas John Thomas and I examined the level and found that in the northern half of the shaft there was a fall about a third of the way along which was about 11 metres long.

'Since this fall completely blocked our way we decided to attack the southern part of the level which we found free, up to the last 45ft. These falls and the lack of oxygen forced us to retire after three days, thus finishing my work for the summer.

'The working during the summer was, I felt, quite profitable and interesting. The opening of 2 adits, the Geo-Physics study, the investigation of the old Plympton water supply, various stopes, adits and shafts, should help us to understand what has been going on in the past, and in the geology.'

Young Mr Howson concluded his missive with 'one statement I feel I must make, and that is we must not stop here, exploration by drilling must be started to keep the momentum we have got now.'

And this was no ordinary student reporting on his working summer, not at all, this was Jay Howson, son of J Beverley Howson, treasurer of the then relatively newly created Hemerdon Mining & Smelting Ltd., who were based in the Bank of Bermuda building, in Front Street, Hamilton, Bermuda.

The list of 'workers' that Jay Howson describes that summer is an interesting one as it included John Thomas, who had first visited the site on behalf of AMAX eight years earlier, and Dr John Rottenbury who was to play a significant role in Hemerdon Mining & Smelting Ltd., who had taken on the Hemerdon leases from Bill Richardson that summer.

Clearly the new lessees were keen to develop the site, and while the operation that Jay Howson describes was clearly quite modest in scale, it was by no means lacking in ambition and probably accounted for more activity at Hemerdon than the site had seen since Richardson had first become involved over a decade earlier.

Why had he not initiated on site investigations of his own? From what little we've seen to date it would appear that, assaying aside, he was trying to get someone else to fund such explorations. On the face of it, it was perhaps because he didn't have sufficient finances himself, or sufficient financial backing, however as events were to unfold over the next few years it seems that William Augustus Richardson wasn't quite the businessman he purported to be, indeed he may well have been a modern day incarnation of one of the many mine 'owners' that we encountered in the nineteenth century.

According to an account published in *Maclean's Magazine* in August 1987 the *'once wealthy Richardson, 68,'* was now *'an old man with cancer living in public housing.'*

Describing him as *'ashen faced and hard of hearing'* the somewhat sympathetic account written by Diane Francis, says that, in court, he *'squinted and cupped his hands behind his ears to understand how the pie he had created would be divided.'*

However, it seems that much of that wealth was made up of monies Richardson had received for various unregistered securities, so-called grubstake securities, primitive IOUs issued to United States and Canadian citizens against future proceeds.

As early as December 1978 the Securities & Exchange Commission had made a note of allegations that Richardson had *'made misrepresentations including representations concerning his use of investors funds and failed to disclose material events, including that he was not a prospector obtaining funds from investors to finance a prospecting expedition.'*

Indeed *'it was alleged that a certain portion of the funds fraudulently raised were used to purchase mining leases that were later turned over to Hemerdon Mining & Smelting, a corporation incorporated by Richardson, in exchange for 5,000,000 shares of Hemerdon common stock.*

'For tax reasons he incorporated his company, Hemerdon Mining & Smelting Ltd., in Bermuda, where certain company taxes do not exist. But in 1976 certificate shareholders mutinied over disputes as to how Hemerdon's five million shares would be divided among them.'

Not surprisingly, perhaps, Richardson lost his first legal battle by default – because he failed to provide the $10,000 for the legal fees. What followed next gives us quite an insight into the Richardson era at Hemerdon and at the Parys Mountain mine, where he also had a 'scheme'.

In 1978 Richardson found a Toronto-based lawyer who he managed to convince that he had been hard done by, and he agreed to act for Bill as long as he agreed to make the lawyer, Ian Outerbridge, a preferred creditor, and submit himself to a psychiatric examination, which he passed … and handed Power of Attorney over to the trustee branch of the accounting firm Clarkson Gordon, who would represent him on a retainer. Although agreeing to represent him, Outerbridge, by his own admission, didn't trust his client. He was also concerned that *'the other side would attack his mental competence. The man is eccentric, but by no means nuts.'*

Within four years the courts had given some 4,000,000 Hemerdon shares to the various claimants and Richardson was left with just 850,000 – which Clarkson, as trustee, refused to release as they were concerned that they wouldn't get paid.

And so it was that Richardson hired some other solicitors to try to get back the Power of Attorney and in June 1982 the Ontario Supreme Court said that he could, but only if all the other creditors agreed, and if Richardson agreed to set aside the money he owed to both Outerbridge and Clarkson. Herein lay another problem, Hemerdon was not yet fully operating and with low tungsten prices the value of his shares had dropped to 25 cents or $212,500 and so Richardson couldn't afford to borrow enough against the value of those shares to pay off Outerbridge and Clarkson.

So what to do next? He decided to take his bid to regain his Power of Attorney to the Supreme Court of Canada. His lack of funds caused him to represent himself and again he lost, and again his debts rose.

The years passed. In 1985 Clarkson, along with other shareholders, swapped stock with the then principal players at Hemerdon – AMAX – and in April 1987 with the share price at a high point they sold up. By that stage the amount owed to Outerbridge, including interest, came to $919,500 with a further $369,000 owing to Clarkson, which was a little over the $1.2m raised by the sale of the shares.

To compound matters Richardson now owed a further $500,000 to creditors – most of it to lawyers he'd employed to fight Clarkson.

In the out-of-court settlement that followed Clarkson and Outerbridge agreed to take just 65% of their fees. A Toronto policeman, Sgt Jake Mol, had agreed to act as Richardson's advisor as he was worried that *'Bill wouldn't get a dime'.*

Certainly there were those who felt he should have got more, but the man himself said he was just glad that it was all over. He died three years later.

Can You Dig It?

While the Richardson saga followed its troubled course on the other side of the Atlantic, Hemerdon Mining & Smelting (UK) Ltd., a wholly owned subsidiary of Hemerdon Mining & Smelting (Bermuda) Ltd. under the chairmanship of Carl Schwarzwalder, commenced the long-awaited drilling investigations at Hemerdon in November 1976.

Paul Williams, who was now running his own firm of chartered surveyors, was also now on site managing the Hemerdon project, along with geologists, John Rottenbury, who as we have seen, had been on site the previous year, and Jean Claude Leroy, who had made many observations – and assertions – on Hemerdon, from afar, for Richardson.

The issues with Richardson appear to have come to light soon after the formation of Hemerdon Mining & Smelting in 1974 and it's interesting to note that while Richardson's name does not appear on the glossy brochure produced by the new company a few years later, that of Ian Outerbridge, the lawyer he initially engaged, and Diana Shwarz, his admin lady, both appear, as indeed do those of John Rottenbury, Paul Williams and Cecil Venn (of Bond Pearce and solicitors for the owners), who between them made up three of the five directors of the UK based subsidiary. Williams and Venn were also listed directors of the parent company, with Paul an executive committee member.

Whatever, the overall role of the 20 directors on that Bermudan parent board, activity at Hemerdon stepped up several gears ... very quickly.

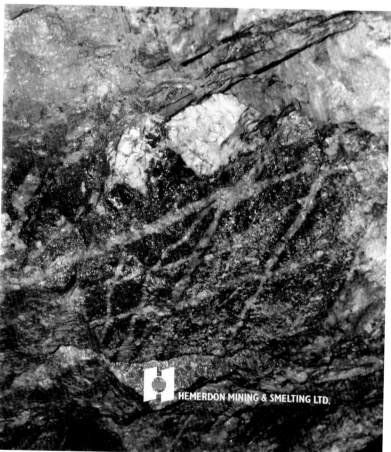

Top: Original AMAX Hemerdon Mine sign. Above: HM&SL prospectus cover: a cross section of the underground workings at Hemerdon illustrating the variety of mineralisation. Left: Chief Geologist Dr John Rottenbury examines a specimen for mineralisation looking for tungsten.

Looking towards Lee Moor, exploration drilling starts at last.

The programme of percussion drilling in late 1976 saw the on-site team make 45 shallow holes, each one no more than 125 feet but as a consequence of the work it became clear that the mineralised deposit was greater than was first thought.

It was at this point that AMAX, who had been watching the site with interest since at least December 1967, when John Thomas first visited Hemerdon, decided to invest in the project.

And so it was that, on 19 October 1977, a five-phase, joint-venture agreement was signed between Hemerdon Mining & Smelting and AMAX Exploration of UK Inc., this being a wholly owned subsidiary of AMAX Inc., the very large and long-established international mining group that had its HQ in Greenwich, Connecticut (AMAX had originally been the nickname for the American Metal Climax, Inc.).

Five months later, and looking to extend the sett, an option agreement was signed by the new AMAX-Hemerdon partnership to look for tungsten on the hitherto un-drilled land administered by English Clays (ECLP).

Encouraged by the feedback received from Germany in January 1978, at their new admin offices located above No.5 Derry's Cross, on the analysis of samples sent to Professor Dr Hansgeorg Forster at the Institute of Mineralogy at Aachen, AMAX Explorations secured an option to proceed from the second to the third phase of their investigations.

Once again the omens were favourable, prompting a move to the next phase, phase four, for a detailed feasibility study, something that Richardson had consistently failed to produce and which potential investors had all been very keen to see. The idea was that on the successful completion of this study AMAX would have a 50% stake in joint venture, with HM&SL (UK) holding the other 50%.

Activity on site was now at a level not seen in over 30 years. By December 1977 there were around 20 people on site and over the next few months that number kept steadily rising.

The drilling programme continued to excite interest. Three-metre-long cylindrical diamond drill cores were cut in half, one half being crushed for assaying, the other half being kept in case further analysis was required. Three main companies were involved; Alfred H Knight Ltd did the bulk of the 9,500 samples that came to be examined but Robertson Research International and Huntings Technical Surveys Ltd. also played a part.

As well as the Hemerdon sett itself, around 200 holes were drilled in the mineralised surroundings of Bottle Hill, Crownhill Down and an area west of Tory Brook.

With attention ultimately fixed on the main site, in October 1978 the green light was given to an 18-month feasibility study that was due to report its findings in March 1981. The anticipated cost of this work was said to be around $10m (in the order of £27.5m in today's terms), with a substantial amount of that cost, almost £1 million it was said, coming from MEIGA (under the terms of the Government's Mineral Exploration & Investigation Grants Act of 1972).

Less than a year later a basic pilot facility had been set up in the existing Second World War buildings and some seven tons of ore per hour were going through the concentrator that had been designed to process up to 3,000 tons per day. The following month, October 1979, confidence in the project was such that AMAX issued two contracts to Matthew Hall Ortech, of Sale, Cheshire, to design, construct and commission a new pilot plant where they could process and sample material at Hemerdon. As well as crushing, screening and sampling the plant was to incorporate heavy medium and other gravity concentration systems. The contract was worth £850,000 (around £4.25m today) to Matthew Hall Ortech.

At last serious money was being invested and in the summer of 1980, in association with Cementation Mining Ltd., of South Yorkshire, work continued on a decline that was being driven through the orebody to bring out bulk samples for metallurgical testing.

As David N Skillings jnr. reported in the June 1980 edition of *Skillings Mining Review*: 'The 9ft square opening is being excavated at 12° a total distance of 350 metres to the 100-metres elevation from which drifting will be commenced to remove representation samples of the mineralisation'.

By this stage the number of personnel working on the site had already more than doubled, with Roger Craddock, the newly arrived project manager being supported by a team of 18 staff members and 28 labourers.

John Abraham in the Hemerdon decline after measuring water flows, the giant tube supplying fresh air to the underground workers; notice metal hoops supporting soft granite roof, more commonly used in coal mines. Right, top: The old mine adit. Middle: The new decline. Bottom: Decline with ore trucks used to haul material.

Roger had until recently, been working at the troubled Bula lead and zinc mine in Ireland which had gone into production in 1977, but which ended up generating more money for solicitors than it ever did for its directors (various court cases would stretch over more than two decades).

Working alongside Roger already by the summer of 1980 were Paul Lister, the mine planning engineer (who would later take over from Roger), John Webber, mining engineer, Ian Davies, environmental scientist, Dr Paul King and his wife Sheila, both geologists, Don Seymour, accountant and Andy Sarosi, senior metallurgist.

It was a young, dynamic but nonetheless experienced team, most of them were in their twenties or thirties, and Andy, a South African, who had previously worked at Wheal Jane tin mine in Cornwall, was no exception. Impressed with the meticulous care that had been taken by Paul and Sheila King in their preparation of geological and mineralogical data, Andy and his metallurgist, Dr Simon Meik, made countless trips to Camborne School of Mines where bench testing was carried out using both hard and soft granite cores obtained from AMAX's extensive drilling programme.

The bench testing included crucial heavy liquid analysis of the ore in order to determine its amenability to the Dense Medium Separation (DMS) process.

The process facilitates the separation (rejection) at the crushing stage, of the light-density barren granite (roughly 80% of the ore weight), from the heavier density wolframite and tin-bearing quartz veins in the ore. Successfully executed it achieves a significant saving in operating and capital costs of the project in not having to grind and process the granite as described earlier.

Above: *1980 The crushing section and conveyor feed-belt to the new mill erected by Matthew Hall Ortech. Left: Images of the bench-scale tests conducted at the Camborne School of Mines, using crushed drill core samples. It was from these tests that the pilot mill was designed.*

Once the bench testing had been done, a flow sheet of the process was arrived at and Alan Smith, a consultant mechanical and design engineer, was appointed to adapt the flow sheet and visualise how the machinery would need to be laid out in the spaces available before working up the engineering design drawings.

Simon Meik had studied magnetic separation for his PhD from Birmingham University and thus provided extremely useful knowledge, as a key element of his thesis had been precisely the separation of the (para) magnetic wolframite (tungsten mineral), from the non-magnetic cassiterite (tin) like that being dealt with at Hemerdon.

The bench testing at Camborne confirmed that the Hemerdon ore would be amenable to DMS process, which, considering the relatively low grade of the ore (0.17% WO_3 and 0.025% sn) would be critical to the viability of the project.

Now just in case anyone reading this is still thinking that the process of removing the mineral from the ore was anything like as simple as the process adopted by the ancient tin streamers, think again, and while we don't want to lose anyone in the technical detail, it's important to give some idea of what is involved with this form of modern-day mining. So, what follows is Keith Loze's account of how Hemerdon tungsten was teased out of the orebody by a series of machines that smashed and separated the mineral from the waste material. It begins with an outline of the flow chart around which the pilot plant was planned.

1. Crushing via jaw-crusher
2. Feed preparation, a grinding mill to create coarse and fine fractions.
3. Dense Media Separation coarse material to DMS float and DMS sink
4. Processing the heavier, sink material
5. Processing the fines via spiral concentrators
6. DMS float and fines tailings taken off to waste
7. DMS sink and fines concentrates upgraded to final product

The pilot plant ended up in operation for around nine months and the processing path, following the outline above, went like this:

1. Outside the 1940s processing plant new buildings were constructed and bulk samples from the decline were crushed in a single toggle jaw crusher, and then sent through a cone crusher and screen to create the feed for the new mill. The product at this stage was now around 9mm top size and stored in a 40-tonne bin.

2. This material was then taken into the mill via a belt conveyor to the washing screens that removed the fines smaller than 0.5mm, the minimum size for efficient DMS.

Top: *Conveyor brings material into the pilot plant.* Bottom: *Screen table sorts by size.*

Dyna-Whirlpool system, a key component of the operation.

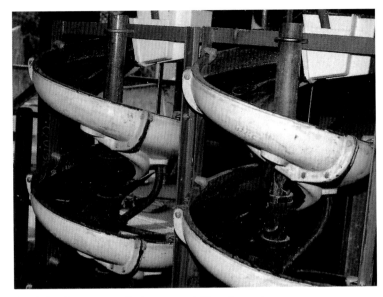

Spiral classifier separates the heavy material from the waste.

3. Dense Media Separation: A Dyna-Whirlpool DMS separator is used by introducing atomised ferrsilicon and ground magnetite in a slurry with a specific gravity 2.65 to 3.00. The two resultant products are DMS float waste, essentially barren granite and quartz veins, and DMS sink, containing wolframite, cassiterite and quartz vein material with wolframite (WO_3 tungsten material), and cassiterite (tin, Sn) mineral attached. The DMS sink was returned to the plant for further processing, meanwhile, the float material – some 90% of the feed material – was rejected and removed as waste.

4. The sinks matter is now ground in a rod mill to a top size of 1.7mm and the ground product screened at 0.5mm with anything over that size going on to be treated in hydraulic jigs, in a machine that vibrates the sinks in water to separate the liberated tungsten/tin material from the bulk of the remaining waste matter to produce a coarse concentrate, assaying at a figure between 30-50% WO_3 and 5% Sn. The tails from the jigs are further ground in a rod mill and passed to tables to recover more wolframite and cassiterite minerals freed by the grinding.

The use of rod mills over ball mills was to minimise the overgrinding of the wolfram. Coarser particles along the length of rods cascading in a rotating mill tend to keep the rods apart so that the finer particles are not pulverised like balls in ball mills.

Nevertheless, there was still a significant level of overgrinding due, mainly, it was thought, to operational issues, like pumping small volumes of coarser heavy material resulted in blockages, and difficulties in maintaining steady feed rates for grinding.

A two-ton bulk sample of DMS sink matter was trial-ground in a rolls crusher and processed in the jigs. This revealed a sizeable reduction in overgrinding with a corresponding improvement in the DMS sink tungsten recovery. This data was used in subsequent feasibility projections.

5. Fines processing: The washed fines from the second feed preparation were cycloned and passed over two spirals (the cyclones remove slimes – clay and ultra-fine size fractions of matter that would otherwise affect the tabling performance).

The concentrate thus produced is screened to produce two sizes that are, in turn, passed onto two tabling stages to produce fine concentrates of around 25% wolfram and 5% tin. The slimes and the tailings from the gravity (tables) section are then de-watered in a thickener and the thickened slimes and sand tailings deposited in the tailings pond. The water recovered in this process would then be re-used.

Throughout the operation sampling was carried out at all stages to help refine performance. The slimes were studied to record their settling characteristics to better inform the design of a tailings dam.

Settling pit looking towards the mine decline.

The pilot plant was projected to produce pre-upgraded concentrate of around 25-40% WO$_3$ and 5% Sn, which in turn could be upgraded by magnetic separation to produce tungsten of a marketable grade – around 65% WO$_3$ – usually referred to as tungsten ore, and tin concentrate – 20% or more Sn. The material extracted from the bulk sampling decline included both the soft and the harder granite. Two batches of pre-tungsten concentrates were produced in separate campaigns. The first batch with a relatively high grade around 55% WO$_3$ was successfully upgraded by magnetic separation to produce a marketable grade of tungsten ore. The results also indicated a relatively small amount of paramagnetic haematite in the feed but not much attention was paid to it.

The second batch was lower in tungsten, around 45% WO$_3$, and the maximum upgrade achieved after magnetic separation was around 55%. The indication being that the main contaminant, haematite, was not ferromagnetic, but exhibited similar paramagnetism to the wolframite making it impossible to separate the two.

Subsequent testing at Leeds University on this pre-upgrade concentrate showed that the haematite could be converted to ferromagnetic magnetite by roasting the concentrate under reducing atmosphere conditions. When subsequently subjected to the magnetic separation process the roasted material achieved a marketable value 66% WO$_3$.

Curiously enough this echoed the 1940s experience at Hemerdon, which described pre-drying the pre-upgraded concentrates in coal fired driers before exposing the material to the magnetic separation process. The inference here being that they too, either wittingly or unwittingly were converting their haematite to magnetic under the reducing atmosphere of burning coal.

Throughout the nine months of the operation of the pilot plant the whole process was heavily scrutinised and when the last test period was signed off there was still a lot more research required before a final plant design could be arrived at.

AMAX had, however, achieved good results not only with regard to their exploration but also in their attempts to overcome the processing of low-grade material.

So the issues that still needed to be resolved were: could they secure the necessary funding, the planning permission and, underpinning the whole endeavour, would the price of tungsten stay high enough to make the whole adventure worthwhile?

Of course, it wasn't just from inside Hemerdon and AMAX that events were being closely monitored during these initial investigations – the outside world was also starting to take quite an interest.

In April 1980 stock market dealings in Hemerdon shares started up again. HM&SL had some 1,550 shareholders with an issued share capital of 5 million 10 cent shares with a further 500,000 shares held in reserve to meet possible claims of those who had invested in the Richardson era. With AMAX investing £3 million in the project to date and a further £4 million expected just to complete the feasibility study, there was an expectation that Hemerdon might at last be due to realise its potential.

As the recruitment drive to start up the pilot plant got under way in 1980 Roger Craddock speculated at a Press Conference in Plymouth that 300 to 350 jobs could be created, if and when a full-scale plant went fully operational, potentially in the second half of 1985.

Carl 'Bud' Schwarzwalder, Chairman of Hemerdon Mining & Smelting Ltd.
According to former AMAX employees whenever Bud came to Plymouth he would always fly into the airport at Roborough and hire the biggest car he could find. With a penchant for electric blue suits, he would walk around the Hemerdon site and greet everyone like a personal friend.

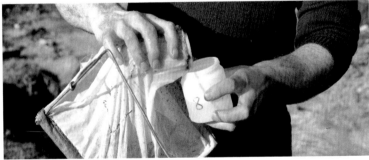

Clockwise from the top left: Surveying the site. Collecting meteorological and atmospheric conditions. Aquatic life sampling. Noise survey. Water sampling.
These images illustrate some of the measures undertaken by AMAX for their comprehensive Environmental Baseline Study. This was supplemented with surveys and plans drawn on site by cartographer John Abraham, all of which was to play an important role in ultimately achieving planning permission for mining at Hemerdon. Now a common-place requirement it was one of the first studies of its kind in the country.

With favourable feedback coming in from the pilot plant, in April 1981 HM&SL chairman Bud Schwarzwalder confirmed that the venture was indeed ongoing and that planning permission was about to be sought for the mine and mill. The number of new jobs being talked about had now escalated to between 300 and 400, with production being spread over 20 years. Shares in Hemerdon Mining & Smelting Ltd. over night shot up from 14p to 92p on the London Stock Exchange.

In October the flamboyant Mr Schwarzwalder was back in town. There was a public exhibition in Harewood House, Plympton from Thursday 8 October through to the following Monday with a planning application due to be officially lodged with Devon County Council on Friday 16 October. The number of new jobs potentially being created for the area had now increased to between 650 and 700: 350 at the mine itself with a yearly payroll of £3 million, which in turn *'through the multiplier effect meant a further 300 to 350 jobs would be created in the Plymouth area'.*

In the meantime, with the work of the pilot plant finished for the time being, there were job *losses* at Hemerdon as a number of the geologists, mineralogists and metallurgists were laid off on 7 August 1981.

'*We didn't see it coming,*' recalls Jane Charley, who had been taken on as a 24-year-old graduate the previous August.

'*I was training to be a teacher and at half term I walked into the AMAX Exploration office at Derry's Cross and asked if they had any jobs for geologists. We chatted and I agreed to help with inputting data. It was in the early days of new technology and I knew how to operate a computer with ticker tape, and so I was taken on.*'

Jane rather conveniently found shared accommodation in Hemerdon House, the Woollcombe property but then in August 1981, somewhat abruptly, found herself standing in the dole queue at Plympton with Doug Oakley, geologist and core logger, John Webber, mining engineer and Phil Lofts, another geologist. Metallurgist Simon Meik was another to get his P45 that month and as a testimony to how well the team at Hemerdon had gelled, a handful of them sailed off into the sunset bound for Cherbourg when they were laid off.

Not long after taking up her post at Hemerdon, Jane had replaced Sheila King, who together with husband Paul, had gone off to South America on a job. Her main task now became analysing the composition of the floats and sinks that were being generated, and to look at the composition of each batch and compile a mineralogy report for each one, with respect to density fraction, presence of wolframite, cassiterite, sulphides and gangue materials.

'*AMAX had sponsored me to do an MSc at Camborne and my experience with an electron microscope was to prove useful.*'

As many of the ad hoc team pulled together to work on the Hemerdon feasibility scheme were relatively recent graduates, there was still something of a student culture at large among them. Consequently it was not difficult to persuade them to join in sporting activities – cricket, football, tug of war – and charity events, in order to engage with the local community, help raise funds for Sparkwell Village Hall, and help sell the idea of a mine in the longer term at Hemerdon.

The Miners' Arms was a regular lunchtime and after-work haunt: '*We worked hard and played hard, regularly working from 8am to 7pm then rolling down to the Miners and staying there until 11pm.*'

Like Jane, Paul Lister also lived near the Miners, sharing with a few others from AMAX, so the pub was a handy local. The Mountain Inn at Lutton was another popular watering hole for the young team, while the Fiesta Suite in town was an occasional late-night venue of choice, as a number of the young singletons were happy to look for partners. Indeed there were a couple of almost in-house romances that blossomed at that time.

Top: *October 1981: Don, Dave and Paddy getting the model out for public display*
Bottom: *Lunch at the Mountain Inn, Lutton, Gaynor Biczecski (secretary), Doug Oakley (geologist), John Webber (mining engineer), Sheila King (geologist), Brenda Hutchins (drawing office), Don Seymour (accountant), Phil Lofts (geologist).*

Top left: *Cricket team includes John Webber, Dave Heywood, Paul Lister, John Abraham and Jane Charley.* Top right: *Phil Lofts' stag night, John Abraham, Ian Davies, Doug Oakley, Paul Lister (front), John Hogan, Chris Marcol, Clive Newall, Roger Craddock, Randy Martin, Dave Heywood.* Above: *7 August 1981, last day for some, hence smoking 'celebratory cigars' John Abraham, John Webber, Dave Cartlidge, anon, Peter Davies, Gaynor Biczecski, Celia Damerell, Dave Haywood, Lesley.* Right: *Ladies football with Jane Charley right back all sporting their AMAX-branded team shirts.*

Senior Mine Planning Engineer Paul Lister, an early 1970s graduate of Leeds University, had been encouraged to foster good relations with the legal representatives that were working for AMAX, in the hope they might get a discount and, conversely, the legal firm had issued similar advice, to their main point of contact, so that maybe they could charge more, which is essentially how Paul came to meet and later marry solicitor Jane Morris – in October 1982 – when they were both 31-years-old.

Paul Lister was, although doubtless no-one considered it at the time, destined to become the longest serving AMAX employee at Hemerdon. However, we're jumping ahead. Back in October 1981, with Planning Application about to go live, Press interest in the Hemerdon Project intensified. Some 600 people had seen the models, and the film of how the development would look when it had been on show, and suddenly all the knock-on effects of having what was potentially a £50m scheme (around £200m in today's terms) on the edge of town started to invite attention.

The South Devon Times who had previously devoted space to the number of jobs that could, or would be, created were now interested in what those living closest to the mine thought.

Violet Hanna, who had family working at the site, interviewed a number of local residents. First up was Jane Wilson, of High Post, Hemerdon, who'd lived in the area over 20 years: *'Attempts to mine wolfram in the past have not proved successful,'* she said, adding, *'one wonders at the optimistic view of today's miners.'*

City businessman and Plymouth Argyle director Peter Bloom who lived as close as anyone, in Drakelands, intended to oppose any development: *'We have lived in the shadow of the mine for several years but never envisaged the type of development that AMAX is proposing.*

'The exhibition at Harewood House gave the impression that people locally would not be adversely affected but this is not so – our homes will go.'

Mr & Mrs John Phillips of the Bungalow, Drakelands, were 'extremely angry' at the prospect of losing their home, Mr Southgate, of Crownhill Down Cottage, was a little more sanguine, and said he'd rather sell to AMAX than ECLP.

Dorothy Lee, and her husband George, had lived at Emarco, Drakelands since the war, indeed 70-year-old Dorothy had been a shorthand typist at the mine at the time, and they were not looking forward to having to move. Neither was Henry Elford of Lower Drakelands.

Meanwhile, the prospect of their being any sort of dump for the waste the mine was likely to generate filled conservationists with 'horror and dismay' and Kate Ashbrook, secretary of the Dartmoor Preservation Association, and Dartmoor commoner and conservationist 77-year-old Lady Sylvia Sayer, both threw their weight behind those opposed to the scheme.

A battle loomed and in December those for the project received a boost when the Royal Dutch Shell offshoot, Billton, offered to invest $15m to buy out HM&SL's 50% stake in the enterprise, although the full package was dependent on planning permission being obtained.

The news provoked a 3p rise in the value of Hemerdon mining shares, they had fallen back to 66.5p, but now they started climbing again.

On the same day it was announced that it was 'highly probable' that the ultimate decision on the planning application would be taken by the Environment Secretary, Michael Heseletine. For the time being, however, South Hams Planning Committee, despite receiving 69 letters of objection, gave their approval for the plan on 15 December 1981.

Councillor Les Savage evidently expressed the general feeling of the committee when he said: *'This development has got to happen because of its importance to the national wellbeing of this country and in terms of jobs.'*

It was by now accepted that Hemerdon housed the biggest known deposit of tungsten in Western Europe and that, if efficiently exploited, could improve Britain's balance of payments to the tune of £22 million (£85m today) as well as pumping around £14m a year into the local economy. Devonport MP, David Owen, was slightly less enthusiastic, noting that the two previous mining ventures had been abandoned raising major concerns in his mind about what might happen to the environment long term in the event of a sudden liquidation. He proposed requiring the developers to have to bank deposits to guarantee restoration work, but the Government rejected the notion on the grounds that restoration and waste disposal proposals would be agreed before planning permission would be given.

Meanwhile, West Devon Tory MP Peter Mills gave his backing to the scheme, as did MP for Plymouth Drake, Janet Fookes, who visited the site in February 1982.

There was a further step in the right direction, when, in June, Devon County Council followed their South Hams colleagues and thus looked certain to back the development at the public inquiry that the Environment Secretary had ordered to take place in September.

At the start of what was anticipated to be an eight-week inquiry the environmentalists began co-ordinating their approach as the Dartmoor Preservation Association joined hands with the Commons Open Spaces and Footpaths Preservation Society, the Council for National Parks, the Youth Hostels Association, the Ramblers Association, the Council for British Archaeology, the Devon Archaeological Society and the Plymouth Federation of the Amenity Services.

In the event, the inquiry opened on Tuesday 7 September and on the very first day, one of the major objectors, the National Farmers' Union, withdrew its objection.

The Public Inquiry opens at Ballard House, 7 September 1982.

The venue chosen for the proceedings was the post-war Ballard Centre, opposite the Crescent, in Plymouth. Nearly 150 gathered to hear the discussions on that first day and it appears that David Widdicombe, QC, representing AMAX, was not entirely wide of the mark when telling the inquiry that *'most of the objectors seemed to be concerned with the tipping of waste on Crownhill Down.'*

Noise, dust, vibrations and water supplies were other concerns although four weeks into the inquiry and few topics were drawing any great crowds. Writing in the *Herald*, Roger Malone described *'the daily gathering of by now familiar faces'* as having *'an air of plodding academic diligence …*

'Officials combat-trained for such endurance tests, stifle sly yawns, and the inspector, Tom Millington, blows his way steadily through a box of Kleenex.

'He is the balance in the scales of justice. On his right, a brace of learned QCs pursuing the commercial cause of AMAX … on his left, district and county council officials, who, barring a bit of nit-picking seem happy to agree.

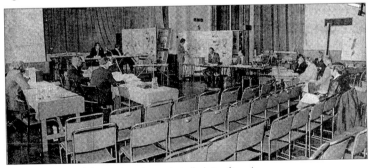

Four weeks in and the numbers have dwindled significantly

'Further out on the limb of a trestle table is Lady Sayer: eloquent crusader, bureaucratic irritant and staunchest defender Dartmoor has ever had. "I don't mind whether I'm popular – I would be dead if I did. This sounds pompous but I know I'm right – this is a fight for environment in the face of greed and materialism," she said. "I think these people have been mesmerised by the fact that AMAX sunk £6 million into the original investigation and the Government added £1.5 million because it supports exploration activities …" [Lady Sayer incidentally had bought a single share in AMAX so that she could attend shareholder meetings]

'After lunch the battle continues. The mountain of literature is reshuffled and the inquiry creaks on towards the projected finish on November 10.'

As October rumbled on more voices of dissent were heard. Colin Kilvington, a soft-spoken marine biologist, questioned the need for tungsten in the current climate, with falling demand and falling prices. Malcolm Todd, Professor of Archaeology at Exeter University, was worried about the potential loss of prehistoric agricultural and burial remains … *'the main period of occupation most probably extending from 4,000 to 500 BC.'*

Dr Tom Greeves spoke of the recreational and educational potential of Crownhill Down, which, he said, *'could enrich the experience of thousands of people in understanding how their society evolved.'*

In all, almost 60 witnesses gave evidence at the inquiry, which, as it transpired, lasted six weeks, and ended on 20 October.

AMAX had done their homework, and done it well, perhaps too well. *'We produced the first full-scale environmental impact survey in the country, we looked at everything, but our opponents ended up using our reports to bash us over our heads,'* recalls Paul Lister.

In addition to the two QCs present throughout, there were seven solicitors present, as well as the Inspector and his assistant, the salaries of the latter two being paid for by the Government. In all the cost in terms of time, paper and money, was immense … as was the amount of time that elapsed before a decision was reached.

It was in July 1983 that the Inspector's report eventually landed on the desk of the Environment Secretary, Patrick Jenkin, and, on 25 July, in his first speech representing the South Hams, Anthony Steen, MP, criticised the Government's slowness and questioned the Parliamentary Under-Secretary for Industry on the deliberations. In response there was a hint that the Government would eventually approve the plans, but there would be a number of conditions to its use and, he added, *'It is likely to be some time before he* [the Environment Secretary] *reaches a decision.'*

Come December that decision still hadn't been made and the Billiton (UK) option was due to run out at the end of the month. However, a few days before Christmas, the Shell-owned company agreed to extend their option for another twelve months. Payment for the extension came in the form of a $500,000 interest-free loan to Hemerdon.

Paul Lister, appointed Project Manager for the development in September 1983, said that he was *'very pleased that Billiton are showing confidence in the project by continuing their option.'*

In the meantime all went quiet on the western front. In March a piece in the *Western Morning News* noted the comments of the keeper of archaeology at Plymouth City Museum, Cynthia Gaskell-Brown. Referring to aerial photographs of the Hemerdon area taken as part of the project by Plymouth City Council and South Hams District Council, she identified possible Iron Age or Roman earthworks, possibly protecting a farmstead from wild animals. She recommended that the 1.5-acre site south of Hemerdon village should be retained as an open space.

The following month the long-awaited news on the 538-acre site looking to accommodate Western Europe's biggest tungsten mine at Hemerdon was released. The plans, it was announced, had been rejected by the Government, Patrick Jenkin, the Environment Secretary, backed the conclusions of the inspector that the scheme was too intrusive.

But: *'the inspector has gone on to suggest changes to the original plan, which might be more "favourably" looked upon in the future.*

'These would involve siting the processing plant lower down the Smallhanger Valley, on a South Westerly direction, and altering the site of the waste tip.'

The residents of Hemerdon were left confused by the ruling while the AMAX response from Paul Lister was upbeat: *'We are encouraged to hear that the Minister has agreed in principle to the idea of the tungsten mine and we are still very keen to develop Hemerdon.'*

Support for the scheme from across the Tamar came at the Cornish Mining Development Association's annual meeting. There, the chairman, Jack Trounson, said that the refusal to give the go-ahead to the mine had been *'planning gone mad'*. He also criticised the delay in announcing the decision almost 18 months after the inquiry took place as *'deplorable'*.

'To say, as the inspector did, that the submitted proposals would have too great an impact on the visual amenities of the area is a complete nonsense. If that were so then the whole of the great china clay industry in Cornwall and Devon should be closed down.'

Trounson pointed out that the mine workings and spoil heaps would be in an area already heavily industrialised by major china clay workings. *'Minerals can only be worked where they exist and this major ore body of tungsten and tin ores could make Britain self sufficient in tungsten and an exporter. In addition it would provide much employment in an area of heavy unemployment.'*

Behind the scenes AMAX were endeavouring to find ways around the Minister's objections and to meet the conditions laid out, it was far from a simple process.

A selection of the free items handed out to interested parties by AMAX to promote public relations, includes drill core, tungsten concentrate, core section, project report and even a Christmas card.

Above: Left, the World War II processing works, right, the new AMAX pilot mill.
Centre right, Crownhill Down, proposed mine waste tipping area, in the distance –
Lee Moor's china clay industry.
Left: The 1986 AMAX proposed and approved plan for the new mine at Hemerdon.

When December rolled around again, no-one was greatly surprised to find that Billiton (UK) were not going to renew their option. In the face of weak mineral prices around the world they had cut their extraction programmes in Canada by 50% and their decision to pull out of the Hemerdon project was more about their own need to adjust their strategy rather than a reflection on the mine's potential.

Falling mineral prices were affecting tungsten too and in February 1985 AMAX chairman Pierre Gousseland announced that the corporation had *'no immediate plans to develop Hemerdon, but it is certainly a major candidate for development, if and when tungsten prices become more favourable.'*

He blamed one of the world's biggest tungsten producers for the situation: *'In 1984 China opened up a new way of selling its tungsten products and some of these people do not seem to be operating with an understanding of the market. They have been selling the products below the price of the ore.*

'One day they will realise what they are doing and the situation will sort itself out.'

Two months later and exactly one year on from the Minister's rejection of the original planning application, AMAX submitted a fresh application to the South Hams local authority.

Differing in certain design aspects and addressing the guidelines of the Minister and the inspector, Paul Lister suggested that *'there was no necessity for a further public inquiry.'*

However, at a packed public meeting in June, in Sparkwell Village Hall, Lady Sayer elicited widespread applause from the 250 assembled there, when she suggested that the newly elected county council should hold just such an inquiry.

The Chairman of Devon County Council's planning sub-committee chaired the meeting and said that the subject would be examined with a 'fresh mind.'

Days later 2,000 copies of an anonymous (later attributed to local builder David Passmore) leaflet were distributed locally calling for a fresh appraisal and/or a public enquiry.

Later, Rob Ruffles' planning sub-committee rejected the proposal by 7 votes to 4, but when in September the revised application came before Devon County Council's planning and transportation committee that decision was overturned with a combination of Labour and Conservative members ensuring an 11-to-6 in favour of the project.

James Mildren, the *Western Morning News* environment correspondent, reporting on the outcome wrote: *'Immediately after the meeting, project manager, Mr Paul Lister expressed his pleasure at the decision which obviates the need for a second public inquiry.*

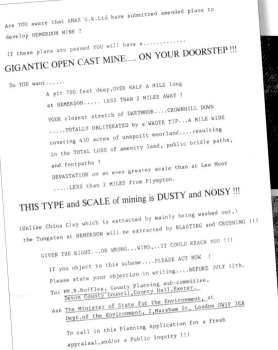

Are YOU aware that AMAX U.K.Ltd have submitted amended plans to develop HEMERDON MINE ?

If these plans are passed YOU will have a.............

GIGANTIC OPEN CAST MINE..... ON YOUR DOORSTEP !!!

Do YOU want......

A pit 700 feet deep,OVER HALF A MILE long at HEMERDON..... LESS THAN 2 MILES AWAY ?

YOUR closest stretch of DARTMOOR....CROWNHILL DOWN ....TOTALLY OBLITERATED by a WASTE TIP...A MILE WIDE covering 430 acres of unspoilt moorland....resulting in the TOTAL LOSS of amenity land, public bridle paths, and footpaths ?

DEVASTATION on an even greater scale than at Lee Moor ....LESS than 2 MILES from Plympton.

THIS TYPE and SCALE of mining is DUSTY and NOISY !!!

(Unlike China Clay which is extracted by mainly being washed out,) the Tungsten at HEMERDON will be extracted by BLASTING and CRUSHING !!!

GIVEN THE RIGHT...OR WRONG...WIND,..IT COULD REACH YOU !!!

If you object to this scheme....PLEASE ACT NOW !
Please state your objection in writing....BEFORE JULY 12th.

To: MR.R.Ruffles, County Planning sub-committee, Devon County Council,County Hall,Exeter.

Ask The Minister of State for the Environment, at Dept.of the Environment, 2,Marsham St, London SW1P 3EB

To call in this Planning Application for a fresh appraisal,and/or a Public Inquiry !!!

Left: The 'anonymous' leaflets that was spread around Hemerdon and Sparkwell. Right: Ellis Daw and tiger Kahn, who takes an unwitting part in the protests.

'He said the company would now need to study the 12 pages of conditions the county council is expected to lay down at its next planning sub-committee meeting.'

It had been a long and tortuous journey, there had been all sorts of bumps along the way and various attempts to derail the project, but now it had approval. Last minute concerns about the health impact on the area had been addressed – or dismissed. Now all that needed to happen was for AMAX or whoever to take it to the next stage. Would it have a detrimental effect on the neighbourhood, would the residents of Hemerdon and Sparkwell suffer? Would Ellis Daw, as he claimed, really have to shut down his Dartmoor Wildlife Park? Until such time as work commenced on site these were all imponderables.

Time is eventually called on the old World War II workings

CRYING WOLF?

In the weeks leading up to the eventual approval of the Hemerdon planning application AMAX had come up with a new cash offer to buy the homes hit by the proposals, in the event of the plans being given the go-ahead. Now that point had been reached, what did that mean for those affected and what was AMAX's next move going to be?

Speaking at a Plymouth Chamber of Commerce meeting on 18 November 1985, Paul Lister ran through the positives that would follow in the wake of the mine's operation: 75% of the 350 workers would be recruited locally and capital costs during the mine's 16-year-life would be 10 million a year.

'We've put the money up for this mine and £10 million has been spent already, it can only be of benefit to the local economy.'

'But,' ran the *Western Morning News'* account of the meeting, 'he could not give a starting date for the mine, which was originally 1988, but has now been postponed. All he would say was that it was a 'viable proposition' and 'planning permission had taken longer than expected.'

A quiet Christmas followed, with little or no activity on site. Then, in February 1986, the news filtered through that the Canada Tungsten Mining Corporation was looking to raise funds to complete a £29.9 million acquisition of AMAX's tungsten interests ... including Hemerdon Ball. Although not the highest grade deposit that Canada Tungsten would have on their books, their President, Wayne Lenton, said that Hemerdon remained well regarded.

'I visited the property some while ago. So far as Hemerdon is concerned we will not be doing anything different to the policy pursued by AMAX. We will continue to rely on the local people who have worked on the property.'

'The main purpose of the transaction with AMAX is to combine the various tungsten interests into one main group so that we have a business where we are the producer and distributor and can run it as a total business.'

'We have every intention of going ahead with the Hemerdon property when tungsten prices recover. The key to the future of the tungsten market and to Hemerdon's future is the marketing policy of the Chinese.'

Paul Lister didn't disagree: 'It's all part of AMAX sorting itself out. It's just a tidying up operation to restructure the company. As far as I'm concerned it doesn't have any direct effect on the work at Hemerdon.

'There's no point digging until it's profitable, but at the end of the day if we cut overheads, it's going to have an effect on when it becomes profitable to start mining.'

The problem was that the price was not right then or for some years after that. Canada Tungsten kept the mine on its books and just before AMAX was sold to Phelps Dodge, it gradually moved the Canada Tungsten portfolio into the ownership of Aur Resources. Then, in 1997, a new concern, North American Tungsten plc acquired all of Aur Resources' tungsten assets with a view to developing three of their dormant mines including Hemerdon.

However, a couple of years later, with the price of tungsten still below the level that would excite investment, the company decided to abandon their interests in the area. There were ongoing annual upkeep costs in excess of $150,000 Canadian dollars, and when their attempts to reduce fees with the mineral rights holders failed they surrendered two of the three mineral rights in 2000 and, three years later, they disposed of the third.

Not surprisingly, when income from those leases stopped, landowner, Jim Woollcombe locked the gates.

'They couldn't pay the leases, and they stopped paying me,' recalled Paul Lister. There appears to have been no formal communication beyond that! And so, that was it, the most promising assault on the Hemerdon tungsten deposit in the second half of the twentieth century just fizzled out, without any fuss or fanfare.

Hale fellow, well met?

Back in 1984 around the time that AMAX were beginning to wonder if the Hemerdon project was worth pursuing, a young lad at Wellington College, Berkshire, was wondering what he could do to avoid studying Latin. He opted for a subject set that included geology, the study of which he found sufficiently interesting to list Exploration and Mining Geology at the University of Wales, Cardiff among the handful of courses he applied for on his UCCA form a year or two later.

Humphrey Hale was from a Devon family but his father, a banker, had moved to the South East for work purposes. While at Cardiff he met fellow student Ian Bruce who had been a mineral collector ever since he'd been able to call himself a collector.

After graduating, Ian formed a company, Crystal Classics, which over the last 30 years has become one of the best known sources of fine and rare mineral samples in the world. Meanwhile, Humphrey went to work in the oil industry, working firstly in the Gulf of Mexico, then in Singapore and then back into Europe where after just one year he was made redundant – via a phone call.

It was then that he met Andy Thompson, a fellow exploration mining geology graduate who had also struggled to find a settled job in the field. And so he had gone off to Australia on a one-year working visa. Ending up in Queensland, a chance meeting with a prospector led to him panning $300 worth of gold and small numbers of rubies and sapphires all in one week.

Taking this to be the opportunity of a lifetime Andy did a deal with the landowner, and headed back to England where he hooked up with Humphrey.

Gold fever pair to head Down Under

1993 cutting from the Reading Evening Post

'When I panned my first ounce I understood gold fever and the magic it holds,' 26-year-old Andy told the *Reading Evening Post*, adding *'If this company is a success we can be millionaires within a couple of years ... but it will take a lot of hard work.'*

The two young men managed to raise £25,000 from friends, family and businesses with intention of buying a gold mine in Australia. The site had evidently been tested to show that there was gold in the ground, but not enough to interest a major mining company.

Styling themselves British Australian Resources Mining (or as their friends would refer to it

mnemonically BARMY) they bought some mining equipment, and headed down under. Liz Parks picked up the story (in 2013) in the *Western Morning News*:

'During an eventful trip which saw an unfriendly local threaten to shoot them, employees stealing equipment and expensive machinery nearly swept away as river levels rose following torrential rain, they called in an expert to assess the data that the project was based on.

'Unfortunately, it was too good to be true and, after the BARMY team had sieved and washed a large section of Queensland dirt, the consultant confirmed that there were only trace amounts of gold present.

'As a result the company was liquidated and although Humphrey can see the humour in some aspects of it, he's also aware of the consequences for investors.

"It was a low point in my own life We set out taking people's money to invest in the operation but we failed".'

Humphrey stayed in Australia moving to Kalgoorlie in Western Australia, where a few years earlier a number of underground mines had been consolidated into the Fimiston Open Pit – the Super Pit – an open-cut gold mine that's over two miles long, one mile wide and over 600 metres deep. The host, since 1992, of the annual Australian Diggers' & Dealers' Conference, the country's premier mining conference, Kalgoorlie, this celebrated mine is still in production and anyone working on it is expected to live in town, which houses a population of around 30,000. There were no fly-in fly-out workers allowed.

Humphrey Hale stayed there until 1998 when he moved to Perth, from where he worked in the industry on a fly-in, fly-out basis. As he told *MiningNewsPremium.net* a few years later:

'I ended up at AngloGold Ashanti where I worked on the Sunrise Dam project near Laverton as an exploration geologist up until the end of 2006 when I was asked to be the inaugural managing director for Wolf Minerals.'

Wolf was created as a result of a co-operative divestment agreement entered into by Ironbark Gold Limited and Graynic, both of them newly created companies themselves (August 2006 and 2005 respectively) in December 2006.

The name 'Wolf', somewhat surprisingly with the benefit of hindsight, was not conjured up with any consideration that the company might come to be involved with a mineral called Wolfram.

At that time the former handed over the two mines, Burrandana and Kiawarra in New South Wales, with Graynic adding a third, at Yanco Glen. Representatives of both companies were invited to join the board and alongside Humphrey Hale as MD, Peter Mullins a former Australian diplomat, was appointed the non-executive Chairman.

In his interview with *MiningNewsPremium.net*, Hale explained the set-up he found in the fledgling operation: *'When I came into Wolf Minerals we had some tin and tungsten tenements in New South Wales and those tenements were highly exploratory. We needed and wanted to expand the company profile and move it forward, so I spent some time looking at opportunities in the tin/tungsten space and I remembered back to my field trip days in the south of England which had fairly strong uranium and tin deposits so I did some research and spoke to an old university friend. He said he could give me some tungsten leads and within five weeks of that phone call we had signed a short-form agreement for the Hemerdon project and it took us a further six months to negotiate the long-form agreement and acquire the project. So within a year we had gone from an IPO (Initial Public Offer) float to a company with a substantial project and it had a great impact on our share price, it took us from 20c per share to \$A2.95 by the end of 2007 and we were the best performing IPO of the year.'*

The University friend in question was Ian Bruce who had already had two very serious mineral-collecting visits to Hemerdon, collecting thousands of specimens and was familiar with its back story.

In September 2007, just a year after the company had been incorporated in Australia, its registered office being in the same building as Ironbark, Wolf was registered at Companies House in London, with offices in Fetter Lane, off Fleet Street.

Alongside Humphrey Hale as MD was Ian Bruce, now listed as a director of Wolf Minerals, as was Jonathan C Downes, the MD of Ironbark and a non-executive director of Graynic. Adrian Byass and Gregory Campbell, two other Ironbark directors, were also part of that early board along with Peter Mullins. Each of them held somewhere between 100,000 and 615,000 shares in the company.

On 5 December 2007 Wolf announced that they had acquired 100% of the Hemerdon tin and tungsten resource. They had paid one million Australian dollars for the deposit plus a further \$160,000 per annum rent together with a 2% net smelter royalty.

In March 2008 the company issued 1,500,000 options exercisable at \$1.50 to it directors, the options carrying an expiry date of 12 March, and on 28 April they issued 3 million ordinary shares at \$1.00 each (the exchange rate then being around 2.3 dollars to the pound).

Having now raised a substantial amount of money and having decided to focus their efforts on the Hemerdon project, on 1 July 2008 Wolf appointed Jennifer Abols as their project manager. A metallurgical engineering graduate of Laurentian University, Canada, Jennifer has recently – November 2019 – been appointed Executive Director of her alma mater and the Goodman School of Mines and CEO of MIRARCO.

Left: *Humphrey Hale and Ian Bruce, two 1992 graduates of the University of Wales, Cardiff pictured 20 years later after they had become directors of the Hemerdon project. Ian knew the Hemerdon site well and had found many rare mineral samples there.*
Below: *A double page spread from the Plymouth Herald in December 2007 re-igniting hopes and fears traditionally associated with any development of Hemerdon.*

Herald online: thisisplymouth.co.uk   The Herald, Wednesday December 5 2007   The Herald, Wednesday December 5 2007   Herald online: thisisplymouth.co.uk   PAGE 5

THERE'S GOLD IN THEM THAR HILLS!

■ The reopening of Hemerdon tungsten mine could generate £20million-a-year, Wolf Minerals Ltd's MD has told **TRISTAN NICHOLS**

MINING on the edge of Plymouth could re-start within two or three years, bringing with it up to £20million per annum over 10 to 15 years.

That's the message from Australian-based mining company, Wolf Minerals Ltd, which has signed a lease to re-open Hemerdon mine more than 60 years after it closed.

The company is planning to conduct an extensive feasibility and public consultation study, costing £8million, over the next six to 12 months, with the aim of re-opening the site within two to three years.

The £60million will be spent on updating mining equipment and manpower and the installation of a road diversion which, it is hoped, will alleviate congestion caused by the lorries.

Around 100 million tonnes of waste will be created and it will be dumped north of the pit on Crownhill Down next to the Imerys China Clay operations.

The company says two or three lorries a day will transfer waste from the site.

The mine, near Plympton, could potentially employ up to 200 people and a further 300 positions indirectly in the Plymouth area.

The re-opening of the mine, which closed shortly after World War Two, is due to the growth of China's economy and the global need for tungsten, a metal commonly used for light bulb filament.

Hemerdon is a hugely important mineral resource, containing one of the largest tungsten and tin deposits in the Western world.

Once fully operational the mine will supply all the tungsten needs for the UK, as well as five per cent of global needs.

Humphrey Hale, managing director of Wolf Minerals Ltd, said: "We are very excited about the project and we are very keen to get on with it.

"It is a terrific opportunity and it feels great to bring mining back to the South West.

"We've searched the world and chosen Hemerdon. It is a world-class mineral deposit."

Funds to mine the site at Hemerdon will be sought via UK and international investors.

Wolf Minerals (UK) Ltd has agreed a 40-year lease with the Hemerdon Mineral Trust on the site which is estimated to hold 40 million tonnes of tungsten and tin ore.

It is envisaged the pit will be 200 metres deep, 540 metres wide and 850 metres long.

Once the open pit has been completely mined, it will become a lake.

Hemerdon already has planning permission in place for mining at the site, dating back to 1986 and valid for 35 years.

Mr Hale said the company intended to actively engage with the community to reassure residents and ease concerns.

He said the consultation – together with the feasibility study – will take around six to 12 months to complete.

"Realistically, with the public consultation we anticipate being up and running and in production in two to three years' time," he said.

"With any major project you have to go to the communities and talk to them.

"We are a public listed company and we have a reputation we want to uphold. We are proud of the way we work and we want to get things right."

As a condition of the planning permission, a road has already been planned within the confines of the mine which leads out through the Hemerdon Estate to the main Sparkwell road at West Park Hill.

Mr Hale added: "We recognise there will be immediate local concerns about reopening the mine. However, we will be dealing with concentrated materials.

"As such there will be no intrusively large lorries transporting material to the docks [at Cattedown] compared with the current mineral operations."

Mr Hale also said while Wolf Minerals (UK) Ltd aims to generate some parts of the mine 24 hours a day, there will be no restrictions in place determining when machinery can operate.

Tungsten is in great demand at the present time and has grown in importance over the last decade.

At the moment the UK is almost totally dependent on supplies of this valuable metal from abroad.

According to the British Geological Survey, there are important deposits of tungsten and tin in China with about 80 per cent world share, Russia, Austria and Portugal.

The price and demand for tin and tungsten is rising very sharply as China is now consuming all its own resources.

China is seeking to expand its sources of supply.

The average amount price of tungsten since 1950 has fluctuated between US \$10 per metric ton until in 1965, rising to US \$170 in 1977 before dropping back to \$60 per metric tonne unit.

At present, the price of tungsten [refer to some of operations] is now operating at approximately US \$250 per metric tonne and costs subject to change.

Once operational Hemerdon would be the only operational tin and tungsten mine in the UK for a single work about 40 years and would signal the reintroduction of mining across the country.

DIGGING DEEP: Wolf Minerals MD Humphrey Hale, in the giant pit where the tungsten ore is buried. Below, abandoned mine-workings at Hemerdon

TUNGSTEN: demand

A MASSIVE boom in demand for tungsten from the Far East, South East Asia and South America has led to the re-opening of Hemerdon mine.

The development of countries including China and India has led to a demand for many metals including steel, nickel and tungsten.

The metals are essential to provide materials to build cars, televisions and construction tools, and even drill bits.

China in particular, which has been an exporter to the UK for decades, is now becoming the consumer in the reverse of trade.

"These countries are developing at a pace that is just unheard of," said Humphrey Hale, managing director of Wolf Minerals Limited.

"We are now seeing the boom in the demand."

Will that change? Mr Humphrey was then asked.

"Our guess is no," he added. "Not for the foreseeable future. We are here for a number of years."

Hemerdon mine closed shortly after World War Two due to the drop in market value of tungsten and tin.

MINE: history

■ DEPOSIT of tungsten was discovered in 1867 at Hemerdon and its 1916 renewed exploration revealed a widespread low grade wolframite deposit.

■ Mineral working was carried out between 1915 and 1920 and again between 1934 and 1944.

■ Hemerdon mine closed shortly after WWII due to the drop of market value of tungsten and tin.

■ A pilot scheme was conducted in the 1980s to consider the viability of re-opening the mine.

■ On Monday Wolf Minerals Limited agreed a lease with Newham Estate and Hemerdon Estate to restart mining at the site.

38,000 tons of ore was mined before the mine closed. A new pilot plant mining operation is to be centred at South Crofty in Cornwall.

The discovery of tungsten at Hemerdon dates back to 1867, before World War One caused a surge rise in the price of the metal. Preparation of the site began in 1917 and mining operations started in 1919.

ONE INSPIRING: Ian Bruce, a director of Wolf Minerals, with a rock sample from the Hemerdon mine

Residents concerned by plans

THE shock announcement to re-open Hemerdon mine has surprised and angered residents.

While many agree the investment in the area will ultimately boost the local economy, they are concerned about the effect on their lives.

Film editor Steve Newsham said there is an upside and a downside to the news.

"In some respects it is good news to more industry in the area," the 57-year-old said.

"The concern is of course that there will be an influx of lorries travelling through the village.

"The thought of lorries using the route through the village is not a good one. It would be completely wrong.

"I am surprised that Wolf Minerals has not spoken to residents before announcing the plans. I don't think it is right to hear it on the news first."

Another resident, Liz Baldwin, said she believes it is "terrible" that residents have not been consulted before the announcement.

"The news will upset a lot of people and come as quite a shock," Mrs Baldwin said.

"This is a tiny community with narrow roads. Our fear is that the lorries will use our village as a through road."

Motorsport photographer James Beerne said he will be contacting South West Devon MP Gary Streeter about the plans.

"It is disastrous," the 34-year-old added.

"My main concern is the influx of lorries coming through here. It is bad enough now because satellite navigation systems seem to steer them here."

Another resident added: "It is appalling that we have not been told first of the plans.

"The noise from the mine will echo through the village."

'DISASTROUS' Hemerdon resident James Beerne is one of the narrow lanes he fears mine traffic will use

'SURPRISED' Left, Hemerdon resident Steve Newsham's concern is that there will be an influx of lorries in the village, pictured above

Within six months of acquiring the project, metallurgical testwork was underway. Wolf commissioned SRK Consulting (Australasia) Pty Ltd who were based in Perth, to produce a resource based on the drilling data as defined by AMAX and this was delivered in March 2008.

The AMAX figures had suggested a deposit of 38.2 million tonnes at 0.183% tungsten (WO3) and 0.029% tin (SN) – the SPK figures were even more encouraging postulating a resource of 82 million tonnes at 0.22% WO3 and 0.022% tin: that is significantly more tungsten and with not quite as much tin, although AMAX, who had drilled over 500 holes for a total of over 35,000 metres, had also reported geological reserves of 73 million tonnes of slightly lower grade WO3 (0.143%)..

To improve confidence further, however, SRK recommended that a small programme of drilling be undertaken to confirm the historical data on which they were basing their figures. Essentially they had just re-assayed around 10% of AMAX's drill cores.

Their initial proposal was for a further five to six diamond-drill holes yielding around 1,100 metres of material.

The directors also decided to commission two scoping studies with a remarkably broad degree of toleration levels – plus or minus 40%.

The idea behind these studies was to provide an evaluation of the operating and the capital cost of mining and processing the deposit. Cube Consulting, based further along Hay Street from Wolf's offices in Perth, were appointed to assess the mining and Ausenco (an international concern with offices in Columbia, Brazil, Thailand, Brisbane and Perth) were charged with evaluating the processing plant and infrastructure that would be required.

Again the feedback was positive, indeed it was described as being 'very robust' and a Feasibility Study, to be overseen by Ausenco, was commissioned with a projected completion in the June quarter of 2009.

At this stage a much higher degree of due diligence was in place than had been the case with Humphrey Hale's first mining experience in Queensland and there was still more to be done.

Initial projections by Ausenco anticipated a throughput of 3 million tonnes of ore per annum, with an average processing cost of around $7.39, with a further admin cost per ton of around $1.68 all against a backdrop of the capital cost of the enterprise which they put at $160,100,000 (around £64m at that time and around £87m today).

Given the price of tungsten in 2008 Wolf reported that they were *'excited and encouraged by the results of the scoping studies and the progress of the ongoing work to confirm and update the 1981 AMAX study.'*

But, as of 26 September 2008 they said that they did *'not endorse the publicly released 1982 Feasibility Study or declare that the approved pit is economic and will be developed. Wolf has yet to complete a detailed economic review of the current feasibility study and approved open pit plan.'*

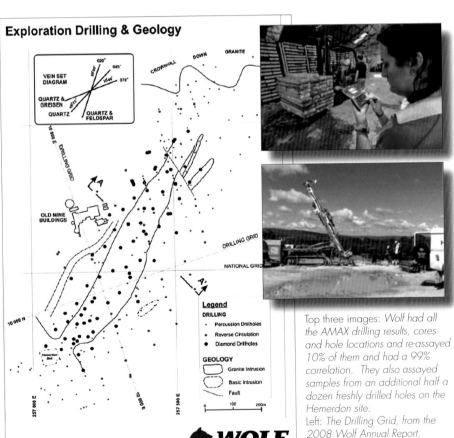

Top three images: *Wolf had all the AMAX drilling results, cores and hole locations and re-assayed 10% of them and had a 99% correlation. They also assayed samples from an additional half a dozen freshly drilled holes on the Hemerdon site.*
Left: *The Drilling Grid, from the 2008 Wolf Annual Report.*

In the event the drilling programme wasn't completed until the beginning of October 2008 and the following month Humphrey Hale told Tristan Nicholls of the *Plymouth Herald* that Wolf were making *'headway with the metallurgical and mining studies which are providing encouraging results'.* He added that an ecological study of flora and fauna had been completed and archaeological studies had begun on the ground and that they would continue into the new year. Humphrey also said that he had met many local people since announcing Wolf's plans the previous December and that he planned to continue the consultations. Contact numbers and an email address were given at the end of the article for those wishing to contact Mr Hale. A website address for Wolf Minerals was also provided. All in all it was a far cry from those distant days when it was extremely difficult for members of the public to get a deeper insight into what was going on other than via the often far from impartial nineteenth-century newspaper accounts.

In November 2009 Councillor Roger Croad, Devon County Council's cabinet member for Environmental and Regulatory Services chaired a meeting in Sparkwell Village Hall to answer questions from residents and whoever about Wolf's proposed changes to the planning permissions. Council Leader, John Hart affirmed that the *'planning permission is current and Wolf Minerals could go ahead with the mine,'* but that it was *'the wish of the County Council to take this opportunity to improve the planning conditions and the final restoration of the site.'*

At that stage it was anticipated that were work to commence on the site it would not be before 2012.

As a consequence of the renegotiation of the planning conditions, minor alterations and improvements to the existing arrangements were agreed and approved by Devon County Council and Plymouth City planners in 2011 and work began on a new 600-metre link road to the mine between Lee Moor Road and West Park Hill, although that was a condition of the AMAX planning consent.

The road was opened on Friday 27 July 2012, by Councillor John Hart. Four months earlier Wolf had received credit agreement from three major banks supporting them. The price of tungsten had risen steadily from around $50 per metric tonne in 2005 to a peak of $500 in 2012 and it was thus no surprise to find that investors were suddenly very interested in what was regarded as being one of the three largest tungsten deposits in the world. As *Financial Times* journalist Kate Burgess reported the following year, the price rises *'triggered a stampede of prospectors, many Aim-quoted [AIM being a sub-market of the London Stock Exchange], vying to restart defunct projects or find new seams.'*

Of course Hemerdon fell into neither of those categories, the price of tungsten, arguably, being the only thing holding back its operation over the last 100 years.

Friday 27 July 2012, Devon County Councillor John Hart, second left, opens the new link road, with Cllr Mark Coker, Humphrey Hale, Gary Streeter MP and Cllr Ian Blackler.

Hemerdon Project

Access to world-class infrastructure in a mining friendly area

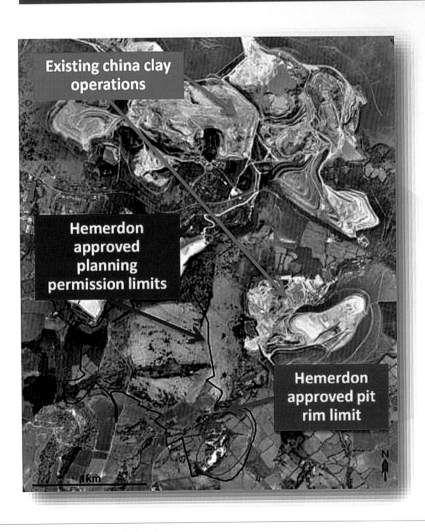

- 40 year lease term
  - 2% NSR royalty to landowners who own all metal mineral rights
- Plymouth 10 kilometres away
  - Excellent transport links
  - 250,000 population
  - Power & water infrastructure
- China clay mines adjacent
- Project will generate approximately 300 direct and indirect jobs during the operational phase
- £10 – 13 million per annum in salaries and wages during the operational phase

Page from Wolf's brochure.

Hemerdon had a number of other advantages too, as Kate Burgess put it: *'There are already two big clay pits close by and a mining community in situ. Unlike rivals, Wolf Minerals has not had to dislodge villages, ship in skilled workers, build airstrips or rely on diesel power. The company can tap into what is already there, which translates into lower than average costs of $105 per MTU of tungsten.'*

With an airport close by, a village even closer, and geologists in Britain charging substantially less for their services, Hemerdon had never looked a better bet.

By this stage Wolf had already taken on their first full-time employee in the UK, 53-year-old Jeff Harrison, who, curiously enough had been at University with Jane Charley, the AMAX geologist who had worked at Hemerdon 30 years earlier. Jeff – who had over 35 years experience in global mining mineral processing, had spent many years in Australia, as well as gaining valuable local knowledge working with Imerys (china clay) in Devon and Cornwall – joined Wolf in May 2010 and quickly became a familiar figure in the local area.

With the Definitive Feasibility Study successfully completed in 2011 and the price at last being right, green lights started to brighten up the prospects. *'The Company,'* ran the wording of the Executive Summary sent out to shareholders in June 2012 *'obtained a credit approved offer of £55 million of senior debt. Wolf followed this up with the signing of a Heads of Terms agreement with offtakers that provided the commercial terms of a five year offtake and an additional £20 million of project funding. Following the year end the Company announced that it had mandated its syndicate of banks to seek revised credit approval to provide senior debt finance facilities totalling GBP75 million (AU$114 million) to fund the commercial development of the Hemerdon project removing the need for the £20 million of funding from offtakers.'*

The three banks involved at this stage were UniCredit Bank AG (an Italian global banking group), ING Bank N.V. (a Dutch-based global bank) and Caterpillar Financial SARL (a German-based loan agency) and although the investment from these partners obviated the need for funding from the offtakers, the agreements subsequently entered into with the American-based Global Tungsten & Powders (GTP) and the Austrian-based Wolfram Bergbau und Hutten were critical to the early confidence shown in the Hemerdon project. Between them these two agreed to take 80% of Hemerdon's expected average, annual concentrate output for a period of at least five years.

It was the £2m funding offer from the Resource Capital Fund (RCF) that had started the ball rolling again in late 2009-early 2010 after a relatively quiet period in which Humphrey Hale was doing his level best to stimulate interest in the Hemerdon project.

Frequently Asked Questions

How large will the site at the Drakelands mine be?

The open pit will be approximately 850 metres long by 450 metres wide and 200 metres deep. The site is approximately 220 metres above sea level

How many tonnes of tungsten do you intend to mine?

It is anticipated that when full production is reached the mine will produce approximately 5,000 tonnes of tungsten concentrate and 1,000 tonnes of tin concentrate per year.

Why is Hemerdon going to be mined as an open pit and not underground?

The Drakelands orebody outcrops at surface allowing for efficient open pit mining. It may be possible in the future to mine at depth by underground mining if economically viable.

How long will the project last?

The current plan is for the Drakelands mine to run for 10-15 years. Exploration drilling has shown that there is significant mineral resource at depth. Any decision to extend the life of the mine below the current planned 200 metres would be subject to future economic viability and a further planning process.

At what times will you be operating the mine?

Current planning permission requirements mean that the processing plant will not work on Sundays. There are also restrictions on using the waste tip at night and on blasting times.

Why has the name been changed from Hemerdon Mine to Drakelands Mine?

The residents of Hemerdon requested the name be changed to Drakelands Mine. Drakelands is the name of the local community in a valley between the pit and new processing plant.

Will there be any danger to health for nearby residents?

No. Dust will be controlled and continuously monitored to meet established planning conditions. China clay operations have been in the area for many years and are mining similar rocks. The milling and processing of tungsten ores is predominantly by crushing and gravity processes, which require no large-scale chemical additions.

How will you control dust from the site?

There is a range of accepted good practices for controlling dust. Most involve spraying water, building wind breaks and hydroseeding. Strict environmental controls have been placed on the mining operation by the local and regulatory authorities including Devon County Council. These will remain in place throughout the project life. Careful monitoring to ensure that the air quality stays within government guidelines will be implemented. Wolf Minerals has already started dust measurements and this will continue throughout the life of the mine.

What noise can be expected from the mining operation and how will you monitor and control this?

Any noise emitted during the operation of the mine will be closely monitored to ensure it is kept within the levels set in the planning conditions.

How will you ensure the overall safety of the mine?

The site will have the appropriate security measures to ensure the mine is only accessed by those with permission to operate on behalf of Wolf Minerals. There will only be one access point to the mine. Staff will be highly trained in mining safety and appropriate health and safety working regulations will be enforced at all times.

There will be Wolf personnel on site at all times, inspecting and monitoring the operation to ensure operations are carried out safely at all times.

How will the mine waste and tungsten concentrate be transported?

Tungsten concentrate will be filled into bags and transported in containers by trucks from the mine site, with around one truck per day leaving the site when at full production.

Waste rock and spoil will be transported by Caterpillar dump trucks using the internal site haul roads.

Where will you dump waste soil and rock?

The mine waste facility will be located at Crownhill Down, off the Lee Moor Road north of Plympton and to the south-east and south-west respectively of the three southernmost china clay workings and mine waste facilities associated with the Lee Moor china clay mining area.

How big will the mine waste facility be?

At its outer edge, the rockfill embankment will be 113 metres high. The mine waste facility will cover 175 hectares. The storage capacity of the mine waste facility will be approximately 30 million m^3 waste rock storage and 10 million m^3 of tailings storage.

Why does the waste facility need to be on Crownhill Down?

The location of the mine waste facility was considered in detail during a full Public Inquiry in 1981 and when planning permission was granted in 1986.

Will the mine waste facility contain hazardous materials?

The material being deposited in the waste facility is classified as non-hazardous.

How will the mine and mine waste facility be restored when it is completed?

Once production is complete, the pit will fill naturally with water to become a lake and the production plant and other infrastructure will be removed.

There is an agreed Restoration Concept with Devon County Council for the mine waste site. This involves the lower levels being planted with deciduous woodland, higher levels to be reinstated as heathland and the top flat levels to be wet areas but with no standing water.

Above: *Wolf's FAQs*
Left: *Jeff Harrison*

Top: *Jeff Harrison at the entrance to the site. As well as purchasing all the property they were looking to acquire in and around the site, the area also had to be fenced off.* Bottom: *The early incarnation of the team pictured outside the offices at Tamar Science Park.*

The RCF arrangement provided a secured development capital facility of $6 million, with repayment term of one year from the date of the first drawn-down, which took place in January 2012.

With funding secured activity at Hemerdon – or Drakelands as it had now been rechristened – everything stepped up a gear. Hemerdon and Sparkwell Parish Council did not like the use of Hemerdon for the mine as it could have had a negative influence on house prices in Hemerdon village. 'We agreed to a name change, Drakelands was adopted as it was the name of the hamlet where we had bought most of the properties.' recalled Jeff Harrison.

After a tendering process had been conducted GR Engineering Services (GRES), a company with an excellent track record for constructing gold mines in Australia, were awarded the Engineering, Procurement and Construction (EPC) Contract to build the processing mill (with associated infrastructure) in March 2013. Although their principal offices were in Perth and Brisbane it was felt that no new mining mill had been built in England for over half a century and that therefore there was not the expertise in Britain to draw on. Furthermore, the company was well-known to the newly appointed project manager Rupert McCracken so he was happy with the choice.

GRES had been invited to complete plant design and engineering for the Hemerdon feasibility study back in January 2010 and now had the job of creating a processing mill that could handle three million tonnes of ore per annum for one of the largest tungsten deposits in the world. Although it was not exactly a run-of-the-mill mill for GRES, they nevertheless felt confident enough to design it in house. Working to a fixed-price, fixed-term budget, GRES were awarded the A$111m (£75m) contract on 6 March and began work on site on 12 June 2013. Encouragingly, their contract fee was £2m below the projected cost that they had outlined in the Definitive Feasibility Study.

Commenting on the Contract award, GR Engineering's Managing Director, Joe Ricciardo said: *'The award of the Hemerdon EPC Contract follows over three years of GR Engineering working closely with Wolf to deliver specialised studies and advice whilst demonstrating the engineering and construction capabilities that are pivotal to the successful delivery of the project. 'The contract is particularly significant for GR Engineering as it is consistent with our growth strategy to expand offshore and to maintain our traditional standing as an EPC contractor that can deliver fixed price, turn-key solutions. GR Engineering looks forward to continuing to work with Wolf to bring the Hemerdon Tungsten and Tin project into production.'*

Meanwhile, with his Plymouth office located at Tamar Science Park, Jeff Harrison's team, including Mineral Manager and Estates Planner, John Briggs, now had to set about purchasing the fifteen or so private properties that currently sat with the sett that Wolf were about to work as well as the china clay land where the Mine Waste Facility was to be located.

'It was an interesting and challenging time,' recalls Jeff.

'Many of the residents had been living under the threat of the mine being developed for decades – since AMAX had first attained planning permission. Soon after acquiring those permissions ourselves we had gone around and arranged to buy the properties in and around the site. We'd negotiated a selling price with all of them, but of course we were not in a position to actually purchase the properties until we had the necessary funding in place to develop the mine, and for that matter, the funding to be able to make those purchases.

'For some of the residents it was very difficult, they realised that they might well have to move and they were generally happy with the price we'd agreed, but because we couldn't tell them exactly when the sale would be completed, it made it difficult for them to look around. Nevertheless a few of them did, and they would ring me and say "Jeff, we've found our 'dream home' when can you complete the sale?" And I'd say "not yet." Their problem of course was that they were now going to struggle to sell to anyone else as their homes weren't long term prospects for anyone.'

As yet, of course, there had still been no commercial mining on site. GRES were contracted to complete the mill by mid-2015 and the contract for actually digging the material out of the open cast mine had been awarded to CA Blackwell, a British-based earthwork-moving concern, founded back in 1956 by Chris Blackwell, specialising in the creation of motorways – they'd also worked on the Olympic Park for the 2012 London Olympics.

The Mobile Plant Mining Contract was an Australian-type contract routinely used in there but very unusual here. Few UK contractors were prepared to bid due to the significant risk being placed on them.

Blackwell's remit here was to begin the pre-strip and mine development by March 2014 by which time all thoughts would be on starting to consider the practicalities of processing the Drakeland's deposit.

After six or seven years of raising interest in the project and, more significantly, raising funding, the without-which-not element that had always eluded Bill Richardson and which was ultimately a non-starter for AMAX because of the poor price at the time of tungsten, activity at Hemerdon had now taken on a markedly different complexion.

A frank conversation between the Wolf chairman John Hopkins, and the man who had brought the project to this point, MD Humphrey Hall, followed.

'Humphrey was asked what qualities he thought would be important in overseeing the construction of the mill and the physical development of the site and he realised right away that the point the chairman was trying to make was that they weren't necessarily part of the skill set of a geologist with a nose for prospecting. A deal was struck and in October Humphrey resigned,' recalled Jeff Harrison.

'Russell St. John Clark will succeed Hale as the new Managing Director and will start with immediate effect. Hale will continue to work with the company in a consultancy capacity for a period of three months to ensure an efficient hand-over and transition,' ran the press statement.

Top: Drakelands farmhouse. Above: Drakelands, former home of Peter Bloom, it was used as the Site Engineering Offices for 18 months during the construction phase.
In November 2013 it was announced that Wolf had purchased, or secured contracts for the acquisition of 15 properties and parcels of land near Hemerdon.

Top: Russell Clark talks up Wolf on TV. Bottom: Groundbreaking day with Jeff Harrison, a South Hams Council representative, Gary Streeter, John Hart, Tudor Evans, Anthony Cobbold, Russell Clark.

'The move,' said the statement, was 'in line with its transition strategy.' With more than 35 years of experience in the industry, 55-year-old Russell Clark had previously been Managing Director of Grange Resources, Australia's largest magnetite producer.

Ushering in his successor, Humphrey was quoted as saying: 'I would like to welcome Russell to the company as its new Managing Director. It gives me great confidence to be able to hand over to someone of his experience and expertise, and his skill sets and experience in managing and operating mining projects will be invaluable to Wolf as the company executes the development strategy to bring Hemerdon into production.'

The following month a glowing report was produced by Breakaway Research, a member of the Sydney based Breakaway Investment Group. Comprehensive, detailed and well illustrated with graphs and computer generated imagery from Wolf, their recommendation from an investment perspective was 'Speculative BUY'.

'Wolf,' they concluded, after assessing the financial packages in place, and global tungsten offer, were now 'clearly in a league of their own as the only company to have the funds in place and 'development ready' to build a meaningful scale operation.'

Still not a single unit of wolfram had been produced.

March 2014, however, witnessed a ground-breaking day, quite literally in the history of the project as work began on the mine itself.

Tim Jones, a former chairman of the Heart of the South West Enterprise Partnership, said the 'revival' of the South West's mineral industry could provoke other investors to look at the region.

'Investment in our mineral assets is something we have been striving for for a long time. We hope to see a long-term future come out of this.'

Chairman of the Plymouth Chamber of Commerce, Paul Woods, agreed: 'It's a substantial investment which has opened up other people's eyes to possibilities here.'

Meanwhile, MD Russell Clark told William Telford at the Plymouth Herald in the second week of March that Wolf had placed its securities in a voluntary and temporary suspension on the Australian Securities Exchange pending the groundbreaking announcement.

'We are looking to raise capital to complete the financing of this project. We are pulling together numerous investments to finalise the funding. Once that's complete we will have the funds we need to completely build the project.'

Thus it was that in May Wolf had issued 608.9 million shares in a bid to bring in working capital. They raised £108.5 million and with their funding now secure, Russell Clark said that the priority now would be to ensure that the project came in on time … and on budget.

GRES were now instructed to start work on site and over the next two years it was estimated that 70% of their £75m contract was spent on subcontracting to UK companies, many of them from Devon and Cornwall. These contracts ranged in value from around £100,000 to £3,000,000. At the top end of the range the Newton Abbot-based Centristic Limited had been awarded the contract to design, manufacture and install 11 conveyors for the mined material throughout the processing stages and provide steel work, pipe work and plate work for the structure of the buildings on the mine site.

It was anticipated that around three dozen Centristic staff – including draughtsmen, engineers, fabricators and site operators – would work on the project between June 2014 and March 2015.

Centristic's operations director James Hepworth told the *Plymouth Herald's* Steve Grant that the company was *'proud to be playing our part in a mining project of this importance.'*

He added, *'As well as direct employment for our employees from this contract we will also be providing work for other Devon firms ... like South West Galvanisers.'*

Another local firm to pick up a sizeable contract were Exeter-based Dawnus who were awarded £1.7 million to supply and install all the concrete structures for the new crushing and processing plant and other operational buildings on the mine site. However after a few weeks they were superseded by a company from the Midlands.

From the other side of the Tamar, where mining historically had played an even greater role, Holman Wilfley of Redruth secured a £150,000 contract to manufacture eight gravity – or shaking – tables to work on the separating out of the tin and the tungsten.

Holman Wilfley director Chris Bailey, who had spent some time working at Hemerdon during the AMAX era, said that *'in the past Holman gravity tables would have been installed in large numbers in support of tin mines across the South West. Today most of the gravity tables used by customers in this country are for separating out metals in recycling plants. We are proud to be associated with a mining project of this status closer to home.'* Interestingly enough, shaking tables have been part of mine processing for over a century. The current Holman Wilfley company inherited the licensed OEM Holman and Wilfley technology from the original manufacturers over 20 years ago making them the only global company that still produces the well established, genuine premium brand gravity tables.

Nigel Jump, Visiting Professor in Regional Economic Development at Plymouth University, observed at the time that *'despite a proud history, mining investment in the South West has been sparse in recent years. Wolf's investment,'* he said, *'is welcome news for supply chains and local employment, especially if it can be sustained and developed beyond the*

Top: *Jeff Harrison and Russell Clark with Chris Bailey at the Holman Wilfley works.*
Bottom: *James Hepworth (Centristic Operations Director), Jeff Harrison, Russell Clark, centre with Roddy Grant (MD Centristic) at Newton Abbot.*

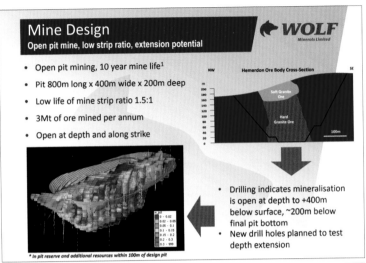

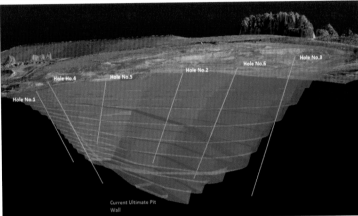

initial phase. It is always good to hear about an export-orientated, high-value-added operation instigating new activity around Plymouth.'

Russell Clark too was clearly very positive about it all too: *'There is a wealth of expertise and enthusiasm in Devon and Cornwall for this project and we are very pleased to be supporting local companies and harnessing their skills to create a world class mine.*

'The Drakeland's Mine, Hemerdon, project will create about 200 direct jobs and pump millions of pounds into the South West and UK economies over the next decade.'

In terms of the operational team, the vast majority were, according to Wolf's inaugural *Newsletter* published in September 2014, *'born in the South West, educated at Camborne School of Mines or have lived and worked locally for many years.'*

Happily the weather was kind over the next few months, and significant progress was made in the construction of the mine. As October 2014 drew to a close Wolf had taken on some 35 full-time employees and at any one time there could be around 300 people working on site.

In December SLR Consultants (a privately owned environmental consultancy set up in the UK 20 years earlier by Alan Sheppard, John Leeson and David Richards), completed a detailed drilling programme around the edges of the open pit and found that the country rock (that surrounding the mineral bearing igneous intrusion) was stronger than first thought. This was good news as it meant that open sides of the pit could be made steeper, allowing an additional four to six million tonnes of ore to be extracted for processing.

By this time Wolf had secured the entire site with fencing and had signs erected advising the public to keep out, primarily for their own safety. Meanwhile, they were busy arranging visits for those curious to see what was happening at Hemerdon. Over 180 villagers had already requested tours, the first of which took place in September and among the first outside groups to be shown around were Plymouth Rotary Club and students from Plymouth University and the Camborne School of Mines.

As the year drew to a close Wolf reported that *'earthworks and concrete works are substantially complete with only minor works outstanding. Structural steel erected has picked up pace with approximately 300 tonnes erected out of a forecast total of 1,266 tonnes.*

'Major mechanical components installed include the scrubber and scrubber screen and associated platework in the Washing and Screening area, the primary and regrind ball mills in the Primary Milling area, along with various other mechanical and platework items in other areas of the Concentrator building. The administration building is complete other than infrastructure services, and the laboratory building is at a similar stage of completion with the external cladding ongoing.'

The weather had taken a turn for the worse, but the report went on to say:

'Construction work continues to progress despite the inclement weather, and the contractors and workers are to be congratulated on the ability to work no matter what the heavens throw at them.'

Wolf graphics showing the extent of the pit and its potential impact prior to restoration work.

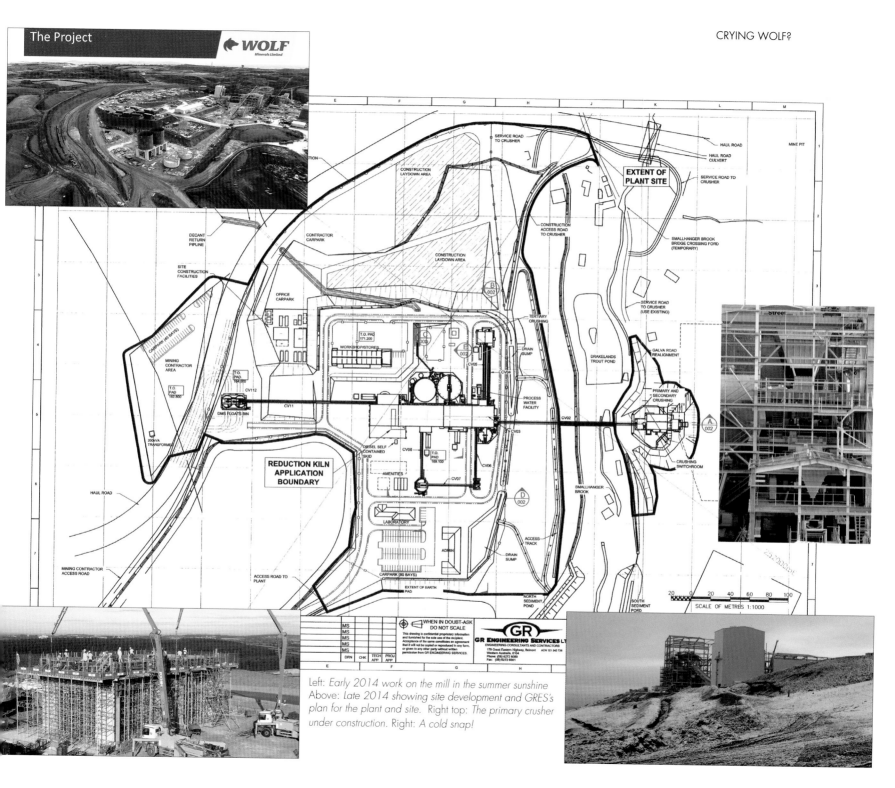

The Project

WOLF
Minerals Limited

EXTENT OF PLANT SITE

REDUCTION KILN APPLICATION BOUNDARY

Left: Early 2014 work on the mill in the summer sunshine
Above: Late 2014 showing site development and GRES's plan for the plant and site. Right top: The primary crusher under construction. Right: A cold snap!

Top: *Wolf's 'We've built a five-star bat hotel' (Russell Clark) with oak cladding and slate roof. Inset: Bat motif on the door. Bottom: May 2014 Mrs Cobbold opens the new bridleway.*

Of course it wasn't all just about the mine, the stringent planning agreements meant that there was a lot of work for the developers to do in and around the site.

An extensive tree-planting programme required the creation of nine hectares of open broad-leafed woodland involving the planting of 40,000 whips in the first two seasons, with further planting to take place throughout the life of the project.

Furthermore, in the initial development of the open pit area *'traditional Devon hedges and stone faced banks, which are nature's corridors had to be removed'* (Wolf Minerals Newletter No.4 January 2015).

'These were carefully dismantled under the watchful eyes of ecologists with reptiles and amphibians removed by hand and carefully relocated, the stone was also saved and stockpiled for future use. One of the compensation strategy projects has involved the construction of a new Devon hedgerow to complete the habitat linkage around the open pit north perimeter for flora and fauna use. The combination of stone walling and the newly planted eastern perimeter bund provides a linkage between the Smallhangar Valley and Hemerdon Ball. The traditional Devon hedge bank is nearing completion spanning approximately 250 metres following which the top will be planted with native hedging species and managed traditionally (ibid).'

Another part of the environmental permitting process concerned the bats that were found using the old, World War II, buildings for foraging and roosting. Wolf had to apply for three separate European Protected Species Licenses (EPSLs) to enable them to remove the existing roosts and create suitable replacements.

Two of the three new roosts were adapted from existing outbuildings – including Drakelands farm barn – while the third was purpose built with oak cladding sawn from wood felled on site during development, and reclaimed slate for roofing.

For horse riders and ramblers new bridleways were constructed around the perimeter of the site and interpretation boards with maps, images and text were proposed to be erected at appropriate locations.

Plans were also at this stage submitted for the new Lee Moor Road, and Wolf management acknowledged that no mine traffic should go through Hemerdon village. In an attempt to mitigate any or all inconvenience for the neighbourhood, temporary and permanent car parking was being surfaced to cut down on the potential amount of mud that might be inadvertently driven off site, and two wheel-washers were installed on site.

To further endear themselves to the local community Wolf, in addition to holding numerous open public meetings, sponsored a wide variety of local causes, including: the provision of a new storage container for Chaddlewood Miners' Football Club; funding the installation of emergency defibrillators for the villages of Sparkwell and Lee Moor and providing a new chain of office for the Stannator of Plympton.

Top: *The new bridleway where it runs past Hemerdon Ball.* Left: *The new Devon hedgerow.* Middle: *Some of the thousands of whips that had been planted by the end of 2014.* Right: *Map showing areas intended for planting.*

In January 2015 Wolf announced that they had appointed Kerry Dee as their Human Resources Manager and she lost no time in appointing Plymouth based national recruitment specialists Astra Recruitment to help with the task of filling the large number of posts that were about to be created. Wolf were currently advertising for operatives to work in the mine processing plant and over 800 people applied for the 40 posts that the company were then looking to fill.

'It was an exciting time building the new Drakelands workforce. The mine was seen as something special and there was great enthusiasm by everyone to make the project a success. In the early years it was a very happy and enjoyable place to work,' recalls the Operations Manager.

One of the first major in-house appointments was that of Charlie Northfield, a Plymouth-born Camborne School of Mines graduate who had over 30 years' experience in the minerals industry throughout the world. Appointed as the Process Plant Manager, Charlie came with considerable experience of managing process plants recovering a wide range of minerals, including gold, tungsten and tin. Well aware of what was on his hometown's doorstep he had been keenly waiting for someone to take on the Hemerdon deposit so that he might have the chance to come back to the area to work.

Meanwhile, Wolf opted to operate an assay laboratory on site, so that rather than send samples away for testing they could all be assayed on site.

SGS (registered as the Société Générale de Surveillance in Geneva in 1919) were awarded the contract to oversee the assay laboratory and as a result of this move Wolf needed to recruit eight technicians, four shift chemists and a laboratory manager.

The rollercoaster that was witnessing the greatest ever assault on the Hemerdon deposit was gaining momentum on a daily basis. Early in 2015 Wolf sought permission from Devon County Council to allow the primary crusher to operate seven days a week like the rest of the plant. Russell Clark had long been unhappy with the situation whereby the primary crusher would have to shut down at 6pm on a Saturday and not start up again until 36 hours later, that is at 6am on Monday morning, effectively making the Drakelands operation a 5.5 day week operation. The main fear was noise but Wolf argued that it wouldn't be an issue and sought a six-month, seven days a week trial period – and in August, just a few weeks before the mine was due to open, permission was granted.

Meanwhile, in other news the mainly Danish-owned DONG Energy were awarded the contract to supply a projected 82GWh power supply to the mine and IFS (a Cambridge-based software development company) were appointed to provide the Enterprise Resource Planning technology – the computing system – for the mine.

To the north of the plant, the new Mine Waste Facility was ready to start taking material from the processing plant and diggers, dump-trucks and other mine vehicles started to arrive on site, although it was not anticipated that the full fleet would be in place much before the end of 2015.

In June the first batch of ore was fed into the process plant marking the completion of the construction phase and the start of the wet commissioning of the process plant, which in turn meant that the plant was almost ready for the full on switch on.

This page: Aerial perspective of the processing plant – centre – with the pit at the top of the picture and the primary crusher just below the pit connected to the mill by a covered metal conveyor, which crosses the Drakelands valley. Drakelands House sits to the left of the conveyor. Left: The first load goes into the primary crusher. Opposite page: various new vehicles including a new, 779 HP, 70-ton-capacity, Cat 775G off-road Caterpillar rigid dump truck and a Komatsu HD785-7 rigid dump-truck. The vehicle is over 5m high, 6.5m wide, and 11m long and has 1200 HP engine, and is capable of carrying loads of 60 tons (or 91 tonnes).

Top: *Australian High Commissioner Alexander Downer.* Middle: *David Fursdon (Lord Lieutenant of Devon) addresses guests and board members at the official opening of the Drakelands Tungsten and Tin Mine 17 September 2015.* Above: *Wolf MD Russell Clark can barely conceal his pleasure at the long-awaited opening.*

WOLF
Minerals

Drakelands Tungsten and Tin Mine

Opened by

David Fursdon Esq, Her Majesty's Lord-Lieutenant of Devon,

and

Mr John Hopkins OAM, Chairman of Wolf Minerals Limited,

17th September 2015

At the beginning of September, with more than 200 people now working for Wolf on site, it seemed that the whole system was good to go. The processing plant had been delivered on time and on budget.

MD Russell Clark announced that 'as part of the commissioning process we have now produced tungsten concentrates to the required specification.

'Overall commissioning activities are going well and the operating teams have learned how to manage the plant in different conditions.

'Commissioning,' he added by way of clarification, 'is a time when all processes and equipment are fully tested and performance established.

'By its very nature it is not unusual to encounter a number of challenges along the way and our teams are working successfully together to address these. It is particularly pleasing that the plant is operating as expected and we are successfully upgrading the ore to produce product that meets our customer's expectations.'

Russell anticipated that the mine would be in positive cash flow within two years.

Company Chairman John Hopkins flew over from Australia as three days of opening events were organised to mark the commissioning of the first new metal mine in the UK for 45 years.

The official opening, on 17 September 2015, followed a similar event held the previous day for Wolf team members and their partners as a celebration of the project and an opportunity for the Wolf Board to thank everyone for their efforts. John Hopkins told the team: 'Just 18 months ago the ground-breaking ceremony was held at this very spot. The Board and I would like to congratulate you on successfully building the project not only on time and on budget but also most importantly, without serious safety, community or environmental breach. What we have here today is the start of a journey, and one where the project has the potential to run stronger for longer, maintaining the 200 permanent jobs that have been created, and becoming one of the most important suppliers of tungsten in the western world. As the Chairman of the Board, I take this opportunity to thank you for your considerable efforts, both past and in the future.'

David Fursdon Esq, Her Majesty's Lord-Lieutenant of Devon, together with John Hopkins, unveiled a plaque to officially open the Project. The event took place in a marquee set up overlooking the mine site and process plant and guests enjoyed the opportunity to meet up and share a local hog roast before proceedings got under way.

The Hon Alexander Downer AC, Australian High Commissioner to the UK, the Chairmen and Leaders of Devon County, South Hams and Plymouth City Councils, representatives of Sparkwell and Shaugh Prior Parish Councils, neighbours and members of the wider local community joined the Wolf Board, staff and project team, investors, financiers and customers in celebrating the achievement.

Wolf Chairman, MD and Board with Cllr John Hart (Leader of Devon County Council), Cllr Ian Bramble (Chairman of South Hams District Council), Cllr Dr John Mahony (Lord Mayor of Plymouth), Cllr John Tucker (Leader of South Hams District Council) and Cllr Tudor Evans (Leader of Plymouth City Council).

Cllr. Tudor Evans, leader of Plymouth City Council, said that *the economic impact of this project will be felt in Devon and in Plymouth. It is fantastic for the local economy. This mine is of truly international significance.'* After multiple false starts across the twentieth century Hemerdon, at long last, was being attacked with the best equipment the modern world could bring to bear on metal mining.

Processing Mill ready for action.

241

Trouble at Mill

With sound financial backing in place and with companies agreeing to take 80% of the output for the next few years it seemed as though everyone involved could at last breathe an enormous sigh of relief and look forward to proving that all those nay sayers who suggested that this was one of the biggest white elephants in the history of white elephants, were wrong. This was no longer the stuff of dreams or La La La Land, where only the **la**bourers, the **la**wyers and the **la**ndowners made money, this was a money-making enterprise that would reap rewards for everyone involved. As 2015 came to a close the company disclosed that it was already looking towards the longer term. *'To this end we have made an application to extend the life of the Drakeland's planning permission as well as undertaking a number of geological projects to further improve understanding of the ore body,'* said Russell Clark.

The original planning permission granted back in 1986 was for a 35-year mine lease and now Wolf were seeking to extend that until 2036. Meanwhile, their 24/7 trial in the processing plant was ongoing and a series of blasting trials had been undertaken in October.

The December Newsletter contained the following statement: *'Blasting – Wolf is likely to begin regular blasting at the mine in mid-January next year, as the ore and surrounding rock waste have become much harder to excavate. A document outlining the particular measures to be taken in respect of members of the public and local community is being prepared, and those local residents that may hear the blasting at their homes will receive a copy of that document early in the New Year, so that they can fully understand these measures. Modern-day blasting uses millisecond delay detonators which allow the use of smaller amounts of explosive to achieve the same effect. The time during which blasting can take place is limited to two periods per day, and no blasting is permitted on Sundays. Blasting is allowed in the mornings between 10.00am and 11.30am, and in the afternoons between 1.00pm and 4.30pm.*

'Wolf will be using blasting "sentries" posted around the perimeter of the mine at locations including public and private rights of way to warn users of imminent blasting. These sentries will be in place before blasting takes place, and will not leave until blasting has finished. A small trial blast has already been carried out at the mine to determine blast characteristics of the ore and waste. Information from this has helped us to design effective production blasts that comply with our planning permission requirements. For blasting activities all relevant regulations will be followed with site
visits and inspections from regulatory bodies to ensure safe and compliant operations.'

As the new year dawned issues emerged concerning one of their major subcontractors as the CA Blackwell Group, who were responsible for the on-site earth-moving operations (here and across half a dozen other open pits across the country) were acquired by the Durham based Hargreaves Services for £11.9m, a move that made the later one of the largest bulk earthworks plant fleets in Europe.

The transaction had little or no impact on the operation at Drakelands; however, the falling price of tungsten undoubtedly did. In January 2016 it was reported that the price of the heavy metal had fallen by half since work had started on the construction of the plant two years earlier and in their interim financial statement for the six months up to 31 December 2015 the company's Perth based accountants, PFK Mack said: *'These conditions … indicate the existence of a material uncertainty that may cast significant doubt about the company and consolidated entity's ability to continue as a going concern … Therefore the company and the consolidated entity may be unable to realise its assets and discharge its liabilities in the normal course of business.'*

The Wolf directors, however, on the face of it at least, remained upbeat, and in January they signed a binding deal with RCF (Resource Capital Fund) to provide standby equity of up to £25 million.

But finance wasn't Wolf's only headache, there was trouble at mill …

'Wolf took over the management of the Process Mill in September 2015 following GRES completing the commissioning phase and demonstrating that the plant could achieve the design throughput for short periods of time – but not successfully completing the performance test, getting the recoveries and tungsten and tin design tonnage (this was never achieved)' recalls Jeff.

'GRES personnel remained on site to 'help' Wolf achieve the design performance. Once it was achieved they would receive their final payment of £7m (this was never achieved and the money not paid).

'It became clear very quickly that the recoveries could not be met, there were problems nearly everywhere and it was difficult to know where to start. Control of material through the plant was often difficult with frequent chokages, spillages and significant plant downtime. The ore was being overworked and quickly slimed – lost to the Mine Waste Facility. Operators were spending more time cleaning up the mess rather than producing tungsten.

'The Wolf Team battled on bravely to try and improve plant performance often working long hours often under difficult working conditions.

'Consultants were brought in to help and advise how to fix the problems. Sadly the GRES Australian site management team and some of the Wolf Australian management team started to try to blame the British workforce for their inability to achieve the required tungsten and tin production. It was suggested I should be more demanding of the workforce and start to discipline and sack people to try to improve plant performance.

'I retired as had been agreed 12 months earlier and was replaced by Alan Fearon on 1 April 2016. Alan was born in Rhodesia and worked most of his career in Australia. He immediately took a much harder line with management and the workforce and started to sack people, due to poor plant availability and lack of tungsten production. Alan lasted a year and failed to improve the plant performance, and the morale of the workforce deteriorated significantly. During this time it was accepted that there were serious design faults with the Process Mill and radical expensive alterations were required which would take significant time to fix.

'The new General Manager was Callum Semple, a mining consultant brought in to do a job, not make friends, but quickly improve the Process Mill and get the plant up to full production. Morale continued to suffer with key personnel starting to resign. One positive move was to bring in another consultant – an experienced process design engineer.

Part of the problem was identified by James McFarlane who was brought into the Drakelands project as the Geology Superintendent, in January 2015, after the plant was up and running and thus too late to have any impact on the design of the mill. He hadn't been there long when he identified a significant part of the problem was that the mineralogy and metallurgy of the deposit had been misunderstood. The tungsten at Hemerdon primarily presents itself as ferberite – which is paramagnetic – and not wolframite – which is weakly magnetic, something that James Cameron had pointed out in some detail back in the 1940s.

Blackwell and Hargreaves-branded vehicles excavating the hematised country rock on site at Drakelands which was then sent straight to the Mine Waste Facility.

Above: A tour party is taken around the vast processing mill during its construction.
Left: Not all the vibrations coming out of Drakelands were good vibrations – cracks were starting to appear from the earliest days of the operation.

The weather didn't help either, the Australian designers had apparently hoisted in average winter temperatures for this part of the world but perhaps not the fact that averages are just that and to end up with an average temperature there are times when the climate can be a good deal colder. The winter of 2016/17 witnessed some particularly cold weather, machinery froze up, weeks of production were lost.

It was all starting to get a little bit tense. The year end figures for 2016 revealed a loss of over A$63m (around £37 million). Wolf put in place a 'turnaround plan' after extending its borrowing to cover the losses.

In the spring of 2017 Russell Clark stood down, he hadn't wanted to move out of Australia altogether and it was clear that Drakelands needed an MD that was prepared to be fully hands-on to turn the situation around.

In April 2017 Wolf appointed 41-year-old Richard Lucas as interim MD and a year later confirmed his appointment which came with a handsome £269,000 salary.

A chartered accountant with the best part of 20 years of financial experience, Richard had already been with Wolf since April 2011, serving as their chief financial officer and company secretary. In that first year as interim MD he managed to secure funding for Wolf's ongoing operation and for growth.

Having upped sticks and moved to Devon it was reported that Mr Lucas had 'initiated and successfully executed a comprehensive operating turnaround ... which has resulted in improvements in concentrate production and sales, as well as operational reliability and performance.'

In August 2017 it received another £5 million as a bridging loan and in the firm's annual report it said that talks were under way to secure a further loan of £10 million to cover the three-month period from December 2017. The stark reality however was that they posted another half yearly loss – of £19.35 million – for the latter part of 2017. The good news, such as it was, was that this was an improvement on the previous year's figures and that production and sales were up by over a third on the corresponding period.

John Hopkins, still in the Wolf chair, said: 'The board is delighted with the progress of Richard and his team over the past twelve months. We have the utmost confidence in Richard's leadership and look forward to his future contribution to the growth and the advancement of the company.'

In March 2018 the 'Beast from the East' the unusually severe cold snap impacted on the operation, but overall, in the early part of 2018, Wolf reported record production at the mine, most of the really low-grade material at the top of the pit had been dealt with and tungsten and tin production was up 41% and 67% respectively. Throughout the year two million tonnes of ore was processed for the first time, but it was well below the projected figure of 3.5 million tonnes. It was now three years down the line not two and the mine was still some way off operating on a positive cash flow basis. In their first two full years of trading they sold just £3.9m worth of tungsten and £321k of tin (2016) and £12.3m of tungsten and £2.4m of tin (2017) and now, not only were Wolf sitting on a bridging loan of £69 million but they were looking to borrow more.

One estimate suggests that revenue close to £100million had been lost because full production had not been reached.

Having said that there was an £11 million pot of money in the bank but that was largely for site restoration work and only to be spent when Wolf were ready to exit the operation.

On a happier note the price of tungsten had risen 6% in the previous three months and it was now at its highest level since 2014, before the mine was fully commissioned.

But, in all honesty, it wasn't anything like enough. The major shareholders and investors had been sensing trouble for sometime. RCF, who had more than a 55% stake in Wolf, had sent their people over to investigate, as did the Todd Group, the American based financial services who held a 23% stake and who at one stage had wanted to go 50/50 with RCF (Resource Capital Fund).

Australian-based Wolf board members flew over – Drakelands was by now almost their sole raison d'être, to see what could be done – but by October 2018 the inevitable was looking increasingly likely.

On 9 October 2018 they announced that unless a new funding package could be secured within 48 hours the mine would be in danger of having to close down.

A statement was released to the stock exchange: 'The company has been working with its key financial stakeholders to develop longer term funding solutions required to provide the company with capital prior to the expiry of the standstill period on October 28, 2018, to progress further production improvements. The company's discussions with those stakeholders are ongoing and the company expects to conclude those discussions this week, following which a further announcement will be made.'

But the next announcement was that the mine had gone into administration, the very next day – 10 October 2018.

Crippled by its borrowings, not helped by the falling price of tungsten soon after they had given the project the green light, the fact that they never hit the level of throughput they were anticipating or the grade of concentrate they were after, they had been struggling from the outset.

The ongoing issues with the problems in the processing plant had meant that they had held back 10% of the £75 million contract payment to GRES. However when issues were raised about the mill design the standard comment from Perth was 'don't worry if something does not work properly there is £7m of GRES's money to fix it!'

The catch was though that if Wolf asked GRES to make changes to their design it would be a variation and have to be paid for by Wolf. Although £7million sounded a great deal of money at the time, Wolf, when at full production, were projected to bring in a revenue of over one million pounds per week, so it was perhaps not such a major consideration in the grand scheme of things.

After much acrimony there was a tentative agreement sorted in April 2018, but in the end it was settled out of court.

There was, nevertheless, a thought process that reasoned that if someone could now pick up the mine, cheaply, out of administration, and not have to pay all of the debt, especially as now the mine was processing the more valuable ore, having dealt with all the really low-grade kaolinised material, then perhaps someone could actually make a go of the operation.

At the end of November 2018, it seemed as though just such a situation might prevail as the press reported that a billionaire Russian oligarch wanted to pump £25 million into reopening the mine.

'Pala Investments, owned by one of the world's richest men – Vladimir Iorich – is understood to be willing to inject the cash into the Drakelands tungsten mine, Hemerdon, after it went into liquidation.'

But he didn't and after that the press went quiet. As of November 2019, when this book was published, nothing further was heard, but with so much investment, so many lessons learned and so much tungsten to be mined, surely this isn't the end of the story.

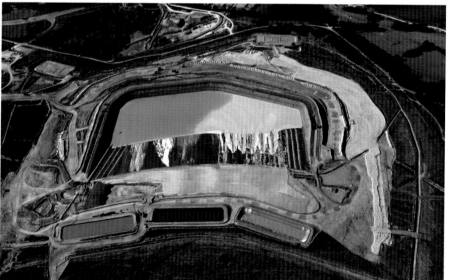

Left: The headline says it all. Top: A lone Wolf employee looks wistfully back at the Drakelands processing mill. Above: What a waste! An aerial perspective of the massive mine waste facility.

245

Back Row L-R Nick Finlayson (Ore Quality Geologist), Andy Nisbett (Ore Quality Geologist), James McFarlane (Mining Technical Services Manager), Laurie Hassall (Senior Mine Geologist) Front Row L-R: Narina Shorland (Senior Mine Engineer), Andy Moore (Project Geologist), Mel Jones (Mine Geologist), Tom Pascoe (Project Geologist), Zoe Scannell (Project Geologist)

Around 250 were working for Wolf when they suddenly went into administration on 10 October 2018. For most it was something of a shock, for some it had been obvious that the situation was precarious at best. A great loss to the area, Drakelands had generally been a happy place to work, muddy, dusty and wet and mucky at the best of times, it was nevertheless impressive and provided opportunities for many mining students who might otherwise have struggled to get a job in the industry. Traditionally an industry dominated by men, with a few bal maidens brought in to do mainly manual work, around 15% of the Wolf workforce were women, most of them on the technical, geological and mineralogical side – although there were no women on the board.

Above left: *Metallurgist, Samantha Bartlett, Ore Quality Geologists, Zoe Scannel and Melanie Jones.* Right: *Their last day! Back row L-R: Andy Moore (Project Geologist), Max Hembroke (Drill and Blast Supervisor), Lawrence Sullivan (Mining Engineer), Nick Finlayson (Ore Quality Geologist), James McFarlane (Mining Technical Services Manager), James Marsden (Junior Metallurgist), Tim Sandbrook (Plant Metallurgist), Chris Ecott (Senior Metallurgist), Doug Caffel (Metallurgy and Process Engineering Superintendent), Michelle Ball (Junior Plant Metallurgist), Zoe Scannell (Project Geologist – and 8 Months pregnant!) Front Row L-R: Anon, Mel Jones (Mine Geologist), Andy Nisbett (Ore Quality Geologist), Chris Savery (Project Engineer)*
Opposite page includes, top left: *Charlie Northfield, Process Plant Manager.* Top right: *Hannah Clarke* Bottom right: *James McFarlane, Geology Superintendent* Bottom middle: *Sam Bartlett, Michelle Ball, Jo Torres.*

TUNGSTEN WEST

ACQUISITION OF THE HEMERDON TUNGSTEN MINE

Tungsten West Prospectus: Drakelands Mine as operated by Wolf Minerals, with open cast pit top left, processing works middle, Plympton in the middle distance and Plymouth Sound far right.

ON THE BALL – AND UNDER THE BALL?

On 10 October 2018, following Wolf's failure to comply with the terms of the Current Standstill Agreement, Uni Credit (acting as facility agent and security trustee) served a formal demand on Wolf UK (as borrower) and Wolf Minerals (as guarantor) for the immediate payment of debts owing to the tune of £63 million.

Unable to obtain further relief, or further short term funding, the Wolf Directors appointed Martin Jones and Ryan Eagle of Ferrier Hodgson to act as their administrators.

Seven days later Wolf UK was ordered to be wound up, and the value of their shares was rated as nil. A little under four weeks later Ferrier & Hodgson published their initial assessment of the situation and their conclusions as to why Wolf went under which, in their eyes, boiled down to three essential considerations:

• Trading losses
• Inadequate cash flow or high cash use
• Inability to obtain new or extend finance facilities

Ferrier & Hodgson's cash flow verdict was that *'throughout the period of analysis and on an annual basis the Company was operating at a loss'* and further *'given that Wolf was operating at a loss since the commencement of its mining operations in June 2015, it is also likely that the Company did not report a profit since on or around that date.'*
The losses shown were A\$1.1m for FY (Financial Year) 2017, A\$12.7m for FY18 and from 1 July through to 30 September 2018 A\$5.09m.
From the Company's banking records the auditors didn't identify any dishonoured payments and their conclusion was *'that the Company was not insolvent prior to 10 October 2018 as it was still in discussions with potential funders.'*
Significantly, towards the end of their 75-page report to the creditors, the Australian-based auditors didn't recommend that creditors resolve to liquidate the Company *'given the recapitalisation sale process afoot.'*
There was clearly still a belief that Drakelands had a working future.
Rumours were rife but there were no apparent takers, until, in March 2019, the company who were one of the largest unsecured creditors of the Drakelands enterprise, Hargreaves (who having bought Blackwells were responsible for all the digging, and transporting activities on site and who were owed £7m at the time Wolf went under) bought the mine out of receivership for £5.4m.

The following month Hargreaves tendered the project and in May a fledgling company, that had been incorporated just twelve months earlier, Tungsten West, secured a pro-tem bid for a stake in the operation.
The initial agreement gave Tungsten West an Exclusivity Period of four weeks, extendable in four-weekly periods, up until the end of November 2019, they also agreed to cover the care and maintenance costs on site – which amounted to the not inconsiderable sum of £200,000 every four weeks.

With 55-year-old, Australian, Stephen Fabian, a venture capitalist with over 25 years' experience in the mining industry, as their founding director, the company is currently presided over by CEO Max Denning (formerly of Brazil Tungsten), while Mark Thompson, (who was involved with the Treliver tin project at St Columb Major a few years ago) is the executive chairman.
As part of their due diligence regarding Drakelands, Tungsten West engaged the services of a number of experts. One or two had valuable first-hand knowledge of the Hemerdon deposit gained during the AMAX period (Dr Simon Meik, the experienced mineral separation specialist) and the Wolf era (James McFarlane, the last, but significantly not first Senior Geologist on site and now a consultant geologist working for Mining Plus). A specialist team critically reappraised every aspect of the Drakelands' operation and the wider deposit.
Initially their test work focussed on the ore sorting and magnetic susceptibility of the granite and killas that were being processed for their tungsten content which confirmed their view that previous attempts to process the material had been based on a fundamental misreading of the material they were attempting to deal with and consequently a misunderstanding of what the best methods were for processing that material.
The tungsten at Hemerdon, as we have noted before and as earlier geologists had concluded, is primarily presented as ferberite (not wolfram),

which is typically very coarse grained – plus millimetre to plus centimetre sized grains – but Wolf failed to appreciate this. And thus their plant wasn't designed with an understanding of the friable nature of feberite and its tendency to slime.

Tungsten West's conclusions clearly put a slightly different spin on the Ferrier & Hodgson assessment. Yes, there had been trading losses, but Wolf's failure wasn't so much due to inadequate cash flow or high cash use, or its ability to obtain new or extended finance facilities, rather it was due to a misidentification of the predominant tungsten mineral in the ore which led them to design and construct an inappropriate processing plant that caused the mine to be 'sub-economic', thus forcing Wolf into receivership.

'After three years of operation Wolf's recoveries averaged only 38% of WO3 versus a design expectation of 65%.' A situation that led to the Offtakers reducing payments by 20%.

The problem, Tungsten West suggest, was due to poor choices of the equipment that was brought on site, starting at the very beginning of the process with the primary crusher. The roller crushers had worked on the softer, kaolinised granite, but when the harder granite started to come through, *'high attrition and wear'* saw regular breakdowns, rising maintenance costs and production time lost, with the obvious knock-on effects for profitability. And yet it had been this hard granite, taken from below the surface from the AMAX decline, upon which the 65% recovery figure had been based.

Jaw and cone crushers should have been used to treat this material instead, the experts said.

But in Wolf's defence the roller crusher had been selected as it would process the softer granite mined in the first few years. It was thought that jaw crushers would continually choke with the clay. The roller crusher was also expected to process the harder granite, but this was not the case. With hindsight some two to three million tons of very soft granite should have gone straight to the mine waste facility as the tungsten was very fine with poor recoveries. The mine should have started up processing the hard granite with jaw crushers.

The agreement to produce concentrate of 65% was a tough ask in the first place: *'Wolf did not have experience in negotiating such contracts and with hindsight they did not get a good deal,'* reflects Jeff Harrison.

Then there was the over-use of pumps which created an over-production of slimes which were effectively taking out almost a third of the WO3 at an early stage of the process.

Another overlooked element in the process was the host killas. The metamorphic rock that contained tungsten is mineralogically almost identical to that of the granite, typically lower grade, but nevertheless well worth processing. Remarkably, they estimate that more tungsten was delivered to the mine waste facility to build it, than was ever delivered to the processing plant. However, it has been suggested that the Wolf processing plant was not able to process the killas as it has a much higher density than the granite.

Again, stressing an over-reliance on the earlier AMAX findings, Wolf didn't include ore sorting in the crushing circuit. The world of mining had moved on in the decades since AMAX had been experimenting and the perceived wisdom is that the ore here is highly amenable to X-Ray Transmission sorting – that is sorting by density within the ore.

The solitude of a redundant open cast pit. Is there life in the old dog yet? Pic: James McFarlane, latterly Wolf's Mining Technical Services Manager now a consultant with Mining Plus.

'We set up a pilot plant with Wolf and showed that we could reduce tonnes going into the mill by almost 80% while recovering ~75% of the tungsten. This would significantly reduce the amount (and cost!) of future processing to still achieve the same amount of concentrate production. A game changer for the project,' adds James McFarlane.

Magnetic separation was also used by Wolf, but only towards the end of the process. Tungsten West believe that it should be used much earlier, removing much of the tungsten before it can be turned into slimes. Understandable if the material that Wolf thought they were looking at wasn't primarily at the ferberite, and hence paramagnetic, end of the tungsten spectrum, but it is.

Returning to the equipment that was actually used in the mill, it seems that there had been a tendency to bring in big bits of kit when it would almost certainly have been better to deploy several medium size pieces of equipment. The issue being that if the big bit of kit, whatever it might be, broke down, the whole process would be held up. There was no obvious 'plan B' whereby other machines could carry on, alongside the bit of kit that was being repaired, thus keep the mill running. Nor was there a stock piling system in place whereby if a piece of equipment failed then material that had already gone through the system and past that point, could then be fed in to keep everything moving.

It was estimated that overall plant availability had been less than 50% across the three years of Wolf's operation, and again this wasn't a funding issue, rather, it is suggested, an original design flaw.

Having identified a number of areas where they felt that Wolf had got it wrong, and how they would get it right, Tungsten West also proposed various measures that they would introduce to further enhance the smooth functioning of a revised processing plant at Drakelands, including the use of leaching in concentrate dressing phase to further reduce the losses of mineral. Leaching, they reason, has shown a 98% recovery rate, compared with the Wolf kiln method that had an 80 to 92% recovery. They also suggest that more effective monitoring could simply be achieved by using more than the eight cameras that Wolf had in use, by introducing real time X-ray fluorescence monitoring and by speeding up the turn-around time for producing assay reports. All of which, they reason, would make it possible to reach meaningful decisions during a shift, a facility that had hitherto been lacking.

In addition to all of these practical considerations, Tungsten West also have their eyes on a further prize, the potentially rich southern extension. First noted back in the late nineteenth century, nothing has been done about it to date because it was felt that there was plenty of ore in the current pit site. Furthermore during the First and Second World War operations here were curtailed because of a rationing of explosives, making investigation difficult. But there is little doubt that the southern extension is as significant, if not more significant, than the existing site.

And so it is that Tungsten West are looking to make a success of a mine that to date has been a sink-hole for shareholders. There have been valuable lessons learned off the back of all those previous assaults on this part of Hemerdon, even though those lessons haven't always been heeded. But as Wolf's former Operations Manager, Jeff Harrison, points out:

'Mines often go bust and the shareholders lose their money. New owners acquire the mine on the cheap, fix the problems and then make the new shareholders lots of money.

'Wolf did many things very well and any new operators will benefit from:

1. Two road projects successfully constructed – costing over £7m
2. Mine Waste Facility ready for re-start – construction cost over £2m
3. Waste water system in place across the site – cost £1m
4. 15 properties and various parcels of land purchased for over £10m
5. A significant part of the £70m process plant and building can still be used including workshops, stores and canteen facilities
6. Internal roads in place plus all external security fencing
7. The Wolf workforce with three years' of processing experience are scattered but still in the local area and many would return to mining
8. Generally good relationship in the local community and seen as managing the environmental aspects of the mine to a very high standard
9. Experienced mining contractors on site.'

What is more mining is undoubtedly a more sophisticated business now than it has ever been. So perhaps, with reserves in other parts of the world reaching the end of their working lives, and with demand for tungsten continuing to rise, then now, at long last, Hemerdon's star is truly about to shine and it will become a viable working mine, bringing wealth and prosperity to this area and all of those involved in promoting it.

And this is what it's all about. A vein of feberite surrounded by quartz from south of Hemerdon Ball. The ruler below indicates a 1cm scale. Originally thought to be wolfram WO_3 the mineral deposit is principally ferberite $FeWO_3$. Hopefully this knowledge, which has been hinted at over many years, will enable a future operator to make a success of this valuable tungsten deposit.

GLOSSARY

Many mining terms were only used within a particular mining district.

Adit: *horizontal level in a mine driven from hillside to allow drainage and hauling ore*

Adventurers: *original prospectors, shareholders or partners in a cost book mine*

Air shaft: *shaft sunk for ventilation*

Alluvial: *mineral gravels that have been washed from the lode*

Arsenical pyrite: *FeAsS when roasted produces arsenic*

Assay: *a chemical analysis to determine the amount of mineral present*

Attle: *refuse or waste often stacked underground*

Bal: *a mine*

Bal maiden: *women working on the surface of a mine*

Battery: *a set of stamps to crush ore*

Black tin: *tin concentrate before smelting*

Blende: *sphalerite, or of zinc, black jack*

Blondin: *aerial ropeway for buckets transporting materials*

Blowing House: *small scale tin smelting furnace*

Borer: *long chisels for drilling holes ready for blasting*

Buddle: *to concentrate ore by separation and settling in water*

Cal: *Cornish for wolfram*

Calcine: *process to drive off volatile matter eg. arsenic, sulphur*

Calciner: *used to produce arsenic from arsenical pyrite*

Carbide: *calcium carbide used in carbide lamps of other lodes*

Cassiterite: *tin ore*

Catch pit: *a reservoir pit to catch tailings sediment*

Caunter Lode: *a lode inclined at a considerable angle*

Chalcopyrite: *CuFeS$_2$ copper ore*

Cockle: *structure of wolfram*

Cost book: *mine development by calls on the adventurers*

Country rock: *rock surrounding igneous intrusions often metamorphosed*

Crosscut: *level driven across the lode at right angles*

Deads: *waste rock stacked underground – non ore bearing*

Decline: *inclined shaft*

Dressing floor: *where ore was produced to remove any waste*

Drill core sample: *cylindrical piece of rock obtained by drilling*

Dump: *a spoil pile of waste material from mining or processing ore*

Elvan: *dyke rock*

Engine house: *built to house winding and pumping engines*

Fault: *a break in earth's crust along which movement has taken*

Fathom: *mine measurement of 6 feet*

Fe: *iron*

Ferberite: *FeWO$_3$ ore of tungsten high in iron*

Flookan: *flukan, flucan, a vein filled with clay*

Footway: *ladderway for miners, access in a mine*

Galena: *Pbs lead ore*

Gangue: *non metallic mineral, eg Quartz, fluorite*

Grass, at: *on the mine surface*

Greenstone: *green rock, dolerite, gabbro*

Grizzly: *a set of bars set to intercept rocks as in a primary crusher*

Gunnis: *a stoped out area, an underground level worked to surface*

Halvans: *waste of copper ore*

Hematite: *Fe$_2$O$_3$ one of the various ores of iron*

Horse whim: *horse driven device used to wind kibbles up or down a shaft*

Hubnerite: *MnWO$_3$ ore of tungsten low in iron*

Ingot: *cast block of metal*

Arsenic crystals

Cassiterite – tin

Chalcopyrite – copper

Hematite – iron

Jurats: *stannators in the Tinners' Parliament*
Kaolin: *china clay, decomposed feldspar in granite*
Kibble: *large, bucket like, used to haul rock or ore up a shaft*
Killas: *metamorphic rock, clay slate*
Launder: *a wooden trough conveying water*
Leat: *man-made ditch to convey water often to machinery*
Level: *underground passage driven horizontally*
Lode: *main ore deposit often near vertical in Devon and Cornwall*
Mallet: *sledge hammer used for hitting borer or drill*
Magazine: *store for explosives, detonators*
Metamorphic: *metamorphosed changed rock surrounding granite*
Mine dumps: *burrows, dump to waste rock on mine surface*
Mine waste facility: *modern term for mine dump*
Mispickel: *arsenical pyrite, the source of arsenic also called mundic*
Mortar stones: *granite blocks in which tin was crushed*
Mouldstones: *granite blocks, often in fine-grained granite*
Mundic: *iron pyrite*
Old men: *early miners or streamers from the past*
Openwork: *a surface working along the lode*
Overburden: *soil or rock overlying the mineral deposit*
Overhand stope: *removing the ore from the lode above the miner*
Pare: *gang or party of miners working together*
Pillar: *leaving blocks of ore or rock to support roof or sidewalls*
Poll pick: *miners pick, one pointed end, the other a blunt hammer head*
Processing plant: *where the ore is processed*
Rise: *underground shaft driven from one level to another*
Scheelite: *ore of tungsten*
Sett: *mine boundary*
Shaft: *vertical or inclined excavation in a mine*

Shaking tables: *used for processing ore by density*
Slimes: *very fine material in water during processing*
Sn: *tin*
Spall: *to hand break ore*
Spalling: *hammer used to break down ore by hand*
Sphalerite: *zinc ore, black jack*
Stamps: *mechanical hammer for crushing ore*
Stannary Town: *four towns in Devon where tin was assayed and stamped*
Stannator: *one of 24 elected officials in each stannary*
Streaming: *winning of tin bearing gravels*
Stockwork: *stringers or veins containing ore*
Stope: *worked out section underground, overhand or underhand*
Streamwork: *where eroded deposited tin is worked*
Sump: *excavation at the bottom of a shaft for collecting/pumping water*
Tailings: *non-metallic matter left after processing ore*
Tailings Lagoon: *store pond for slimes from processing ore*
Tin stone: *small grains of tin in rock*
Tin straw: *small sample bars of refined tin — nb not hollow*
Tribute: *when miners work for a fixed percentage of profits from sale of ore*
Tributers: *groups of miners to work at agreed rates*
Tut work: *work paid for percentage value of ore raised*
Underhand stoping: *when the miner works the lode below him*
Wheal: *a mine*
Whim: *mechanical apparatus for winding ore to grass*
Windlass: *mechanical apparatus for winding material to surface*
Winze: *underground shaft sunk from one level to another below*
Wolfram: *(FeMn)WO3 one of the ores of tungsten*
Zinc blend: *sphalerite ore of zinc*

Galena – Lead, silver

Ferberite – tungsten

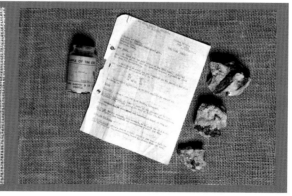
Bottle sample of tin concentrate, returned from smelter after assay. WWII assay terms and conditions from Williams Harvey. Specimens on ferberite and cassiterite from Hemerdon.

BIBLIOGRAPHY

Account of the Rise of Mining in the County of Devonshire from the time of the Phoenicians to the Present, **Geoffrey Chowen** (1863)

Agricola, Georgius, Dover Publications (first published 1556)

Alluvial Records of Medieval and Prehistoric Tin Mining on Dartmoor, Southwest England, **Thorndycraft, Pirrie, Brown,** Geoarchaeology (2004)

Archaeological Survey of an Area Surrounding Hemerdon Ball – Report of Devon Committee for Rescue Archaeology, For AMAX (1979)

Ashburton, The Dartmoor Town, **Francis Pilkington**, Penwell Ltd (1978)

Bal Maidens, Women and Girls of the Cornwall and Devon Mines, **Lynne Mayers**, Blaize Bailey Books (2008)

Britannica, Antiqua Illustrata, **Aylett Sammes,** London (1676)

Book of Devon, **Sabine Baring Gould**, Methuen (1920)

Castle Street, The Pottery, Plymouth Excavations, **Cynthia Gaskell Brown**, Plymouth City Museum and Art Gallery (1979)

Chronicle of Britain and Ireland, editor **Derrik Mercer,** Jacques Legrand Publishing (1992)

County of Devon, The Chorographical Description or Survey of the, **Tristram Risdon**, Rees & Curtis (1811)

Current Archaeology Magazine, How a New Town revealed communities spanning millennia, **Gareth Chaffey and Matt Kendall**, Issue 342, Sept 2018

Dartmoor a New Study, **Crispin Gill**, David & Charles (1970)

Dartmoor and its Antiquities, An Exploration of, **John LW Page**, Seeley & Co (1892)

Dartmoor and Prehistoric to Early Medieval Tin Working, **Henrietta Quinell**, Dartmoor Tin Research Group (2017)

Dartmoor Pictorial Records, **Robert Burnard's**, W Brendon & Son (1891)

Dartmoor Stannaries, The, **Paul Hambling**, Swift Print (1995)

Dartmoor Tin Industry, The, A Field Guide, **Phil Newman**, Chercombe Press (1998)

Dartmoor Worker, **William Crossing,** Peninsula Press Ltd (1992)

Devon and Somerset Mines, Roger Burt, **Peter Waite, Ray Burnley**, University of Exeter and The Northern Mine Research Society (1984)

Devon (A New Survey of England), **WG Hoskins**, Collins (1954)

Devon Pewterers from the Fourteenth Century to about 1750, **Ronald F Homer**, Dev.Assoc.Trans. (1995)

Devon Roads, **Michael Hawkins**, Devon Books (1988)

Devon Tin Industry, The, An Archaeological and Historical Survey, **Tom Greeves**, University of Exeter PHD thesis (1981)

Domesday Book, Devon, Parts 1&2, **John Morris**, Phillimore (1985)

Echoes of an Ancient Forest, **William Crossing**, Forest Publishing (1994)

Forest of Dartmoor, **The, Rev Henry Breton**, Forest Publishing (1990)

Fortunate Islands, The, The Story of the Isles of Scilly, **EL Bowley**, WP Kennedy (1945)

Geology of Devon, **EM Durrance & DJC Laming**, University of Exeter Press (1982)

Geology of Hemerdon Wolfram Mine, The, **James Cameron**, IMM (1951)

Hemerdon Wolfram – Tin Mining, The, **Ernest Terrell**, Mining Magazine (1920)

Hemerdon, An Evaluation Case History, **JE Christoffersen & PM King**, AMAX

Hemerdon Mining & Smelting Ltd., Booklet for Shareholders

Hemerdon Project, The, AMAX (1979)

Hemerdon Project, Report on the, AMAX (1981)

History of Devonshire, The, **Richard Polwhele**, Cadell, Johnson and Dilley (1797)

History of Metals, A, **John Webster**, Kettilby (1671)

Industrial Archaeology of Dartmoor, **Helen Harris**, Peninsula Press (1986)

Industrial Archaeology of Plymouth, A Guide, **Cynthia Gaskell Brown** (1973)

Industrial Archaeology of the Plym Valley, **Ernie Hoblyn**, Amberley (2013)

Industrial Archaeology of The Tamar Valley, **Frank Booker**, David & Charles (1967)

Medieval Monasteries, **CN Trueman**, History Learning Site (2015)
Metalliferous Mining Region of South-West England, The, vol II, **HG Dines**, Her Majesty's Stationery Office (1956)
Minerals of Britain and Ireland, **AG Tindle**, Open University
Miner's Friend, The, **Thomas Savery**, London (1702)
Mines of Cornwall and Devon, An Historic Photographic Record, **Peter Stanier**, Twelveheads Press (1998)
Mines of Devon, **AK Hamilton Jenkin**, Landmark Publishing (2005)
Mines of Devon and Cornwall, booklet (1856)
Mining for Tin on Dartmoor in the Eighteenth to Twentieth Centuries, **Phil Newman**, Dartmoor Tinworking Research Group (2017
Mining Skill, Progress of, In Devon and Cornwall, Historical Notes, **RN Worth** (1872)
Northwestern Iberian Tin Mining from Bronze Age to Modern Times: An Overview, Dartmoor Tin Research Group (2017)
Notes on the West Devon Mining District, **CF Barclay** (1931)
Norman Conquest, The, **HR Loyn,** Hutchinson University Library (1965)
One Man's Moor, an Exploration of Dartmoor, **William D Lethbridge**, Halsgrove (2006)
Oxford Companion to Food, **Alan Davidson**, Oxford Companions (1999)
Pilot Plant, AMAX (1980)
Place-Names of Devon, The, **JEB Gover**, **Allen Mawer, FM Stenton**, Cambridge University Press (1961)
Plymouth, A New History, **Crispin Gill**, Devon Books (1993)
Plymouth Mineral Mining Club, Journals of, various
Plymouth Municipal Records, Calendar of the, **RN Worth**, William Brendon & Son (1893)
Plympton's Old Metal Mines, **Bert Shorten** (1985)
Pre-Historic Times as Illustrated by Ancient Remains and the Manners and Customs of Modern Savages, **John Lubbock** (1865)
Proposed Bulk Sampling and Pilot Plant, AMAX
Romans on Dartmoor, **Tom Greeves** (online)
Shaugh Parish, The Book of, It's A Shaugh Thing, **Don Balkwill**, Halsgrove, (2008)
South West England, **Aileen Fox**, Thames and Hudson (1964)
South West Highways Atlas for 1675, The, **Paul White**, Tamar Books (2005)
Scilly, Ancient, **Paul Ashbee**, David & Charles (1974)
Skillings Mining Review (June 1980 & 7 January 1984)
South West to 1000 AD, The, **Malcolm Todd**, Routledge (2017)
Sparkwell, The Book of, with Hemerdon & Lee Mill, A Parish Portrait, **Pam James**, Halsgrove (2001)
Stannaries, The, A Study of the English Tin Miner, **George Randall Lewis**, Cambridge Harvard University Press (1924)
Stannary Law, A History of the Mining Law of Cornwall and Devon, **Robert R Pennington**, David and Charles (1973)
Survey of Cornwall, **Richard Carew**, AM Kelley (1602)
The Old Men of the Moor, **Mary and Jessica Walmesley**, Arthur Stockwell Ltd (1982)
Three Hares, The, A Curiosity Worth Regarding, **Greeves, Andrew, Chapman**, Skerryvore Productions (2016)
Through England on a Side Saddle in the Time of William and Mary, **Celia Fiennes**, Sutton Publishing (first published 1697)
Tin & Tungsten in the West of England, **Ernest Terrell**, Mining Magazine (1915)
Tinworking in the Cornish Landscape, **Peter Herring**, Dartmoor Tin Research Group (2017)
Travels in Tudor England, **John Leland,** Stroud (1998)
Tungsten, The Story of an Indispensible Metal, Tungsten Institute Washington DC
Worth's Dartmoor, **RGH Worth**, David Charles (1967)

Looking back across the partially built processing mill at Drakelands towards Derriford.